CONRAN
COOKBOOK

THE PURCHASE AND PREPARATION OF FOOD

CONRAN
COOKBOOK

THE PURCHASE AND PREPARATION OF FOOD

TERENCE AND CAROLINE CONRAN

ARTISTS HOUSE

Executive Manager   Kelly Flynn
Compiling Editor   Freda Parker
Art Editor   Ruth Levy
Production   Peter Phillips
Contributors   Maria Kroll
                     Ann Sayer
Photographers   Clive Corless
                     Christine Hanscomb
                     Terry Trott
Illustrators   Ingrid Jacob
                     Andrew Davidson
                     Paul Brooks

Edited and designed by the
Artists House Division of
Mitchell Beazley International Ltd
Artists House
14–15 Manette Street
London W1V 5LB

An Artists House Book
© Mitchell Beazley Publishers 1980 and 1986
Text © Conran Ink Limited 1980

ISBN 0 86134 090 6

Typeset by Hourds Typographica Limited, Stafford.
Reproduction by La Cromolito s.n.c., Milan.
Printed in Italy by Poligrafici Calderara, s.p.a., Bologna.

CONTENTS

GLOSSARY

Glossary of North American cookery terms with their British equivalents.

North American	British
broiler	grill
chocolate:	
bakers' chocolate	chocolate for cooking
bitter chocolate unsweetened cocoa powder	plain chocolate
cocoa powder	cocoa powder
cornstarch	cornflour
corn syrup	golden syrup
cream:	
light cream	single cream
heavy cream	double cream
whipped cream	whipping cream
eggplant	aubergine
endive	chicory
fava beans	broad beans
graham cracker	wholemeal digestive biscuit
molasses	black treacle
rutabaga	swede
sugar:	
confectioner's	icing
lump	cube
superfine	castor
vanilla extract	vanilla essence
wax paper	greaseproof paper
zucchini	courgette

INTRODUCTION

This book is about food, and is intended as a reference book for cooks; but unlike most other cook books, it does not have a bias towards the terms and usages of *haute cuisine*. Quite the reverse, this is the book for home cooks who want practical information and a straightforward approach.

It is concerned with food in all aspects — it is about raw ingredients and their preparation, with suggestions on cooking and presentation. Stated so baldly it sounds a dry affair, but where food is concerned, the matter can never really be dull. Food has a marvellous sensuality about it; even the simplest raw vegetable has a vitality and beauty of its own. The colors, textures and smells of food are all stimulating to the cook, inspiring a desire to cook in the same way that a writer wants to write or a painter to paint. And, like a painter or writer, the cook never knows exactly what will emerge at the end. Predictability would be boring, but luckily good ingredients are so individual — one tomato varying from the next according to the sun, the soil, the season — that there are constant surprises to keep up interest.

Many variations can be made on each theme too. Every time a dish is cooked, there is a feeling it can be improved upon, that it can be done a little differently from the time before. But to do this, one must be intelligent and well informed; the wider the knowledge, the more interesting and successful will be the experiments. This book hopes to provide a knowledge of a vast range of different foods, so that the cook – like someone with an extensive vocabulary — can be fluent and confident. Take, for example, olive oil: when you see it in the ingredients for a recipe, you may go straight to the supermarket and buy an olive oil that has been blended to appeal to the majority, and which therefore cannot afford to have much character. But, if you first find out about olive oil and then try all the different qualities and pressings with their strong individual flavors, you will be in a much better position to judge what the true olive oil taste is like, and which particular oil would be best suited to your purpose. Whether it is oils or cheeses, this book will encourage you to learn to seek out and try individual foods sold in specialist stores or markets where the produce is not designed for mass appeal, and different foods are consequently allowed to have a character of their own.

As a matter of fact, all good food starts with the shopping — certainly living out of a freezer is convenient, but it does away with a good deal of enjoyment. The seasons and their differences are part of the experience of life. If you constantly eat frozen green peas throughout the year, where is the pleasure when the first young peas appear in the spring?

Obviously it is madness not to freeze or preserve food when it is in abundance, and would go to waste otherwise, but does it make sense to ship or fly food many thousands of miles so that we can eat it all the year through? And surely shopping for fresh food in the market is a much more inspiring and entertaining performance than burrowing in the freezer for anonymous-looking if carefully labelled frosty packages.

Simplicity does not mean dullness. There are countless tastes, flavors and experiences available to people who take the trouble to find and try them. This book is intended to help you to do so.

Caroline Conran
Terence Conran

FISH

Fish is a food of tremendous character and charm. To a cook with true feeling for raw materials, there is great satisfaction to be found in the beauty of form, the shimmering colors of scale and skin, and the distinctive flavors and textures of fish of all kinds. Cooking becomes more of a pleasure if one can make an occasional experiment or discovery, and among fish there are endless discoveries to be made.

CHOOSING FISH

There is no excuse for bad fish being offered for sale any more, now that refrigerated equipment makes it easy to transport fish for long distances in a freshly caught state. What we are more likely to see in fish shops these days are fresh fish that have been in the shops too long, or fish that have been in and out of the freezer several times, thawed out and sold as "fresh." Unfortunately, the tell-tale signs of a thawed-out fish are less easy to detect than those of a stale fish. If you are not an expert, the best fish to buy are those you see in a crate, packed in ice and obviously straight from the wharf or wholesale market. These fish will have been chilled – not blast-frozen – immediately after they have been caught.

However, with frequent visits to the fish dealer it soon becomes easy to recognize the differences between good, fresh fish that have simply been chilled, stale fish and thawed-out frozen fish. Don't be afraid to sniff the fish if you are suspicious, or to ask pertinent questions. Here are the signs to look for – remembering that the fish is likely to be only marginally on the stale side rather than offensively bad.

FRESH FISH

A really fresh fish looks almost alive and ready to swim away. It gleams, it slides and slithers springily through your hands as though it would like to escape. Its color is bright, its flesh firm and rigid yet elastic to the touch, and the skin will shine with a viscous slime that is clear and evenly distributed.

Eyes
Bright, bulging eyes with black pupils are a clear indication of freshness. The eyes of stale fish have greyish pupils with red rims, and are dull and sunken.

Gills
These should be clean and bright red. Dirty, dark or slimy gills are a sure sign of a bad fish.

Smell
Fresh fish smell fresh and pleasant, while quite obviously, the more offensive the odor, the staler the fish will be.

FROZEN FISH

Commercially frozen fish, usually in fillets, are sold from freezers in stores and super-markets. But there are other fish, usually sold whole, that have been frozen and thawed out, and are sometimes sold with no sign to indicate their previously frozen state. This is an unfortunate deception. Genuinely fresh fish must be eaten as soon as possible after they are caught or bought, but these thawed-out fish are usually imported and have travelled some distance. As long as you are aware of their condition, they need not be shunned – often they are the only chance you will have of tasting unusual fish from far away. To detect a badly thawed-out fish, look for a sad appearance and dull, flabby skin that has lost its natural slime and shininess.

STORING FISH

There is only one essential piece of advice on the storing of fresh fish – don't. If you must keep it overnight put it, well wrapped in several layers of newspaper, in the coldest part of the refrigerator. Fresh mackerel, herrings and sardines should be eaten the day they are purchased.

FREEZING FISH

Domestic deep-freezers simply do not act fast enough to prevent large ice crystals forming in the flesh of a fish. The jagged crystals puncture the delicate tissues, resulting in the loss of texture, juices and flavor. So if you want a freezerload of fish as a standby, you would be well advised to buy commercially frozen fish, which should keep for two to three months.

There is a way to preserve a degree of texture and flavor using a domestic deep-freeze, and this is called glazing. First clean and gut the fish in the normal way, then place it, unwrapped, in a freezer set to fast freeze. When the fish is reasonably solid, dip it into cold fresh water. A thin film of ice should instantly form. Return it to the freezer immediately and, when the ice has set

Fresh fish have bright, bulging eyes and skin that shines with a clear, natural slime

A fish with dull, discolored, sunken eyes and lifeless skin is well past its prime

solid, repeat the process two or three times until the fish is completely encased in a good coating of ice, then store it in a freezer bag in the usual way.

Fish that best withstand the freezing process are those with fine-grained flesh, such as the sole and its flat relations. Salmon, and other fish with flesh that falls into flakes, can be frozen but are decidedly nicer fresh; the flesh becomes a little soft with the freezing and thawing process. The shorter the time any fish remains frozen, the better it will be.

Frozen fish should be defrosted before cooking. If cooked from frozen, the outside is overcooked before the inside has had time to thaw out, which is less than ideal.

SALTWATER FISH

Fish from the sea can be roughly divided into those that have white flesh and those that are oily. Within these broad categories exist several natural culinary groups, such as the flat fish, the cod and its relatives, the sea basses and porgies, and the oily mackerels and herrings. The great ocean fish, such as tuna and swordfish, have a category of their own, and there is a section for the multitude of fish, such as red snapper and skate, that do not fall easily into categories.

French names have been given in case you wish to sample something new from a restaurant menu, before deciding whether to add it to your own repertoire.

FLAT FISH

All flat fish are fine fleshed, white, delicate and lean, and two – turbot and Dover sole – rank in the top echelon of all sea fish.

Dover sole (*sole*)

The true Dover, or Channel, sole is perhaps the cook's perfect fish, a fact reflected by its prominence on restaurant menus in England and Europe. The flesh is firm, white and delicate and keeps well (in fact sole tastes better if it is at least 24 hours old). It lends itself to almost any cooking method and is excellent with a multitude of sauces, but is at its finest simply cooked on the bone and served with butter, parsley and lemon. Only poor quality fish need dressing up.

Buying guide: available fresh all year in Europe. There is no true sole in American waters – although a number of flounder-like fish are labelled sole – but imported Dover sole is available in larger East Coast cities. Buy whole if serving plainly broiled or fried; in fillets if serving in a sauce. Each fish provides four good fillets. The price of Dover sole has become inordinately high, but a 7–8oz/200–225g sole is enough for one person,

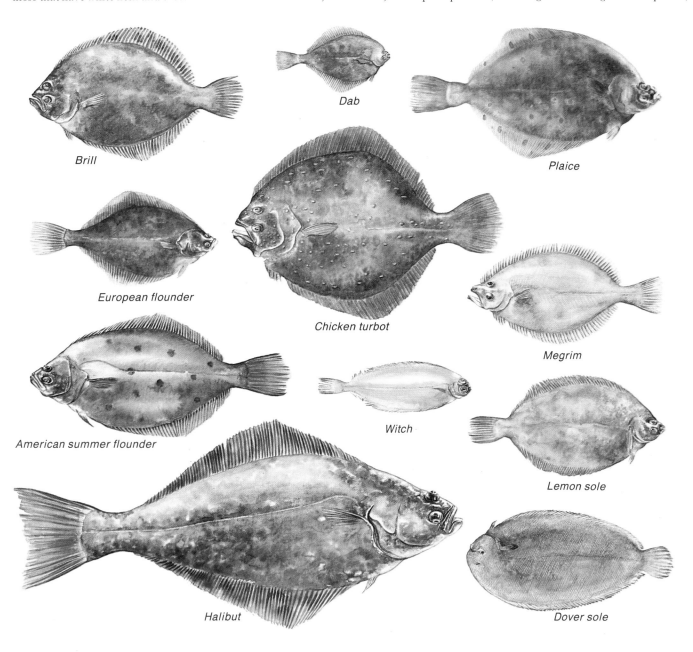

Brill

Dab

Plaice

European flounder

Chicken turbot

Megrim

American summer flounder

Witch

Lemon sole

Halibut

Dover sole

though vegetables will be needed if it is to be served plain.

Best cooking methods: broiled, fried or *à la meunière*, or filleted and poached in sauce.

Flounder (*flet*)

In America, the flounder family includes the excellent summer flounder (also known as fluke), the winter flounder and the grey and lemon sole. These are all quite good eating when freshly caught and are often used in recipes that call for Dover sole or turbot since they respond to the same methods of cooking.

Buying guide: year round for American flounder, with the exception of fresh summer flounder. Sold whole and in fillets.

Best cooking methods: a good-quality thick flounder can be poached like turbot; a thin one should be fried gently in butter or cooked like sole.

Turbot (*turbot*)

Turbot is one of the finest of sea foods. Its flesh is the firmest and most delicate in flavor of all the white fish and has to be paid for dearly these days, but any opportunity to buy it should not be missed. Recognize turbot by its knobbly brown skin and awesome size: a whole fully grown specimen can weigh up to 28lb/12kg and makes a handsome centerpiece on the fish dealer's slab, usually white belly uppermost. If you can't manage to cook a whole turbot, you can buy fillets or steaks, but remember that they take less time to cook.

Buying guide: available all year, sold whole, in fillets and in steaks. The flesh should be creamy white; a bluish tinge means that it is stale. Imported turbot may be found in large American cities.

Best cooking methods: turbot is so excellent that it suits any cooking method, but is best simply poached or broiled and served with parsley sauce, lobster sauce or hollandaise.

Halibut (*flétan*)

A giant among flat fish, the halibut can grow up to 6ft/2m long and is not in fact, particularly flat. It is a medium to darkish brown on top and pearly white underneath. It has almost as good a flavor as turbot, although it doesn't hold its succulence so well. It is, however, cheaper than turbot.

Buying guide: available all year. Best when small: a young halibut, called chicken halibut, weighing less than 3lb/1.5kg is a very good-looking lunch or dinner for 4–6 people, depending on how it is served. Larger halibut are sold in steaks, cutlets and fillets. Avoid frozen halibut, which is dull and dry.

Best cooking methods: poach or bake, with a good sauce – lobster, egg or parsley – or melted butter. Also good when eaten very fresh, as in a seviche.

Lemon sole (*limande-sole*)

A delicious-sounding fish, lemon and sole being such a good combination of tastes, lemon sole in fact neither tastes of lemon nor is it a sole (it belongs to the dab and plaice family and corresponds to the American yellowtail flounder). A pleasant-looking, yellowish-brown fish, it has a fresh salt-and-iodine taste and benefits greatly from total freshness. Soft textured but pleasant, it is best simply cooked with few additional ingredients.

Buying guide: available all year, sold whole or in fillets. Frozen fillets tend to be somewhat woolly.

Best cooking methods: use simple dab or Dover sole recipes. Filleted, egg-and-crumbed and fried, lemon sole makes a good children's lunch.

Plaice (*plie or carrelet*)

Dark brown with russet spots on its upper side and white on its underside, plaice is a mainstay of every English fish and chip shop, its mild, soft flesh heavily encased in batter and deep fried. It is certainly a perfectly palatable fish when served this way, provided it is quite fresh. Gently poached in milk, it is particularly good fish for children and invalids. American plaice can be prepared in the same way.

Buying guide: available all year. Sold whole or in fillets.

Best cooking methods: deep fry in a good batter or in egg and bread crumbs and serve with hollandaise or tartare sauce, or poach and cover with a cheese or parsley sauce.

Dab (*limande*)

Looking like a small flounder with rough skin, the European dab is not the most exciting of fish although its flesh is soft, fragile and easily digested. It can grow up to 12in/30cm long but is usually smaller. The American sand dab, or rust dab, is slightly different but prepared in the same way.

Buying guide: best in autumn and winter. Sold whole or in fillets.

Best cooking methods: broil whole like a piece of toast, or fillet, egg-and-crumb and fry for breakfast or a light supper dish.

Brill (*barbue*)

A very good European fish akin to turbot, brill has a mixed-tweed coloring and is smaller than its cousin. Its flesh is softer and not so gelatinous as that of turbot but it is sweet and delicate to eat.

Buying guide: available all year, sold whole or in fillets.

Best cooking methods: recipes for turbot, halibut and sole suit brill.

Megrim (*cardine*)

A small, yellowish-grey, rather transparent

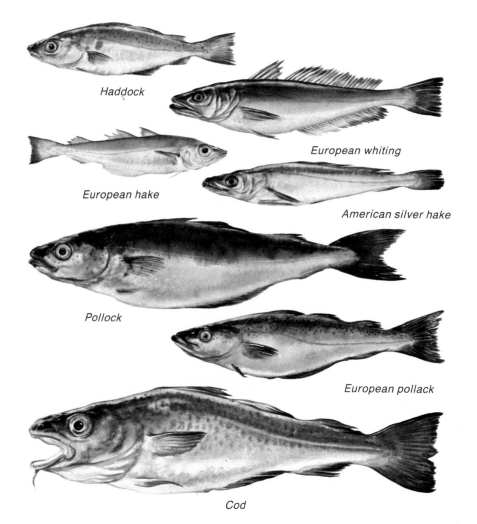

Haddock

European whiting

European hake

American silver hake

Pollock

European pollack

Cod

fish, megrim is also known as whiff, sailfluke, West Coast sole, white sole and lantern flounder. Not a particularly good fish, it has the advantage of being cheap and, like rock sole or dab, it makes a reasonably good contribution to fish soup.

Buying guide: autumn and winter, sold whole or in fillets.

Best cooking methods: as for lemon sole or plaice, but probably best filleted and fried with the added texture of crisp bread crumbs to help it along.

Witch *(plie grise)*

Also known as Torbay sole, witch sole, witch flounder or pole flounder, this long, narrow, cold-water fish is shaped rather like a sole and has sandy-brown coloring. Cook it in exactly the same ways as sole, but witch is a duller fish so use a little more seasoning, herbs and spices.

THE COD FAMILY

This large family of white-fleshed fish, including such cornerstones of the fishing industry as cod, haddock and whiting, keep their succulence best when lightly poached, fried in batter or bathed in a good light homemade sauce.

Cod *(cabillaud)*

The cod is a handsome fish with a skin of greenish bronze dappled with yellow. The flesh is succulent and comes in large flakes – a really fresh fish will produce a curd between the flakes, rather like salmon. The cod has an excellent roe – used in taramasalata – and its liver produces a disagreeable but effective vitamin supplement. An adult cod can weigh up to 80lb/36kg; small cod, or scrod, just as good, about $1\frac{1}{2}$–$2\frac{1}{2}$lb/ 700g–1kg.

Buying guide: available all year, but best in winter. Fresh cod is sold mainly as steaks and fillets. Never buy fillets or steaks with yellow or pinkish patches on the flesh. Frozen cod, although reliable, lacks the flavor of really fresh cod, but is certainly a better buy than cod of dubious quality.

Best cooking methods: the flesh falls naturally into large, firm flakes and keeps its texture well. It is splendid poached and excellent in fish pies, croquettes, salads and fish cakes. Also bake, broil, fry or deep fry with good homemade sauces such as hollandaise or tartare. In Britain poached cod is traditionally served with slices of lemon and horseradish relish, but nowadays you are more likely to be offered aïoli (mayonnaise heavily flavored with garlic). In order to whiten and tenderize the flesh, it is a good idea to rub it with a cut lemon half an hour or so before cooking.

Haddock *(églefin or aiglefin)*

Fresh haddock is sometimes preferred to cod, but haddock is really no better a fish. It has a fresh marine flavor, a light, firm texture and is blessed with fairly good keeping qualities. It looks like cod, but has a greyer skin, larger eyes and a marked black lateral line. Haddock is also smoked.

Buying guide: available all year, best in winter and early spring. Fresh haddock is usually sold in fillets.

Best cooking methods: deep fried and served with French fries, in fish pie (especially good mixed half and half with smoked haddock) or any method suitable for cod.

Hake *(merluche)*

An elongated, deep-water member of the cod family, hake appears on some French menus as white salmon *(saumon blanc)*, and is familiar – although probably unrecognized – all over the United States as "deepsea fillets." Silver hake, from America's East Coast, is a particularly fine fish which also goes under the name of whiting (not to be confused with the European whiting, a lesser fish). Hake is most popular in Spain, fried in beaten egg or in an escabeche – a cold hors d'oeuvre of fried fish in herby marinade, but it is sadly becoming an increasingly rare sight in the fish shops of northern Europe, and no opportunity should be missed to buy it though it does tend to be expensive. It has tender, flaky flesh, somewhat lighter than that of cod, with a delicate flavor. It also has the advantage of possessing comparatively few bones, which are fairly easy to remove.

Buying guide: fresh hake must be very fresh and is sold whole, in fillets and in steaks. It is also sold frozen.

Best cooking methods: deep fried in batter, pan fried, baked with pine nuts, bread crumbs and cheese, or poached and served on a bed of spinach or sorrel mixed with fresh cream.

Whiting *(merlan)*

This is a common but unexciting European fish not found in American waters (in the United States whiting is another name for silver hake). It is grey and white with a pointed head and backward-slanting teeth. A really fresh whiting is quite good, light and easily digestible, but a tired and travelled specimen will be dry, dull and tasteless.

Buying guide: available all year but best in winter. Sold whole, usually between $\frac{1}{2}$ and 1lb/225–450g, or in fillets.

Best cooking methods: flake and use in fish cakes, purée for mousses and mousselines, poach and serve with a julienne of vegetables, or fry fillets covered with egg and crumbs – serve with fresh tomato sauce.

Pollock *(lieu noir)*

Firm textured and strong flavored, it is one of the mainstays of the ocean-fresh and deep-sea fillet markets. The off-putting greyish flesh whitens considerably during cooking, even more so if rubbed generously with lemon juice beforehand, and although pollock does not have the succulence of cod it is fine for everyday fish cakes and fish pies. Smoked and served with hot toast, it makes a passable substitute for smoked salmon pâté.

Buying guide: available all year, sold in fillets or steaks.

Best cooking methods: in well-seasoned soups, pies and fish cakes.

Pollack *(lieu jaune)*

This European fish, also called lythe, is somewhat short on flavor and needs a little help in the form of a good sauce like hollandaise, or interesting seasoning.

Buying guide: available all year, best in autumn and winter. Sold whole, in fillets or steaks.

Best cooking methods: as for cod, but best in pies, fish cakes and fish soups.

Ling

The flesh of the fresh fish is well flavored and can be used in fish pies and soups of all kinds.

Cusk

This is eaten in pies and soups, and sometimes steamed with a cream sauce.

Pouting

This should be eaten very fresh indeed as its main claim to fame is that it goes bad very quickly – it is sometimes known as stinkalive. Cook like whiting.

BASS, BREAM, PORGY AND GROUPER

Firm and white fleshed, these fish go well with strong Mediterranean flavors – saffron, fennel, olive oil, tomatoes, white wine and garlic. They are delicious grilled whole over charcoal in the open air, or baked with olive oil and herbs.

Bass *(bar, loup de mer)*

Sea bass, whether one of the North American varieties – striped bass, black sea bass, rock bass – or the beautiful silver bass of the Mediterranean and warmer northern European waters, is the ideal fish for a splendid meal at home. It is just the right size for a small family and has delicately flavored milky flesh.

Buying guide: available all year. Sold whole or in steaks and fillets.

Best cooking methods: bass up to 2lb/900g can be grilled whole – in France they are cooked on charcoal with herbs and a handful of fennel twigs is put on the fire. Bake larger fish, and bake or poach steaks and fillets. Bass is also excellent in salads or seviche, or, for an unusual dish, steamed on a bed of seaweed.

Porgy or bream *(daurade)*

Some species of sea bream are distinctly better than others: the finest is the Mediterranean gilt-head, with its gold spot on each cheek and its compact body. The red bream, the only good bream found in northern European waters, is a large fish usually sold in fillets and only recognizable by its orange-red skin. Porgies and scups, the American East Coast bream, are quite small. They all have rather coarse but juicy flesh and a pleasant taste that suits fairly strong accompanying flavors. They must be scaled – ask your fish dealer to do this for you, or cook the fish with its scales intact and carefully remove them with the skin just before serving.

Buying guide: available all year but best in autumn. Sold whole or in fillets.

Best cooking methods: season well and broil or bake in foil, or roll in cornmeal or flour and fry briskly in oil. Make two or three slashes on each side with a sharp knife if cooking whole, so that the heat may quickly penetrate the thicker parts, thus ensuring that the whole fish cooks evenly.

Grouper *(mérou)*
A delicacy in Mediterranean countries, grouper are not widely available in northern Europe, which is a pity because their flesh is particularly firm and well flavored. America enjoys a number of varieties – red grouper are found from Virginia down to Florida, and the Gulf has black grouper or yellowfish. In California, grouper can often be found in fillets labelled golden bass.
Buying guide: sold whole, weighing up to 15lb/6kg, and in steaks and fillets.
Best cooking methods: as for sea bass.

OILY FISH
Absolute freshness is essential – all oily fish are inedible when stale. The traditional accompaniments of mustard for herring and green gooseberry for mackerel counteract their natural oiliness.

Mackerel *(maquereau)*
The mackerel is one of the easiest of all fish to recognize – the taut, steel-blue skin, mottled on the back with blues and greens and a pattern of blackish bands, is so smooth that it looks almost enamelled. The belly is pearly white, the inside of the mouth black. If the natural markings have lost their brilliance and the fish does not positively shine up at you, do not buy it. The pink-tinted flesh is firm, richly flavored, very oily and rich in vitamins.

Buying guide: at their best in April, May and June, when they are in roe. Mackerel are sold whole, usually weighing about 1lb/450g which will serve one person as a main course, two as a first course.
Best cooking methods: grill; good stuffed; soft roe can be mixed with the stuffing, but a hard roe is better baked under the fish. Also bake, or poach in white wine or roll fillets in oatmeal and fry them like herring. Sauces for mackerel, apart from gooseberry, include mustard and horseradish.

Horse mackerel *(chinchard)*
This somewhat off-putting name belongs to a group of fish regarded as poor man's mackerel. They lack the fine markings of the true mackerel and are not considered a high-quality fish, being rather coarse and bony.
Buying guide: available all year. Sold whole – a large one will feed two people, a small one, one person.
Best cooking methods: treat as mackerel, but they will not respond as well, or braise.

Bluefish *(tassergal)*
Familiar along America's East Coast in summer and in the warm waters around Bermuda, the bluefish can be identified by the blue-green sheen along its back. The flesh is rather soft and goes best with sharp accompanying flavors – lemon juice, capers or green gooseberries.
Buying guide: most seasonable in spring, summer and autumn. Usually sold whole – 2–3lb/900g–1.5kg is a manageable size, but it can be up to 10lb/4.5kg.
Best cooking methods: brush with melted butter and broil or bake with a little white wine and butter, or poach whole and serve with melted butter.

Herring *(hareng)*
Herrings are rapidly becoming less available because of overfishing. This is a pity because they are a tasty fish and rich in protein, fat, iodine and vitamins A and D. They produce a pervasive smell while cooking and need cleaning and may need deboning before cooking, but this is a simple job.
Buying guide: available all year but best from spring to autumn. Choose herrings that are large, firm and slippery. They are usually sold whole.
Best cooking methods: pat with seasoned oatmeal and fry in a little lard or butter, or score, brush with fat and broil. Never discard the roe, which is very good.

Smelt *(éperlan)*, argentine and atherine *(pêtre)*
Although unrelated, these bright, silvery, semi-transparent little fish are very similar in size, appearance and taste. About 7in/17cm long, they spawn in fresh water. The smelt is the superior of the three: it has a delicious scent when very fresh – some say of cucumber, others of violets. They all need delicate handling – leave the head and tail on and clean them through the gills.
Buying guide: best in winter and spring, but there are good and bad smelt years so buy smelt whenever you see them – it may be a long time before you see them again.
Best cooking methods: traditionally they are strung on a skewer through their heads, dipped in milk and flour and deep fried.

Sardines *(sardines)*
Fresh sardines are a delight, but they must be fresh. They travel badly so are usually only found close to where they are caught, such as the Mediterranean coasts of France

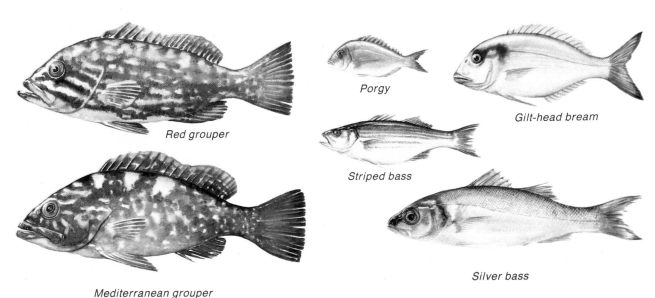

Red grouper

Porgy

Gilt-head bream

Striped bass

Silver bass

Mediterranean grouper

and North Africa (the true Mediterranean sardine is named after the island of Sardinia). When you do find them in fish markets, they are simplicity itself to prepare. Cut the head almost through from the backbone, pull, and as the head comes off the gut will come with it.

Buying guide: at their best in spring. Fresh sardines are sold whole; sizes vary so judge by eye how many you need per person. Also sold frozen – the finest are from Portugal.

Best cooking methods: fry in olive oil, or coat lightly with salt and olive oil and grill, preferably over charcoal. Eat them with chilled rough wine and fresh bread.

Anchovy (*anchois*)
Seeing fresh anchovies for the first time, with their slim bodies and sparkling silvery greenish-blue skin, comes as something of a surprise when one's only previous acquaintance with this useful fish has been as canned fillets. To enjoy their delicate flavor at its best they should be straight from the sea, which ideally means the Mediterranean, but some varieties do appear in northern European and North American waters.

Buying guide: sold whole.

Best cooking methods: fry or broil as sardines. Also delicious marinated in lemon juice, or boned and fried with garlic and parsley.

Sprats (*sprats*)
These are worth some attention if only for their superabundance in European waters, which means that they are very cheap. Tiny silvery fish, they look rather like small herrings but are shorter and stouter.

Buying guide: a winter fish, said to be best when the weather is frosty.

Best cooking methods: sprats are very oily so are best when broiled, or dusted with flour or oatmeal and dry fried in a pan sprinkled with salt.

Whitebait (*blanchaille*)
The small fry or young of herrings and sprats, whitebait are the most delicious little fish. Bright, silvery and slender, they are scarcely more than 1½in/4–5cm long. Whitebait are eaten whole so there is no need to clean them – simply rinse them gently.

Buying guide: traditionally February to August. Allow about 4oz/12g per person.

Best cooking method: the best and only way to cook whitebait is to dip them in milk, shake them up in a bag of flour and deep fry them. They should be so crisp that they rustle as they are put on the plates.

THE GREAT FISH

The great ocean fish make firm, meaty eating. Their flesh is inclined to be dry, so marinate it in oil, lemon juice or white wine and herbs before cooking.

Tuna (*thon*) **and bonito** (*bonite*)
The tuna family is related to the mackerel and includes the bluefin, the albacore, the skipjack and bonito. When you see fresh tuna, don't be put off by the ugly, stained look and close-grained texture of the flesh – it improves during cooking. Much drier than canned tuna, it needs plenty of oil and seasoning. Bonito can be treated as either tuna or mackerel.

Buying guide: available all year. Sold in steaks and occasionally very small ones are available whole.

Best cooking methods: broil, or bake in slices not less than 1½in/4cm thick, basting often with oil, salt and pepper, or slice very

quickly into small scallops, dust with flour and fry gently in butter and oil for 2–3 minutes on each side.

Swordfish (*espadon*)
Familiar in Mediterranean waters and popular in America as "the steak of the sea," the swordfish is only a very occasional visitor to northern European waters. It makes delicious eating, but the flesh is close grained and inclined to be dry so is often marinated in wine, oil and herbs before cooking.

Buying guide: sold fresh in steaks; also sold frozen in countries which import it.

Best cooking methods: broil or grill and serve with plain or herb butter, or seal in butter and then bake in a sauce. Also excellent as kebabs.

Sailfish, spearfish and marlin
(*voilier, makaire, marlin*)
Well known to American sport fishermen, these majestic fish are spectacular fighters and highly prized trophies. But if you don't want to put them on the wall, all three make very good eating.

Buying guide: not commercially fished, but occasionally sold as steaks in ports near the fishing grounds.

Best cooking methods: as for swordfish.

ASSORTED FISH

Many fish do not fall naturally into a culinary category except that they are good to eat. For many of them their looks are not their greatest asset, but it is a pity that they should be so often passed by in favor of their better known and more comely cousins.

Monkfish, angler fish (*lotte, baudroie*)
This fish is sometimes muddled with the angel fish, which is also known as monkfish

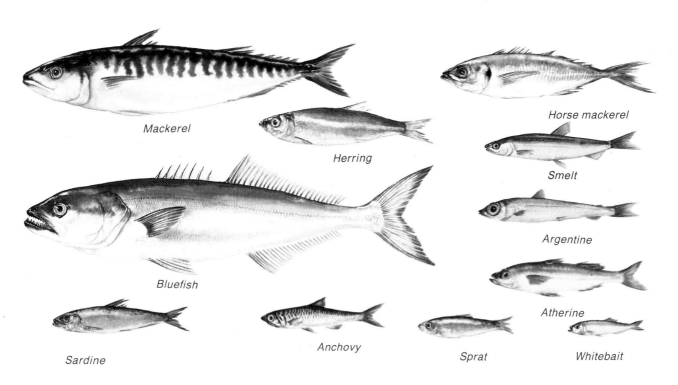

Mackerel

Herring

Horse mackerel

Smelt

Argentine

Bluefish

Atherine

Sardine

Anchovy

Sprat

Whitebait

but is a member of the shark family. Certainly there would be no confusion if the fish dealer would leave the monkfish intact, but it is usually sold headless. The flesh is firm, very white and has the succulence of lobster, and its taste is more associated with shellfish than with fish. It is also called goosefish.

Buying guide: available all year. Ask for a good tail piece – 3lb/1.5kg for six people. It can then be sliced or cooked whole.

Best cooking methods: can be treated almost as meat – it is sometimes roasted and called *gigot de mer*. It can also be poached like cod, but allow twice as long for the cooking, or split the tail in half, brush with oil and broil well on both sides. Simplest and best of all are small scallops marinated in lemon and garlic, dusted in flour, and fried in butter.

Skate, ray (*raie*)

Only the wings of skate are eaten – they contain no real bones but strips of gelatinous cartilage from which the flesh comes off in long succulent shreds. Fresh skate is covered with a clear slime, which reappears when wiped dry, and the flesh should be pearly white, resilient and not flabby to the touch. Don't worry if there is a slight smell of ammonia, this disappears during cooking. Large skate are generally kept by the fish dealer for a day or two in chilled conditions as they are inclined to be tough when very fresh.

Buying guide: best in autumn and winter. Small wings are sold whole; otherwise choose a thick middle cut.

Best cooking methods: the classic French skate dish is *raie au buerre noir* – skate poached in court bouillon and served with browned butter. It can also be broiled, deep fried or poached. The skin is easy to remove after cooking, simply scrape it carefully from the thicker part towards the edge. Because of its gelatinous quality, skate makes a good fish stock or aspic.

Red mullet (*rouget de roche*)

The mullet families can be confusing. There are two species of fish – not related – called mullet in European waters. One is the grey mullet, the other the red mullet, by far the finer of the two species. In America the term mullet applies to fish of the grey mullet family; fish belonging to the red mullet family which inhabit American waters are known as goatfish or bellyfish.

The Mediterranean red mullet is a superb fish, deep rose with a faint golden bar along each side. The flavor is quite distinctive, something between shrimp and sole. This is the ideal fish to cook with strong Mediterranean flavors – garlic, saffron, rosemary and fennel. Its liver is often left in during cooking and provides an added richness of flavor, giving red mullet its nickname of sea woodcock.

Buying guide: best in summer, but if they seem to be bent sideways they have been frozen and have just thawed out. Sold whole: always ask for the liver to be left in.

Best cooking methods: ideal for fish terrines, mousses or pâtés. Also excellent broiled, baked or *en papillote* – red mullet is seldom cooked with water.

Grey mullet (*muge, mulet*)

There are several varieties of grey mullet, known variously as striped mullet, black mullet, jumping mullet and lisa, and they are too frequently neglected in favor of the more highly prized red mullet, which is in fact no relation. Grey in color, it has large thick scales and a heavy head with thick, delicate lips. The flesh is coarse and slightly soft, but the flavor is very good, particularly if heightened with fennel or Pernod.

Buying guide: available all year. Sold whole; look for firm fish caught at sea rather than flabby fish caught in estuaries – their flavor will be muddy.

Best cooking methods: slash the sides and broil or grill, or, if the fish weighs more than 2lb/900g, fill with herbs and garlic, coat with olive oil and bake. Do not cook with water, unless using as an ingredient for a rich fish soup.

Pompano (*pompano*)

One of the finest fish in the sea with firm, white, meaty flesh, pompano are found fresh in Florida and appear on the menus of expensive restaurants elsewhere – notably in New Orleans, where Antoine's *pompano en papillote* is a specialty. California pompano are not related to the Florida pompano but to the butterfish. Pompano are occasionally exported to northern Europe from the Mediterranean.

Buying guide: when available, sold whole, about 18in/45cm long, or in fillets – excellent from any part of the body.

Best cooking methods: brush with melted butter and broil, or poach in white wine. Pompano can also be stuffed and baked. Crab meat or shrimp sauces make a good accompaniment.

Dolphin fish (*dorade tropicale*)

Nothing whatsoever to do with the true dolphin, the dolphin fish is a Caribbean export. It is also found in the Mediterranean, where it is often called lampuga. Easily recognized by its high ridge of fin, it has a strong, excellent flavor.

Buying guide: when available, sold in steaks or fillets. Steaks are better.

Best cooking methods: bake, broil or fry, with lemon and garlic.

Red snapper (*vivaneau*)

You will need to live close to the southern Atlantic or Gulf coasts of America to enjoy this blushing, large-eyed fish fresh from the sea. These snappers will be weighty fish, pleasantly textured and well flavored – a 2–5lb/900g–2kg fish, stuffed and baked, makes a delicious meal.

Buying guide: sold whole or in steaks and fillets when fresh, also available frozen.

Best cooking methods: bake, broil or poach.

Garfish (*orphie*)

The green and silver garfish – no relation to the freshwater species of fish more correctly called gars – is a pleasant fish to eat although not perhaps of the first order. The flesh is a rather poor greyish-purple in its raw state, but it whitens during cooking and the bones have a rather startling advantage – they are bright copper green, quite harmless (caused by a phosphate of iron) and easily picked out on the plate.

Buying guide: worth trying whenever you see them. Sold whole.

Best cooking methods: cut the fish into segments, and fry or bake with garlic, or poach and serve with dill or fresh tomato sauce. Highly gelatinous, garfish is also good in fish pie.

Sea robins or gurnards (*grondins*)

A large family of sweet-tasting fish, sea robins – or gurnards, as they are known in Europe – have several culinary uses and the advantage of being quite cheap.

Buying guide: because they are so ugly they are seldom sold, but if you do find one ask the fish dealer to skin it for you.

Best cooking methods: excellent in fish soups, they can also be baked with white wine, egg-and-crumbed, whole or in fillets, fried and served with a Provençal or tomato sauce.

John Dory (*saint-pierre*)

This grandly ugly Mediterranean fish belies its appearance and is, in fact, one of the most delicious of fish – firm, delicate and excellently flavored. The dark circles on its sides are said to be the marks of St. Peter's fingers, hence the name St. Peter's fish.

Buying guide: buy whenever you can find it. Remember that almost two-thirds of its weight is taken up by its excessively large bony head and its gut.

Best cooking methods: small ones are excellent in bouillabaisse. Larger ones can be cooked whole or in fillets, as for sole.

Dogfish (*aiguillat, roussette*)

The dogfish is a variety of small shark, usually presented for sale minus head, tail and fins and called euphemistically huss, flake, rigg and even – quite shamefully – rock salmon. The flesh is white or slightly pink and firm textured, and deserves more attention than it gets.

Buying guide: available all year.

Best cooking methods: cut into pieces, dust with well-seasoned flour and fry gently, or coat with batter and deep fry.

Sea lamprey (*lamproie*)

A legendary fish that resembles a thick eel, the sea lamprey is distinguishable by the seven holes that lie behind its eyes and have given rise to its nicknames of flute and *septoreils*. It has a thick body, dark grey with mottled markings, and no scales. The flesh is richly flavoured, firm and fatty.

Buying guide: best in autumn.

Best cooking methods: prepare and cook as for eel, but scald before skinning. It can also be pickled in vinegar, or stewed with port.

Conger eel (*congres*)

The conger is one of two edible seawater eels

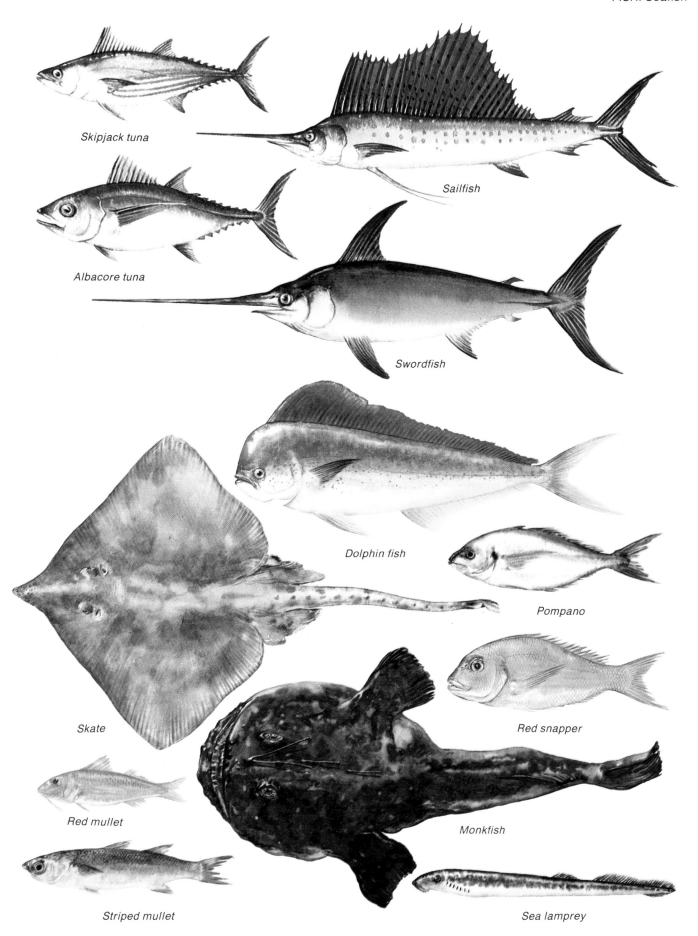

Skipjack tuna

Sailfish

Albacore tuna

Swordfish

Dolphin fish

Pompano

Skate

Red snapper

Red mullet

Monkfish

Striped mullet

Sea lamprey

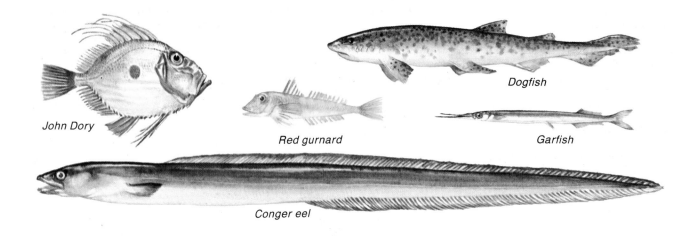

John Dory

Red gurnard

Dogfish

Garfish

Conger eel

– the other is the moray, which is really only suitable for bouillabaisse. If you can contemplate eating conger, it makes a good meal, in spite of its long, sharp bones.

Buying guide: spring to autumn. Ask for a thick cut from the head end.

Best cooking methods: use in fish soups, fish mousselines and terrines. A good-sized cut can be roasted, basted with cider and butter, or poached in cider.

FRESHWATER FISH

Lake and river fish are often more frail than sea fish. Their tissues and organs take up a larger proportion of their bodies, and their skin, once scaled, is easily torn.

The flesh is much lighter, tends to be dry and is often riddled with a structure of hair-like forked bones of amazing intricacy. Because of the vulnerable nature of fresh-water fish, it is imperative that they should be eaten in their freshest possible state.

It has been said that freshwater fish should never touch another drop of water once they have left it, so when they are cleaned and scaled they should be wiped down without washing whenever possible, and baked, grilled, broiled or fried in preference to being boiled or poached. If liquids are used they should be wine, cider, or melted butter or cream rather than water.

The exceptions to the no-water rule are members of the salmon family – these are exquisite poached in a court bouillon or *bonne-eau*, and one of the most delicious of dishes is a *truite au bleu*.

When cleaning a freshwater fish, be sure to remove the gills and see that no weed is left in its throat, as this can give a sour and reedy taste. Take particular care to remove the blood that lies along the backbone – this comes from a main vein and must be cleaned away until there is not a trace left.

If you can choose your fish, take those with a silvery or green rather than brownish hue – the brown fish are more likely to have come from slow-moving, muddy haunts. Various remedies have been suggested – keep the fish alive in a tank of clear water for

a day or so, or pour a tumblerful of vinegar or a couple of handfuls of salt into its mouth as soon as it is killed, or bake it unscaled in clay, which means that the mud-flavoured skin and scales can be removed all at once. But in fact there seems little point in trying to rid fish of their inherent taste, so if you dislike the flavour, choose some other fish that has a different character.

Most freshwater fish need quite a lot of salt and other seasoning – in Spain, river fish are gutted, rubbed in salt and left for several hours or even buried in salt overnight to make the flesh firmer and tastier. If your fish has been caught by an angler and there are herbs growing near the pool or river, such as thyme, watercress or mint, it is a good idea to gather these and take them home for flavoring the fish, which may already have been feeding on them and have a suspicion of their aroma in its flesh.

Small river fish have such a plethora of tiny bones that they are best either soused or pickled, so that the bones are softened by the vinegar, or used in a fish soup or a matelote. If the fish are very small they make an excellent mixed fry of the sort often served in France in the region of the Lot river as a *friture de la Dordogne*, and the bones can be happily crunched along with the crisp brown skin.

Salmon *(saumon)*

Known as the king of fish, the salmon is a majestic creature whose life is mysterious and exhausting. Spawned in fresh water, it spends most of its life in the sea, only returning to fresh water – usually to the river where it was born – to spawn. In fresh water salmon take no sustenance, so on their way back to the sea, when they are known as kelts, they are miserably thin and spent and certainly not fit to eat.

A Scotch or Irish salmon in good condition, in May, June or July, is considered to be the best in the world. It is a glossy steely blue fish shading to bright silver underneath, with black spots on the head and upper part of the body and fine pink flesh. Choose a short, round one with a

small head and broad shoulders (the head can represent a fifth of the total weight of the fish).

Salmon from Norwegian waters are also excellent, and so are those from Greenland. Of the Canadian and American West Coast salmon, the tastiest are the red-fleshed chinook, or king salmon, and the sockeye. Cook it simply and serve unadorned except for an appropriate sauce or mayonnaise and boiled new potatoes. If you are presented with a salmon straight from the river you will need to clean it, but leave on the head and tail. After cooking, skin it very carefully, in one piece.

Buying guide: spring and summer. Sold whole or in steaks. When really fresh there is a creamy substance between the flakes of flesh which sets to a curd when cooked. Avoid steaks that look soft, greyish, oily or watery. Allow 6–8oz/170–225g per person.

Best cooking methods: unless you have a truly enormous fish kettle, the best way to cook a salmon whole is to bake it in foil. If you do have a large fish kettle, or can borrow one, poach the salmon in a court bouillon at the lowest possible simmering point for a really succulent result. Hot, salmon is best with hollandaise or perhaps mousseline sauce, or with *beurre blanc*, lobster sauce or plain melted butter, with or without *fines herbes* – chervil, tarragon or parsley (salmon steaks can be brushed with butter, grilled and served with the same kinds of sauce). Cold, salmon is best eaten with plain or green mayonnaise or with horseradish in whipped cream and served with thinly sliced cucumber and boiled potatoes.

Salmon trout *(truite saumonée)*

Salmon trout – closely related to the brown trout found in rivers and lakes – is perhaps the perfect fish. As the name suggests, it combines the best of both the salmon and the trout: it has the superior texture of trout, being less dense and more succulent than salmon, but has salmon's excellent flavor and pale pink-colored flesh. Salmon trout is also a much more useful size than salmon for cooking whole as it usually weighs less than

5lb/2.5kg, although it can grow to 10lb/4.5kg or even more.

The correct name for salmon trout is sea trout and that, too, is apt since the fish is really a trout that has taken it into its head to wander down to the sea to feed, returning to fresh water to spawn. It is a beautiful silver fish with a small head, not as pointed as that of the salmon and with dark X-shaped spots on the gill cover.

In the northern states of America and in Canada, various species of trout found in rivers and lakes and occasionally available in fish markets are often referred to as salmon trout.

Buying guide: spring and summer. Sold whole. Allow ½lb/225g per person, but, as it is a filling fish, less will do.

Best cooking methods: salmon trout can be dealt with in the same ways as salmon and is particularly good baked in foil. Poached, it makes a delicious summer lunch. Allow the same cooking time as for salmon, or a few minutes less, and use the same sauces as you would for salmon.

Trout *(truite)*

The rainbow trout is a familar and delicious fish – it appears almost unfailingly on restaurant menus and a very neat parcel of food it makes, just the right size for one person, pretty to look at and sweet and succulent to eat. The hatchery rainbow trout is the most familiar, white fleshed and delicate and deserving better treatment than the usual sprinkling of almonds. A hardy fish, it responds well to freezing and frozen rainbow trout, wrapped individually in plastic bags, are quite a good buy. It is often possible, too, to buy extra large rainbow trout up to 3–4lb/1.5–2kg. These are hatchery trout and may have been fed special food to give a pink tinge to their flesh. They are also a good buy if you come across them.

Brown trout, the wild native trout of English rivers and streams, are a beautiful brown with red and dark grey spots. They are usually only available to the families of fly fishermen – a great pity, for they are quite delicious. In America, however, the brown trout has thrived since its introduction at the end of the last century, and is a hardy and popular fish.

Take care when cleaning trout to wipe rather than wash it. Remove the gills but leave the head on – the eyes will turn quite white as the fish is cooking. The skin can be removed after cooking, if wished, in one whole piece.

Buying guide: available all year, fresh (hatchery) or frozen. Sold whole. Allow one trout per person, unless the trout are particularly large.

Best cooking methods: trout can be poached in a court bouillon, served *à la meunière*, baked, broiled or fried, or smoked in a home smoker. It can also be cooked in beer with horseradish and served with horseradish sauce, and another good, if surprising, sauce

is a purée of green gooseberries. If the trout is still alive or is extremely fresh it can be cooked *au bleu* in water with vinegar in it; served with hollandaise or mousseline sauce it is well worth the trouble. In Sweden trout is boiled in a very little salt water and served with butter.

Char *(omble)*

The arctic char of northern Europe and Canada, the char *(omble-chevalier)* of the deep lakes of the French and Swiss Alps, and the Dolly Varden, brook trout and lake trout of North America (also chars) all belong to the enormous and excellent salmon family.

The arctic char is a silver, salmon-like fish with a pink underside, which flushes deep red during spawning. It has firm, delicate flesh and makes a delicious meal. Arctic char used to be so prolific in the Lake District of northern England that potted char became a famous breakfast delicacy, but these days its numbers have lessened considerably. In France, the *omble-chevalier*, which resembles trout, is eaten throughout the summer and is definitely worth ordering if you see it on a menu. The Dolly Varden, brook trout and lake trout are also very good table fish and deservedly popular.

Buying guide: the arctic char is best in early autumn; American chars are available all year. Small brook trout are sold whole, each enough for one person. Lake trout are larger, and these and arctic char can be cut into steaks, or cooked whole.

Best cooking methods: as for trout or salmon. Steaks can be poached for a few minutes with bay leaves and eaten cold.

Grayling *(ombre)*

A delicious, thyme-scented fish, called by St. Ambrose the flower fish or flower of fishes, grayling should be eaten if possible as soon as it is caught because the delicate flavor is fugitive. It is a graceful fish, silver with finely marked geometric scales and a long spotted back fin. It cannot survive in even slightly polluted water and only thrives in cold, crystal-clear, turbulent rivers, often living alongside trout and eating the same food. A very fresh grayling has much in common, in taste and texture, with trout, and bears up well in comparison.

You will probably have to catch your own grayling to try one. Scale it before cooking – scald with boiling water and use a knife or a fish scaler, or try picking the scales off with your fingernails. Grayling never weigh more than 4lb/2kg, and are usually less than 2lb/900g.

Best cooking methods: brush with butter, flavor with thyme – especially if you find thyme near the brook where the fish was caught – and grill, broil, or fry gently in clarified unsalted butter.

Carp *(carpe)*

One of the hardiest of all fish, the carp is known to have existed in Asia thousands of years ago and is reputed to live to a grand old age. A somewhat lumbering fish, in its

natural state it lives in slow and often muddy rivers or lakes, but it can survive well in domestic ponds and is extensively farmed.

The common or king carp is covered with scales, but variants have been bred such as the crucian, mirror, spiegel and leather carp with just a few large scales that can be picked off with your fingernails, or with no scales at all. To scale a common carp, pour some boiling water over it first, but better still ask the fish dealer to scale it for you. A compact and meaty fish, carp needs to be cooked with plenty of interesting flavors.

Buying guide: at their best in late summer and autumn. Sold whole, usually a good size for four people.

Best cooking methods: stuffed and baked, or poached and served with horseradish or sorrel sauce. A baked carp can be served on a platter, surrounded by fried gudgeon if that is what the day's catch has consisted of – the small fish have just their bodies coated with eggs and crumbs, leaving their heads and tails free as if they were in a muff, and are then deep fried. Jewish recipes for carp are excellent.

Pike *(brochet)*, **pickerel** *(brocheton)* **and muskellunge**

The predatory pike is quite handsome in its way, especially the younger fish, or jack, which has bold markings on a golden brown or greenish silver background. An adult pike can weigh up to 40lb/18kg or more, and the flesh is white and firm. The muskellunge of northeastern and north central North America can grow even larger, but the pickerel, or young pike, of the eastern and southern states is much smaller, usually around 5lb/2.5kg. In France pike is much admired, and quenelles de brochet, the lightest of fish dumplings, served with a white wine sauce, is a classic dish.

The theories about cooking pike are many: it should be bled to remove the sharp, reedy taste; it should have quantities of salt forced down its throat and be left to hang overnight to dissolve the bones; it should not be washed because its natural slime keeps it tender. However, a medium-size pike is perfectly good cooked without any of these refinements. Simply scale it before cooking – pour a little boiling water over it first. Watch out for the bones when you eat it, for they are vicious and plentiful; and don't ever eat the roe, which in some cases can be poisonous.

Buying guide: best in autumn and early winter. If you do see pike for sale, a small, whole one is best. Large pike are usually cut into steaks.

Best cooking methods: pike tends to be dry and a very large one may also be tough, so steaks should be marinated before being fried or broiled. Small pike can be poached and served with *beurre blanc*, melted butter, parsley sauce or caper sauce. Best of all, you can make it into quenelles. In Scandinavia, pike is broiled and eaten with horseradish.

Perch *(perche)*, **pike perch or zander** *(sandre)* **and yellow perch**

The perch is a beautiful little fish, pale greenish-gold with a white or yellowish belly and superb coral-colored fins. The back has dangerously sharp spines and the scales are stubborn, but the fish is well worth the trouble of preparing; it is firm fleshed, delicate and light, and has a very good flavor. It is a fish that should only be eaten when it is gleamingly fresh.

Looking somewhat like a cross between pike and perch, with a bony head, thick skin and spiny dorsal fin, the European pike perch is reared, like trout, in special conditions for fast growth. Even so it is a most delicious fish with firm, white wonderfully flavored flesh, more interesting than trout and well worth purchasing whenever you see it. The American pike perch is also known as the yellow pike perch, blue pike perch and walleyed pike.

The yellow perch, sold in many American midwestern markets, is a popular pan fish, known as "yellow ned" in many localities. It is closely related to the common perch and can be cooked in the same ways.

To prepare perch and pike perch for cooking, first carefully cut off the spines and fins with strong scissors, then bend the fish over and scrape the scales that will be raised a little from their usual flat position. The procedure is slightly easier if you hold the fish firmly by the tail with a cloth or paper towel, or you can sprinkle your hands with salt. A pair of stout scissors is also useful for opening the fish to gut it.

Buying guide: these fish are sold whole. Smaller fish are more delicate to eat than the large ones.

Best cooking methods: perch and pike perch are probably best fried slowly in clarified butter, about ten minutes on each side for a 1½ lb/ 700g fish. They can also be baked, boiled or broiled. Perch *maître d'hôtel* is perch split, seasoned and broiled with a dressing of butter and chopped parsley poured over it before it is sent to the table. This is simple and good.

Shad *(alose)*

The shad is a large migratory member of the herring family which spawns in fresh water. White fleshed and nutritious, it has a good flavor but also, unfortunately, a multitude of fine wire-like bones. The roe is particularly good – it is even classed as an aphrodisiac by more hopeful gourmets.

The allis shad, which can grow up to 2ft/ 60cm long, and the smaller twaite shad *(alose finte)* are caught in the Loire and Garonne rivers of France in the springtime, when they are full-roed. The American shad *(alose canadienne)* has been successfully transplanted from the Atlantic to the Pacific and the roes are sold frozen and canned as well as fresh.

Remove as many of the bones as possible before cooking shad, using tweezers if necessary. When the fish is cooked, cut it through in lengthwise parallel strips about 4in/10cm apart and remove any accessible bones before serving, moving your finger over the surface of the flesh to detect the hidden ones.

Buying guide: best in spring when full-roed. Usually sold whole; a 3lb/1.5kg shad will feed six. Ask the fish dealer to scale and possibly bone the fish when he cleans it.

Best cooking methods: stuff with sorrel and bake, or bake and serve on a bed of sorrel. If the roe is not cooked with the fish, it can be cooked *à la meunière* or gently baked in butter. Shad can also be filleted, with the skin left on and gently broiled. Serve with fresh tomato sauce, *beurre blanc* or sorrel purée mixed with fresh cream.

Sturgeon *(esturgeon)*

A huge and somewhat prehistoric looking creature, the sturgeon spends most of its life in the sea, but is most sought after when it comes into rivers to spawn. It can grow up to 20ft/6m or more and the beluga sturgeon – usually a more modest size and the source of the most expensive caviar – can live to the ripe age of 100. Sturgeon are still caught in some American and European rivers, but they are most plentiful in the Caspian Sea, using its southern rivers for spawning. The flesh is white, very firm, rich and close textured, and is frequently likened to veal. It is inclined to be dry and is improved by being steeped in a white wine marinade before it is cooked.

Buying guide: best in spring. Usually sold in large pieces or as steaks.

Best cooking methods: broil or fry in butter, like veal, or poach in white wine and serve with a creamy sauce. In France, a luxurious version is sturgeon poached in champagne. It is also very good smoked, like salmon.

Eels and elvers *(anguilles)*

Eels have a life cycle as strange as that of any fish. The European eel is spawned in the Sargasso Sea and promptly travels up to 4,000 miles/7,000 km to find the fresh waters of its ancestors, where it will spend most of its life, only returning to the Sargasso to spawn and then die. (American, Australian and Japanese eels have spawning grounds closer to land, but still have a very long way to travel.)

By the time they reach the river mouths the larvae have grown into elvers 2–3 in/5– 8cm long. These little creatures, looking like transparent spaghetti, are good to eat, rather like whitebait but not as crisp. By their second winter in fresh water the elvers have become small yellow eels, which are not so good to eat. These then mature into the familiar silver eels, velvety brown on their backs and silver below, and excellent to eat

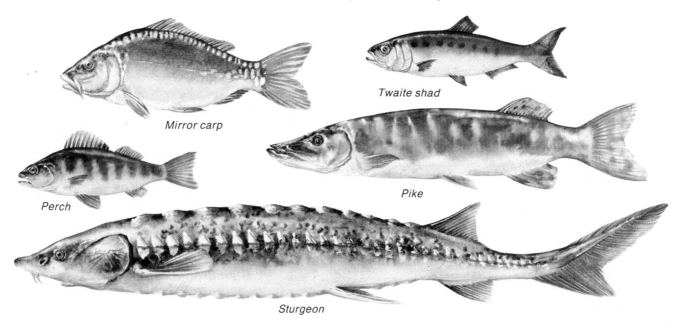

Mirror carp

Twaite shad

Perch

Pike

Sturgeon

– meaty, even textured, succulent and very rich.

Buying guide: elvers appear in the spring; eels are in season all year but are best in autumn. Try to buy live eels – they become tough and go off instantly once killed. If you flinch at the prospect of dispatching a live eel yourself, ask the fish dealer to kill and skin it for you and chop it into 1 in/2.5 cm lengths, but ask for 3 in/8 cm pieces, which look better and are better able to keep their moisture during cooking.

Best cooking methods: jellied eels and "eel pie and mash" with a kind of parsley liquor or sauce have long been a speciality of London's East End, and jellied eels are an English seaside treat. You may prefer to stew your eel in red wine, wrap it in bacon and sage leaves and broil it, or sauté it with a few bay leaves and serve it with green sauce. Elvers should be washed and tossed dry in a cloth, dipped in flour, then cooked immediately in hot oil. In Spain they are served in a fried tangle with a fiery fresh tomato sauce.

Other freshwater fish

The following freshwater fish are not commercially fished or grown in hatcheries, and are unlikely to be found in a fish market – they are trophies for the angler rather than the cook.

Barbel

Respected by European anglers as one of the hardest freshwater fish to catch, the barbel does not make very good eating, the flesh being somewhat coarse and flannelly. It must be cleaned and soaked and rinsed and soaked again before cooking, and the roe is slightly poisonous. Cook in the same ways as catfish.

Bass

A collective name for a large family of bony fish with spiny fins, which includes the magnificent sea bass. All make good eating.

Cook small ones whole, baked and stuffed, or broiled with fennel stalks. Fillets from larger fish can be poached or served *à la meunière*.

Bleak

A small, slim, silvery fish found in the rivers of northern Europe, which can be cooked just like a whitebait.

Bluegill

A popular fish with anglers, this dry but well-flavored member of the sunfish family is best when pan-fried. It is also known as bream and sun perch.

Buffalo fish

A popular freshwater fish from the Great Lakes and the Mississippi Valley which makes good eating. It is often smoked, but can be prepared as for carp when fresh. Other varieties are the common buffalo, the red mouth, the prairie buffalo and the big mouth rooter.

Burbot

This handsome golden fish is the only member of the cod family to inhabit fresh water, and it is found in Europe, Britain and the United States. Burbot has good, firm, fatty flesh and a richly flavored liver that can be sliced to release its oils and baked or poached with the fish. The fish may also be cooked in red wine, or served with a tomato, cheese and cream sauce. Burbot is best in summer.

Catfish

So called because of the long barbels that hang about its mouth like drooping cat's whiskers, the catfish is a particularly hardy creature. It is easily transplanted from one region to another, and is a candidate for intensive fish culture. It should be skinned before cooking, and is usually deep fried as fillets and served with tartare sauce. It also makes a good basis for a fish soup that should include plenty of tomatoes, garlic, herbs and white wine.

Chub

A fish that precisely fits the description "cotton wool stuffed with needles," chub is watery flesh, full of small forked bones and not really worth eating. If, however, you do catch one and don't want to waste it, try stewing it, frying it or baking it in foil with herbs. It should be cooked as soon as possible after being caught as the flavor deteriorates in a very short time.

Crappie

Known to anglers as white crappie, this is an excellent Mississippi Valley and New England freshwater fish. It is related to the delicious calico bass or black crappie and is usually fried.

Dace

The European and American dace are completely different fish that happen to have the same name, but neither is of much culinary interest. Both may be rolled in flour and deep fried, or fried in butter (preferably over an open fire on the river bank just after they have been caught).

Gudgeon

Found on the sandy bottom of many rivers and lakes in Britain and Europe, gudgeon are delicious little fish which can be crisply fried like whitebait, and served with lemon and chopped parsley.

Lake herring/cisco

A whitefish found in plentiful supply in the Great Lakes, lake herring, nicknamed cisco, make good eating and can be used for trout, smelt or salmon recipes.

Roach

A quite well-flavored British and European fish, roach sadly defies much enjoyment because it has such quantities of bones. Larger specimens (around 3 lb/1.5 kg) can be scored and fried in butter, or baked in white wine. The roe, which is greenish, is good, and becomes red when it is cooked.

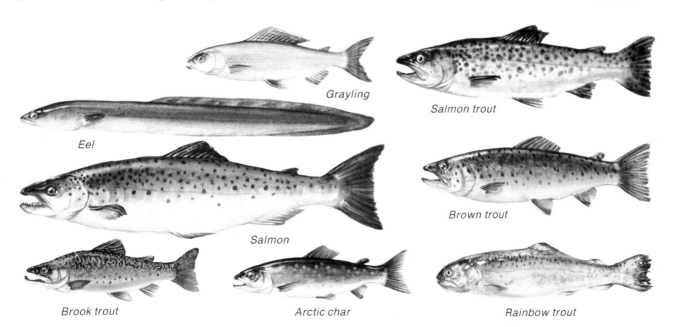

Grayling

Salmon trout

Eel

Salmon

Brown trout

Brook trout

Arctic char

Rainbow trout

Sheepshead

Not to be confused with the saltwater red bream, for which sheepshead is another name, this fish is found in fresh waters of the American Middle West and southern states. It is a relative of croakers and drums, and can be either poached or pan fried when very fresh.

Tench

This fish, which is said to be best when taken from fast-running waters in Britain, must be scaled, cleaned and soaked in cold water before cooking. The flesh is rather flaccid and has a somewhat muddy flavor, but it may be cooked in a matelote together with eel, carp and pike, or fried or baked and served with an interesting sauce that should include such strong flavors as herbs, cloves, garlic or shallots. Tench are in season between autumn and spring.

Vendace and powan

Known collectively as whitefish, these fish, which slightly resemble salmon in appearance, are found in cool, clear lakes of northern Europe, including the lochs of Scotland and Ireland. Both fish may be treated as for grayling.

RECIPE SUGGESTIONS

Fish pie

¾ lb/340 g fillet of fresh haddock	
1 small whole smoked haddock, about 1 lb/450 g	
⅔ cup/1.5 dl milk	
1 bay leaf	
2 lb/900 g potatoes	
butter and milk for mashing	
4 hard-boiled eggs	
½ stick/55 g butter	
2 tablespoons/15 g flour	
3–4 sprigs fresh tarragon or parsley, chopped	
salt and freshly ground pepper	

SERVES 4–6

Preheat the oven to 325°F/170°C.
Put both kinds of fish into a baking dish or roasting pan with the milk, ½ cup/1.5 dl water and bay leaf and poach in the oven for 15 minutes. The fish should be just cooked, with a creamy liquid coming to the surface.
Meanwhile, peel the potatoes and start them cooking in salted water.
Turn the oven up to 425°F/220°C, alternatively, heat the broiler.
Flake the fish, taking care to remove the skin and all the bones. Melt half of the butter in a small pan, stir in the flour and make a sauce with the liquid in which the fish was cooked. Drain the potatoes, using some of their liquid to make the sauce the consistency of thick cream. Taste it to see if it needs more salt—it probably won't. Put the fish and the hard-boiled eggs, peeled and chopped, and the tarragon or parsley into the sauce. Mash the potatoes and season well.
Put the fish mixture into a pie dish or gratin dish, cover it with a nice even layer of mashed potatoes, dot the top with thin slivers of butter and either bake for 15–20 minutes until nicely browned, or brown it under the broiler.
ALTERNATIVES: *cod, hake, halibut.*

Cod poached whole

1 cod, about 7 lb/3 kg	
few strands of saffron (optional)	
for the court bouillon:	
fish bones	
1 onion	
4 carrots	
few sprigs of parsley and a sprig of thyme	
1 bay leaf	
2 tablespoons salt	

SERVES 8–10

To make the court bouillon, put the fish bones, the peeled onion, carrots, parsley, thyme and bay leaf into a large saucepan with 5 quarts/4.5 liters very well-salted water and bring to the boil. Simmer for 20 minutes. Remove from the heat and allow to cool to room temperature.
If you are using saffron, put a few strands into the cod's belly. Make two straps of silver foil by folding two 18 in/45 cm square sheets into 2 in/5 cm strips. Place the straps in the pan of court bouillon, lay the fish on top of them and join the strap ends at the top. These are for helping to lift the fish out in one piece when cooked.
Bring the court bouillon slowly to boiling point, turn down the heat until the water is merely swirling, not bubbling at all, and cook at the barest simmer for about 25 minutes. A knife inserted at the thickest part of the fish behind the head should show that there is no trace of pink next to the bone. Serve with new potatoes, young carrots, small beets, green beans and aïoli, or with hard-boiled eggs, potatoes, carrots and butter.

Truite au bleu

4 fresh trout	
6 tablespoons wine vinegar	
1 tablespoon salt	

SERVES 4

Bring 2½ quarts/2.25 liters of water to the boil with the vinegar and salt.
Meanwhile, if the trout are alive bang them on the head with a knife-sharpening steel or other heavy implement. Clean them carefully and remove their gills, but do not wash or wipe them, and handle them as gently and carefully as possible so that the natural coating on the skin is not disturbed. Slip them into the boiling water and simmer for 5–10 minutes, according to their size, until cooked. Drain well and place on a folded white napkin. Serve with melted butter or beurre blanc.
This recipe is most valuable to those who can obtain freshly caught trout with their skin still covered with a smooth natural slime, which turns a delicate cloudy blue in the cooking process. However, ordinary store-bought trout are also excellent cooked this way, although they will not be the same lovely color.

Poached salmon

1 salmon, about 3–3½ lb/1.5–2 kg	
5 quarts/4.5 liters court bouillon	
2 glasses white wine	

SERVES 6–8

Clean the salmon, remove the gills and wipe with a paper towel to remove any blood. With the court bouillon at a lukewarm temperature, add the white wine. Slide in the fish and bring the liquid, which should just cover the fish, up to simmering point. From this point it should simmer gently for 5–6 minutes per 1 lb/450 g (a smaller fish needs a shorter cooking time). Never let the liquid boil.
Lift the fish out and let it stand on a rack, covered with a clean cloth, over the hot liquid for 5 minutes to drain and set. Serve hot with hollandaise, new potatoes and peas, or cold with mayonnaise.
ALTERNATIVES: *salmon trout, char, pike, perch.*

Halibut in cider

4 fillets halibut about 1 in/2.5 cm thick	
1 small shallot or ¼ onion	
2 tablespoons/30 g butter	
salt and freshly ground pepper	
1¼ cups/3 dl hard cider	
2 egg yolks	
⅔ cup/1.5 dl heavy cream	
juice of ½ lemon	
1 tablespoon chopped parsley	

SERVES 4

Peel and finely chop the shallot or onion. Melt the butter in a frying pan and gently sweat the chopped shallot or onion. Remove the pan from the heat and put in the fillets of fish, seasoned with salt and pepper, turning them in the butter until they are well coated. Pour in the cider and put back over a gentle heat. Poach at a slow simmer for 10–15 minutes. Remove the fish to a serving dish and reduce the cooking liquid by half. Whisk the egg yolks and cream together in a small saucepan, add the reduced cider and whisk over a gentle heat until slightly thickened, then add the lemon juice and parsley. Taste for seasoning. Spoon over the pieces of fish and serve with small, plainly steamed new potatoes.
ALTERNATIVE: *turbot, flounder.*

Carp with thyme stuffing

1 carp, about 2–2¼ lb/900 g–1 kg	
2 tablespoons/30 g butter for basting	
4 tablespoons heavy cream	
for the stuffing:	
1 onion	
½ stick/55 g butter	
½ cup/55 g fresh white bread crumbs	
½ teaspoon chopped thyme	
1 teaspoon chopped parsley	
1 teaspoon grated lemon rind	
salt and freshly ground pepper	

SERVES 4

Ask the fish seller to scale the carp and cut off its head so that it can be gutted without opening the stomach. Keep the head. Make certain that the inside is very well cleaned and washed out.
Preheat the oven to 350°F/180°C.
To prepare the stuffing, chop the onion finely and sweat it in the butter in a small frying pan, without letting it brown. Stir in the bread crumbs, thyme, parsley and lemon rind and season with salt and pepper. Stuff the fish with this mixture and put it in a buttered baking dish. Put the head back in place, dot the carp with butter and bake for 20 minutes, basting it from time to time. Add the cream and bake for another 10 minutes. Serve with buttered potatoes and quarters of lemon.
ALTERNATIVES: *shad, grayling or bluegill.*

PREPARING FLAT FISH

1 TRIMMING

Flat fish are usually gutted on the boat as soon as they are caught, so preparing them for cooking is a simple task. First, snip off the tough upper pectoral fin. The fish here is a small halibut.

Slice down one side of the fish, edging the knife between the flesh and the bones. For the second fillet, slice away the flesh from the opposite side. For the third and fourth fillets, turn the fish over and repeat the process.

Trim the tail and cut away the dorsal and anal fins.

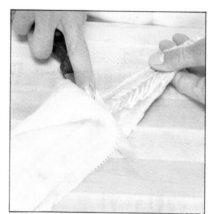

To skin the fillets, hold each firmly by the tail end and work a sharp filleting knife down the length of the fillet, keeping the blade as close to the skin as possible.

Cut off the head just below the gills.

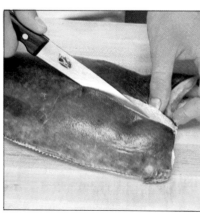

3 SKINNING

To skin a flat fish that is to be cooked whole, first make a nick in the skin across the tail end on the darker side. Run a finger up either side of the fish between the skin and the flesh.

2 FILLETING and SKINNING

Make a slit down the backbone from top to tail.

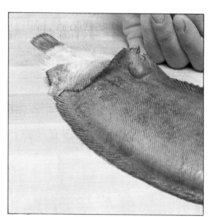

Ease the skin away from the flesh, pulling towards the head. If the skin proves too slippery to grip, dip your fingers in salt. If you want to remove the white skin from the reverse side, turn the fish over and repeat the process.

PREPARING ROUND FISH

1 SCALING

Hold the fish by the tail. Scrape away the scales with the back of a knife, working towards the head.

Slit open the fish's belly and ease out the guts. Finally, rinse the fish thoroughly, inside and out, under cold running water.

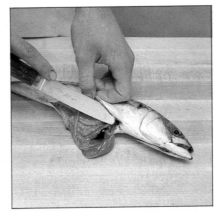

2 CLEANING

Before cooking a fish whole, it is important to remove the bitter-tasting gills. Lay the fish – in this case a mackerel – on its back and ease open the gill flaps.

3 FILLETING

Starting just behind the head, cut into the back of the fish, sliding the knife closely along one side of the backbone.

Push the fan of gills out from between the gill flaps, sever and discard them.

Continue slicing down the length of the fish, severing the fillet just below the gills and at the tail.

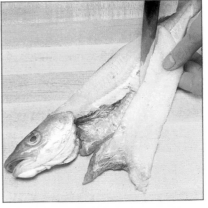

Trim off all the fins with blunt-ended scissors.

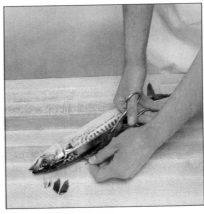

Cut the second fillet from the opposite side of the backbone. Skin the fillets in the same way as illustrated for flat fish.

PREPARING ROUND FISH

4 BONING

Cut down into the head and, when the knife is almost through, ease the head away from the body, taking the guts with it.

Slice down the back of the fish, keeping the knife close against one side of the backbone. Do not puncture the belly. Open out the herring like a book.

Turn the fish flesh side down and cut away the backbone and small adjoining bones.

Discard the head, guts and bones. This method of boning a herring is particularly suitable when the fish is to be stuffed.

5 SALMON SCALLOPS

Take a tail end section of fresh salmon.

Cut it lengthwise along each side of the backbone, starting at the tail and cutting as close to the bone as possible. Discard the backbone and skin each fillet.

Slice each fillet into two thin slices, using a long, sharp, flexible knife.

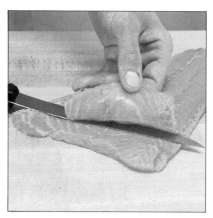

Place each slice of salmon between two pieces of dampened wax paper and gently but firmly flatten the fish into scallops, using a rolling pin or a cutlet beater.

SMOKED FISH

Fish must be salted before smoking. This process, which entails either soaking the fish in a brine or rubbing into it a generous amount of dry salt, improves both the flavor and the keeping qualities. After salting, the fish is cold- or hot-smoked. The protein content remains unchanged, calories are diminished.

Store-bought smoked fish will keep for about three days, or up to twenty days in a freezer. Home-smoked fish should be eaten at once. Only dried and salted fish keeps indefinitely.

COLD-SMOKED FISH

Cold-smoking takes place at temperatures of around 75°F/24°C, which smokes the fish but does not cook it. Products of the cold-smoking process are either eaten raw, like smoked salmon, or may require further cooking, like kippers or finnan haddie.

Smoked salmon

Smoked salmon should be fresh and succulent, melting away under the knife as it is sliced. The best of all is the pale pink-gold, rather under-salted salmon. Buying a whole side has the advantage of giving you both the denser, saltier, lower cuts and the fatter middle. To slice the salmon, go across the grain of the flesh – that is, cut from the shoulder towards the tail. You need an extremely sharp, long, flexible knife – one with a wavy edge is best.

Kippers

Split washed herrings are briefly brined, hung on "tenterhooks" to dry, and then smoked for 4–6 hours.

Buy a fat kipper – lean kippers tend to be dry. And buy your kippers fresh and loose – frozen kippers, although they keep their texture fairly well, do not taste as good, and boil-in-the-bag fillets make very dull eating.

Finnan haddie – smoked haddock

Smoked haddock is eaten hot. Broil, or poach it for a few minutes in milk or water, then simply serve it with butter, or use it to make dishes such as the creamed finnan haddie of New England, or the Anglo-Indian kedgeree, or the poached smoked haddock of Scandinavia.

Finnan haddie has a distinctive pale color due to the method of curing it.

Smoked halibut

Young halibut are sometimes lightly smoked. Their taste is delicate, their texture firm, and they are served in the same way as smoked haddock.

Bloaters, harengs saur

Bloaters are in-shore herrings that are lightly salted and then smoked without the gut being removed. Bloaters are silvery in appearance and the flesh is soft and moist. They do not keep as long as kippers and must be gutted before they are served.

Smoked sturgeon

Smoked sturgeon resembles nothing so much

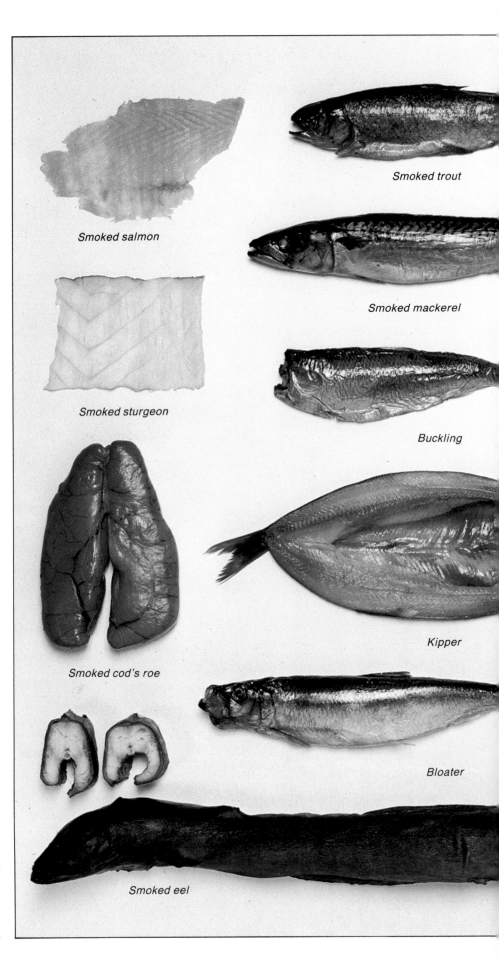

Smoked salmon

Smoked sturgeon

Smoked cod's roe

Smoked trout

Smoked mackerel

Buckling

Kipper

Bloater

Smoked eel

Arbroath smokies

Finnan haddie

Smoked haddock

as smoked turkey both in color and taste. It is, however, more delicious still, more buttery and melting in the mouth, and of course a great deal more expensive. Eat it like smoked salmon.

Smoked roes
Fish eggs from any number of species are smoked and eaten with enjoyment. Smoked roes should be firm and moist with no signs of skin breakage. Smoked cod's roe is deliciously grainy and glutinous. Serve as a first course like pâté, or use it to make taramasalata.

HOT-SMOKED FISH
Hot-smoking takes place at temperatures of about 180°F/82°C and is the method used for eel, trout, buckling and mackerel, which are smoked and lightly cooked at one and the same time. They are bought ready to eat and can also be served hot.

Smoked trout
The best smoked trout has gone into brine as soon as it left the water. It is drawn only after it has been drained, and is then ready for smoking. Serve smoked trout for a summer lunch or supper with lemon wedges, thin brown bread and butter, and horseradish mixed with a dash of the heaviest cream.

Smoked mackerel
Silvery-gold smoked mackerel can be very good indeed. As it is not a very subtly flavored fish, it emerges from careful kippering tasting straightforwardly of itself and is, usually firm and juicy. Best bought loose and whole, it is also available filleted and packed in heat-sealed envelopes. Eat smoked mackerel cold with horseradish sauce or lemon.

Bucklings
A good fat buckling can be an almost triumphant rival of a smoked trout. It is good eaten with brown bread and butter and lemon wedges, and also good mashed to a paste.

Sprats, sild and brisling
These are all small herrings which when smoked are simply served with dark bread, butter, lemon and a glass of beer. As well as being candidates for smoking they also sometimes find themselves canned as sardines.

Arbroath smokies
These are small smoked haddock that have been beheaded and gutted but not split, and hot-smoked in the round. To serve, open the fish out, remove the backbone, put butter and some freshly milled black pepper inside, close it up again and heat it gently under the broiler or in the oven.

Smoked eel
Smoked eel is very rich, oily and filling, and is usually served with pepper, lemon juice and brown bread and butter. Pinky-beige smoked eel fillets laid over a plateful of golden scrambled eggs, bordered with triangles of fried bread, make a first course that is especially delicious.

PICKLED AND SALTED FISH

The pickling process is particularly suited to oily fish, such as herrings. They are steeped in a vinegar or brine solution which halts enzyme action in the same way that cooking does.

Gravlax

This is a most delicious Swedish specialty – it is fresh raw salmon pickled with dill, sugar, salt, white peppercorns and sometimes cognac. It is eaten raw with a rather sweet mustard sauce.

Salt herrings

They should be soaked for up to twelve hours, filleted and chopped for salads or bathed in sour cream for an hors d'oeuvre.

Maatjes herrings

These are the best salt herrings. They are lightly salted fat female fish with translucent, slippery flesh of a beautiful old-rose color. They need no soaking.

Rollmops

These are herrings – boned and halved lengthwise – that have been rolled up tightly around peppercorns and slices of onion and fastened with a toothpick before being put into jars to which is added hot, spiced white wine vinegar.

Bismarck herrings

These herrings, blue of skin and white of flesh, are first steeped in white wine vinegar. They are drawn, boned, topped, tailed and split and kept for 24 hours layered in a dish with seasoning and onion rings.

Soused herring

Many people like to souse herrings at home by steeping them in a vinegary marinade to which herbs and spices are added.

Anchovies

Preserved salted anchovy fillets usually come canned in oil, those in olive oil being the best. Anchovies are good for salsa verde, braised veal, stews, pizzas, and for eating with egg mayonnaise, with sliced tomatoes and in potato salad and salade niçoise.

DRIED FISH

This earliest method of preserving fish is the precursor of modern freeze-drying. Salting is another way to extract moisture from fish, thus discouraging decay.

Dried cod, stockfish

Dried to a flatness and hardness resembling hide, cod – ling, haddock, pollock – spring back to life when they are soaked. The revived fish is often eaten with yellow peas, and also appears in a fish pudding, light as a soufflé, which is served with hollandaise sauce. In Holland, Belgium and Germany, stockfish is often soaked in lime water before being cooked. Some of the best recipes for dried cod are Basque, and variously involve the fish – bacalao – with garlic, oil, tomatoes, pimentos, onions and potatoes.

Bombay duck

This is the most famous of the various Eastern dried fish. It is found in Indian deli-catessens, and provides seasoning for the rice that is eaten with curry. Made from cured bommaloe fish, Bombay duck smells awful when you buy it. Toast it slowly until its edges curl and no trace of the objectionable smell remains. Then crumble it and sprinkle over cooked rice.

Dried shark's fin

This is delicately flavored cartilage of the fin, which requires soaking overnight, or even longer, in many changes of water, until it has become like a firm jelly. Its gelatinous properties have been likened to those of calves' feet.

SALTED ROES

Into this category fall the costly caviar and its less exotic alternatives.

Grey mullet roe

Known as tarama in Greece, the salted, dried, pressed roe of the mullet is considered a great delicacy. As the name suggests, it makes taramasalata – one of the "cream salads" of the Middle East. For this purpose the roe is divested of its skin, pounded with oil, lemon juice and crushed garlic and bound with soft white bread crumbs.

Caviar

The fish that are used for commercial caviar production are the sevruga, the large osetra and the giant beluga, which has a huge roe to match.

Caviars come in a variety of sizes and colors. Sevruga is small grained and greeny-black. Osetra, larger grained, may be golden-brown, or bottle-green, or slate-grey; it can also be pale – almost bluish-white. Beluga, the largest and the best, is grey.

First-grade caviar is sometimes pasteurized, which lengthens its shelf life. Non-pasteurized caviar is kept refrigerated at 32°F/0°C: warmer and it goes off; colder and its flavor is ruined. The contents of an open container should be kept covered in the refrigerator and eaten within a week.

This also applies to pressed caviar – which has been poured into cheesecloth bags and drained of some of its liquid. The eggs, of course, are squashed in the process, and what emerges is a fairly solid mass, saltier than malassol, but tasting more intensely of sturgeon, since 2lb/900g of caviar are reduced to make 1lb/450g of pressed. In the USSR, where large helpings of second-grade caviar are fairly unceremoniously served, it is often eaten with blinis – fat little buckwheat pancakes – and sour cream. But as a rule it is best with a little lemon, some fresh Melba toast and unsalted butter.

Keta – red caviar

This is made from the roe of the salmon. It is bright orange and large grained, not so much an imitation caviar but a fresh-tasting product in its own right.

Lumpfish roe

The pink eggs of the arctic lumpfish are salted, colored black and pressed. Sold as German or Danish caviar, it is usually used to make an impression on canapés.

CANNED FISH

Fish is one of the few foods that stand up well to the business of canning. Canned tuna and sardines, for example, have become foods worth eating in their own right.

Salmon

Canned salmon comes in many grades, from the not-so-good bright red to a more acceptable pink. It can be good and is useful in fish-

Rollmops

Dried shark's fin

Salt herring

cakes and patties.

Sardines

Good brands of sardines have been gently brined, correctly dried and lightly cooked in olive oil, and stored for about a year, so that the flavor of fish and oil are mingled. The sardines caught off the west coast of France are the best and the most expensive. Eat sardines bones and all, with dark bread and butter and a squeeze of lemon.

Pilchards

These fish, slightly larger than sardines, are never as good as sardines.

Tuna

The best canned tuna is taken from the albacore, the king of the tunas, which alone is permitted to be described as "white meat". Use canned tuna for the classic *vitello tonnato*, cold veal with a creamy tuna sauce. Buy good-quality tuna, which come in solid pieces, packed in oil rather than water.

Jellied eels

This traditionally Cockney delicacy is difficult to find freshly cooked. But it is sold in cans, and makes a good appetizer: serve it with little bunches of watercress.

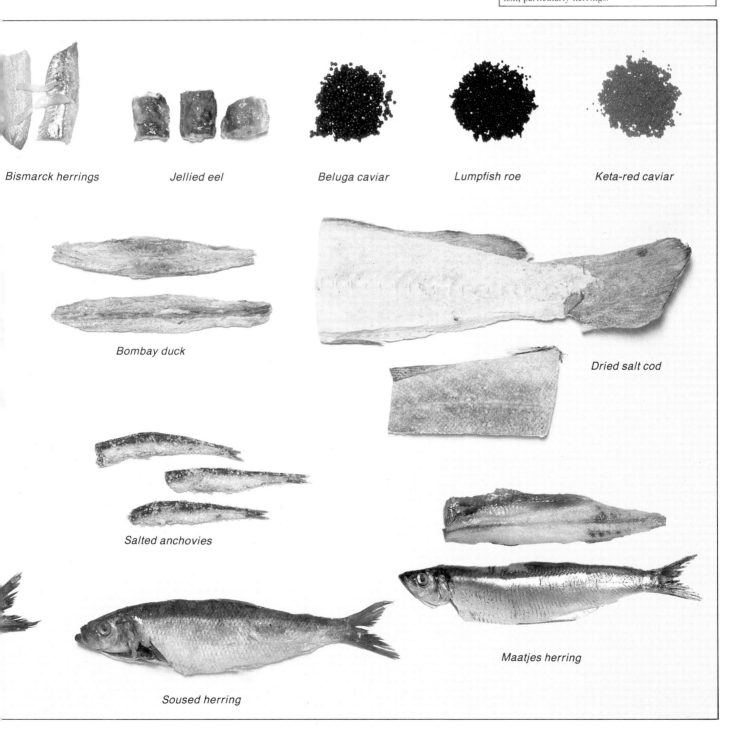

Bismarck herrings

Jellied eel

Beluga caviar

Lumpfish roe

Keta-red caviar

Bombay duck

Dried salt cod

Salted anchovies

Maatjes herring

Soused herring

Live crab

Small live lobster

Live crawfish

Cooked crawfish

_Cooked brown
shrimps_

Cooked shrimps

_Cooked
Dublin Bay prawns_

Cooked crayfish

SHELLFISH

Although overfishing and pollution have taken their toll of shellfish, there are signs that things are improving. Waters that were a hazard to the health of both shellfish and consumers have been radically cleaned up, and new farming methods are making it possible to harvest fast-growing shrimps, prawns and lobsters, for example, in large quantities.

If you are buying cooked shellfish, a quick sniff should distinguish the freshly cooked from the fading. Shrimps and prawns lose the color in their shells and become lighter as they dry up. Lobsters and crabs also lose weight – choose heavy specimens with tension in the tail or claws. If they are floppy and unresisting they are likely to be stale. If you want to cook them live, plunge them into fast-boiling salted water, seawater or court bouillon. Take care not to overcook them – all shellfish toughen and become rubbery if they are cooked for too long.

CRAB (crabe)

To pick the meat out of a crab is a labor of love but always worth the effort – the flavor and texture are almost equal to that of lobster, and certainly much less expensive. The large crabs with fiercesome claws found all around the British coast, the sweet spider crabs beloved of the French and the soft green-backed shore crabs which are a Venetian specialty are all delicious. In America the crab really comes into its own, with an abundance of blue crabs from the Atlantic and Gulf coasts, the superbly flavored Pacific Coast crab, the Dungeness, the Florida stone crabs, the Alaska king crabs and the rock crabs found on the California and New England coasts.
Buying guide: Alive or cooked, choose crabs that feel heavy for their size and smell fresh and sweet, with no hint of ammonia. About 1lb/450g of crab in the shell or ¼lb/115g of crab meat is usually sufficient for each person, depending on how it is prepared.
Best cooking methods: The best crab is the one you boil and dress yourself, eaten cold with mayonnaise and dark bread and butter. Hard-shelled crabs are also good steamed, and can be used to make a very delicious bisque. Soft-shelled crabs can be eaten *à la meunière,* or be broiled or deep fried.

LOBSTER (homard)

Lobsters from colder waters are generally the finest; the best are the superb Irish and Scottish lobsters and those from Brittany, on the European side of the Atlantic, and the northern lobsters from Maine to Nova Scotia on the American side. The cock lobster is firmer-fleshed than the hen and has meatier claws, but the hen has a more delicate flavor, a broader tail and the delicious coral, or roe, which turns scarlet when cooked and makes excellent lobster sauce.
Buying guide: Fresh lobsters are available all year, but are at their best and most abund-

ant during the summer. Choose a lobster that is heavy for its size and has both its claws – sometimes a claw is lost in a fight, and some of the best meat is in the claws. Alive, the best way to buy lobsters, the shell is dark blue or green; if already boiled, the shell should be bright red. If the lobster is pre-cooked, check that its tail springs back into a tight curl when pulled out straight. This shows that it was cooked when alive. If you are brave enough, give it a sniff underneath, too, to make sure it is quite fresh.

If you intend to cook the lobster yourself, make sure you get a lively specimen and, again, that it is a heavy one – sometimes lobsters get quite thin in captivity waiting for someone to come along and buy them. To keep a live lobster in the refrigerator, but not for more than a day or two, roll it loosely in newspaper to prevent it crawling about, enclose it in a paper bag pierced with air holes and put it in the vegetable crisper.

If called upon to face cutting a live lobster in half or in pieces before cooking, lay it on a board, stomach upwards, and cover the head and claws with a wet cloth to protect your hands. Hold it down firmly and with a strong, sharp, pointed knife make a swift incision in a head-to-tail direction at the point where the head and tail shells meet. This severs the spinal cord. Leave for a few minutes for the reflexes to cease, then cut the lobster in pieces, or split it in half lengthwise through the stomach shell and open it out flat, or cut it in half right through the hard back shell. Clean it, removing the sand sac, if any, from the head and reserving any coral and the delicious creamy tomalley or liver to use in lobster sauce. Cook the lobster immediately.

Small lobsters are usually the most tender: a 1lb/450g lobster will feed one person, so you may have to buy several. Large lobsters are also excellent. Never have anything to do with a dead uncooked lobster.
Best cooking methods: The simplest are best: broiled, boiled, steamed or grilled, served with melted butter and a little lemon juice or a good mayonnaise. Keep the shells to put into fish soup or use them as a basis for lobster bisque or lobster sauce.

CRAWFISH (langouste)

Slightly paler than lobster when cooked, it has dense white flesh, well flavored but inclined to be coarse. The choicest meat is in the tail, and there is a lively market for frozen tails.
Buying guide: Fresh is best, in late spring or early autumn. Choose specimens without eggs, as those with eggs are not considered to be wholesome. Otherwise, follow the same guidelines as for buying lobsters.
Best cooking methods: When fresh, they are best eaten simply boiled with melted butter. Anything left makes a fine salad, with mayonnaise, or a very good bisque together with some shrimps or prawns in their shells,

with plenty of cream and Madeira or brandy. Otherwise, use the same recipes for crawfish as for lobster.

CRAYFISH (écrevisse)

A sweet-fleshed miniature of the lobster, the crayfish (alias freshwater lobster, crawdad and crawfish) is the only edible freshwater shellfish. Once a great feature of country-house tables in Britain, crayfish are still relished in France and Scandinavia.

Buying guide: There are a number of cultivated varieties of crayfish which are available from good fish dealers. If you buy them fresh, make sure they are lively – they spoil very quickly once dead. Allow at least 10–12 crayfish per person, depending on your recipe.

Best cooking methods: Put some smooth stones in the bottom of a large pot of water – this will keep the heat up so that the crayfish don't suffer when they are dropped in. Bring the water, into which you have put plenty of salt and fresh dill, to a rapid boil. Drop each crayfish in separately so that the water keeps boiling all the time and cook for about five minutes, until they turn bright scarlet. Turn off the heat and let them get cold in their liquor. The French cook them *à la nage* – in a well-flavored court bouillon – and serve them in an appetizing scarlet mound with hot melted butter, or cold with mayonnaise.

DUBLIN BAY PRAWNS (langoustines)

Whether you meet them as *langoustines* or Dublin Bay prawns, Norway lobster (their Latin name is *Nephrops norvegicus*) or Italian scampi, these pretty pinky-orange-shelled creatures with their pale claws can be treated as exceedingly large shrimps or very small lobsters, depending on which way you like to look at them.

Buying guide: If you are lucky enough to find them fresh, they will most likely be pre-boiled. Usually only the tails are sold. For four people buy 2lb/900g in their shells, half that amount if they are already shelled. Always available frozen.

Best cooking methods: Cook them in their shells in gently boiling, well-salted water for not more than ten minutes and eat them with melted butter. Cold, they make a very good salad with oil and vinegar dressing or mayonnaise. They are also excellent grilled over charcoal with oil and garlic – even frozen ones are good cooked in this way.

SHRIMPS AND PRAWNS (crevettes)

There are so many species in the shrimp family that anything more than 2–3in/5–7cm long is called in Europe a prawn. In the United States, classification is usually by size, from the large and luscious Gulf Shrimp (10–12 make 1lb/450g) to the tiny coldwater specimens which need 100 or

more to tip the scales.

Fresh caught and freshly boiled, *crevettes grises*, the little brown shrimps, are more delicate than their larger cousins, these are delicious with lemon and dark bread and butter, or potted and served with lemon and hot toast. Brown shrimps turn browner when cooked; pink shrimps are greyish-brown when caught and turn pink when they are cooked.

Buying guide: Fresh prawns and shrimps should be springy with bright, crisp shells – avoid any that are soft or limp or have a smell of ammonia about them.

Best cooking methods: Make an incision along the shrimp's back and remove the dark vein, then simply drop them into a large pan of boiling seawater or salted water and simmer them for a minute or two, depending on their size.

OYSTERS (huitres)

Oysters are a shellfish you either love or loathe.

There are a number of varieties of oysters, some distinctly finer than others. The best European oysters include the Whitstable, Colchester and Helford, and the Belons and green Marennes from France. In America the East Coast yields the fine Eastern or American oyster, more commonly known as the Blue Point. On the West Coast the tiny Olympia oysters and the much larger, tougher Pacific oysters, or Geigers, are found. There are stringent regulations to keep oysters safe from pollution, but if you have one that tastes bad, spit it out.

Oysters are best eaten raw, on the half-shell. Serve them in the deep halves of their shells, on a bed of crushed ice, and take care not to spill the liquid they contain – it has an exquisite salty, marine flavour with a hint of iodine.

Buying guide: These are best in late autumn and in winter, when they are not spawning. They can also be bought canned or frozen, but these are only for cooking.

Best cooking methods: Portuguese and Pacific oysters, which must be chopped as they are rather tough, are used for cooking.

SCALLOPS (coquilles St. Jacques, vanneaux)

Europe can boast the best of the many species of scallop that abound, including the most common great scallop, the pilgrim scallop and the queen scallop. American scallops – the large deepsea variety and the small, tender bay scallops – are sold without their coral or roe, although in Europe this is considered to be the best part.

Buying guide: Three or four large ones per person is usually sufficient but if using queen or bay scallops, allow between 10 and 15 per person.

Best cooking methods: Do be careful not to overcook scallops or they will be tough –

small ones only take a few seconds, large ones a minute or two at the most. They can be fried or baked in the oven, in butter with parsley, garlic and lemon juice, or sautéed and served with a little port and cream stirred in to make a sauce, or broiled with bacon on a skewer, made into a chowder, or lightly poached or steamed and served in a white wine sauce, sprinkled with bread crumbs and browned under the broiler.

CLAMS (praires)

North America is the place to appreciate clams: aficionados can distinguish between long necks and little necks, cherrystones, quahogs and razors, surf clams, butter clams and pismo clams.

Buying guide: Since clams vary so much in size from one variety to another, ask the clam-seller how many to allow for each person. Canned clams are also widely available.

Best cooking methods: The soft or long-neck varieties such as razor and Ipswich clams can be eaten raw just like oysters, and so can small hard-shell clams such as cherrystones. Larger ones like quahogs can be steamed and ground for chowder, fried in olive oil with lemon juice and parsley, broiled with butter, bread crumbs and garlic.

MUSSELS (moules)

If you are collecting your own mussels, make sure that they are living in unpolluted water and known to be safe. Do not collect them in the heat of summer (when there is not an "r" in the month) and discard any that are even remotely damaged.

To clean mussels, put them in salted water with a sprinkling of oatmeal or flour for an hour or two so that they rid themselves of grit, then scrape the shells – clean with the back of a knife and rinse thoroughly in cold water. Pull out the stringy beard and cut it off, and rinse the mussels again in a bowl of clean water. It is important to discard any that float to the surface or whose shells are damaged or open.

Buying guide: Mussels are happily inexpensive. The medium-size or smaller ones are best; large mussels are not so appetizing. Always buy more mussels then you need, to allow for those you have to discard. For two people, buy a quart (about 2lb/900g).

Best cooking methods: One of the best-known recipes for mussels is the excellent moules à la marinière. They can also be used, once opened, like snails, broiled with bread crumbs, garlic, parsley and butter, or in a garlicky tomato sauce.

COCKLES (coques, sourdons, maillots)

These have long been a favored shellfish in Britain, traditionally sold with winkles and whelks at the seaside and outside London pubs.

Buying guide: At their best in the summer, cockles are usually sold boiled. At seaside stands they are accompanied by salt, pepper, vinegar and dark bread and butter.

Best cooking methods: Eat cockles raw, or boil them in a court bouillon until their shells open. They also make a splendid soup, combined with mussels, garlic, potato, bacon and milk, and are a good addition to risottos and fritters, or they can be stewed with their juices in a thick tomato sauce and served with pasta.

RECIPE SUGGESTION

Scampi in cream and wine

1 lb/450 g shelled large shrimps or Dublin Bay prawns
½ lb/225 g button mushrooms
few drops of lemon juice
¾ stick/85 g butter
sprinkling of flour
salt and freshly ground pepper
1 small glass dry white wine, preferably Meursault
3 tablespoons light cream

SERVES 4

Drain any water off the shrimps and pat them dry. Wash and dry the mushrooms and sprinkle them with a few drops of lemon juice. Melt half the butter in a frying pan. When it is hot, sprinkle the shrimps very lightly with flour and fry them a few at a time until they are just beginning to brown—they only take a minute or so—turning them once. Remove them to a dish and keep hot. Add the remaining butter to the pan and sauté the mushrooms without letting them get too brown—they should be light golden. Remove them to the same dish as the shrimps, season with salt and pepper and keep hot. Add the wine to the frying pan and reduce it to two tablespoons, then add the cream and swill it around. Let it boil until it starts to thicken. Pour this mixture over the shrimps and mushrooms and shake the dish to blend it with the other juices, which will make a thin and delicate sauce. Serve with plain boiled rice.

Belon oysters

Mussels

Portuguese oysters

Cockles

Clams

Scallops

PREPARING PRE-COOKED LOBSTER AND CRAB

1 LOBSTER

If you wish to remove the claws and legs, simply twist them off. Dressed lobster dishes are usually presented with the claw meat already extracted.

Pull the halves apart to expose the flesh. This fine female lobster has an excellent red coral, and also some darker external roe, which is unusual. Both are edible and should be reserved.

To extract the meat from the claws and legs, crack them open, using the back of a knife or, as for crab, a hammer or nutcracker.

Discard the white gills, which will be found in both halves in the top of the head, and the intestinal canal, which runs down the middle of the tail. As well as the coral, the creamy green tomalley, or liver, should also be reserved to make lobster sauce.

Splitting a lobster in half is easier to do in two stages. First, draw a sharp knife through the head from the shoulder up towards the eyes.

2 CRAB

Hold the crab firmly in one hand and give its back underside a sharp thump. This should loosen the body and legs from the shell.

Reinsert the knife and draw it in the opposite direction, cutting down to the tip of the tail and splitting the lobster completely in two.

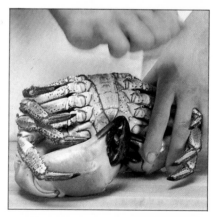

Stand the crab on its head and, pushing against the body with your thumbs, lever away the back end of the shell with your fingers.

PREPARING PRE-COOKED LOBSTER AND CRAB

Pull the body and the legs away from the shell.

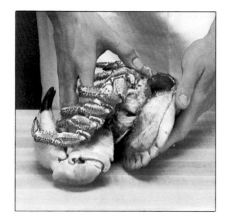

Twist off all the legs and claws. To expose the body's white meat, make two cuts, one on either side of the bony central peak. The two cuts should meet in a V shape at the peak of the body. This divides the body in three. Discard the middle bit which contains no flesh.

Remove and discard the messy bundle of intestines. This will be found either in the shell or still clinging to the body. Comb it gently with a fork to remove any brown meat that is adhering to it.

With a skewer, dig out the white meat from the two outer pieces of the body. This requires a little time and patience if you are to avoid crushing the brittle inner shell. The meat on the plate shows how much you can expect from half the body of a large crab.

Scoop out the brown creamy meat from inside the shell.

Crack open the claws and legs with a hammer or nutcracker and extract their meat. The meat on the plate is the amount obtained from one claw and one leg.

Discard the grey gills, known as dead men's fingers, which lie on either side of the body.

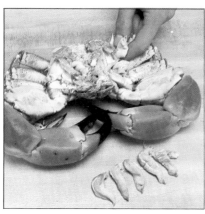

Mix together the white meat from the legs, claws and body, and serve it with the brown meat.

PREPARING SHELLFISH AND SQUID

1 SHUCKING OYSTERS

Hold the oyster steady and insert a strong, rigid knife between the two shells, just next to the hinge. The knife used here is a special oyster-shucking knife, and the oyster is an English Whitstable.

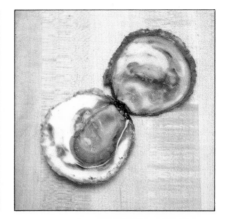

Turn the oyster over to display its more attractive side, and serve it with its own marine-flavored juices in the rounded shell.

Keep a firm grip on the oyster and, pushing against the hinge, twist the knife until the hinge breaks.

2 SCALLOPS

Lever the shells apart with the end of a strong broad-tipped knife.

Open the oyster and sever the muscle that adheres to the rounded shell.

Sever the scallop from the rounded shell by carefully sliding a knife underneath the adhering muscle.

Run the knife underneath the oyster to free it from the flat shell.

Rinse the scallop under cold running water, pull away the film of membrane, or "beard," and discard it.

Keep the scallop under running water and, holding back the white flesh and coral with your thumb, push away the black intestine and sever it.

Feel inside the body for the transparent cartilage, or "quill," draw it out and discard it.

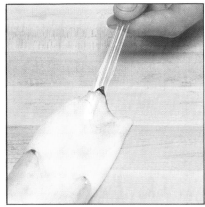

The cushion of muscle and the delicious orange coral are now ready to cook.

Wash the body thoroughly, inside and out, under cold running water and then separate the two flaps from the body. You will find that they pull away quite easily, as if held in place only by suction.

3 SQUID

Grasp the squid with one hand and with the other reach inside the body and pull the head and tentacles away.

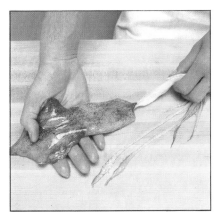

Cut the tentacles from the head. If the long, narrow ink sac is present and still intact, you will find it attached to the head; remove it carefully and put it aside to use in an accompanying sauce. The remains of the head, which contain the entrails, can now be discarded.

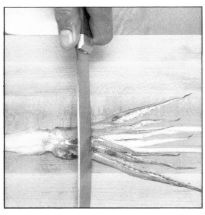

Pull off and discard the body's mottled skin.

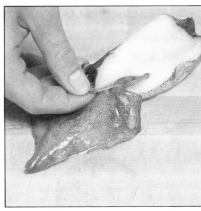

Cut the body into thick rings, slice the flaps in broad strips and cut the tentacles to a manageable size. The squid is now ready to cook.

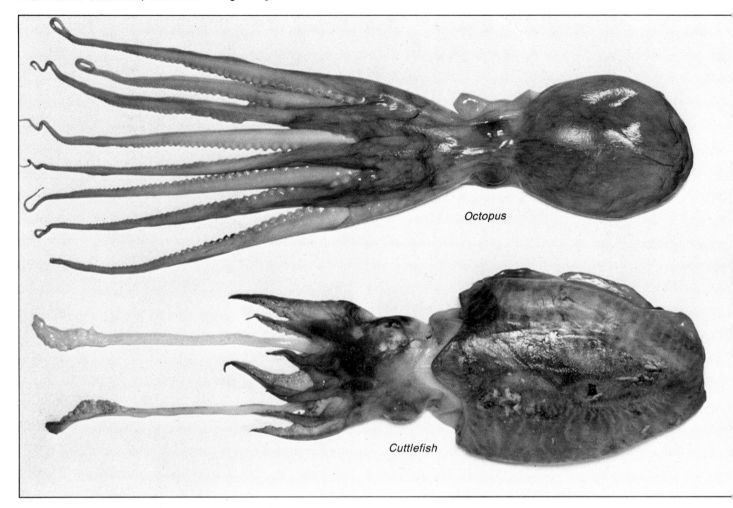

Octopus

Cuttlefish

Many creatures are so strange and so lacking in allure that they are usually, for want of a better label, called "miscellaneous." But unappetizing though they may look, with their spiny, jelly-like or leathery exteriors are delicious.

OTHER SEAFOODS

If you gather seafoods yourself, always remembering that any living thing gathered from the sea and its shores is potentially dangerous if it comes from a polluted area, and that many varieties are simply inedible. If in any doubt about the safety of your haul, check with an environmental health officer.

SQUID, OCTOPUS AND CUTTLEFISH

The Mediterranean countries understand best how to deal with these extraordinary creatures, having eaten them in great quantities since the earliest days of civilization. They also play an important role in the cooking of China and Japan. All are at their sweetest and tenderest when small; larger specimens can be improved by soaking for several hours in a marinade of wine vinegar, sliced onion, salt and pepper.

Squid

Familiar in Mediterranean dishes as kalamari, calmar or encornet, calamaro or calamar, squid is delicious to eat if you understand the principle that the cooking must be either very brief or very long – anything in between and your squid will be as tough as rubber. Once cleaned, the pocket can be stuffed with ground meat and the chopped legs and baked in a tomato-and-garlic-flavored sauce, or sliced in rings and fried plain or dipped first into a light batter. Larger specimens can be stewed gently with olive oil, or wine and tomatoes.

It is a pleasure, in Spain, to be served with two little dishes at the same time, one holding a fragrant stew of the legs, with onions and garlic, and the other the sliced, crisply fried rings of the body. Squid can also be boiled very briefly – more than a minute or two, when they lose their pearly transparent look, will toughen them – and then put into a seafood salad. The tiniest squid, with fragile bodies no more than 3in/8cm long, can be very quickly deep fried in a coating of beaten egg and flour.

Octopus

This can be very tough, and the larger it grows the tougher it gets, so it is a wise precaution, having removed the beak and head (if the fish dealer has not already done so) and turned out the contents of the body, to pound the legs and body with a mallet or a steak beater until they are soft. The octopus contains its ink within its liver and this is sometimes used to make a very strong and heavily scented gravy.

Octopus can be stewed or stuffed and baked like squid, but a large specimen will need up to two hours or more to become tender. Little ones can also be fried gently in olive oil and make a delicious salad, often eaten warm, with lemon juice, olive oil, garlic and chopped parsley.

Cuttlefish

Often gracefully camouflaged by striped markings, the cuttlefish has a larger head than the squid and a much wider, dumpier body. Inside lies the white shell, or cuttlebone, found washed up on beaches. More tender than octopus or squid, cuttlefish can be cooked in the same ways and very small ones are delicious deep fried. They are cleaned and prepared in the same way as squid. The ink, or sepia, can be used to make a sauce in which the cuttlefish can be stewed, and goes into the Italian dish risotto nero, black rice.

Ground cuttlebone was once used as tooth powder and as jewel polish.

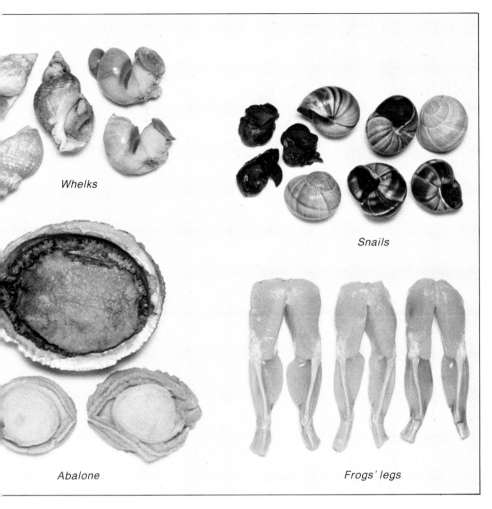

Whelks

Snails

Abalone

Frogs' legs

meat needs to be tenderized by vigorous beating and can then be stewed in a wine sauce with herbs and spices, or thinly sliced and deep fried. It also goes in chowders or can be eaten raw in a salad with a good vinaigrette.

"FRUITS" OF THE SEA

Sea urchin, oursin
The sharp-spined sea urchin is plentiful in many parts of the world. Best for eating are the green sea urchin and the black sea urchin. These can be lightly boiled and are sometimes pickled, but are best eaten fresh, raw and straight from the shell. To accomplish this the sea urchin is cut in half, ideally with a *coupe-oursin* designed for this task. This exposes the rose-colored or orange ovaries, which are simply given a drop of lemon juice and scooped out with pieces of fresh crusty bread. The crushed corals can also be used in omelets and as a garnish for fish.

Sea anemone and tomate de mer
These inhabitants of rocky pools are sometimes eaten in Japan, Samoa and France. The snake-locks anemones, known as *orties de mer*, are carefully gathered in France and marinated, dipped into a light batter and fried. They also go, together with a few red *tomates de mer* and a great many shellfish, into a Mediterranean soup.

Figue de mer, violet
This very odd, leathery skinned creature is particularly relished in Provence, accompanied by white wine. Found anchored to rocks or the sea floor, siphoning water in through one spout and out of the other, it is cut in half and the yellow part inside is eaten raw.

Bêche de mer
Also known as sea cucumber, because of its shape, and as sea slug, trepang and balatan, this warm-water creature is sliced and eaten raw in Japan with soy sauce, vinegar or mustard, and several species are smoke-dried and used in soup. In China it is known as *hoy sum* and has a reputation as an aphrodisiac.

Jellyfish
The Chinese are great users of dried jellyfish, primarily to add texture to a meal, and slabs of dried jellyfish can usually be found in the more specialized Chinese supermarkets. If the jellyfish has been salted it will need to be washed and allowed to soak for some hours in several changes of fresh water. Once soaked, it can be cut into slivers and stir-fried with chicken, or scalded, which produces crunchy curls which are served with a sauce of sesame-seed oil, soy sauce, vinegar and sugar. In Japan jellyfish is cooked into crisp-textured strips and eaten with vinegar as a side dish.

SINGLE-SHELLED CREATURES

These all belong to the same family that includes the familiar garden snail. They all move on a muscular "foot" and can go into fish soups, sauces and stews, as well as being tasty snacks when simply accompanied by plenty of vinegar, pepper and dark bread and butter.

Abalone, ormer
These white-fleshed shellfish with their curiously ear-shaped shells, the inside gleaming with pearly colors, can still be found fresh around the Channel Islands and the Breton coast at certain times of the year, and in the warm waters off California.

Fresh abalones, even little ones, need to be well beaten to make them tender. Very small abalones can then be eaten raw with a squeeze of lemon juice, larger ones are usually thinly sliced and marinated in white wine, oil, herbs and chopped shallot and then fried very briefly in butter – over-cooking only toughens them. They can also be used like clams in soup or chowder. Canned abalone is a good substitute for fresh, but dried abalone is not worth the effort of making it edible – it needs to be soaked for four days before anything can be done with it.

Winkles or periwinkles
In England they are eaten with bread and butter and a pot of tea, and make a tasty snack on seaside piers, accompanied by vinegar. In France you are likely to be given a plate of *bigorneaux* with a glass of kir – cassis and white wine – in an Alsace brasserie while waiting for your pork knuckle and sauerkraut or your slice of foie gras. Whatever the circumstance a long pin is indispensable for wheedling the little shellfish out of their shells. To cook winkles, boil them in their shells in salted water for about 10 minutes. Eat only the first part of the body – the second part is easily separated.

Whelks
These handsome shellfish with their ribbed, deeply whorled shells are usually sold already boiled. They are eaten with vinegar and brown bread and butter, like winkles, but are a much more substantial mouthful and easier to remove from their shells. The large "foot" is the part that is usually eaten. Whelks can also be used in fish soups and stews.

Conch
The term conch is often used to include the winkle and whelk, but what is usually thought of as being the best of the family is the large Caribbean conch. Fresh conch

SAMPHIRE AND SEAWEEDS

Seaweeds are a rich source of minerals as well as of intriguing textures and flavors. Most are at their most luxuriant in early summer. If you gather your own, cut the plant well above its base so that it can grow again, and always wash it thoroughly in fresh water before cooking. Most of the better-known seaweeds can be found in dried form in health food stores or oriental supermarkets and can be restored by soaking.

Samphire

Also known as sea fennel and Peter's cress, or *herbe de St. Pierre*, this green plant can be found growing on seaside cliffs. It is quite common along southern European and Mediterranean coastlines, but in England is found only in East Anglia, where it can sometimes be bought in bundles, along with the similar but unrelated marsh samphire,

from the fish market. The flavor of fresh marsh samphire is salty and iodiney – like seawater but green; it is the crisp texture that is interesting.

Samphire can go fresh into salads and is often steeped in vinegar to make a delicate pickle. In East Anglia it is greatly appreciated as a vegetable, simply boiled and dipped in melted butter, then drawn through the teeth like asparagus to strip the succulent part from the thin central core.

Laver

With its delicate taste of the sea this reddish-purple seaweed was very popular in England in the eighteenth century. It is seldom eaten in the West today, except in Wales, where it is enthusiastically boiled until it turns into the spinach-like purée called laver bread. Although why it should be called bread is a mystery. The purée is then mixed with oatmeal, shaped into small flat cakes and fried with bacon for breakfast, or heated through with a knob of butter and the juice of an orange or lemon to make a sauce to eat with

mutton. In China, laver is dried and then simmered to produce a nutritious jelly. In Japan, where it is cultivated and called *nori*, it is pressed and dried in thin sheets, toasted lightly and wrapped around rice balls or crumbled over rice as a salty garnish.

Carragheen, Irish moss

This pretty red-tinged plant is common along most northerly Atlantic shorelines. It can be used fresh or dried, when it bleaches to a creamy white, and is an important source of agaragar, a vegetable gelatine much used in the food industry. The traditional way to make a carragheen jelly is to simmer the moss in milk or water until most of it dissolves, strain and leave it to set. The result is very nourishing, and if you don't like its faint taste of the sea it can be flavored with vanilla, honey or fruit.

Kelp

A number of large seaweeds are popularly known as kelp and have long been used as a source of food and of medicine, being particularly rich in iodine. Much liked in Japan,

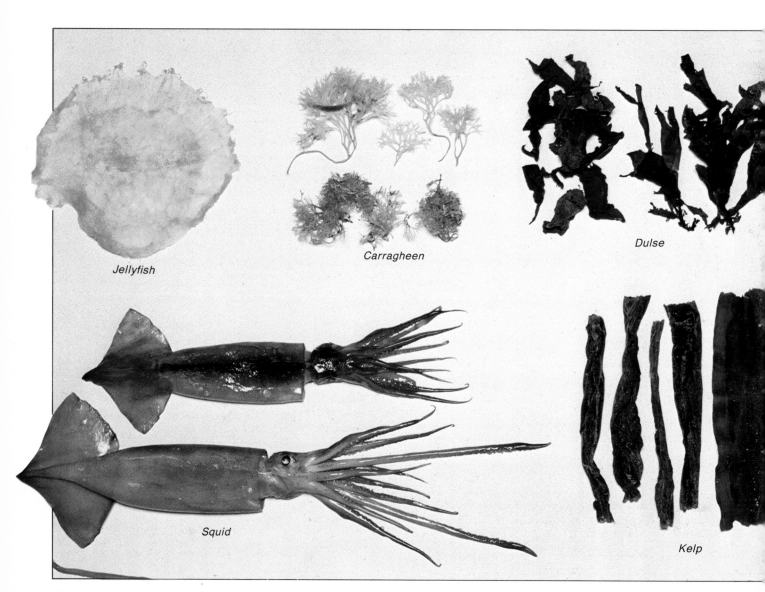

Jellyfish

Carragheen

Dulse

Squid

Kelp

where it is called *kombu*, kelp finds its way to the table as a delicate salad vegetable, a seasoning for root vegetables, a garnish for rice or fashioned into miniature baskets, deep fried and stuffed with vegetables. It is also used for making soups and stocks or can simply be cooked as a vegetable.

Dulse

Another of the familiar purplish-red seaweeds, dulse is to be found growing plentifully on rocks and on larger weeds. It can be eaten raw as a salad and around the Mediterranean it sometimes goes into ragouts, but it is a very tough, rubbery plant and needs to be cooked for up to five hours. Dried it can be chewed as a rather unconventional appetizer, without any further preparation, or used as a relish. It has a salty fish-like flavor.

Wakame

A rich source of minerals, this dark green seaweed is much used in Japan. The soft leaves go into salads or are cooked with other vegetables, and both leaves and stems are used in soups.

Wakame

Winkles

SNAILS

The snails the French prize most are the hefty specimens from the vineyards of Burgundy, where they are fed – like the snails of ancient Rome – on grape leaves until they have grown fat and luscious. The classic way to prepare snails is the Burgundian way, in which case they become *escargots à la bourguignonne*, served sizzling in their shells with great quantities of rich garlic butter and fresh crusty bread for mopping. However, as there are never enough Burgundian snails to meet the demand, the alternative is a smaller striped snail, the *petit gris*, which makes up for its lack of size by being sweet, tasty and tender. A drawback is that the *petit gris* shells, unlike those of the Burgundian snails, may be too fragile to be used once their occupants have been removed. Instead use the little ceramic pots called *godets*, easily washed and always ready to be used again. Other essentials for the dedicated enjoyment of snails are the dimpled plates called *escargotières*, which hold six or twelve snail shells or *godets*, tongs for picking up the piping hot shells and special forks which have two prongs for twisting the snails out of their shells.

The business of preparing live snails means that it is much simpler to buy snails canned, already cleaned and ready to cook, or cooked and only needing to be reheated and combined with their sauce. As a change from garlic butter, snails are very good simmered in olive oil with garlic, tomato and fresh rosemary or mint the traditional dish to serve on Midsummer's Eve in Rome.

FROGS' LEGS

Like snails, frogs' legs as a delicacy have long been associated with the French. Escoffier, the "king of chefs," is credited with making them acceptable to the English: in the 1890s for a party held by the Prince of Wales at the Savoy Hotel, London, he prepared what he called *nymphes à l'aurore*, frogs' legs poached in white wine and served cold in aspic with a little paprika to evoke the rose-gold glow of dawn. Presumably he called his frogs' legs "nymphs" out of delicacy of feeling for the English diners. When he wasn't preparing them for the Prince of Wales, Escoffier simply seasoned them with salt and pepper and sautéed them in butter, serving them with a squeeze of lemon juice and a sprinkling of parsley.

Today those who know their frogs still go frogging in likely streams and lakes, but not all frogs are edible and what appears frozen and canned in the shops and on restaurant menus will have come from special frog farms. They are light and easily digestible, rather like chicken in flavor – in China, where frogs' legs are much enjoyed at banquets, they are known as "field

chickens." In America frogs' legs are often big enough to be southern-fried like chicken legs, but the smaller legs are usually more tender and have a subtler flavor. But Escoffier's way is still the best, first blanched and skinned, and then cooked gently in oil or butter for about five minutes until golden brown and served with lemon and a sprinkling of parsley, or they can be poached in a little white wine and served hot with a creamy sauce. They can also be prepared *à la provençale*, with garlic and tomato.

RECIPE SUGGESTIONS
Seafood salad

36 mussels
8–10 baby squid
24 large shrimps, fresh or frozen
½ lb/225 g prawns, shelled
1 tablespoon lemon juice
6–7 tablespoons olive oil
½ dried red chili pepper, finely chopped
salt and freshly ground pepper

SERVES 6

Scrub and wash the mussels, put them in a large pan with 1¼ cups/3 dl boiling water and shake them over a moderate heat until they have opened. Scoop the mussels out of the pan with a slotted spoon, reserving their liquid. Clean and wash the squid and cut them into rings, keeping the tentacles whole.

Bring the mussel liquid to the boil, adding a little boiling water if it becomes too scant. Drop in the pieces of squid and let them cook gently for about 1–2 minutes. Remove them quickly, and if you are using raw shrimps or prawns drop them into the same liquid and poach for 3–4 minutes, until tender. Shell the mussels and arrange them, the shrimps and the prawns on a plate with the squid rings and tentacles. Squeeze the lemon juice over the shellfish, then pour on the oil. Scatter the chopped chili pepper over the top and season with salt and pepper.

Squid risotto

1 lb/450 g small squid
2 tomatoes
3 cloves garlic
1 large onion
3 tablespoons olive oil
1 tablespoon chopped parsley
1 glass white wine
1 cup/170 g round Italian rice
1 teaspoon tomato paste
salt and freshly ground pepper

SERVES 4

Skin, seed and chop the tomatoes and peel and chop the garlic and onion. Clean the squid, cut it into thick rings and then cut the rings in pieces.

Heat the olive oil in a fairly wide, shallow pan or sauté pan. Sweat the onion in the oil, without browning, then add the garlic and parsley. Fry gently for 1 minute and then add the squid and the tomatoes, turning them over in the oil. Add the wine and a ladleful of water and stew the squid for 30 minutes, covered. Add the rice, another ladleful of water and the tomato paste. Season with salt and pepper. Keep stirring the rice, adding more water as it becomes absorbed. The rice takes about 30 minutes to swell and cook, by which time it is creamy and a marvellous pink-brown color.

MEAT

Meat is such an important part of our diet, so delicious and so
expensive that it makes sense to buy it as intelligently as possible.
If you always go to a high-class butcher, possibly one who buys meat
by the carcass and hangs it until it has reached the peak of juiciness
and flavor, you will seldom have a disappointing piece of meat.

CHOOSING MEAT

In America legal standards demand that meat is graded "prime," "choice," "good" and "standard," but in England the word "prime" is merely an adjective used by the butcher to describe the best meat he has.

All meat destined for the table is carefully raised: special attention is paid to the ratio of fat to lean while the herd is still on the hoof, the animals' diet is carefully supervised, and they are rested before slaughter in the cause of tenderness. The finer the herd, the more care is lavished upon them and the more delicious is their meat.

The look of meat

At a really good store all the cuts, even the cheapest, will look appetizing. They should look silky, not wet. All boned, rolled cuts should be neatly tied, not skewered, since piercing causes a loss of moisture during cooking and may introduce bacteria into the center of the meat. Barding should be neat, complete and even. Where there are bones, these should be sawn smoothly, not jaggedly chopped, and meat should be neatly trimmed, particularly chops and steaks, with excess fat removed.

Tenderness

No matter where and how a carcass is divided, most of the best meat of each animal comes from the hindquarters and loin, and the tenderest meat of all comes from the parts that have had the least exercise. Exercise means the development of muscle fiber and of the connective tissue that holds the muscles together in bundles, and it is connective tissue that is primarily responsible for toughness.

The tender cuts with little connective tissue respond to dry heat (roasting, frying and broiling), but the others need slow cooking in moist heat (braising, stewing or boiling), which breaks down the connective tissue into gelatine.

There are ways of preparing tough meat in the kitchen so that it arrives at table full of flavor and juice. Try marinating it in a marinade including wine, lemon juice, vinegar, yogurt, or even pulped tomatoes. Oil, too, is used in many marinades to add succulence. Of course, lengthy cooking in moist heat must follow to complete the process, but this is no disadvantage since the tougher cuts need time, above all, to develop their flavour to the full.

Ageing

This improves the taste and tenderness of meat. Carcasses to be aged are hung in a refrigerated chamber, their moisture evaporates, and enzymes in the meat break down tendons and tough tissues. Beef should be aged for 10–14 days, lamb for no more than four days. Pork and veal are not aged, nor is kosher meat.

Storage

All cuts of meat will keep best when they are lightly covered – and when they are not so tightly packed as to rule out the circulation of air. A loose foil wrap that allows the passage of air will do almost as well, but never put meat away wrapped in plastic.

COOKING PROCESSES

On the whole, it is wisest to use the correct cooking process for each cut: dry heat for the tender ones; moist for those not so tender.

Broiling

The meat, first brushed with butter or oil to prevent drying out, is seared on both sides close to the source of heat to produce color and flavor. It is then removed a little away from the heat to finish cooking more slowly. Salt should not be added until halfway through the process, as its moisture-retaining properties would inhibit searing and browning.

Frying

Choose a frying pan with a good, thick base, and make sure it is the right size. Meat has a tendency to stew in its own juice in an overcrowded pan, and if the pan is too big, a large surface area of fat is exposed that could all too easily burn. A very good reason for not allowing this to happen is that the pan juices, deglazed with a little wine, water or stock, make the best possible accompaniment to fried steaks or chops.

Roasting

Top quality meat goes into a hot oven in an open pan, so that it is browned on all sides and the outside seared.

Roasting times and temperatures vary according to type of meat, cut and quality, but after the initial searing it is a good idea to lower the oven temperature so that the interior of the meat cooks slowly.

There are two golden rules for all cuts: do not add salt until after roasting, and let the meat sit in a warm place for at least 20 minutes after it comes out of the oven to allow the juices time to settle.

Braising and pot roasting

Large pieces of medium quality meat respond well to these processes.

Braising needs a pan with a tightly fitting lid on which the steam from the cooking meat can condense, falling back onto the meat and basting it as it cooks.

This usually takes about 30 minutes per 1lb/450g with 30 minutes over, but times vary according to quality.

Pot roasting in a covered pot dispenses with the liquid, relying only on the steam from the meat, which condenses on the lid and bastes the meat. Pot-roasted meat needs to be started off with a little fat in the bottom of the pan in order to brown it and to prevent its sticking and burning.

Stewing

A tougher cut of meat does best when cut across the grain into smallish pieces, cooked long and slowly in a little liquid. The liquid is provided by the meat juices plus whatever is specified in the recipe. When it is tender (which may take from $1\frac{1}{2}$–$3\frac{1}{2}$ hours depending on the type of meat), the gravy may be thickened.

Boiling

Simmering in liquid is the best way to render large pieces of meat tender, but such good things as *boeuf bouilli* and all the other cuts eaten in the rich broth characteristic of the process need at least a medium quality meat.

Once the liquid has reached boiling point, turn it down to the gentlest of simmers. If meat is subjected to the intense heat of rapidly boiling water, the gelatinous connective tissue will dissolve and the meat will become tough and dry, while at a gentle simmer the connective tissues melt gradually, keeping the meat succulently moist and tender.

MEAT FOR THE FREEZER

Buy meat which has been blast-frozen when it is in season. Many independent butchers have blast freezers and will sell you any quantity you require, from a small bag of chops to half a carcass. To take up less space large pieces should be boned before freezing, and all excess fat removed.

To buy meat by the whole, half or quarter carcass seems an economical way of shopping, but only if you do not eat your way through your investment faster than you normally would, just because it is there.

Storing meat in the freezer

Limits are placed on the storage times for meat, not because the meat will become unsafe to eat but because the quality deteriorates. Meat storage times are determined largely by the fat content, as fat eventually turns rancid even in the freezer. Meat that has been inadequately wrapped for the freezer will develop freezer burn, which manifests itself in greyish-white or brownish patches. These are caused by dehydration on the surface.

The meat will be perfectly safe to eat but will taste dry and unpleasant, so be sure to wrap meat securely in something tough and expel all the air before sealing.

Cooking frozen meat

All meat tastes infinitely better if properly thawed before cooking. Boned and rolled roasts must never be cooked from frozen, as the inside and outside surfaces of the meat will have been handled, and it is therefore important to destroy any bacteria which may be present by thorough cooking.

To thaw large cuts, allow 6–7 hours per 1 lb/450 g in the refrigerator, in its own wrapping. This is much the best way, as the slower the thaw, the more the juices get reabsorbed; but only about 2–3 hours per 1 lb/450 g are needed at room temperature. Cook the meat as soon as it has thawed out – while still cold to the touch. If left thawing longer than necessary, the juices have further opportunity to escape.

Steaks and chops need about 5 hours in the refrigerator to thaw properly – 2–4 hours in the warmth of the kitchen, but if you are in a hurry, warm water helps as long as the package is watertight.

APPROXIMATE MAXIMUM STORAGE TIMES FOR MEAT

Uncooked Meat	In a Cool Place	In a Refrigerator	In a Freezer
BEEF	2 days	3–5 days	12 months
VEAL	2 days	3–5 days	12 months
LAMB	2 days	3–5 days	9 months
PORK	2 days	2–4 days	6 months
GROUND MEAT	same day	1–2 days	3 months
VARIETY MEATS	same day	1–2 days	2 months
Cooked Meat			
CASSEROLES With bacon	1 day	2 days	3 months
Without bacon	1 day	3 days	6 months
HAM	1–2 days	2–3 days	2 months
MEAT PIES	1 day	1 day	3 months
ROAST MEAT Sliced in sauce	1–2 days	2–3 days	3 months
Whole roast	1–2 days	2–4 days	2 months
PATE	5 days	7 days	3 months
STOCK	1 day	2 days	a month

Courtesy of the Meat Promotion Executive of the Meat and Livestock Commission, London

APPROXIMATE COOKING TIMES FOR MEAT

Meats and Cuts	Roasting	Pot Roasting/Braising	Boiling
	Minutes per 1 lb/450 g and temperatures		
BEEF Tender cuts rare:	15 + 15 over Hot	30–40 stove top	
medium:	20 Hot	40 in a warm oven	
Coarser cuts	20 Fairly hot		1 hour at a steady simmer
Boned/rolled	30 Fairly hot		
VEAL Thin cuts and cuts on bone	25 + 20 over Fairly hot		
Thick and boned and rolled cuts	35 Warm	40–50 in a warm oven	
LAMB Tender cuts	20 Fairly hot (+ 15 over for large cuts)	Total of 2½ hours in a warm oven	30
Smaller cuts for casseroles and stews		Total of 1½ hours in a warm oven	
PORK Small, thin cuts	30 + 20 over Moderate	60 stove top	
Thick cuts	35 + 25 over Moderate	60 in a warm oven	
Pickled cuts			Your butcher will advise

CHOOSING BEEF

The color of lean beef varies from coral pink to a deep burgundy red. The color variations of the lean indicate the age, sex and breed of the animal, not the eating quality. Freshly cut surfaces of any piece of beef will be bright red, deepening to a brownish-red on exposure to air – thus a well-aged piece of beef will have a dark, plum-colored crust. The color of the fat will vary according to diet – grass-fed beef has yellowish fat, the fat of barley-fed beef is whiter. Something positive to look for is marbling – the lean of good roasting beef should be well endowed with flecks and streaks of fat that melt during cooking, basting the roast from within and guaranteeing tenderness.

The quality of ground beef is fairly simple to judge – it should look red. If it is pink, the proportion of fat will be too high.

As a provider of beef, the steer (a young castrated male) is the undoubted king. Different countries consider him to be at his peak at different ages – from ten months to six years old – but all agree that a steer, and perhaps a heifer (a cow that has not calved), produce the most succulent meat. Working animals, bulls and cows, are far less good.

COOKING WITH BEEF

When beef is good and succulent, little is needed by way of added flavors. Horseradish or mustard makes a good accompaniment to roast beef, but the gravy of roast beef is nicest when the pan juices are simply reduced with a little boiling water and perhaps some red wine, and plainly seasoned with salt and pepper. Most vegetables go with beef – carrots being the traditional accompaniment to British boiled beef, cabbage is usually served with corned beef, and the Sunday roast beef comes to the table with roasted potatoes, parsnips and often a golden Yorkshire pudding.

Tastes in beef-eating have changed over the years. There was a time when beef was considered at its best when roasted to a crisp. Today more and more people are enjoying their roasts and steaks on the blue side of rare, and even raw. The Italians (never renowned as great eaters of meat) have introduced a new delicacy – raw tenderloin cut transparently thin like smoked salmon.

Broiling and frying

Timing depends so much on the thickness of the steak that you can only be sure whether it is done to your liking by pressing it with your finger as it cooks. If the steak feels soft and wobbly, it is very rare, or *bleu*; a little give and it will be medium rare, or *saignant*; firm, and it will be well done; if it feels hard, it will be quite spoiled.

Roasting

The finest cuts of prime beef respond best when roasted at a high temperature, which makes them crisp on the outside, leaving them a tender rosy pink within. Overcooked

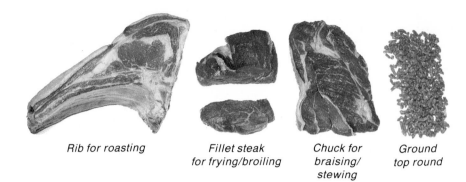

Rib for roasting   Fillet steak for frying/broiling   Chuck for braising/ stewing   Ground top round

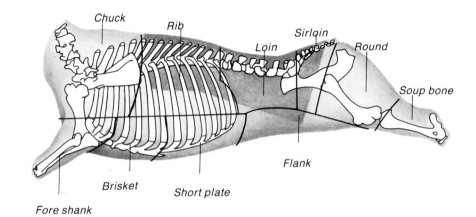

Chuck   Rib   Sirloin   Loin   Round   Soup bone   Flank   Short plate   Brisket   Fore shank

beef turns leathery, even when it is meat of the very best quality. For prime cuts such as sirloin, allow 15 minutes per 1lb/450g and 15 minutes over at a temperature of 425°F/220°C for the larger cuts for rare meat; 20 minutes to the 1lb/450g for medium. The coarser cuts, such as top round, make juicier eating when roasted more slowly – allow 20 minutes per 1lb/450g at 375°F/190°C for thin pieces, or for cuts with the bone in, and 30 minutes per 1lb/450g for thick pieces, or those that are boned and rolled.

Pot roasting and braising

Allow 30–40 minutes per 1lb/450g over medium heat, and 40 minutes per 1lb/450g in the oven at 325°F/170°C for pot roasts.

Braises need about the same time, but a great deal depends on the quality of the meat for this and for the other processes.

Boiling

The tougher boiling cuts may need up to 1 hour per 1lb/450g of beef at a gentle simmer.

THE CUTS

Because butchering techniques vary from country to country, and indeed from region to region, the various cuts for roasting, pot roasting, braising, stewing and boiling differ slightly all over the world. It remains true, of course, that in the case of cattle (as well as the other animals raised for the table) the very best and most expensive cuts come from the back half of the animal, and most of the very best of those from the fleshy hind-

quarters; but the actual names of the cuts and their shapes differ considerably, as do the direction of the grain and the way the bones are dealt with.

Cuts for frying, broiling and roasting

These are the top quality cuts that respond best to cooking in dry heat.

The loin

This provides the tenderest meat that beef cattle or other animals have to offer. The most luxurious piece of all is the tenderloin or fillet – a strip of practically grainless flesh running inside the rib cage, parallel with the spine. Some butchers offer the tenderloin in its entirety: it may be roasted, having been larded with strips of fat to keep it moist, or enclosed in a pastry case to make *boeuf en croûte* (which is also known as beef Wellington in memory of the Duke of the same name). In this case a stuffing goes between the pastry and the meat to add moisture. The tenderloin is often cut into steaks – the thinnest part makes fillets mignons; next come tournedos, which may be wrapped around with white pork fat; then come larger slices, called tenderloin or fillet steak. Next to these lies the Chateaubriand, a steak so hefty that it is considered a meal for two hungry people.

Raw ground tenderloin, spiced to taste with cayenne, Tabasco, Worcestershire sauce and capers and bound with a raw egg, makes a classic steak tartare. Cut into fine strips, tenderloin is used to make *boeuf stroganoff*.

There are many people who consider any part of the tenderloin too bland, soft and woolly, much preferring for texture and flavor rump steaks, porterhouse steaks, sirloin steaks and T-bones (which include the end of the sirloin and a piece of tenderloin), or entrecôtes (cut from the thin end of the sirloin nearest the rib cage).

The various national schools cut their steaks differently, some leaving the tenderloin to form part of larger steaks. But this does not really affect the cook, since the principle of cooking steak remains constant and the various forms of serving it differ only in the presentation. As steaks that are broiled are sealed so fast that they do not make their own juice, it is usual to send them to the table with one of the compound butters. Steaks may also be fried – usually tournedos are cooked by this process, and served on a piece of fried bread to absorb the juices that spurt when the meat is cut. Fried or broiled, steaks are much enhanced by light sauces such as a simple shallot sauce; a light sauce of egg yolks, lemon juice and parsley; a classic hollandaise or béarnaise; or even a raw relish of shallots, lemon juice and oil similar in texture to a salad dressing. Crisp French fries and a green salad are the best accompaniments.

The sirloin is part of the loin, which may be sold in a single piece for roasting, either on or off the bone, with or without the tenderloin which is then called the undercut. A sirloin, on the bone and complete with the undercut, makes a wonderful meal, so good in fact that the gourmand King Henry VIII was moved to knight it – hence Sir Loin. When two unboned sirloins have not been severed at the backbone but arrive looking like an enormous saddle, the cut is known as a baron of beef, but this noble joint is very rarely encountered except at large banquets.

In America and France the sirloin is often cut into enormous steaks, which are cooked on the bone and carved into slices at the table. In Britain steaks, with the exception of the Chateaubriand, are usually cooked in individual portions.

The rump end of loin yields roasts and beautiful juicy steaks for broiling and frying. There will be a few tough sinews running through the meat and these should be lifted out with a sharp knife.

The rib

When Americans say roast beef, what comes to mind are the great standing roasts from the rib section. The English equivalent to this roast is the forerib – the traditional "Sunday joint" served with Yorkshire pudding. This piece may be bought on or off the bone, but with the bone is sweeter. Serve with roast potatoes and lightly cooked vegetables, not forgetting the horseradish sauce. The French rib roast is boned and rolled, served *au jus* (with its pan juices) accom-

panied by French fries and a simple green salad.

Cuts from farther down the rib cage – the short plate – are best braised or pot roasted, but they can be used for roasting. They are juicier when left on the bone but tricky to carve. The thin ribs, known also as oven busters, have a lot of fat and bone, which can be removed by the butcher.

For stewing, pot roasting and boiling

The cuts used for these processes are the tougher pieces that benefit from slow cooking in moist heat.

The round

This yields boneless cuts, called topside and silverside in England, from the top of the leg. Together they make the very best *boeuf bouilli*, France's classic boiled beef dish, which is eaten in its bouillon with boiled potatoes and the vegetables that were cooked alongside it; little gherkins called cornichons are often served separately. Top round (the inside leg) is a good braising and pot-roasting meat – being very lean, it usually gets a wrapping of fat. Top round can also be roasted, although it may well be rather on the dry and tough side. It remains much juicier when it is kept very rare, in which case it is also excellent cold.

Bottom round (the outside leg) is much like top round in character. Roasting is not advised, as it is slightly less tender (and slightly cheaper) than top round, but it makes nice pot roasts and good stews.

Tip roast

Whole, it can be roasted or pot roasted and cut into cubes it makes excellent daubes and stews like *boeuf burguignonne*. It comes from the underside of the hind leg where the leg meets the flank.

The shoulder

It is known as chuck in the United States and chuck or blade in England. Blade steak is cut from the flat of the shoulder blade. When scored across with a heavy knife to cut through all the fine connecting tissues, it can be fried like a regular steak. Chuck is excellent for stews, goulash, pies and daubes.

Meat from the neck is bony. Trimmed and boned it is used for stews. On the bone it is a good addition to the stock pot.

Brisket

It is fatty meat that needs pot roasting or braising, and is nicer when it has been marinated. It is sold on or off the bone and is very economical. It is made into corned beef, in which case it is boiled and often eaten cold, cut into very thin slices.

Flank

The thinner end of flank is used for making stock, curries and stews. Towards the leg end, the flank becomes more tender.

Skirt

Skirt is a lean muscle from this region. In England it is used with the drier chuck for

steak and kidney puddings and pies. In America this muscle is called London broil, and is first scored like the blade steak, then slowly broiled and served cut across the grain in thin strips.

The fore shank

Gives gelatinous stewing meat with a lovely flavor.

The hind shank

Has a lot of gristle and sinew, but tastes delicious.

Marrow

This is a delicious fatty substance to be found inside the large bones of beef and veal. In young animals and in the shorter bones of older animals, the marrow is red; in the leg bones of older animals it is yellow, and it is this yellow marrow that is regarded as a delicacy. Beef leg bones are fairly widely available, already cut into pieces.

Marrow makes a wonderful addition to stocks, in which case the split bones are boiled along with the other ingredients to give up their goodness. If you want to use the marrow for sauces or for spreading on toast, the bones should be soaked overnight in cold water, then wrapped in foil and cooked in a fairly hot oven for 45 minutes. The marrow can then be scooped out from the center of the bones.

RECIPE SUGGESTION

Boeuf en daube

2¼ lb/1 kg top round or tip roast of beef
¼ lb/115 g bacon in a piece
1 large onion
3–4 large cloves garlic
3–4 tablespoons olive oil
¼ bottle red wine
small glass dry white vermouth
bouquet garni of 3 sprigs thyme, 1 bay leaf and a strip of orange peel
1 tablespoon tomato paste
⅔ cup/1.5 dl beef stock
salt and freshly ground pepper
¼ cup/115 g pitted black olives

SERVES 6

Preheat the oven to 290°F/150°C.
Trim the meat and cut it into large pieces. Dice the bacon, rind removed, and blanch it for 4–5 minutes in boiling water. Peel and chop the onion and garlic.
Heat the olive oil in a flameproof casserole and fry the drained dried bacon, the garlic and the onion for 5–10 minutes. Remove them to a plate, then brown the meat rapidly on all sides. It is best to do this in two batches. Bring the wine to the boil in a separate pan. Return the onion and bacon to the casserole, pour the vermouth over the meat and then the boiling wine. Add the bouquet garni, tomato paste, a little stock—as necessary—and some pepper. Do not add much salt yet as the bacon and subsequently the olives will probably make it salty enough. Cover, and cook in the oven for about 2 hours or until tender. Add the olives and cook for a further 30 minutes. Taste the sauce for seasoning and serve.

CHOOSING VEAL

Good veal comes from the same breed of cattle as good beef. There are two types of veal: the first comes from milk-fed calves or vealers slaughtered between eight and twelve weeks of age, and the second from grass-fed calves, which are between four and five months old.

Milk-fed veal should be the palest pearly pink. It should look firm and moist but never wet, and have bright, pinky-white, translucent bones. Grass-fed veal is a little darker in color, but never red. Redness is a sure sign that the animal had grown too old before slaughter. If veal has a brown or grey tinge, it means that it is stale and should be avoided. Veal has a little marbling, which should be hard to spot as the fat is practically the same color as the meat. If there is too much marbling and too much covering fat, then it means the calf has been overfed. What fat there is should look like white satin, and there shouldn't be much of it except around the kidneys.

COOKING WITH VEAL

Because it hasn't much marbling, there is little interior lubrication while the meat is cooking, and veal can be dry unless other fat is added by way of larding or barding for roasting, or by using plenty of butter, good olive oil or bacon in sautéed, pot-roasted and stewed dishes.

The flavor of veal is unassertive, so a strongly flavored garnish is often welcome: the combination of veal and anchovies dates from the earliest times. Lemon and orange often feature in the best sauces, as does white wine and, particularly, Marsala. In Italy, a roast of veal may be studded with strips of anchovies; in Parma, they slit a leg cut of veal and introduce strips of paper-thin smoked ham. Scallops and cutlets of veal may also appear under a slice of mildly cured ham on which a generous slice of cheese is gently melting.

Onions have a special affinity with veal, not only because of their taste but because of their slippery texture – they are often put into the pan alongside a roast. As for accompaniments: any really fresh-looking vegetable is good, as is salad. Veal is pale, so dark green spinach or beans will provide a beautiful background. Potatoes, of course, go with veal in almost any form, and so do rice and noodles. Golden saffron rice is the traditional side dish for osso bucco, and a ring of snow-white rice often surrounds a blond blanquette or a fricassée of veal. (A fricassée differs from a blanquette only in the lack of cream and eggs in the sauce.) Tagliatelle is often served with veal, the slippery texture compensating for any possible dryness in the meat.

All veal bones are extremely gelatinous, and give an excellent texture to sauces and stocks: if the butcher has trimmed the meat

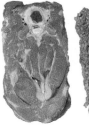

Loin for roasting   Tenderloin, chop and scallop for frying/broiling   Neck for braising/stewing   Ground veal

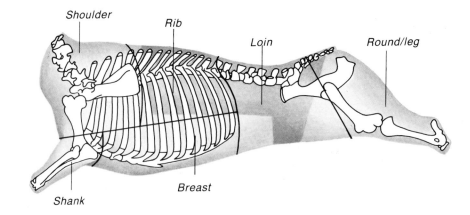

Shoulder · Rib · Loin · Round/leg · Shank · Breast

for you, be sure to carry a few of the bones home with you and add them to the pot when braising a piece of veal, removing them before you dish up.

Broiling and frying

Because of the lack of interior fat, the smaller cuts – chops, cutlets, scallops, medallions and the like – are more often fried than broiled.

Thin scallops should be fried quickly over a medium heat; chops should be first seared over high heat and then cooked on slowly, otherwise they will become tough and dry. Because of the high temperature of the initial cooking, chops will need to be fried in oil or in an oil and butter mixture, but scallops can be successfully fried in unsalted butter.

Veal can be rather indigestible and nasty unless it is thoroughly cooked, so wait until the juices run clear, with no tinge of pinkness, before withdrawing it from the heat.

Roasting

Baste veal frequently if you do decide to try roasting it – pot roasting and braising are often more successful with this dry meat. Roast for 25 minutes per 1lb/450g and 20 minutes over at a medium temperature – about 375°F/190°C – for cuts that are thin or on the bone; 35 minutes per 1lb/450g at 325°F/170°C for those that are thick or cuts that have been boned and rolled or stuffed.

A hefty cut, like a leg, will preserve its succulence better if sprinkled with flour and covered with slices of bacon before it goes in the oven. The lean little roasts, such as a

boned loin, should be threaded through with strips of pork fat (larded) or covered with a lattice of pork fat (barded). This extra fat will keep the meat moist.

Pot roasting and braising

This is the best method of cooking a large piece of veal. Add some little onions, potatoes or carrots to the pot to help produce the moisture which will prevent the veal from drying out. In Italy, a good-sized carrot is sometimes inserted through the middle of the meat for the same purpose.

Allow 40–50 minutes per 1lb/450g at 325°F/170°C, basting the meat frequently with wine and butter.

Stewing

Veal is good stewed in a flavorsome broth which is thickened and enriched at the end of the cooking time with egg yolks and cream.

Boiling

This is more strictly speaking, poaching and should be only a mere simmering: add a split calf's foot, and reduce the cooking liquid after the veal has been removed to make a beautiful aspic, having carefully skimmed off the scum which rises to the top of the pot at the beginning.

THE CUTS

Like beef, cuts of veal vary according to the various butchery techniques. However, since calves are smaller than full-grown beef cattle, there is not quite so much scope for variations and not as much difference between the cuts. In fact most countries follow the economical French style of butchery for veal – and that involves trimming away all gristle and sinew most meticulously and dividing the meat neatly along the natural seams in the muscles.

Cuts for frying, broiling and roasting

Veal needs plenty of additional fat to prevent it from drying out completely in the dry heat of these processes.

The leg

Only the hindlegs go by this name, as the forelegs are called shanks. This large and fleshy joint is almost always divided into the hock end and the fillet end. These cuts can be roasted under a layer of bacon or, better still, braised with vegetables to keep them moist and juicy.

The round roast, or fillet end of the leg – the top slices of which go by the name of round steak or cutlets – is the equivalent of a top round of beef. A boneless round roast makes a succulent meal – it is particularly good stuffed with a moist mixture of pork fat, anchovy fillets and currants and then braised in a web of caul fat.

The most delicate leg meat is from the muscle that runs vertically along the thigh bone. In French butchery it is sold separately as the *rouelle*, but in general, leg of veal cuts tend to be sliced crosswise, containing some of each of the three muscles, which are very similar in taste. So, whether on or off the bone, a cut of center leg makes good eating. It is this bit that is used for the famous Italian dish *vitello tonnato* – always eaten cold and coated with a sauce of tuna fish pounded to an emulsion with olive oil, lemon juice and capers.

The sirloin

This is situated at the point where leg meets loin and is usually boned and rolled for slow roasting and braising.

Scallops

It is from the fillet end of the leg that the best scallops are cut, across the grain and on the bias. Of course, many stores sell thin pink slices of fatless, trimmed veal under the name of escalopes, scallopini or scallops from other parts of a calf's anatomy, particularly the ribs, but first-rate butchers only recognize those from the leg as the real thing. Ask the butcher to press them flat for you for extra tenderness, and when you egg-and-crumb these diaphanous slices, you get the perfect scallops *panés*. These are classically served with a slice of lemon, perhaps a rolled anchovy and possibly some chopped hard-boiled egg arranged in a circle around it, and a few scattered capers.

If you find that you have to pound the scallops yourself, do take care not to beat the life out of them – a well-cut scallop will only require a gentle flattening. If you don't possess a cutlet beater, then use a rolling pin or ease the meat into shape with the heel of your hand.

There are many, many ways to serve veal scallops. This rich diversity is in part due to the fact that the scallop is one of the mainstays of Italian cooking, and it features often in the varied cuisines of France, Germany and Austria.

In Italy, for instance, a great favorite is saltimbocca – which means literally "to jump into the mouth." This is a dish of small scallops rolled up around a stuffing of prosciutto ham and fresh sage.

Piccate, or scallopini, are tiny scallops traditionally dipped in flour and fried in butter. Ideally, they come from the same part of the leg as scallops; they are usually sautéed and served with a good sauce.

In France, veal scallops are often simply browned in butter, with the last-minute addition of a handful of finely chopped shallots or scallions.

The Germans and Austrians are of course famed for their *Weinerschnitzels* – traditionally these are dipped first into flour, then beaten egg, then bread crumbs and then briefly deep fried in hot oil.

Loin of veal

This roasting cut, contains the tenderloin, which is the equivalent of beef tenderloin. It may also contain the kidneys. But these, as well as the fillet, are often removed to be sold separately: the tenderloin to make nice little medallions that look like tournedos. The loin can be divided into chops or sold whole for roasting.

When roasting a loin, keep it very well basted with butter or bacon fat, or cook it in a covered casserole to keep it moist.

Rib

This is the section that is divided into delicious veal chops, which should not be cut too thin. Chops should be cooked very gently after browning or they may become dry. Like scallops, which are also often cut from these parts, cutlets usually have their garnish sitting on top: a poached egg and a cross of anchovy fillets earns them the suffix Holstein; and fontina cheese, prosciutto, small white mushrooms and of course anchovies may all feature.

The middle neck

This forms part of the shoulder in the United States, and provides veal cutlets, which the Americans call shoulder chops, the French *cotelettes découvertes*. Smaller than chops, they are prepared in much the same way, though they are sometimes sealed in butter and enclosed in a paper case together with a farce of shallots, onion, mushrooms and parsley and baked in the oven, to be served *en papillotte*. When the cutlets are not quite severed at the base, and teased around to form a crown of veal, the onion and mushroom stuffing may go into the center. Off the bone, the meat of the middle neck is used for pies, *blanquette de veau* and goulash.

For braising, pot roasting and boiling

Veal adapts particularly well to moist heat, absorbing both moisture and any flavorings added to the pot.

Shoulder or oyster of veal

This is a fairly lean cut suitable for slow roasting or pot roasting. It is almost always sold boned and rolled, often with stuffing, although it is vastly preferable to make one's own. For this purpose, good butchers often leave an empty pocket in the center. Boned and cubed shoulder is a prime candidate for blanquettes and fricassées – especially when mixed with the meat from the breast region. It is the traditional cut for veal Marengo, which unlike its namesake, chicken Marengo, requires no truffles, crayfish or fried eggs. A traditional veal Marengo is a simple braise made with plenty of oil, garlic, tomatoes and mushrooms.

Ground shoulder, flavored with marjoram and rosemary and bound together with egg, makes delicious meatballs – made more delicious with the addition of a sauce of white wine, cream and finely chopped shallots.

Neck of veal or stewing veal

Use for braised dishes as it provides meat that is suitable for long simmering. Ground, it makes good meat loaves, meatballs and stuffings, and can be used in pâtés. Ground veal, in fact, is an ingredient in many classic forcemeats for stuffing pork tenderloin, poultry and game birds.

Breast and flank of veal

These are often seen boned, and provide a vehicle for some very good stuffings. Traditionally, something green is included in these: spinach, perhaps, or peas, or pistachio nuts. Served cold, a stuffed breast of veal, simmered, gently pressed and allowed to cool in its own gelatine, makes a beautiful summer lunch. A breast is also very good hot – casseroled together with a chunk of salt pork and some large, juicy onions.

The shank or foreleg

This is a tough, sinewy but well-flavored piece of meat consisting mainly of bone, which, sawn into thick slices, makes one of the most delicious veal dishes – osso bucco.

Light veal or beef stock

3 lb/1.5 kg veal and beef bones, chopped up by the butcher, ¾ lb/340 g beef shank, 3 quarts/2.75 liters water, 2 onions, 3 leeks, 2 carrots, 2 sticks celery, bunch of thyme, parsley and bay leaf, 6 black peppercorns, glass of white wine (optional), pinch of salt

Cover the bones and meat with cold water and bring slowly to the boil. Skim off the froth and scum that rise and cook very gently for 4–5 hours on top of the stove or 45 minutes in a pressure cooker. Add the vegetables, chopped, the herbs, peppercorns and glass of wine (if using) halfway through the cooking time, but not more than a pinch of salt until later. If you hate the smell of stock cooking, bring it to the boil on top of the stove and then transfer it, covered, to a very slow oven.

Spring lamb that has been weaned will be much the same size as milk-fed lamb: a whole leg may just feed four people. Summer and autumn lamb has flesh that is darker than Easter lamb. Lamb only qualifies for the name when it has been slaughtered before its first birthday. After that, it becomes hogget, then mutton.

Yearling mutton gives delicious meat; it is a little darker and a little stronger tasting than lamb. The expression "mutton dressed as lamb" arose because all too many butchers used to try deceiving their customers (and thrifty hosts their guests), but there is really no mistaking the two kinds of meat: mutton is dark red, not pink, and there should not be too much fat. Although mutton used to be as despised as lamb was admired, it is just the right sort of meat for the heftier regional dishes. Ironically, now that supplies of good lamb are quite constant – not least because this meat freezes particularly well – people who actually want to buy good old-fashioned mutton often have great difficulty in finding it.

CHOOSING LAMB AND MUTTON

When buying lamb or mutton, go for the leanest piece you can see – even the fatty cuts vary greatly in their proportions of fat to lean. Avoid those with fat that looks brittle and crumbly or discolored – the most appetizing-looking pieces will make the best eating and have the most flavor.

Some of the most delicious lamb comes from sheep that have grazed on salt marshes: the *pré-salé* lamb – "pre-salted" lamb – of France's Atlantic coast is world-famous. Most lamb for the table comes from lowland farms where the sheep are fat, but some prefer the leaner lamb from the hills: Welsh lamb, small and slender-boned, is a good example of this superb meat. Hillside lamb is a touch gamier in flavor, and there are many recipes for cooking lamb like venison, using the traditional marinades and the same accompaniments: rowanberry or red currant jelly, or a compote of cranberries.

COOKING WITH LAMB AND MUTTON

Lamb is basically a tender, succulent meat, so take care not to overcook it – generally, lamb should be pink and juicy inside.

Broiling and frying
Chops and steaks of lamb, nicely trimmed, are equally good broiled or fried. The timing depends on the thickness of the pieces. Test them by pressing them with your finger during cooking: when they are becoming firm but still supple, they are done.

Roasting
Much depends on the age of the animal and the quality of the meat.

The timing varies according to whether

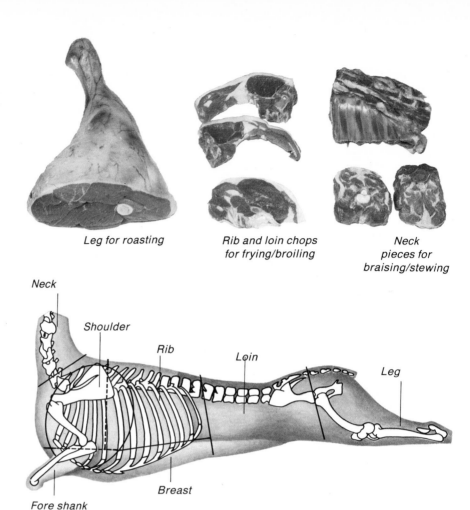

Leg for roasting

Rib and loin chops for frying/broiling

Neck pieces for braising/stewing

Neck

Shoulder

Rib

Loin

Leg

Breast

Fore shank

you like your roast rosy pink or well done. A leg of lamb should be pink within, most gourmets would agree, although not everyone shares the taste of the French, who like it rose-red in the center. The rib end, saddle and loin are best fairly rare – cook all these prime quality cuts at 375°F/190°C, allowing about 20 minutes per 1lb/450g and maybe 15 minutes over for larger cuts, but test by piercing: when the juice runs red, the meat is rare; rosy, it is fairly rare; and when the meat juices run clear, the meat is thoroughly cooked.

The shoulder and all boned, rolled cuts, including stuffed, rolled breasts, are better when they are well done: cook them at 325°F/170°C, allowing about 30 minutes per 1lb/450g.

Pot roasting and braising
This is done at an even lower temperature: 300°F/160°C, allowing about 2 hours for a leg or shoulder, 1½ hours for casseroling smaller cuts, and a lamb stew should be ready for eating after 1½ hours of cooking.

Boiling
Takes about 30 minutes per 1lb/450g for larger cuts of mutton, but it is best to cook them well before they are needed, since they taste nicest reheated and, since mutton for boiling tends to be rather fatty, it gives you a chance to lift off the fat, which solidifies when the dish has cooled. If there is not time

to wait for this to happen, the broth can be defatted either by careful skimming, or by plunging ice cubes into the liquid and lifting out the fat when it congeals.

Because all lamb fat congeals so quickly, it is important to take your stew to the table in a preheated dish and to serve it as soon as possible on very hot plates.

THE CUTS

Most large cuts of lamb can be roasted; even the fattier ones will taste good.

Leg of lamb, or gigot
This succulent piece, simply roasted on the bone, is one of the greatest cuts of meat there is. It may be subdivided into the shank and the sirloin end. The sirloin end, in turn, makes leg steaks. Divested of all membranes, this fleshy steak, cut into cubes, makes lovely little kebabs.

The leg or gigot is also sold boned. It is usually rolled, but is sometimes left flat – in America this version is called a butterfly leg of lamb. In whatever form, this cut makes a lovely roast. Leave on the papery outer skin to ensure even cooking, and if you want to make this extra crisp, dredge it with a little flour after basting.

Serve young lamb with mint sauce and spring vegetables; autumn lamb with root vegetables. If you braise half a leg on a bed of vegetables and use cream and tarragon in the sauce, it becomes *agneau jardinière*, but what is particularly delicious and all too rarely encountered is a noble, very English, boiled leg of lamb – the shank end – served with caper or onion sauce.

In France the centerbone is sometimes removed from the sirloin end of a gigot, leaving only the shank bone in place: this makes carving easier when the meat is served.

Center roast

Lying between the leg and the sirloin, this piece is sometimes sold as a separate cut for roasting. Often it is cut into the juiciest steaks – expensive, since each leg yields only two or three. In some schools of butchery it simply forms part of the leg itself. The two legs, center roast, sirloin and loin make a very impressive cut called a baron of lamb.

Loin

Two joined loins make a saddle, very good for parties. This is sometimes decorated at one end with the kidneys, and a bas-relief of braided fat running its length. The single loin may be bought on the bone, but it also comes boned and rolled, often around the kidneys – slices of this are called kidney lamb chops.

The loin is often devided into chops – each with a small T-shaped bone dividing the two pieces of lean. There are a hundred ways of garnishing chops; left plain, fried or broiled, serve them pink inside with watercress and mashed potatoes. Loin chops can be boned and trimmed of any excess fat until only the eyes remain.

The rib

This cut, which the French usually call the *carré*, and which is sometimes referred to as rack of lamb, lies next to the loin. If you mean to roast or braise it in the piece, ask the butcher to chine it for you, to enable you to carve neat chops after cooking. Two racks placed opposite each other, fat side out, bones in the air and interlinked like swords at a military wedding, make a good party piece called Guard of Honor. A good, moist stuffing goes in between the two pieces of meat, the same type that you would put into the center of a crown of lamb, which is made from the identical two cuts, joined at both ends. The rack, trimmed and chined and with the ribs removed, can also be neatly rolled and divided into noisettes.

Sliced, the rib end or rack gives chops that are a fraction less juicy than loin chops, but still very good. When they are "frenched" – trimmed with the elegance and care that most French butchers bestow on all the meat they handle, so that in this case the bones are pared of fat – they may come to table with a paper frill at the end, and are sometimes eaten with the fingers. The farther back the chops lie, the leaner they are; towards the front, they tend to become quite fatty.

Chops are often egg-and-crumbed. When they are served with a sauce made of vegetables, ham and herbs, all chopped finely, moistened with stock, thickened with cornstarch and flavored with red currant jelly, they become Reform cutlets – named after the London club where they are still served in this way. But elegant classic garnishes – truffles, creamed mushrooms, foie gras, asparagus tips – also find their way onto lamb chops and cutlets.

Shoulder of lamb

Easy to cook, this makes a sweet and juicy roast. It is fattier than the leg, and harder to carve, especially when it is on the bone, but is often a more succulent meal. Boned and tied, it may be stuffed – whether it comes as a long roll or, as in France, in a kind of melon-shaped bundle also known as a ballotine, or *épaule en ballon*. The shoulder also provides blade and arm chops which are good for braising.

Shoulder, trimmed of all fat and membrane, is the cut that is often ground up, perhaps together with meat from the foreshank, for use in moussaka, stuffed peppers, grape leaves and the like. In the Middle East this cut of lamb is sometimes pounded to the consistency of an ointment: this smooth paste, which also involves burghul, is called kibbeh – it is formed into little patties which are eaten raw with onions.

Shoulder chops

Lying underneath the shoulder blade next to the rack, shoulder chops are a decidedly fatty cut, but useful for broth, lamb stew and Lancashire hotpot (unless you make this in the traditional way, with rib chops standing upright in a deep earthenware pot).

Neck and fore shank

Both of these cuts are very economical buys. They are used in the same way as shoulder chops, but have more bone, gristle and fat. Use them to make a good Irish stew – a dish which used once to be made with kid, but lamb is now almost always used. Because they are fatty, use plenty of potatoes to soak up the juices.

A top layer of thickly cut slices of potato benefits from the rich aromatic fat that rises as the meat cooks. A shepherd's pie, with its covering of mashed potatoes, works on the same principle, as do casseroles or haricots of lamb where dried beans act as the blotting paper. Essentially, haricot, ragout and navarin are all stews – although a *navarin printanier* only applies to a more spring-like dish, in which carrots, turnips and peas feature as vegetables. Pilafs, too, feature stewing lamb and rice.

Breast of lamb

This thin, fatty cut tastes better when it has been slowly cooked. The breast cage makes riblets for barbecuing; the less bony parts can be boned, stuffed and rolled, or tied flat, like a sandwich, with the stuffing in the middle. Boneless breast can be simmered, cooled, cut into squares, egg-and-crumbed and fried; these morsels are called epigrams, a charming name and a good dish.

KID

When it comes to athletic lamb from craggy hillsides with no pasture to speak of, the meat is not notable for its succulence. This is where kid, better adapted to such regions, is much preferred to lamb.

Cooked in oil and wine with garlic, wreathed in rosemary or myrtle, young kid, creamy white and tender, makes the festive dishes in such places as Corsica and Sardinia, while lamb is for every day. Saudi Arabia, too, feasts on kid: rubbed with coriander, ginger and onion juice, stuffed with rice, dried fruits and nuts, and served with clouds of rice and hard-boiled eggs. Lamb can, of course, be substituted – as far as recipes go, the two kinds of meat are interchangeable. But as the taste of kid is bland, it needs plenty of flavoring.

RECIPE SUGGESTION
Gigot d'agneau

1 leg of lamb, weighing 4 lb/2 kg, boned
2 cups/340 g dried navy beans or green flageolets, soaked overnight
1 ham bone or a 1 lb/450 g piece of bacon or salt pork
3 cloves garlic
handful of parsley, chopped
¾ stick/85 g butter
salt and freshly ground pepper
1 large onion
1 tablespoon pork drippings, or butter and oil mixed
2 tablespoons tomato paste or 3–4 tomatoes
1 glass white wine

SERVES 6–8

Put the dried navy beans or flageolets in a heavy pan together with the ham bone or whatever piece of pork or bacon you have. Cover with plenty of cold water, bring to the boil and simmer gently for an hour to an hour and 30 minutes.

Preheat the oven to 425°F/220°C.

Peel and chop the cloves of garlic and cook gently with the parsley in a little of the butter, without browning. Allow this mixture to cool and then push it into the cavity in the leg of lamb. Add salt, pepper and a lump of the remaining butter. Roll up the leg and tie it at 1½ in/4 cm intervals with string. Rub the outside with the last of the butter and some salt, and roast for 30 minutes, basting and turning from time to time.

Turn down the heat to 350°F/180°C and cook for a further 40 minutes to an hour, depending on how you like your lamb.

Peel and chop the onion fairly finely and sauté gently in the pork drippings or butter and oil. Stir in the tomato paste and let it reduce. (If you are using fresh tomatoes instead of tomato paste, skin and chop them, and reduce them considerably before adding them to the softened onions.) Add the white wine to the onion and tomato and a cupful of the beans' cooking liquid, simmer a minute or two, then stir in the strained cooked beans. Let them simmer very gently until the meat is ready.

When the lamb is done, remove it from the pan and keep it hot. Spoon all the fat off the juices in the roasting pan, then stir these juices into the beans. Season the beans and transfer them to a heated dish. Carve the lamb and lay the slices down the middle of the dish of beans.

ALTERNATIVE: *you can serve this dish sprinkled with finely chopped garlic and parsley mixed with bread crumbs – which you quickly brown in the broiler.*

CHOOSING PORK

In the case of meat from animals slaughtered between four and six months – called, respectively, young pigs and mature hogs by the trade – make sure that there is a good proportion of lean meat to fat, and this applies even more to porkers, which is what pigs are called between six months and one year. By this time, the meat has darkened to rose-pink and the bones, pinkish in young animals, are white. Deep rose-colored meat, white brittle bones and rough skin are signs of a porker's unduly advanced age; red meat with a dried-up look is not worth bothering with. If you notice brown or yellowish stains on the skin, if the meat looks wet and slippery rather than damp, the meat will be of poor quality, and if there is any kind of smell, the meat is stale.

COOKING WITH PORK

Although all cuts of pork taste rich, not all of them are liberally lubricated from within. The leg, for example, does not have much in the way of intramuscular fat, so meat from this part of the animal may appear to be on the dry side, and to remain as juicy as possible should be slowly cooked.

All cuts of pork without exception need to be well cooked – partly because raw pork may contain microscopic parasites which are killed only when the meat reaches an internal temperature of about 140°F/60°C, and, just as important, because underdone pork tastes very unpleasant.

The humbler cuts of pork are cooked and served with plenty of fat on the meat, and so the best accompaniments are mealy – beans, dried peas and lentils, which will absorb some of the fat.

Chestnuts have the same effect, and in Spain and Portugal potatoes are added to braised or stewed fatty pork dishes about half an hour before serving to soak up the fat that has risen to the top of the pot.

The more expensive, less fatty cuts of pork – leg and loin – are more often served with fruit or vegetables that provide a contrast to the rich, dense meat. Apples are probably the best-known accompaniment, while in Tours, cutlets or fillet steaks of pork are cooked with prunes. In Denmark prunes are used to stuff a loin roast, and a mixture of soaked, dried fruit is used in Poland. In the Rhineland, the mealy and fruity elements are combined in a dish called Heaven and Earth – puréed potatoes and apples.

For moistening purposes, beer, wine and stock are occasionally used, but cider is the liquid most associated with pork.

By way of herbs, pork takes kindly to the warm flavor of fennel and caraway seeds, as well as to the bitter flavor of sage. Some people in England still make their own sage and onion stuffing for their Sunday roast of pork – much nicer than the ready-made variety. In Italy, pork is often cooked with

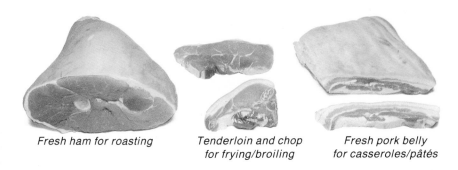

Fresh ham for roasting *Tenderloin and chop for frying/broiling* *Fresh pork belly for casseroles/pâtés*

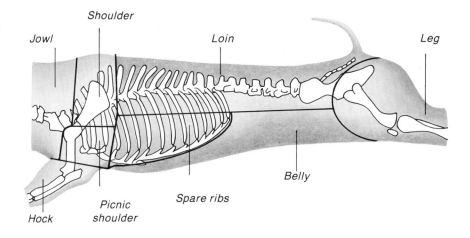

Jowl *Shoulder* *Loin* *Leg* *Belly* *Spare ribs* *Picnic shoulder* *Hock*

rosemary; it is good also with juniper berries and with thyme, and, of course, a loin of pork is wonderful with truffles.

As for vegetable side dishes, all the members of the brassica family, led by sweet-and-sour red cabbage, are naturals for pork. The more delicate roasts, such as leg or loin, look most appetizing with something fresh such as little carrots or turnips, leeks, bright green cabbage or spinach. Young peas and artichoke hearts in butter make one of the best combinations. A plain lettuce salad, eaten from the same plate after a broiled or fried chop, and bathed in the meat juices, is extremely delicious.

Broiling and frying

A medium chop should take about 20 minutes at medium heat. Turn it from time to time as it cooks, and test it by piercing – when the juices run clear, it is ready to serve.

Roasting

Allow a full 30 minutes per 1lb/450g for smaller, thinner cuts, plus 20 minutes over, at about 350°F/180°C and 35 minutes per 1lb/450g and 25 minutes over, for thicker pieces like leg or a shoulder cut. If you buy pork with the skin, ask the butcher to score it closely and deeply with his special knife, right through the rind to the fat, to help the heat penetrate to the center. In many countries, the skin is peeled off the meat before it is sold and supplied separately, to be cooked alongside the meat, enriching the gravy. It turns into the hardest leather by this process. (The Normans found this *cuir bouilli* an

effective protection against their enemies' arrows.) So if you like crisp crackling – and many people think this is possibly the best part of a piece of roast pork – do not allow the meat to sit in the fat in the pan or you render part of the skin inedible. Instead, roast the cut on a rack, having rubbed the skin with oil or salt (but not both together) for extra crispness. Increase the oven temperature a little before the end of cooking and do not baste the crackling during cooking – it just makes it tough.

Braising and pot roasting

On top of the stove, simmer pork over a medium heat, or set the oven at 325°F/170°C.

Boiling

It is not very usual to boil fresh pork, except, of course, for the feet, but any of the pickled cuts make perfect candidates for boiling, or rather simmering. These may need soaking beforehand: ask the butcher for how long, as he alone knows for how long the meat has been salted.

THE CUTS

There is no single cut of pork that cannot satisfactorily be roasted – the pig is too lethargic a beast to develop much by way of tough muscle and connective tissue. The coarser cuts with little visible fat may be better casseroled or slowly stewed. A coarse, fat cut will still make a lovely braise or stew, provided it is trimmed of most of the fat, which would make the sauce too rich.

The leg

A whole leg makes a really imposing dish. But even a small one – and one from a pig should weigh no more than 6–7lb/2.5–3kg – can be rather daunting, so it is usually divided into the shank or leg end and the fillet end, which the French confusingly call *jambon frais* and which in America is referred to as the fresh ham rump.

The shank end

It is easier to cook evenly when it is boned and rolled, but it then looks less handsome on the platter. When cooking it on the bone, it is a good idea to protect the thinner bony bit by wrapping it in foil halfway through the cooking time, leaving the meatier end exposed to the full heat.

The rump end

This is cooked as a roast, or may be cut by the butcher into lean slices about $\frac{1}{2}$–1in/1–2.5cm thick. Such a slice makes a huge meal – cook it as you would a steak. The rump end of leg may be cut into cubes to be cooked as kebabs.

A leg is sometimes, especially in Italy, first simmered in milk and then cooked on in the oven, surrounded by quantities of garlic (the milk ends up as a light, golden gravy), while some countries pickle the leg, to be boiled and eaten with the mash of green split peas that is known and loved as pease pudding in the north of England.

The loin end

This fleshy part of the loin is usually cut into delicious large chops – the butterfly chops of America – but this is another cut that may be roasted on the bone or off, seasoned with sage, rosemary or thyme.

The loin

Delicate and very tender, the loin itself makes a wonderful meal if boned, filled with chopped garlic and a couple of mushrooms or even truffles, and rolled and roasted. On the bone, a loin cut is sometimes served sitting on a bed of unsweetened apples and sweet chestnuts.

It is the loin that provides most of the pork chops: to be fried plain or broiled after being lightly brushed with oil, or pounded, egg-and-crumbed and fried *alla milanese*, or braised, moistened with beer or cider.

Chops taken from the sirloin end of the loin may bring with them a slice of kidney and a portion of the fillet or tenderloin.

The tenderloin

In young pigs the fillet or tenderloin is usually much too small to be separated out, but many butchers remove it in its entirety from larger carcasses, where it may weight about 1lb/450g. Trimmed of its fat, it is good roasted – perhaps scored down the middle and stuffed, or wrapped in bacon and roasted whole like a miniature roast. It may also be cut into medallions or scallops, but their taste, like those of veal, from which they are almost indistinguishable, is delicate, so some interesting flavoring is needed to give them character: in France apples or prunes

are used as garnish for fillet cuts, which are lovely cooked with crushed juniper berries, and in Germany they are cooked with caraway seeds or a rich sauce made of sour cream and the delicious pan juices.

Blade or shoulder

This rather rich cut can be roasted, or ground up or chopped for pork pies or meatballs and for the famous scrapple of Philadelphia – a cooked mixture of pork and cornmeal, sliced and fried in bacon drippings.

Meat from the shoulder can be sliced into steaks that are particularly good when cooked over charcoal.

Picnic shoulder and hock

An awkwardly shaped piece which is often divided into a variety of cuts for stewing, but whole it makes a good, large, economical roast, although the meat is marginally coarser than that of the leg. This cut is a particularly difficult one to carve unless you know exactly how the bones run, but the butcher will advise you if you ask him, or will even bone and roll it for you.

Spareribs

These come from the upper part of the rib cage and are either sold in sheets or separated into meaty single or double bones, each with its cartilage. The sheets of ribs are sometimes cooked sandwiched together with a stuffing in between: the Pennsylvania Dutch like to spread this sandwich with apples, the Germans with cabbage and caraway. The separated ribs are barbecued and often eaten with a sweet-sour sauce, said to have been introduced to America by Chinese railway workers, who used to cook this meat as they worked on the line.

Chinese spareribs

These have very little meat on them, but are extremely good barbecued and served with chili sauce. Eat them with the fingers, allowing about 3lb/1.5kg for 2 people because these spareribs are so bony; they are just the lower ends of the rib bones.

Pork belly

The abdominal wall provides rather fatty meat; it is usually cured for bacon and is good for enriching dishes of beans, lentils and cabbage and is useful in pâtés. If you can't find fresh pork belly use salt pork – preferably a piece with a good streak of lean – that has been soaked to freshen.

SUCKLING PIG

These young pigs, which have been slaughtered between the ages of three and eight weeks, contain proportionally little meat, however what there is, is perhaps the sweetest and richest of all pork.

In northern Spain, suckling pigs are a specialty. These Spanish suckling pigs start their short lives on a diet of mothers' milk and wild herbs. They are traditionally roasted in a slow-burning wood oven and served with potatoes and applesauce.

Choosing suckling pig

You will need to order one specially from your butcher. They range in size from 6–20lb/2.5–9kg, and a medium-size one will be a good buy as it will have developed enough meaty parts without sacrificing any of the tender succulence of the smaller pigs. As a rough guide, a 12lb/5.5kg pig should feed about 10 people.

Roasting a suckling pig

Suckling pig, which should have been cleaned for you by the butcher, can be stuffed with any stuffing suitable for pork (a combination of bread crumbs, parsley, onions, sausage, chestnuts and brandy is good), or simply brushed with oil or rubbed with coarse salt and lemon juice and sprinkled with herbs. Place the suckling pig on a rack and prick the skin before and during roasting to allow the fat to ooze out into the roasting pan. It won't need basting and the skin will turn a shiny crisp brown. A medium-size stuffed pig will take about 2½–3 hours to cook, an unstuffed one will be ready in 2 hours. Allow 20 minutes per 1lb/450g at 350°F/180°C.

RECIPE SUGGESTION

Roast loin of pork

1 loin of pork, weighing about 3¾ lb/1.75 kg, skin on
2 cloves garlic
a little wine vinegar or lemon juice
2 nice sprigs rosemary
1 glass white wine or cider
2 teaspoons flour
¾–1¼ cups/1.5–3 dl chicken stock
salt and freshly ground pepper

SERVES 6–8

Preheat the oven to 350°F/180°C.
The loin should be on the bone, but chined by the butcher. Score the skin well to make crisp, manageable crackling.
Place the loin, skin side up, on a rack in a roasting pan. Tuck the rosemary under the pork and push the unpeeled garlic cloves between the meat and the fat or next to the bone. Rub the surface with lemon juice or vinegar and fine salt but no oil or other fat.
Roast the pork, without basting, for 2 hours, putting it low in the oven if the crackling is getting too dark on the top. Remove the meat to a heated dish and keep it hot for at least 15–20 minutes, covered loosely with foil or an old-fashioned meat cover, so that it can relax. This makes the meat juicier and easier to carve.
Meanwhile, make the gravy; spoon most of the fat from the roasting pan and remove the rosemary. Retrieve the cloves of garlic and crush them, then add the glass of wine or cider and stir and scrape the roasting pan over a rapid heat, to dissolve all the meat juices from the sides and bottom. When the wine has reduced considerably, add the flour to the pan, stir it around and break up the lumps, then add the stock, stirring all the time. Let the gravy cook for a few minutes, season it and then strain through a conical strainer into a gravy boat or pitcher. Serve the loin of pork with this gravy, applesauce and roast potatoes.

Some of the best dishes in the world are made with humble pieces of meat that are collectively known as variety meats. They are treated with special respect in France and the Mediterranean countries, where their distinctive flavor and textures are preserved by careful cooking.

Luckily, many of these meats are among the most economical buys. While some of them, particularly those from veal, may command a high price, only small amounts need to be purchased because of their rich flavor and lack of bones, while meats from less expensive animals are full of wholesome flavor. Whichever type you buy, make sure it is fresh and cook it as soon as possible.

SWEETBREADS

A fine delicacy, sweetbreads are sold in pairs, being two parts of the thymus gland found in the throat and chest of young animals. The rounder, fatter one is the better of the two. (The sweetbreads that come from the pancreas gland and are sometimes referred to as stomach sweetbreads, or beef breads, are coarser than true sweetbreads.) Veal sweetbreads are the best, especially the very large ones from milk-fed veal. They are whiter and larger than lamb's sweetbreads, less fussy to prepare and have a finer flavor. Pork sweetbreads are small and not particularly good.

No matter how they are to be cooked, all sweetbreads need to be prepared first to make them white and firm. One of the best ways of cooking them after the initial preparation is to egg-and-crumb them and fry them gently in butter until brown.

BRAINS

Calf's brains are decidedly the best, although lamb's brains are also quite good. Neither pork nor beef brains are eaten with any enthusiasm. Like sweetbreads, brains need preparation before they are used. They can then be gently fried or poached. *Beurre noir*, with a few capers added, is the classic sauce. Brains are also good *à la meunière* – fried and served with brown butter (*beurre noisette*), lemon and parsley.

LIVER

Fresh liver is the most nutritious of all variety meats. It is sold either whole or in slices and is often already trimmed, but if it still has a thin covering of membrane, this needs to be removed or the liver will curl up in the pan. Less delicate livers such as pork or beef liver will become more tender if they are soaked in milk before cooking.

Calf's liver

Pale and plump, liver from milk-fed veal is the most delicious but it is expensive. Liver from grass-fed veal will be thinner, darker and not as mild. Fried liver is delicious if it is cooked very lightly and rapidly and is still rosy inside – over-cooking makes liver tough, dry and leathery. In the famous *fegato alla Veneziana*, calf's liver is cut into the thinnest slices, fried for mere seconds and served on a bed of golden fried onions. Liver is also good with bacon and watercress.

Lamb's liver

This is a deeper color than calf's liver and has a less good flavor but is as tender. It is served in the same ways as calf's liver.

Pork liver

Its texture is granular and its taste rather powerful. It is best used in pâtés, or braised in one large piece with wine and vegetables.

Beef liver

This is the coarsest and strongest flavored of livers and is eaten braised with onions. Simmer it for 1–2 hours until tender and serve with mashed potatoes.

KIDNEYS

All kidneys, whether they come encased in their fresh white surrounding fat or not, should be firm and smell sweet. Once they have been skinned, halved, and their gristly core has been removed, they can be broiled or sautéed briefly or simmered slowly and for a long time – anything in between and they will be tough and rubbery.

Veal kidneys

These multilobed kidneys will be very large and pale when they come from milk-fed veal, and darker and much smaller from grass-fed veal. They are best when grilled over charcoal and served with bacon, or briskly browned in butter to seal in their juices. The piquancy of a mustard and cream sauce is the perfect complement. They can also be roasted, encased in their own fat. This takes about an hour and the resulting kidneys will be pink and succulent.

Lamb's kidneys

These have a mild but delicious flavor and are excellent fried in butter. With the two halves not quite severed they form an essential part of a mixed grill.

Pork kidneys

These are larger than lamb's kidneys and thought by some people to be strong flavored, but they are tender enough to be broiled or fried and are a favorite dish on the menu in French brasseries. They are also good cooked slowly in wine and served with boiled potatoes to offset their richness.

Beef kidneys

They are only suitable for braising or in steak and kidney pies where they provide just the right strong flavor.

TONGUE

While tongue can be purchased fresh, it is more usual to find it salted and possibly smoked. It is a very smooth meat: beef tongue is best; veal tongue, although good, has less flavor and lamb's tongue is inclined to be rather dull.

Whether fresh or salted, choose a tongue that feels soft to the touch. Soak salted tongue overnight if necessary to remove the salt and then simmer it with vegetables and herbs until tender. Skin it carefully and serve it hot with salsa verde, walnut or raisin sauce, and mashed or boiled new potatoes. Cold, it is usually eaten with pickles, horseradish or mustard, and green salad.

Pressed tongue can be made by placing a weighted plate over a warm, cooked tongue, curled up in a round cake pan with a spoonful or two of its own cooking liquid.

TRIPE

Usually from beef or calf, tripe is the lining of the first and second stomachs. It comes in a variety of textures, some honeycombed, which are considered the best, some just slightly rough and some smooth. In France it is cooked with wine and vegetables; in Italy with wine and parmesan. An authentic *tripe à la mode de Caen*, the Normandy dish flavored with vegetables and Calvados, needs about 12 hours of simmering before it is at its gelatinous best.

Always buy tripe that looks white and fresh. Pickled tripe will need to be freshened before it is cooked.

HEARTS

A heart is a hard-working muscle and is never especially tender. Beef heart is particularly tough and is best sliced and braised with plenty of onions to give it a good flavor. Lamb's, veal and pork hearts, being more tender, can be blanched, stuffed, wrapped in bacon and roasted. Italian cooks like to fry sliced veal hearts very fast with chili peppers and serve them with lemon.

HEADS, TAILS AND FEET

Although not always available, heads, tails and feet are often well worth the trouble and the long, slow cooking needed to make them tender and to bring out their velvety gelatinous qualities.

Heads

Daunting to look at, the head of a calf, pig or sheep can be a lengthy business to prepare, but an obliging butcher will do this for you and split it into manageable pieces.

Pig's head

This makes brawn or head cheese, the chopped meat suspended in a translucent aspic flavored with herbs, spices and vinegar (heads are very gelatinous) and eaten cold with mustard and green salad.

Calf's head

Cooked, boned and chopped and covered with a vinaigrette containing capers and onions, makes the *tête de veau vinaigrette* sold readymade in charcuteries.

Sheep's head

Makes a broth much liked in Scotland but thought depressing elsewhere.

Calf and pig's ears

Braised pig's ears sometimes appear in *choucroute garnie* – garnished sauerkraut – beloved in Alsace, and they can be coated with egg and bread crumbs and fried.

OXTAIL

Oxtail stew, in winter, is one of the very best and most warming dishes. Choose an oxtail with a high proportion of lean, and with fresh, creamy fat. Allow a whole oxtail for two to three people. It needs long, slow cooking to develop its excellent gelatinous texture. The large amounts of fat that rise to the surface will be easier to remove if the stew is made the day before serving and allowed to get completely cold. Oxtail stew reheats particularly well.

FEET

Calf's foot and pig's feet both yield plenty of gelatine – the type with which to fill a home-made meat pie.

Pig's feet

These are sold fresh or pickled. They are usually split in half and can be quite plump and meaty. Often they are just simmered and served hot with sauerkraut or cold in their own gelatine, and they are very good cooked and then bread crumbed and broiled, served with mustard, or fried and served with tomato sauce. Pig's feet go into some stews, and they strengthen the jellying powers of stocks and consommés.

Calf's foot

This can be stewed and goes into the making of jellied stocks and glazes.

GELATINE

Extracted from calf's feet, pig's knuckles and the like, gelatine is sold either in powdered form in individual packets, or in shiny sheets. A good gelatine will have virtually no taste and will dissolve into a clear liquid – so necessary when making galantines, when the meat and vegetables shine through the aspic. Sheet or leaf gelatine is less likely than powdered to go lumpy. Do not boil gelatine but dissolve it with a little liquid in a cup standing in a shallow pan of hot water.

RECIPE SUGGESTION

Foie de veau lyonnaise

1 lb/450 g calves' liver, thinly sliced	
4–6 onions	
2 tablespoons/30 g butter	
1 teaspoon olive oil or lard	
salt and freshly ground pepper	
½–1 tablespoon wine vinegar	

SERVES 6

Peel and slice the onions and fry them in the butter and oil or lard over a fairly gentle heat until they start to brown. Cover the pan, turn down the heat and cook them gently for 10–15 minutes until they are very soft. Push them to one side of the pan or remove them to a plate. Season the slices of liver with pepper and fry them in the same pan over a moderate heat for about 3 minutes on each side. Put the onions on top of the slices of liver, throw the vinegar into the pan, let it sizzle, season with salt and more pepper and serve straightaway.

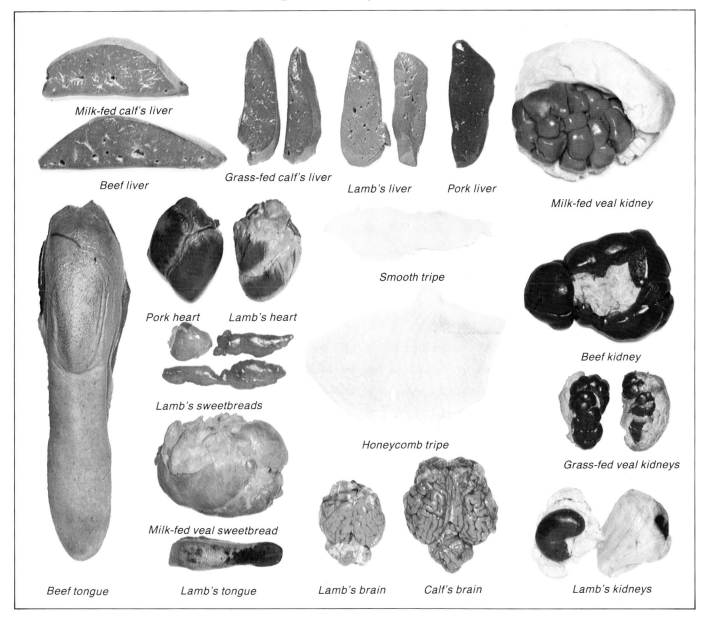

Milk-fed calf's liver

Beef liver

Grass-fed calf's liver

Lamb's liver

Pork liver

Milk-fed veal kidney

Pork heart

Lamb's heart

Smooth tripe

Beef kidney

Lamb's sweetbreads

Milk-fed veal sweetbread

Honeycomb tripe

Grass-fed veal kidneys

Beef tongue

Lamb's tongue

Lamb's brain

Calf's brain

Lamb's kidneys

PREPARING TENDERLOINS, SCALLOPS AND ROASTS

1 BEEF TENDERLOIN

With the rounded, neater side of the meat uppermost, start cutting and pulling away the fat from the wide end.

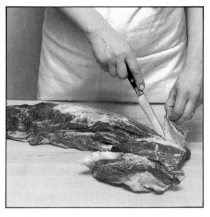

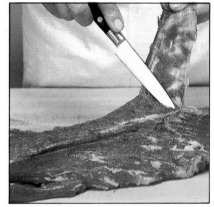

Return the meat to its original position and with the aid of a sharp knife pull off the covering layer of sinew. This should leave the meat completely free of fat, sinew and gristle.

Cut away all the fat and gristle that lie along one side of the tenderloin.

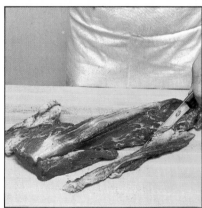

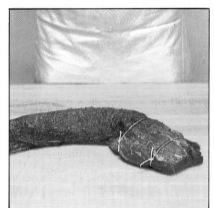

Prepare the meat for roasting whole by securing any loose ends neatly with trussing string.

Sever the large lump of fat that is attached to the wide end.

Alternatively, trim the tenderloin to neaten it, and cut small filets mignons from the thin end, medium-size tournedos from the center. The wide end can be used as a Chateaubriand: wrap it in a clean cloth, turn it on its side and flatten it to half its original height.

Turn the tenderloin over and pull and cut away the strip of gristle and fat.

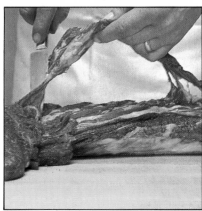

In this way the tenderloin has been divided into a Chateaubriand (bottom), three tournedos (top) and three filets mignons. Use the trimmings for beef Stroganoff or steak tartare.

2 PORK SCALLOPS

Take a tenderloin of pork and slit it down the middle, being careful not to cut right through it.

Open the meat out like a book and place it on a dampened piece of wax paper.

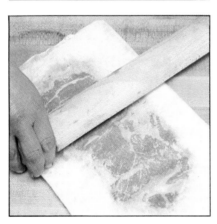

Cover the meat with a second piece of damp wax paper and flatten it gently but firmly with a rolling pin.

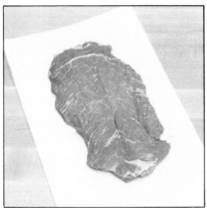

Here, the scallop is ready for use. Alternatively, cut the scallop into smaller pieces and use as scallopini – small scallops.

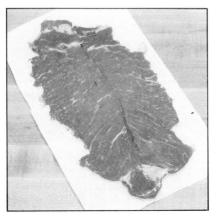

3 VEAL SCALLOPS

Cut even slices from a leg cut of veal, using a very sharp knife.

Flatten each slice between two pieces of dampened wax paper in the same way as for pork scallops. Here, a scallop is compared with a freshly cut slice.

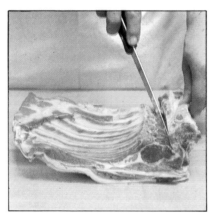

4 RACK OF LAMB

Take two racks of lamb from the rib section and, if the butcher has not already done so, cut away the bony part, or chine, from the meaty end of each rack, using a strong, sharp knife or a cleaver.

Peel the fatty skin from each rack, exposing the layer of fat beneath.

PREPARING ROASTS (CONTINUED)

Strip off the first 2in/5cm of flesh from the tapered ends of the ribs.

Bend each of the racks backwards, with the skin side innermost, to make a semicircle. Truss the racks together to make a complete circle or "crown".

Rack of lamb trimmed to this stage can be roasted without further preparation.

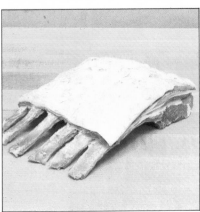

7 SADDLE OF LAMB

Lay the saddle skin side down and cut away the kidneys and their surrounding fat.

5 GUARD OF HONOR

To make a Guard of Honor, fit the two racks together, interlocking the rib ends, and secure them in place with trussing string. You can now, if you like, push stuffing between the two racks.

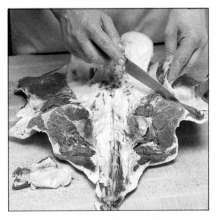

Trim the fatty ends of the skirt on either side of the saddle.

6 CROWN ROAST

To prepare a Crown Roast, make a short incision between each rib on the inside of the thicker, meaty end of each rack. This makes the racks more flexible.

Cut away the fat and sinews that lie along and to either side of the saddle's central bone.

Turn the saddle over and slice away the fat, leaving only a thin protective layer on top of the meat.

Stuff the pig with herb stuffing and sausage meat.

Tuck the flaps under the saddle to make a neat roll and tie securely with trussing string. Prick the large sinew all the way down the spine to prevent contraction during cooking. The kidneys can be skewered to the saddle for flavor and decoration.

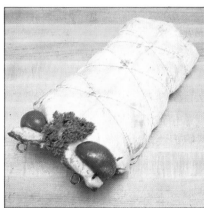

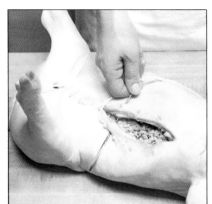

Sew up the belly, using a trussing needle and string.

8 ROAST PORK

Before roasting pork, score parallel lines across the skin at ½ in/1 cm intervals and rub salt into the cuts. This will turn the skin and fat crisp and appetizing during cooking.

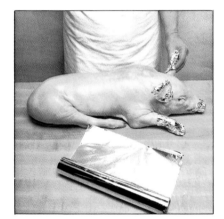

Wrap the feet, ears and nose in foil to prevent them burning.

9 SUCKLING PIG

Dry the inside of the pig with a paper towel. Suckling pig will have been gutted for you by the butcher.

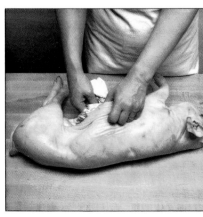

Arrange the pig in a roasting pan, tucking the feet well under the body. Put an apple or a block of wood in the mouth. Brush the skin liberally with oil. It is now ready for the oven.

PREPARING CHOPS

1 LAMB

Take a chined rack of lamb and cut cleanly between each rib with a sharp knife.

Trim the fat from the outside edge of each chop.

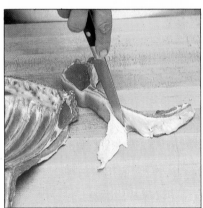

Cut away the awkward corner bone, using a cleaver.

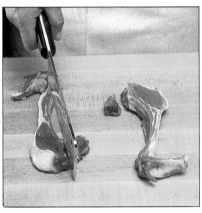

Trim the rib bone ends to neaten the shape of the chops.

2 PORK

Trim the skin from the chop if the butcher has not already done so.

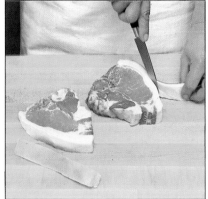

If it is a thick chop, slit a pocket in the meat, cutting into the fatty edge. An alternative method is to slit open the eye of the chop to create a neat hollow.

Push the stuffing into the slit or hollow, using a teaspoon, and pack it in well.

Cut several nicks in the fat to prevent the chop curling during cooking.

TRIMMING AND BONING

1 OXTAIL

Oxtail is usually sold jointed and needs only to be trimmed of any large lumps of fat. Generally only the meatier upper joints need trimming.

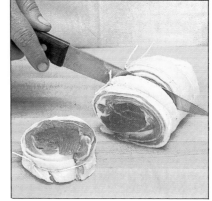

Divide the roll into noisettes by cutting between the pieces of string with a sharp, long-bladed knife.

Here the oxtail is fully prepared. The discarded fat is on the left-hand plate.

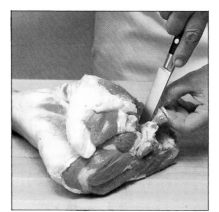

3 LEG OF LAMB

Take hold of the broad, curved hip bone, which protrudes at the wider end of the leg, and carefully run a sharp knife around it. Pull the bone out of the meat.

2 LAMB NOISETTES

Take a trimmed and chined rack of lamb and carefully cut the rib bones away from the flesh with a sharp, short-bladed knife. On the right of the picture lies the chine bone, which has been cut away from the rack.

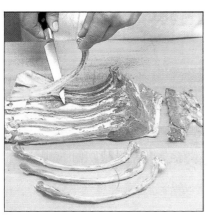

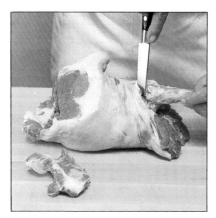

Approach the leg from the narrow end, grasp the shank bone, cut it away from the flesh and lift it out.

When all the ribs have been removed, roll up the boned meat, starting from the meaty end. Trim any excess fat from the scraggy end and tie the roll at 1 in/2.5 cm intervals with trussing string.

Sit the meat up with the wide end uppermost and tunnel into the cavity left by the hip bone, cutting closely around the middle bone.

TRIMMING AND BONING (CONTINUED)

When all the flesh has been cut back from the middle bone, pull the bone out of the hip cavity. Trim any excess fat from the meat.

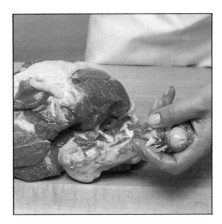

Cut into the joint between the foreleg and the middle bone and then bend the foreleg back until the joint breaks. Remove the foreleg.

Arranged counter-clockwise around the meat lies a lump of excess fat, the hip bone, the middle bone and the shank bone. Above the shank bone lies the continuation of the shank, which may well have been severed by the butcher.

Grasp the exposed end of the middle bone and cut back the meat in the same way as with the foreleg, keeping as close to the bone as possible. Avoid piercing the surface of the skin. Pull the middle bone apart from the shoulder blade to which it is attached and prise it from the center.

Tuck the shank end of the meat into the cavity left by the bones and truss the meat as shown.

Turn the meat around so that the triangular shoulder blade is nearest you. Insert the knife into the side of the meat where you can feel the shoulder blade and cut the meat away from either side of the flat bone. Pull this last bone out and trim any excess fat from the meat.

4 BONING A SHOULDER OF LAMB

Lay the shoulder skin side down and take hold of the exposed end of the foreleg. Cut around the bone with a sharp knife, pushing the meat back as you progress towards the joint.

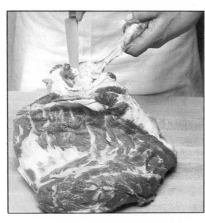

Roll up the boned meat with the skin outermost and secure it with trussing string. The three bones that have been removed are, from left to right, the shoulder blade, the middle bone and the foreleg.

BONING AND STUFFING

5 BREAST OF VEAL

Starting from one corner of the breast, peel off the thick skin, easing it away with a knife wherever necessary.

Make sure that every bone is removed. Feel the breast carefully for any lingering flexible ribs or bits of bone.

Cut back the natural flap of meat until three or four white bones are visible.

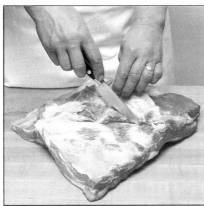

Spread an herb stuffing over the boned breast.

Lift out the first few bones, cutting them away from the flesh with the point of a knife.

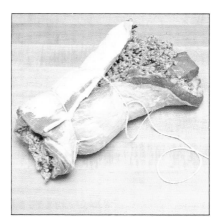

Carefully roll up the veal, tucking one edge neatly under the other.

Continue along the breast, cutting away the long, slender ribs.

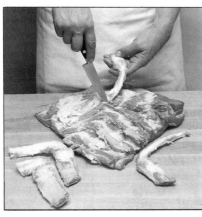

Tie the breast securely with trussing string. It is now ready to go into the oven.

PREPARING VARIETY MEATS

1 LIVER

Pull the thin veil of membrane away from the liver. The liver used here is a calf's liver.

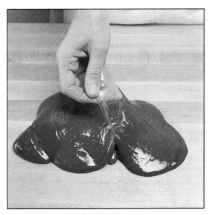

Cut away any fat and gristle that might be adhering to the liver.

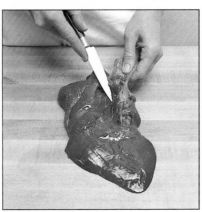

Cut the liver into slices about ¼ in/5mm thick.

2 KIDNEYS

Peel away the casings of fat and the thin inner membrane. These are lamb's kidneys.

Slice each kidney open and snip out the pale inner core with a pair of kitchen scissors.

Veal kidneys are prepared in a similar way. Peel off the surrounding fat with a very sharp knife or pair of scissors, remove the thin inner membrane, then cut out the gristly core that runs through the center of the kidney.

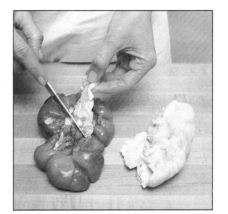

3 HEART

Snip out the pipes and tendons from the core of the heart with a sharp pair of scissors. The heart being prepared here is a pork heart.

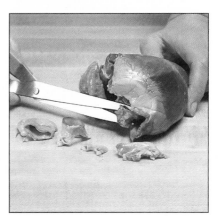

Hearts need to be soaked in cold water for an hour before they are cooked to draw out the blood.

4 *BRAINS*

Soak the brains in tepid water for 1 – 2 hours to whiten them.

5 *SWEET-BREADS*

Soak the sweetbreads in salted water for 2 hours, changing the water from time to time, until they lose all trace of pinkness and turn white.

Carefully remove as much as possible of the skin and membrane with a sharp pair of scissors.

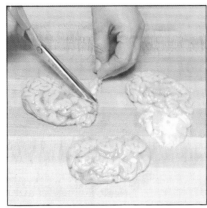

Put them in a pan of cold salted water, bring to the boil, simmer for 2 minutes and then rinse them under cold running water. This process stiffens the sweetbreads and makes them easier to handle.

Pick out as many of the red veins as possible with thumb and forefinger.

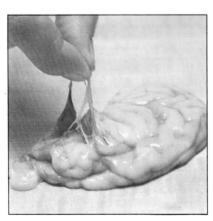

Peel away the skin, connective tissues and gristle – some sweetbreads will fall naturally into smaller portions. These are veal sweetbreads; lambs' sweetbreads are prepared in the same way.

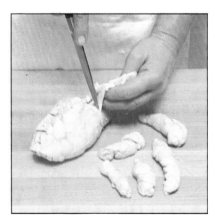

Simmer the brains for 15 minutes in salted water acidulated with lemon juice. If they are still too delicate to handle, chill them in the refrigerator or freezer until firm. Finish by removing any remaining veins, after which the brains will be ready to use. These are calves' brains.

The sweetbreads are now ready to be flattened between two plates for an hour before being poached or fried.

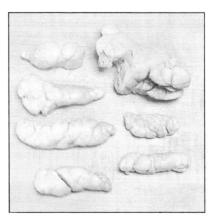

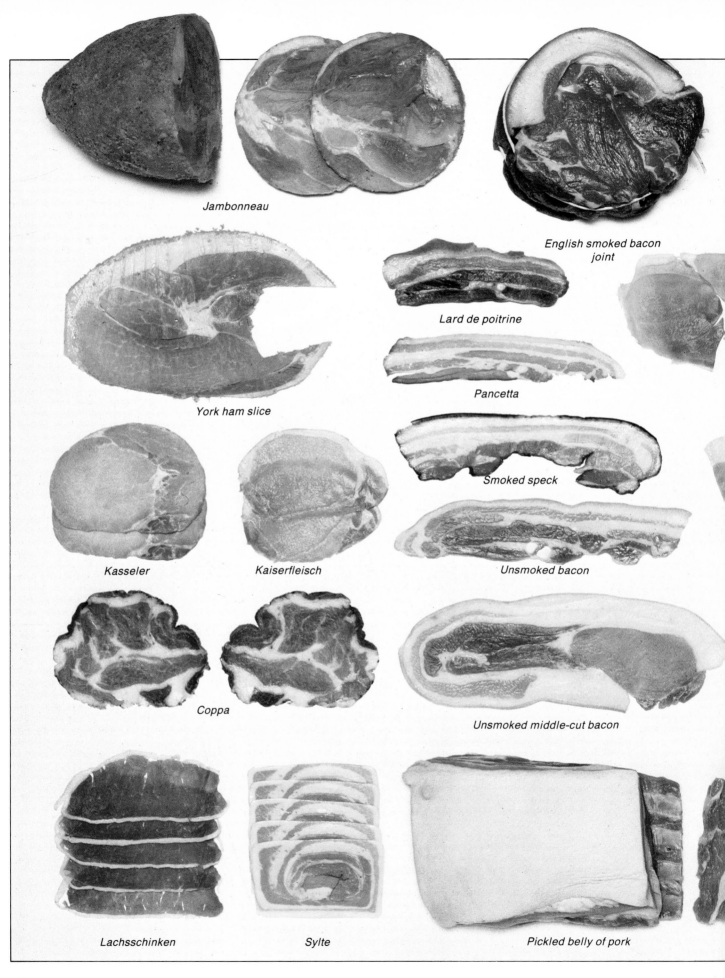

Jambonneau

English smoked bacon joint

Lard de poitrine

York ham slice

Pancetta

Kasseler

Kaiserfleisch

Smoked speck

Unsmoked bacon

Coppa

Unsmoked middle-cut bacon

Lachsschinken

Sylte

Pickled belly of pork

Jambon de Bayonne

Parma ham

Black Forest ham

Westphalian ham

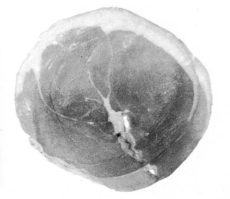

Jambon de Grisons

HAM

Pigs used for ham tend to be longer and leaner, as well as older and heavier, than those that yield fresh pork for our tables.

Not all hams are smoked: some of the finest are simply salted, either in a bath of brine, often with brine first injected into the flesh to speed up the process before it goes into the bath, or by the dry-salt method, which involves repeated massaging, rinsing and drying. This is a slow process, but ensures that the minimum of salt necessary for preservation penetrates the meat; the brine treatment is faster but tends to introduce more salt into the flesh. In both cases, certain flavoring agents – herbs, spices and sweeteners – may be added. When sugar is added the ham may be labelled "sweetcure."

Boiled and boiling hams

Whole boiling hams may be bought cooked or uncooked. If you mean to have a stately boiled ham for Christmas, make your enquiries in good time, since you (or your supplier, who may boil to order) will need time to soak the ham for several days, to simmer it for about 45 minutes per 1lb/450g, to cool it in its own liquid, and then to skin it and perhaps to glaze and bake it, or simply to egg-and-crumb it.

Boiled ham is a most versatile meat: it can be served whole as a hot main course with parsley or Cumberland sauce and young vegetables, or plain with velvety spinach. It may also be eaten with stout vegetables, such as roots or any type of cabbage, or dried peas and beans, which may themselves be cooked together with a ham bone, or a piece of bacon. Sliced reasonably thickly, it often comes in a mustard, cream, tomato or Madeira sauce, although gourmets insist that a spoonful of champagne is all the moistening a first-class boiled ham really needs.

When buying a whole ham to cook at home, do not be put off by a little bloom or mold on its rind, since this indicates that the ham is cured to perfection. It must, however, be scraped off before the ham is cooked.

York ham
Firm and tender, this is the best known of the British boiling hams. It is delicately pink, with fat that is white and translucent. It is cured by the dry-salt method and smoked over oak sawdust until it develops its fine, mild flavor.

Suffolk ham
Traditionally cured in brine with spices and honey, this ham is then smoked and hung to mature. During this process it develops its characteristic blue mold and a full, delicate flavor.

Bradenham ham
With its coal-black skin and deep red flesh, this is another famous English ham. It is cured with molasses and so has a sweet but robust flavor. If bought uncooked, it should be soaked for at least a week before cooking, otherwise it will tend to taste very salty.

Gammon or Wiltshire ham
Unlike true hams, which are first cut and then cured, English gammon is cured as part of the whole bacon pig, which is then divided into various cuts. It is extremely mild and does not keep so well as most other hams. Like bacon, it is sold smoked or unsmoked and comes in a variety of cuts such as steaks, the little wedges called slippers, the lean fine-grained corner and the succulent middle gammon, as well as the bony hocks. It is best boiled and served with root vegetables or dried peas or beans.

Virginia ham
This is among the so-called "country-cured" hams of America. Pigs destined to become Virginia hams are fattened on peanuts and acorns, and the meat is usually smoked over some scented hickory and applewood.

Smithfield ham
This ham is cured and smoked in Smithfield, Virginia. It comes from pigs that feed on peanuts, and is spiced with pepper and heavily smoked.

Kentucky ham
This is another American country ham and is perhaps a little drier than the Virginia hams. It owes its flavor to a large proportion of clover in the young pigs' food and a diet of grain towards the end of their lives.

Prague ham
It is traditionally salted and then mildly brined before being lightly smoked over beechwood embers, from which it emerges as perhaps the sweetest of all smoked boiling hams.

Jambon de Paris
In France, ham for boiling is sold as jambon de Paris, and boiled ham as jambon glacé.

Jambonneau
This small ham from the shank part of the leg is sold covered in bread crumbs and ready to eat.

Other boiled hams
Like the small jabonneau, "half-hams" comes from the meaty, more expensive rump end of the leg, or from the bonier but cheaper shank portion. Hams are also sold boned and these are usually bought by the slice. Some are just boiled, while others may have been baked or topped with bread crumbs.

Hams may also be bought canned, the best known being the Dutch, Danish and Polish. Lean and full flavored, they are boneless and ready to eat, but taste better baked with cider, brown sugar, mustard and cloves.

Kaiserfleisch and Kasseler

Other cured pork products include the delicate smoked Austrian Kaiserfleisch, and the Kasseler so popular in Germany, Denmark and Poland. Taken from the loin of the pig, these cuts look like a row of pork chops, but they may also be bought by the cutlet, boned or unboned, or sliced. Austrians eat Kaiserfleisch with bread-based dumplings and red cabbage.

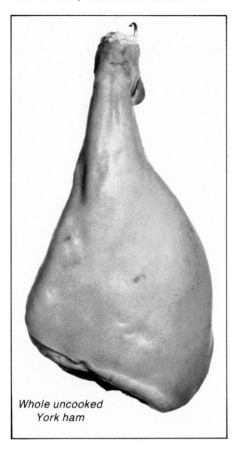

Whole uncooked York ham

Raw hams

Parma ham

When you go into a shop in Italy to buy prosciutto, you will be asked if you want it *cotto* (cooked) or *crudo* (raw), but outside Italy, prosciutto means raw ham, and the best comes from Parma.

Parma ham is lightly salted and air-cured for many months. A crown stamped upon its golden hide tells you that it is the genuine article from local pigs.

Eat Parma ham in transparently thin slices with melon, fresh figs, or simply butter.

Culatello

Looking like a half-size Parma, culatello comes from the choice rump end of the leg. It is less fatty and more spicy than a whole Parma.

Coppa

This is the cured, unboiled shoulder and neck portion of a pig, and is fattier and less expensive than prosciutto. It can also be thinly sliced and served as an antipasto.

Bayonne

Wine plays an important part in the curing process, and accounts for its special taste. Locally, Bayonne ham is eaten with eggs or added at the last moment to stews, but it is most delicious eaten raw like Parma ham, but sliced more thickly.

Westphalian ham

Traditionally, it is smoked over ash or beech with a bit of juniper until it is a deep golden pink. Juniper berries used in the cure give it its special flavor. Eat it thinly sliced on dark bread such as pumpernickel.

Black Forest ham

Strongly brined and strongly smoked, has well-flavored flesh and milk-white fat. Its robust taste goes well with sourdough bread.

Jambons de campagne

The Dordogne area of France is well known for its splendid farm-cured hams, often rather salty and hard as the cure is very heavy, but delicious sliced thickly and served with unsalted butter and French bread. Spanish and Italian country hams are also excellent.

Jambon de Grisons

It is first lightly salted and then dried in the cold, clear air of the Alps.

Lachsschinken

It can be bought sliced or in its expensive entirety, but should be eaten thinly sliced or minutely diced, with crusty buttered rolls.

Jamon serrano

Cured in the Sierra Morena mountains, it is delicious on rough peasant bread. It is reputed to be the sweetest ham in the world, and although it is produced in other parts of Spain, the variety from Huelva is thought to be best.

BACON

Bacon may be bought smoked or – if you can find it – unsmoked, or "green." You can tell the difference if the rind is still on. Smoking makes the rind look golden and the flesh a nice deep pink. Unsmoked flesh is pale pink, and the rind looks anything from off-white to dark cream.

Bacon roasts

The leaner cuts are good hot or cold, boiled with onions and root vegetables, or first boiled and then liberally basted with fruit juice or cider and roasted. Broil or fry bacon chops and steaks and serve them with applesauce.

Fat bacon

Whether you buy pancetta, lard de poitrine, poitrine fumé, speck, paprikaschinken, or tocino, what you carry home is cured pork belly – either sliced or in a slab that can be cut into chunks for use in stews and soups.

Pancetta

It goes into such Italian dishes as *spaghetti alla carbonara*, other pasta sauces, risotto and bean casseroles.

Lard de poitrine

Lard de poitrine is given a proper bacon cure and comes smoked, when it is called poitrine fumé, or green. It is used to enrich stews and farces, and is an essential part of coq au vin and many beef stews.

Poitrine fumé

This is splendid sliced and fried like bacon, or added to omelets.

Speck, spek

Is basically fat with a thin layer of lean. Speck yields such a quantity of drippings that part of it is often poured off and eaten on bread. The rendered fat is also used as a frying medium for potatoes or mushrooms, and for browning pieces of beef or veal before roasting.

Breakfast bacon

When streaky bacon appears in fried slices for American breakfasts, it tends to curl up: the pigs' diet causes their fat to be on the soft side, so that it melts easily causing the bacon to become crisp and crumbly. In other parts of the world, crisping is only possible if streaky bacon is sliced extra thin.

Lean bacon cuts are also made from the back of the pig, and those cut from the meaty leg area are considered to be very good. In England, top back slices are lean; middle-cut bacon slices have long tails of streaky attached and a good eye of solid pink meat at the top end. The oyster-cut from the hind end of the back comes sometimes in the piece and sometimes sliced, and is beautifully succulent. Shortback, with a nice edge of fat and plenty of lean meat, may come in thin slices or in thicker ones, which are meant for broiling. Long back slices are the leanest and most expensive of all.

SALTED PORK

The petit salé of France, the pickled pork belly of Great Britain, and the salt pork of the United States fall into a category all of their own, being not fully cured but lightly salted in brine.

Petit salé

It is eaten in the traditional French potée, a rich cabbage soup containing other cured meats and vegetables. It may also sit in pink and white slices on top of puréed peas and beans, or on a dish of cabbage, when it is called *petit salé aux choux*.

Pickled pork

This meat may need soaking before it is simmered with carrots, turnips, rutabagas or other root vegetables. Pease pudding is its traditional British accompaniment.

Salt pork

The streaked salt pork from the leaner end is what goes into Boston baked beans. Salt pork is also known as sowbelly and is chiefly used as a flavoring agent.

Sylte

This is pickled pork belly, rolled around crushed peppercorns and mustard seed. It is delicious thinly sliced and often appears at Scandinavian cold tables.

SALTED BEEF

There are many ways to treat a salted cut of beef, most of them a welcome legacy from kosher Jewish cuisine.

Salt beef

This is simply beef soaked in brine – the addition of saltpeter makes it red, as in its natural state it is greyish-brown. Some types of salt beef are so heavily brined that some soaking will be necessary before the meat goes into the pot, while others may be ready for cooking just as they are, so check with your butcher. Salt beef – bottom round is the traditional cut – is often boiled with plenty of carrots and served with potatoes.

Corned beef
Corning is the old term for salting, and corned beef is the term used in America to describe the salted and well-spiced briskets that go whole into a New England boiled dinner and chopped into corned-beef hash. To most Europeans, however, corned beef means canned pressed, salted beef, pink in color and usually caked with fat, that is eaten without further cooking.

Pastrami
In the Balkans, the word pastrami is used to describe any kind of preserved meat from beef, pork and lamb to goose. Elsewhere, it has come to mean salt beef that has been smoked and seasoned, usually with black peppercorns. Since the people of Romania, above all other Balkan countries, excel in making pastrami, their method is the model for the rest of the world, and the words "Romanian style" often feature on the packaging. Sold cooked in slabs or slices, it is good with rye bread.

DRIED BEEF
This is beef spiced and salted and then air-dried to the very essence of beefiness.

Bündnerfleisch
Grisons in Switzerland is the home of this mountain air-cured beef. As it tends to be dry, scraped slivers of it are eaten with an oil and vinegar dressing.

Bresaola
The Italian counterpart, is a specialty of Lombardy and is similarly served, although the usual dressing is made with oil, chopped parsley and lemon.

Chipped beef
This is a rather poor American relation sold ready-sliced. It is sometimes served in a cream sauce on toast, or is mixed with scrambled eggs.

SMOKED MUTTON
"No sort of meat," say the Scots, "is more improved by smoking with aromatic woods than mutton." The people of Norway are in perfect agreement Norwegian *fenalar* is smoked and air-dried until it develops a highly concentrated flavor, to be enjoyed with crisp Norwegian flatbrød and butter. The Scottish mutton ham has a rich, interesting flavor and is good sliced and eaten raw, or braised with vegetables.

SMOKED POULTRY AND GAME
Unlike hams, poultry and game are always hot-smoked, or first cooked and then smoked. They can be bought whole or sliced and resemble ham in flavor, but are as perishable as fresh-roasted birds. Smoked guinea fowl, smoked chicken and smoked turkey breasts offer plenty of delicate flesh;

smoked duck is excellent and smoked quail extravagant, but the most prized of all is smoked goose breast from the Baltic coast of Germany, where the geese tend to be the most bosomy. Also excellent is smoked reindeer meat from Scandinavia, particularly from Lapland.

CONFIT D'OIE, CONFIT DE CANARD
An everyday food in southwestern France, where vast numbers of geese and ducks are fattened for foie gras, confits are simply salted pieces of goose or duck preserved in fat. Confit can be bought in jars and will keep for several months, but all that is needed to make it in one's kitchen is the bird, its rendered fat and coarse salt. The salted meat simmers in the fat until it is well permeated, then it is drained, scored and covered with the strained fat.

A portion of confit is an essential ingredient in a cassoulet, but confit can also be eaten on its own, gently sautéed in a little of its preserving fat.

RECIPE SUGGESTION
Spinach and bacon salad

1 lb/450 g fresh young spinach leaves	
1 avocado	
6 thick slices bacon	
1 teaspoon olive oil	
for the dressing:	
4 tablespoons olive oil	
1 tablespoon white wine vinegar or sherry vinegar	
small pinch of sugar	
salt and freshly ground pepper	

SERVES 4–6
Make the dressing first, mixing the ingredients together with a fork. Wash, drain and dry the spinach, shaking it well in a cloth, a third at a time, to get all the moisture off the leaves without bruising them too much—spinach leaves are very fragile. Halve the avocado, remove the seed, skin the halves and cut them into either thin slices or fairly small dice. Toss them in a bowl with about 2 teaspoons of the dressing to keep them a fresh green. Cut the bacon into strips and fry them in the olive oil. While they fry to a crisp brown, put the spinach into the bowl with the avocado and dress it lightly with the remaining salad dressing. When the bacon is brown, pour it—still sizzling—with all its fat, over the salad and serve at once.

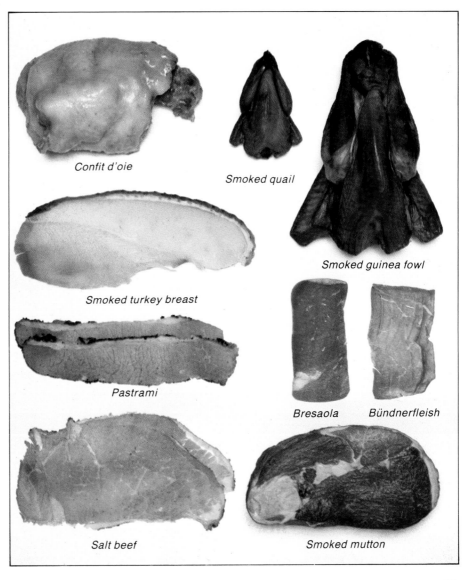

Confit d'oie

Smoked quail

Smoked guinea fowl

Smoked turkey breast

Pastrami

Bresaola *Bündnerfleish*

Salt beef

Smoked mutton

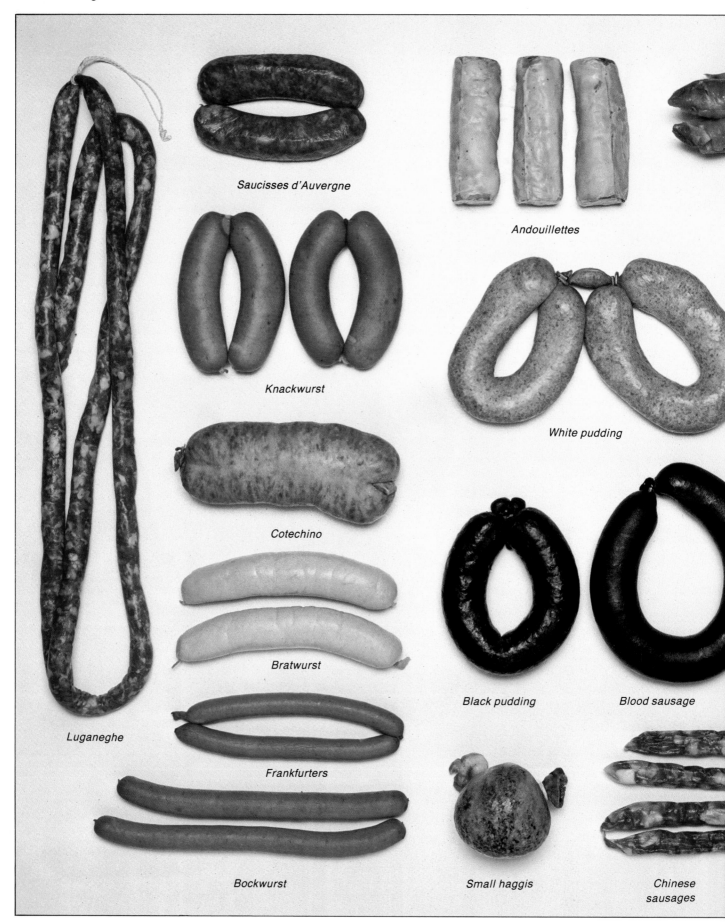

Saucisses d'Auvergne

Andouillettes

Knackwurst

White pudding

Cotechino

Bratwurst

Black pudding

Blood sausage

Luganeghe

Frankfurters

Bockwurst

Small haggis

Chinese sausages

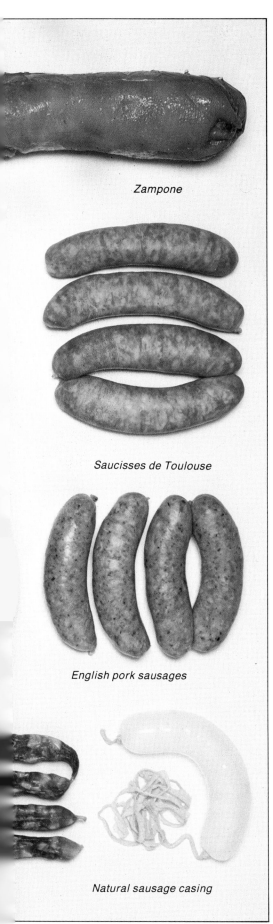

Zampone

Saucisses de Toulouse

English pork sausages

Natural sausage casing

SAUSAGES

When country people killed their own animals, particularly pigs, to provide themselves with meat, there was always a tremendous amount of work to be done to make sure that every part of the animal could be either eaten at once or, for the most part, stored for later use.

The liver, heart, kidneys and so forth were eaten at once, while legs, bellies, shoulders, feet and heads were salted for the winter, and all the scraps were gathered together, and turned into sausages, with the animals' own guts serving as casings. These sausages were either spiced, to help prolong their life by a few days, and eaten fresh, or dried and preserved by various means for eating later.

Most interested sausage eaters prefer their sausages in natural casings. It can be recognized by the fine, slim knots between the links; artificial casings tend to untwist, leaving air spaces between the individual sausages.

FRESH SAUSAGES

These should be treated like fresh meat and eaten within a few days of purchase, or they develop a strange flavor.

English and American sausages

Usually bought by weight, these can be made from fresh pork, or, less good, from fresh beef, or a combination of the two. Sage is their usual seasoning and the best are made of pure, coarsely chopped pork. (Slender, half-size sausages, filled with pork or beef, are called chipolatas in England.)

Unless they are labelled 100 percent meat, sausages are likely to contain a cereal binder. They also contain a good deal of moisture, since crushed ice is introduced into the sausage machine to prevent overheating the meat as it is ground up.

Weisswurst and bratwurst

These fine-grained, pale, almost white sausages are usually made of veal. Called "frying sausages," they may indeed be fried, or they may be first poached and then briefly broiled. They are of a fine consistency and have a delicate taste.

Saucisses

Small fresh sausages in France generally go under the name of saucisses, while larger ones are saucissons. All are made of pure meat, which is so important when making saucisses *en brioche* and other sausage pastries if the result is to be light and delicate. Throughout France there are any number of excellent locally made country sausages in which a wide variety of seasonings is used.

Saucisses de Toulouse

These delicately seasoned sausages are made from coarsely chopped pork and are an essential ingredient of cassoulets.

Saucisses d'Auvergne

These are saucisses fumées, or smoked sausages. They are eaten broiled or fried, and combine their rich flavor beautifully with a hot potato salad.

Kielbasa

In Poland any number of fresh sausages, called kielbasa, are added to hearty *bigos* – cabbage and meat stews – but elsewhere kielbasa refers to a particular garlicky and spicy sausage sold either fresh or fully cooked. It is good broiled and served with sauerkraut and a mild mustard.

Luganeghe

This sausage from northern Italy, made of pure pork shoulder seasoned with Parmesan cheese, is made in enormous lengths; it is slim, unlinked and cut to the customer's order.

Salsicces or Italian sausages

Seen hanging in Italian shops, Salsicces have a rustic flavor and may be highly spiced with chili peppers, or very mild, especially if they are made simply with ground pork and pancetta. In America salsicces are seasoned with fennel seeds and are usually referred to as Italian sausages.

OTHER COOKING SAUSAGES

Apart from fresh raw sausages, there are those that have been treated in some way to preserve them. Some, such as the frankfurter, have been fully cooked, but are reheated and served hot. Others have been salted and smoked and then left to mature but still require further cooking.

Frankfurters

It is the light smoking that gives the skins of frankfurters their familiar color. Unless marked kosher, in which case they are made of pure beef, frankfurters contain a mixture of finely ground beef and pork, and are usually quite highly spiced and salted. Genuine frankfurters are always sold in pairs – the best are fresh, while those that are heat-sealed in a vacuum pack come next. Canned varieties are inferior.

When frankfurters appear in long rolls as hot dogs or dogs (or, today, foot-longs), they owe their name to America.

Knackwurst

This short, stumpy sausage is made of finely ground pork, beef and fresh pork fat, flavored with salt, cumin and garlic. Saltpeter is added to give the meat a good color. Knackwurst are usually sold in pairs or in long links.

Bockwurst

These sausages are prepared in the same way as frankfurters. The Berliner bockwurst is a smoky red sausage, while a Düsseldorf favorite is bockwurst wrapped in bacon with mustard.

Saucisson-cervelas

This is similar to the small French saucisse except that it has matured longer and is therefore drier. It is best poached and served with *choucroute* or a hot potato salad. The English version, the saveloy, is a poor and stodgy shadow of its French relation.

Cotechino

From northern Italy, this sausage is made of pork moistened with white wine and subtly seasoned with spices. It comes in various sizes and is usually salted for a few days. It is one of the essential ingredients of *bollito misto* – an Italian dish of mixed boiled meats.

Zampone and stuffed goose neck

Besides guts, stomachs and bladders – other parts of animals can be turned into interesting sausages.

Zampone

This specialty of Modena in Italy is one such example and is really a cotechino stuffed into a boned pig's foot. Fresh, it needs soaking and then simmering for an hour, but those that are packaged are pre-cooked and only need heating through.

Stuffed goose neck

The fat skin of a goose is used in a similar way. The filling consists of innards – liver, stomach, heart – perhaps morel mushrooms, air-cured bacon, bread crumbs, and an egg for binding it all together. It is sewn up or tied at both ends and may then be fried to a golden brown, poached and pressed between boards and eaten in slices, or simply poached in stock fortified with a little white wine.

Chinese sausages

These sausages are cured and air-dried. Salami-like, dark red with white bits of fat, they need no further cooking. They flavor a number of Chinese chicken and vegetable dishes, and are sometimes mixed with rice.

Andouillettes and andouilles

Andouillettes contain tripe and chitterlings, which are pork guts boiled to a gelatinous tenderness. They often come covered in lard, and are broiled and eaten with mashed potatoes or fried apples. The larger andouilles, which may be black skinned, are hung to dry and are sliced and eaten cold.

PUDDING SAUSAGES

These are the ancestors of all the fresh sausages and contain cereal as well as meat.

Black puddings

These get their color from pigs' blood, their richness from cubes of pork fat and their body from oatmeal – at least in Scotland and northern England. Elsewhere, other cereals, even bread crumbs, may be used. The French *boudins noirs* may, variously, also contain onions, apples, chestnuts, eggs, garlic and the leaves of chard. They are simmered by their makers, but may afterwards be boiled, baked or fried.

White pudding

Made of white meat with bread crumbs or ground rice, cream and perhaps eggs, these are first simmered, and may be gently fried or broiled or wrapped in buttered parchment paper and baked.

Blood sausages

These are also known as black sausages, but differ from black puddings in that they have fewer cereal additives and less seasoning. They always contain pigs' blood.

Blutwurst

There are many varieties of German blood sausages, but perhaps the blutwurst is the best known. It is made of diced bacon, veal or pork lungs and is seasoned with cloves, mace and marjoram. It is often served with boiled potatoes and cooked apples.

Morcilla

Made and smoked in Asturias, Spain, this blood sausage is made of pigs' blood, fat, spices and onions, and is an essential ingredient of *fabada asturiana*, or bean stew. There are two varieties – ordinary morcilla which has a strong smoky flavor, and morcilla dulce, which has a sweet, spicy flavor that is slightly reminiscent of a rich Christmas pudding

Haggis

In Scotland, haggis is created with reverence and solemnly piped in on special occasions. It is made of roughly chopped, freshly cooked sheep's pluck (liver, lungs and heart), toasted oatmeal, onions, suet and herbs, all loosely packed into a sheep's stomach, which is then sewn up. The filling swells as the haggis is boiled and makes it look like a greyish rugby ball. A haggis merely needs to be steamed to heat it through, but it must be piping hot to be good.

Faggots

These little round parcels are made like crépinettes but contain pigs' fry – liver and lungs – cereal and fat salt pork or bacon. They are wrapped in caul fat – the fatty membrane from around the stomach and guts of a pig, previously soaked and softened in warm water – and are cooked slowly in the oven. Also known as poor man's goose or savory duck, they are best when homemade from good ground meats, with plenty of onion, nutmeg and other spices. If caul fat is a problem to obtain, they may be put unwrapped into the oven, sitting closely together in the pan.

HOMEMADE SAUSAGES

Once you have made fresh sausages you will realize how simple the procedure is and nothing can be more rewarding than to see links of fresh homemade sausages emerging in your own kitchen.

Sausage meat

A basic sausage meat consists of about one-half lean to one-half fat. For pure pork sausages; use lean meat from the shoulder, neck or loin, and add fatback in an equal quantity. For other sausages, veal and game such as hare and venison can be used, and smoked fish is good. Fatback is the best fat to use for any type of sausage, but any scraps of fat from the belly or even the fat trimmed from pork chops or spareribs can be used. Trim the fat of any rind or gristle, cut it into cubes with the meat and put them through a grinder, or chop briefly in a food processor. Take care to remove gristle and strings from the chopped meat. The ground ingredients should be mixed well before the seasonings of your choice are added.

Casings

Some sausages such as crépinettes, cayettes and faggots are merely encased in caul fat. Others can be skinless, in which case they are bound with eggs or dipped in beaten egg and bread crumbs or simply floured. Sausage meat can also be poached in a muslin bag, but natural casings are best.

Casings can be bought in small sets from butchers' suppliers or through mail order. The small $1\frac{1}{4}$ in/3 cm hog casings usually come in approximately 20 ft/6 m lengths and can be cut as required. Store them, in salt, in a screwtop jar in the refrigerator.

Stuffing sausages

It is not difficult to force the freshly ground, seasoned meat into the casings, you only need a funnel and a pastry bag, some string, a prodder, such as the handle of a wooden spoon, and a faucet.

After disentangling and soaking the casing, slip it over the faucet and run cold water through it, cutting out any bits with holes. Then cut into convenient lengths and wrinkle each one up over the funnel, leaving a good bit dangling at the end. Tie it up and start feeding in your mixture; force out any air bubbles, and tie or twist the casing at intervals. Dry for about 24 hours – in an airy place in cool weather, on a rack in the refrigerator if not – and then cook in the usual way.

SLICING SAUSAGES

These are always cooked or smoked and are eaten cold. They are best bought uncut or freshly sliced; once they are sliced they don't last very well. Those sold presliced in vacuum-packed bags are frequently mass produced and of inferior quality.

Mortadella

Made of finely ground pure pork, this is the best and most famous of all slicing sausages, patterned perhaps with green flecks of pistachio nuts and white cubes of fat. The best come from Bologna, where only the best ingredients are used, and flavorings include wine and coriander.

There are, however, other varieties: some good, some very pasty. Although not made in Bologna, they are still called Bologna sausages or baloney. It comes in a variety of shapes: variously sized balloons, rings and sticks, and even a square one to fit bread baked in pans. They vary in texture and flavor depending on whether they are made of pork, beef or veal, or mixtures of these meats, and the spices used.

Jagdwurst

This sausage owes its character to quite sizeable pieces of pork fat and rosy pork meat embedded in its pale pink paste, which is slightly porous due to the fact that it has been made by a process which involves the use of moist heat.

Bierwurst

Although much larger in circumference than jagdwurst, this sausage has a similar paste. Ham bierwurst, or bierschinken, shows bits of ham in each of its large slices. It is also known as ham bologna in America and is often flavored with garlic.

Mettwurst

The word mett is the medieval name for lean pounded pork. There is grosse mettwurst, which is coarse in texture and red, and feine mettwurst, which is smooth and pink.

Zungenwurst

When a blutwurst is interlarded with bits of tongue, it becomes a zungenwurst. Bits of pork fat and a lot of pigs' blood, heated carefully to setting point without curdling, make this black sausage, which does not usually contain any cereal additives.

Hungarian brawn sausage

Reminiscent of a head cheese, Hungarian brawn sausage, also known as presswurst, consists of meat from the pig's head, neck and feet, blood and seasonings. Cased or uncased, it is cooked, lightly pressed and cooled until the mixture jellifies. Sage is the most usual flavoring.

Sulzwurst

Similar to brawn, this sausage is made of large pork pieces. It can be eaten spread on bread, or with sliced onions and an oil and vinegar dressing.

CERVELAT SAUSAGES

Almost always smoked, cervelats are far less stiff than salamis because their maturing time is half as long. There is, however, a slight resemblance between the two. They are always moist, and being made of finely pounded meat and fat, they have, when cut, a velvety surface and a color of mottled pink. Fat or thin, cervelats are always pliable and look rather like large frankfurters.

German cervelats

Made of finely ground beef and pork, these are very popular in Germany and are exported in various diameters. They are mild, delicate and easy to slice.

Plockwurst

With its smoke-darkened skin and dark meat, which contains a high proportion of beef, this sausage often comes studded with whole peppercorns.

Katenrauchwurst

This cottage-smoked sausage is produced in some quantity. It is made of coarse pieces of pork, is dark and firm and should be cut diagonally in thick oval slices.

Danish cervelat

Air-dried and hot-smoked, this is rather a bouncy cervelat. Its skin is usually varnished and looks a glossy red.

Thuringer

Among the American cervelats – also sometimes called summer sausages because their surfaces do not sweat so badly in the hot months – is the coriander-spiced variety called Thuringer.

SALAMIS

The Italian salamis – and there are almost as many regional variations as there are villages in Italy – may be considered by purists to be the only authentic salamis, but it is worth noting that most of central Europe has made this type of tightly stuffed sausage for a number of centuries, they are not pale imitations of the Italian original but indigenous sausages.

Most salamis, wherever they are made, consist of a mixture of lean pork and pork fat and sometimes beef. Occasionally veal takes the place of beef, and sometimes wild boar is used. They can be flavored with red or white wine, with rum, with peppercorns, fennel or garlic, or with paprika.

Only a few types of salami are smoked, but all are matured for from a few weeks to a few months. During this time they lose a good deal of weight in the form of moisture, while the flavor of the meats and the seasonings becomes more concentrated.

Buy salami that is a fine fresh red or pink, not brown or greasy, on its outside surface. If you squeeze it and it gives a little you can be sure that it will be fresh and fragrant. The harder the salami sausage, the more thinly it should be sliced; cut it at an angle.

Genoa salami

This is one of the salamis that traditionally contains a high porportion of veal. To make up for the possible dryness of this meat, a little more pork fat than usual goes into the mixture, so that the result is quite fatty.

Salami de Felino

Made near Parma, this pure pork sausage is among the best of all the Italian salamis. Since it is made by hand, it is less geometrical than most of the others. It contains white wine, garlic and whole peppercorns, and is subtle in flavor and succulent in texture. It does not keep well, but when sent abroad is encased in wax for a longer life.

Salami Napolitano

Seasoned with chili pepper, this salami is made with pork and beef. It is usually garlicky and extremely peppery and hot.

Salami Finocchiona

This pure pork salami has the unusual but very good flavor of fennel seeds. A similar salami, known as *frizzes,* is flavored with aniseed and comes in both mild-sweet and spicy varieties.

German salami

Because this is not usually cured for long, it is fairly moist. It is mild with a whiff of garlic and usually has a medium texture.

Danish salami

This is bright pink or red because it usually contains coloring. This is one of the types that is salted and then sometimes hung over smoke, which is just cool enough to make the flavor more interesting and to brown the casing but not warm enough to cook the meat. Danish salami tends to be fine textured, rather fatty and to have a bland flavor.

Hungarian salami

This is not necessarily made in Hungary; other countries also produce this type, which contains paprika as well as other peppers. It is surprisingly mild and is often smoked. Since it is matured for about six months, it is one of the really hard salamis and ideal for slicing.

Saucisson de Lyon

In France, salami is known as saucisson sec. Perhaps the most famous is the saucisson de Lyon, which, with its cross-cross cording, is made of pure pork. Cording is used to keep the salami straight while it dries. It is coarsely cut and a good rose-pink color, and has an excellent flavor.

Garlic sausage

Many of the sausages of France are flavored with garlic. However, the one known as garlic sausage is different insofar as it is only lightly spiced, so that the taste of garlic predominates.

Chorizos

These are popular throughout Spain and are coarsely textured and quite spicy. In Spain they are widely used in cooking, and elsewhere they are usually sold air-dried and are suitable for slicing or cutting into chunks. Chorizo de Lomo is one of the finest chorizos for slicing and eating.

Salsicha

This Spanish sausage is similar to a salami and is usually served as a snack. It is made of finely chopped pork, pork fat and whole white peppercorns.

SMALL SALAMIS

These are usually bought whole and can be short or long.

Rosette

Perhaps the finest of the Lyonnaise sausages is the rosette, which is slowly matured and, due to its extra fat and thick casing, is more moist than other salamis.

Kabanos

These slim, garlic-flavored sausages of Polish origin are smoked until they show wrinkles. Too thin to slice, they are bought whole and eaten in chunks.

Landjäger, gendarmes, cacciatore

Landjäger and gendarmes presumably owe their names to uniformed officials who used to patrol and administrate the German and French Alpine regions, carrying a good supply of these hard, salami-type sausages in the pockets of their tunics. The sausages are usually smoked in little frames, which accounts for their strap-like shape.

The Italian version, called cacciatore, or hunter's sausage, is somewhat thicker than the others. It is not usually smoked but briefly cured and matured and is just about large enough to slice.

Pepperoni

This Sardinian salami can be mild or spicy. It is usually eaten hot, or sliced into a pepperoni salad or onto pizza.

PÂTÉ-TYPE SAUSAGES

Some sausages such as liver sausages, leberkäse and teewurst can be soft in consistency and are meant for spreading, while others are firm enough to be sliced.

Liver sausages

These may be large or small, curved or straight, finely milled or coarse, and their paste may also contain chunks of fat, bits of liver (which is especially good in the case of goose-liver sausage), truffles and any number of fine chopped herbs. Some liver sausages are soft and pasty and meant for spreading, while others, such as the Strasbourg liver sausage, which also includes pork

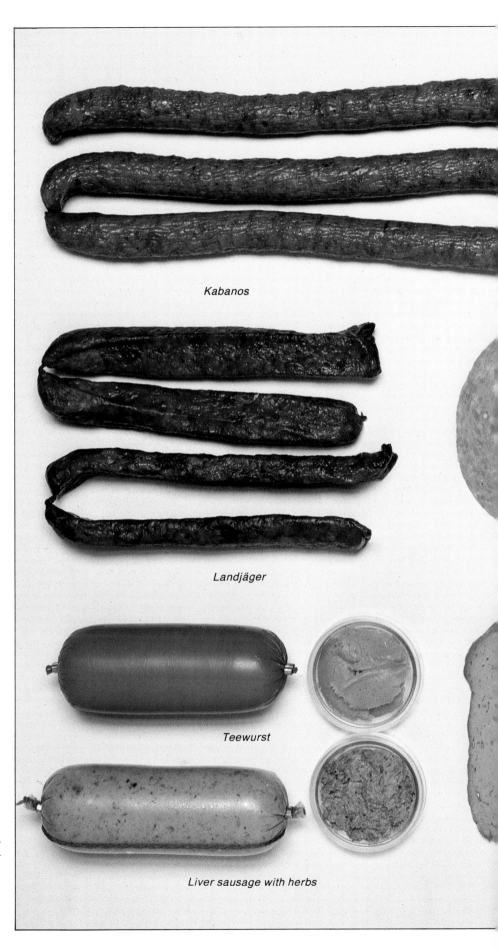

Kabanos

Landjäger

Teewurst

Liver sausage with herbs

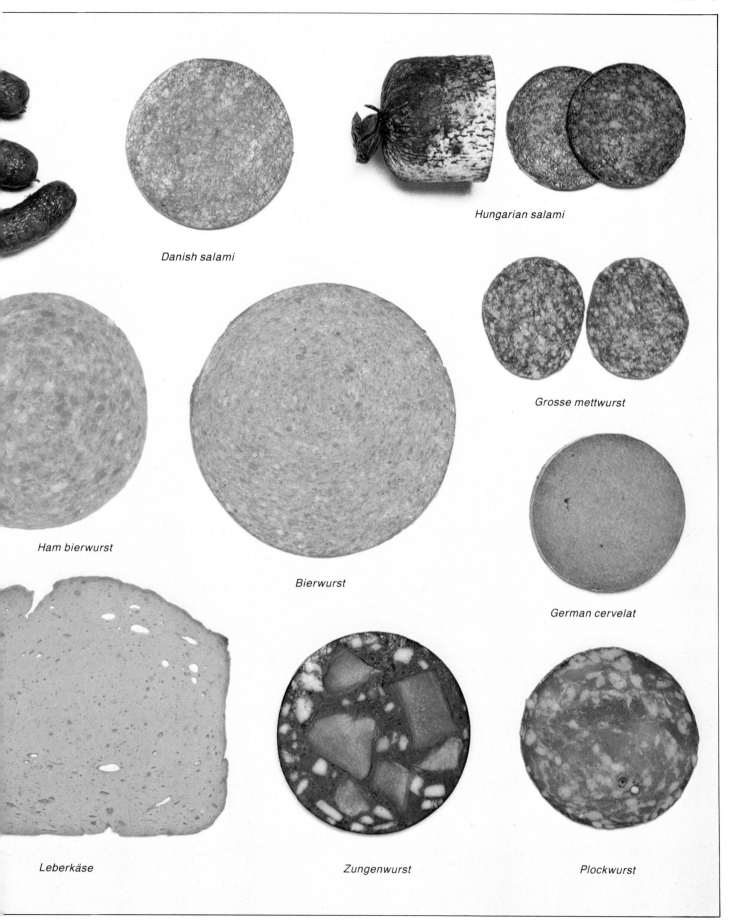

Danish salami

Hungarian salami

Grosse mettwurst

Ham bierwurst

Bierwurst

German cervelat

Leberkäse

Zungenwurst

Plockwurst

meat and is smoked, are meant to be thickly sliced.

All liver sausages can be eaten as they are, but occasionally form an essential ingredient of cooked dishes. Flavorings, besides herbs and truffles, may include nutmeg, cinnamon, browned onions or anchovies; where anchovies predominate, the liver sausage is known as a sardellenwurst.

Most liver sausages are made of pork liver mixed with pork or veal – some may contain other innards as well as liver – but there are also pure liver sausages. Calves' liver sausages are particularly good, and there are also sausages made of poultry livers.

Teewurst

This is the name given to small sausages of the spreadable variety. They are usually made of a spiced, finely pounded mixture of pork and beef.

RECIPE SUGGESTION
Sausage and mushroom pie

1 lb/450 g sausage meat
1 clove garlic
3–4 sprigs parsley, chopped
generous pinch of dried thyme
2 sage leaves, chopped
grating of lemon rind
salt and freshly ground pepper
grating of nutmeg
½ onion
¾ lb/340 g mushrooms
3 tablespoons/45 g butter
flaky pastry made with 2 cups/225 g flour
1 egg, beaten

SERVES 4–5

Peel and crush the garlic and mix it, together with the chopped herbs and lemon rind, into the sausage meat. Season with salt, pepper and nutmeg. Peel and chop the onion finely and slice the mushrooms thinly. Melt the butter in a frying pan and sweat the onion. Add the mushrooms, season, and cook gently until soft. Allow to cool.
Preheat the oven to 425°F/220°C.
Roll out about two-thirds or rather less of the pastry into a rectangle, 12–14 × 8 in/30–35 × 20 cm, and lay it on a greased baking sheet. Take one-third of the sausage meat and pat it out in the middle of the pastry, leaving a margin of about 2½ in/6 cm all around. Place a layer of mushrooms on this and press them in lightly. Spread more sausage meat, more mushrooms and finish with a layer of the sausage mixture. Pat it into a nice even rectangular shape. Bring up the sides of the pastry, folding it over the sausage meat. Cut off any excess at the corners. There should still be a rectangle of sausage meat visible at the top.
Roll out the remaining pastry into a rectangular lid for the pie; cut even parallel slashes in it at ½ in/1 cm intervals, leaving a margin of ½ in/1 cm uncut all the way around. Brush lightly with water, and place it, moist side down, on top of the pie—the filling should just be visible through the slashes. Brush the pie all over with beaten egg. Allow to dry for 10 minutes, then brush a second time. Dry for a further 5–10 minutes.
Bake for 15 minutes, then turn down the temperature to 350°F/180°C and continue to bake for a further 30 minutes. Allow to cool—if possible overnight— and serve in thickish slices.

RECIPE SUGGESTIONS
Yellow pea soup

½ lb/225 g dried yellow peas, soaked overnight
1 carrot
2 potatoes
1 ham bone or piece of bacon soaked overnight or ½ lb/225 g salt pork
2¼ quarts/2.25 liters water or ham stock
bouquet garni of 1 sprig parsley, 1 sprig thyme and 1 bay leaf
salt and freshly ground pepper

½ lb/225 g smoked boiling sausage, sliced
⅔ cup/1.5 dl heavy cream or ½ stick/55 g butter

SERVES 4–6

Peel and coarsely chop the carrot and potatoes and put them in a large pan with the drained peas and ham bone, bacon or salt pork. Cover with the cold water or stock, add the bouquet garni, pepper and a very little salt and bring to the boil. Skim and allow to simmer for about 1¼–1½ hours until everything is tender. Remove the ham bone or bacon and the herbs. Purée the soup using the fine blade of a food mill or liquidize it in a food processor.
Return to the pan and taste for seasoning. Add the

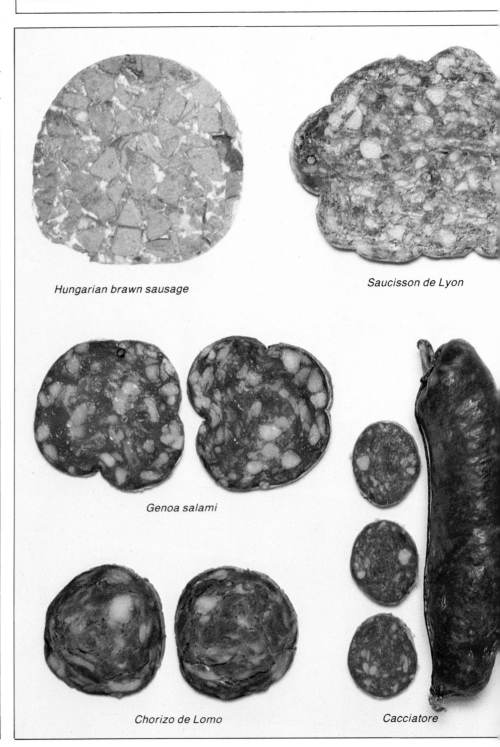

Hungarian brawn sausage

Saucisson de Lyon

Genoa salami

Chorizo de Lomo

Cacciatore

sliced boiling sausage, simmer for 15 minutes and serve very hot. This soup is very delicious with cream stirred into it, but is more traditionally served with a knob of butter added to each bowl and plenty of freshly ground black pepper.

ALTERNATIVE: **Lentil soup**. *Substitute brown or green lentils for yellow peas, add 4 sticks of celery to the carrot and potatoes, and add a teaspoon of olive oil to each bowl in place of cream or butter.*

Veneto polenta

3¼ cups/450 g coarse yellow cornmeal (polenta)
1¼ teaspoons salt

SERVES 6

Bring 2 quarts/1.75 liters of salted water to the boil and turn down the heat until it is simmering steadily. Take a handful of cornmeal at a time, and pour it into the pot in a thin stream, letting it trickle out between your fingers. At the same time keep stirring it continuously with a wooden spoon. The stream of cornmeal should be so thin that you can see the individual grains as they fall. Keep stirring all the time or lumps may form. If they do, you can crush and dissolve them against the side of the pan with a wooden spoon. Keep stirring over a low heat for 20 minutes—the polenta is done when it pulls away from the sides of the pot.

Serve it piping hot, with melted butter, or wet a large clean board or wooden platter and pour the polenta onto it in a large golden pool. It will spread and set. Let it cool and slice it for frying or broiling to eat like bread or to serve with game and stews. Slices of polenta are especially good fried in butter and serve topped with Gorgonzola cheese. Italian housewives fry **Luganeghe** in oil, with tomatoes or sage, and serve it with polenta.

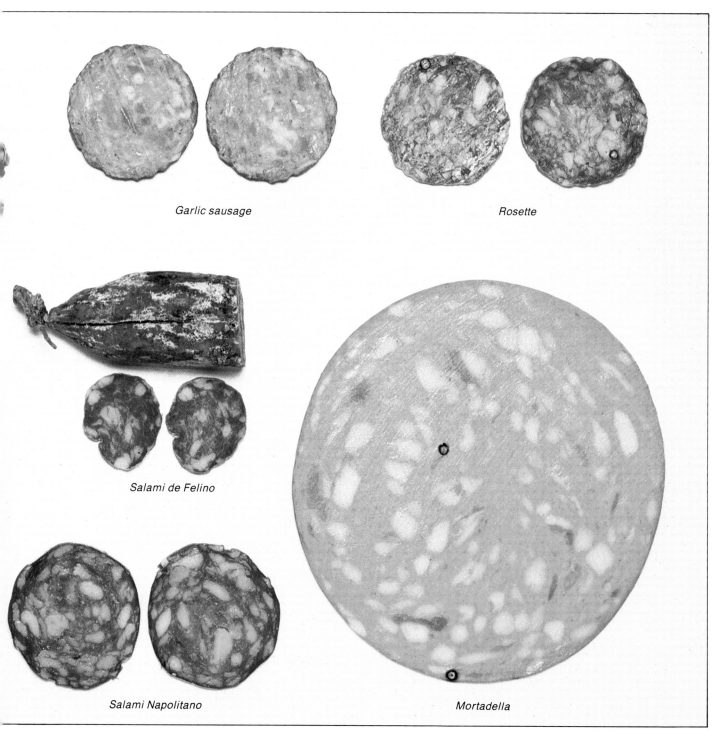

Garlic sausage

Rosette

Salami de Felino

Salami Napolitano

Mortadella

GAME AND POULTRY

One of the pleasures of autumn is the arrival of game on our tables.
In Great Britain shooting begins in August with the open season on
grouse – the "Glorious Twelfth" and by the 13th grouse features on
the menu of every stylish restaurant. Game – furred or feathered –
is usually served with a great deal of ceremony with a flourish of
traditional accompaniments.
Poultry used to be a rare Sunday treat but in recent years it has
moved out of the luxury class to become an everyday treat.

GAME – FURRED

In town game is a luxury but in the English countryside where, even if there is no local dealer selling game fairly cheaply during the open season, you are likely to be given some as a present. The only drawback is that it probably arrives in the kitchen with its fur and guts intact, but once you have mastered the art of preparing it for cooking, this meat above any other is worth your time, skill and attention. Apart from the subtlety of flavor and texture, it is also considered to be one of the healthiest of meats.

To tenderize the more athletic and older creatures, a marinade is useful. This, as a rule, contains vinegar to break down tough fibers, oil to add succulence, and wine, herbs and spices to permeate the meat with flavor. There are cooked and uncooked marinades, the cooked ones being more powerful. The marinade should completely cover the meat, which should be turned periodically during the time it is steeped. This period may vary from a mere 12 hours or so for a hare to at least two weeks for a haunch of wild boar.

All game is protected by laws, which vary from country to country. These are laid down to prevent the shooting of creatures that are too young, to allow mating and the rearing of young to take place and also because the game population of any given area varies from year to year. As a further safeguard, the numbers of any species allowed to be shot by each sportsman are also limited in many parts of the world. Some species of game have been hunted almost to extinction; the American buffalo is an example, but fortunately it has been reintroduced and may now only be hunted on game farms, under strict control.

VENISON

Once bagged, deer becomes venison. It does not matter whether it started life in the wild as red deer, roe deer, fallow deer, white-tailed Virginia deer or the black-tailed variety called mule deer, or even as reindeer, caribou, elk or moose. Nor does it matter if these animals have been bred especially for the table, lived in the wild or, as in the case of roe and fallow deer, in parks; wild or semi-tame, they all become venison.

Venison is not always easy to obtain, since the hand-reared variety is mostly sold to hotels and restaurants, while the wild deer shot by the sportsman is usually sold privately. When venison does appear it is usually in the most expensive stores. It is, however, sometimes to be found in country shops or market stalls, costing rather less than beef, only to be ignored. Contrary to custom, unfamiliarity seems to have bred contempt, but venison prepared with real devotion makes a memorable meal.

The buck is supposed to be better than the doe, but neither should be eaten too young since the flesh, although tender, will not have had time to develop its characteristic flavor. The tendency these days is towards fresh venison, but if a gamy taste is preferred the animal should hang, head down, in a cool, airy place free of flies for 12 to 21 days, depending on the weather – the cooler the weather the longer it can hang.

The saddle, the loin and the haunch, which is the whole leg, make the best roasting cuts. The loin can also be eaten as chops, while the rest of the animal is usually used for ragouts, game pies and pâtés. The head is rarely used in the kitchen, although smoked reindeer tongue is a delicacy in Scandinavia, as is smoked and salted reindeer meat, and moose in all forms.

When buying venison, make sure that the flesh is dark and close grained and that the fat is clear and bright, but trim off the fat before cooking because it is not good to eat. Venison is by nature a dry meat and the fat should be replaced by pork or bacon fat before cooking, the venison having been placed first in a marinade of oil, vinegar, spices and plenty of red wine to which juniper berries have been added. In Italy, venison is sometimes soaked in olive oil with excellent results.

When it is time to cook the meat, lift it out of the marinade and wipe it dry. Then wrap it in a jacket of good white pork fat or, even better, lard it with thick strips of pork fatback, and cover it all over with oiled parchment paper, tying it on with string. Alternatively, instead of parchment use a jacket of aluminium foil, which does the job just as well. When cooking venison, it is usual to allow 25 minutes per 1lb/450g for the buck and 20 minutes for the doe, in a fairly hot oven. It is cooked when, on piercing the skin, the juices run clear. Any sign of blood indicates that the meat needs more time.

Venison has a strong but muted flavor, sometimes described as old lamb that tastes of beef. It needs the encouragement of some sharp, sweet, spicy or piquant accompaniment to taste at its best, so serve it with red currant or rowan jelly, cranberry sauce, spiced cherries or Cumberland sauce. Other flavors that marry well with venison include those of juniper berries, rosemary, Seville orange or lemon juice and spices such as cloves, cinnamon, mace, allspice, nutmeg.

Among the many dishes that have an affinity with venison are wild rice, which is traditional – but expensive – with all game in America; and the noodles or dumplings, made of pasta dough, eaten in southern Germany, Switzerland and Austria, where venison is also sometimes served with a sauce made of sour cream blended with the pan juices. This sauce also accompanies it in northern Germany and in Scandinavia, where it is mopped up with mashed potatoes or potato dumplings. Spiced red cabbage often appears with venison in these countries, and chestnut purée is invariably served with it in France, while celery or celeriac complement its taste and suedelike texture beautifully.

Hare

The flesh of the hare is a dark mahogany brown regardless of the color of its coat, which varies from species to species. In the Champagne district of France, the much-prized hares are golden, while northern France offers a mottled variety. German hares are almost russet colored, English hares are fawn to grey and the Scotch blue hare of the Highlands is the color of Scotch mist.

The blue Scotch hare is a first cousin of the arctic hare of America, called the snowshoe rabbit; this name is an example of the linguistic confusion that has overtaken the hare, which is not helped by the fact that the highly palatable, domestically bred Belgian hare is, in fact, a rabbit. Jack rabbits are actually American hares, which becomes clear when it comes to eating them as there can be no confusion between the strong, gamy flavor of hare and the mild, more delicate taste of rabbit.

The hare, a common but usually distant sight in open farmland in autumn, is surprisingly large when seen close to. Its hind legs are heavily built for speed and it is these and the fleshy saddle that are particularly esteemed in *haute cuisine*. A cut consisting of the back or saddle goes under the culinary name of *râble*, and when the hind legs are included it is called *train de lièvre* or *baron de lièvre*. These are the classic cuts, but a tender, less muscular foreleg can be more succulent than either.

Hare is best eaten when young and luckily its age is easy to determine. A leveret, as a hare under one year of age is called, has a white belly and pliable ears, easily split skin and a barely noticeable harelip. Its claws are almost hidden under the fur of its paws and it is also easily recognizable by its fur, which should be soft and smooth – the fur only becomes matted with advancing age. Long sharp claws and yellow teeth are a definite sign of adulthood.

Leverets are always tender and although the doe remains so during its second year the buck begins to become tough. A hare is usually hung for a few days by the feet. It is then paunched, or gutted, and skinned, after which the inner bluish iridescent layer of muscle that covers the saddle must be removed. If the hare is bought from a game dealer, he will perform this service and probably also joint or truss the animal. Hares are sold minus their heads and innards, but ask for the liver, taking care to remove the gall, which lies between the lobes. You can use the liver to make a forcemeat stuffing, which can be pushed into the diaphragm cavity to make the traditional British "hare with a pudding in its belly."

Hare should be well marinated and then larded or wrapped in pork fat to counteract its tendency to be dry. It can then be roasted slowly and served quite rosy if young and tender. The larger the hare, the longer it

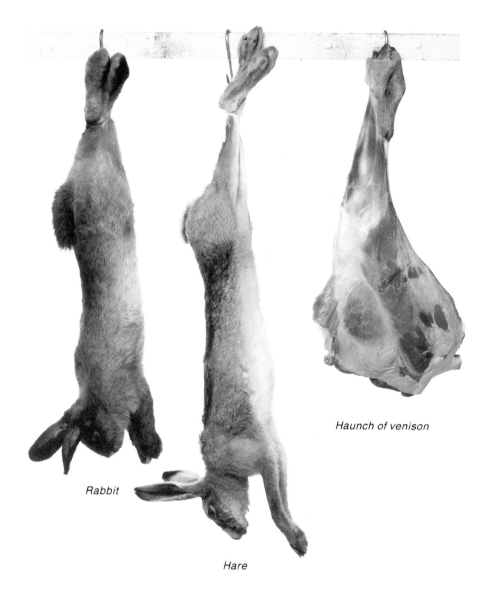

Rabbit

Hare

Haunch of venison

should be cooked – give it 20 – 25 minutes per 1lb/450g in a medium oven.

Allow about 6oz/170g of hare per person if you plan to jug it. The original method was to place it in a jug with herbs, vegetables, spices and port and then to put the jug in a pot of boiling water. Nowadays, however, jugged hare is often stewed or braised in the normal way, and it is a good idea to keep the saddle separate and roast it for another meal. Recipes for jugged hare often tell you to collect some of the hare's blood in a paper cup attached to its nose as it hangs head down, gutted, but still in its fur.

A few drops of red wine vinegar in the cup will prevent the blood coagulating. If the blood has not been kept or the smell of it is too overpowering, a fine jugged hare can still be made without it.

The flavor of hare, which should never be high, is improved by the addition of cloves in moderation and red wine in abundance, and also by port, red currant jelly, fat bacon, mushrooms, shallots, juniper berries and cream, particularly sour cream. In France noodles, in Italy polenta and in Switzerland celeriac purée are served with roast or braised hare.

RECIPE SUGGESTION

Cranberry sauce

1¾ cups/170 g cranberries
3 tablespoons brown sugar

Pick over the cranberries, discarding any that are soft. Put all the ingredients in a small saucepan with 3 tablespoons of water and bring to the boil. Simmer for 15 minutes until the berries burst. Allow to cool, then mix to a ruby-colored mush. Cranberries have a sweet-acid, slightly spicy taste that is very good with turkey, pheasant and hare.

RABBIT

The rabbit is both the ancient enemy and old friend of the countryman; ancient enemy because it eats crops and old friend because it can, in turn, be eaten.

Wild rabbit, still rampant – although reduced in number wherever that unfortunate disease myxomatosis has struck – are stronger tasting and, with age, ranker than tame ones. They are also less plump and tender. Perhaps the best is a fat white rabbit that is not too young, when it is tasteless; not too old, when it becomes dry and tough; and certainly not stale, when it becomes yellow and discolored and loses its resilience and glossiness.

Rabbits are paunched, or drawn, as soon as they have been killed and can be eaten immediately. They do not have to be marinated or hung, although a large, elderly, wild rabbit will develop a good aroma if it is marinated. When choosing rabbit in its fur, pick one that is plump and compact rather than heavy, long and rangy. If buying it skinned, look for pink meat and do not be put off by a bluish sheen. Frozen rabbit pieces have a mild but good flavor and are best in ragouts and mustard sauce. Allow half a rabbit per person.

Although it has a definite flavor of its own, rabbit also makes a good vehicle for other flavors. This works to the cook's advantage in the case of cooking the wild rabbits of Provence, which feed on the tender shoots of wild rosemary and thyme and come with an added herby flavor. Backyard bunnies, however, brought up on lettuce leaves and dandelions, are unlikely to offer unexpected flavors, so it is worth adding a variety of herbs and spices to make them more interesting.

Apart from the famous French rabbit dishes such as *lapin aux trois herbes* or *lapin au moutarde*, there are some splendid traditional English recipes such as rabbit pie, flavored with salt pork or bacon, grated lemon rind and nutmeg, or rabbit stew with bay leaves, carrots and onions. In some parts of England the stew is moistened with cider, which gives a delicious flavor.

In Spain, rabbit is practically a staple food. When it is not roasted, covered in olive oil and sprinkled with sprigs of rosemary or chopped garlic and parsley, it is stewed in wine or served in a light case of potato pastry. In Italy it is cooked with Marsala, tomatoes, eggplant, ham or bacon, and Sicilians, true to their early Moslem heritage, eat it with pine nuts and an *agro-dolce* sauce made with raisins, herbs, stock and vinegar.

Scandinavians roast rabbit like hare and serve it with red cabbage; and when rabbits used to be regarded as "frontier food" in America, pioneers used to enjoy them in a delicate fricassée.

WILD BOAR

Any wild pig, male or female, once killed becomes wild boar. Pig sticking, that dangerous sport, is almost a thing of the past, and although wild pigs still roam the woods of the world, especially in the Causse district of southern France, most of the wild boar – or *sanglier*, as wild boar is also known – found in a butcher's or in a game and poultry store have been reared in boar pens, an environment as close as possible to the wild woods, but where the animals can be fed and can raise their young successfully.

A young wild boar is called a *marcassin* up to the age of six months, after which time it becomes a *bête rousse*. After it is one year old it does not make such good eating, and in old age (wild boars can live up to the age of 30) only the head is still considered to be edible.

Wild boar meat should be dark, almost black, with little fat. It tastes of pork with strong gamy overtones and, like pork, has a certain natural succulence. While *marcassin* may need only hanging, a *bête rousse* is usually tougher and requires marinating as well as hanging before being cooked. The top part of the leg and the saddle make noble roasts; the smaller cuts such as steaks and

PREPARING RABBIT OR HARE

1 SKINNING AND CLEANING

Cut off the head at the back of the neck and the feet at the first joint. Then, with a sharp knife or pair of scissors, slit the belly from just below the rib cage to the rear vent.

Holding the flesh from inside the slit, start pulling away the skin and fur, working towards the tail end.

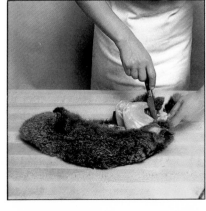

When you have pulled the hind legs out of the skin, sever the tail from the rest of the body.

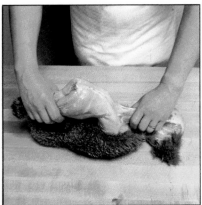

Grip the animal by its hind legs and pull it up and away from the skin, working towards the shoulder.

Ease the front legs free and then pull the animal right out of its skin.

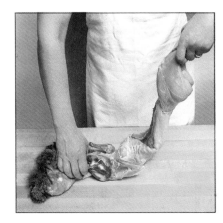

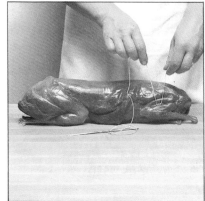

Bend back the forelegs to sit neatly under the body and truss them in place by drawing a threaded trussing needle through both the legs and the body.

Remove all the entrails, reserving the heart, liver and the kidneys.

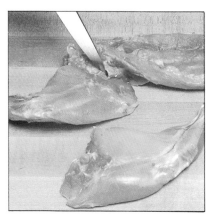

3 JOINTING

Take a skinned and gutted rabbit or hare and cut off the hind legs by inserting a strong, pointed knife into the ball and socket joint, just above each thigh. Cut the forequarters off in one piece, slicing cleanly through the rib cage.

2 ROASTING WHOLE

Take a skinned and gutted rabbit or hare – in this case a hare is being used – and sever the sinews behind the knee of each hind leg. This prevents the legs contracting and distorting during cooking.

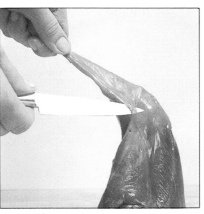

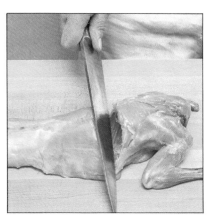

Cut the forequarters off in one piece, slicing cleanly through the rib cage.

Tuck the hind legs under the body and tie them in place with trussing string.

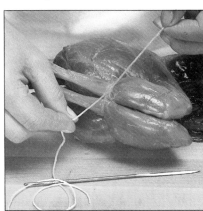

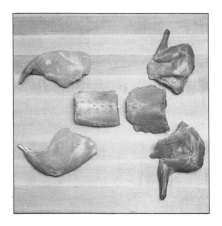

Split the forequarters down the middle and, if you do not want to keep the saddle whole for roasting, cut the remaining body or saddle into serving-size pieces. The forequarters, saddle and hind quarters of this rabbit have divided into six pieces.

chops are often broiled or braised. But no matter how you cook wild boar it is a lengthy operation and, again like pork, it must be cooked right through with no trace in pinkness.

In elegant French country restaurants the mounted mask of a ferocious boar with its tusks at a war-like angle may look down on you as you are served, in the autumn, with *marcassin* accompanied by chestnut purée and a poivrade sauce, which owes its flavor to wine, spices and cognac. In German country inns wild boar is served with a sour-cream sauce, plain boiled potatoes and a side dish of golden chanterelles. As with venison, a spicy accompaniment is required such as cranberry sauce, spiced cherries, or bottled sour cherries poached in red wine flavored with cinnamon.

Since boar is eaten wherever it is found, and the method of its preparation follows national traditions, it is no surprise that it is made into curry in India. In America, where boar was introduced from Germany in the early twentieth century, its steaks are broiled and eaten with a sweet pepper and mushroom sauce, flavored with plenty of garlic and onion. It is also often marinated in cider and served with applesauce.

GAME – FEATHERED

Once the "Glorious Twelfth" has arrived do not be in too much of a hurry for your first taste. Most game needs time to hang to develop its flavor and tenderness, especially if you like the *haut-goût* – although the day is passing when pheasants were judged fit to eat only when head and tail feathers fell out of their own accord, and when maggots showered down from them like so much rice. Today the ripeness of game birds is judged by smell and by the condition of the bird around the vent. This becomes moist and fragile when the bird is well hung – don't worry about a blue or greenish tint to the skin. A high bird smells powerfully gamy while a bird that is rotten smells bad, like any other bad meat.

Hang pheasant, partridge and grouse heads up; hang wildfowl, including geese, by the feet. Apart from helping the meat to mature slowly and magnificently (especially in cold weather, best for the slow mellowing of game), this helps to retain moisture – and if game has a fault, it is that it tends to be dry. If very smelly once plucked, it is helpful to wipe the meat with a cheesecloth dampened with diluted vinegar.

WILD GEESE

These migratory birds fly vast distances and as a result are normally less well covered and more muscular than the fat domestic goose. Choose a young bird with bright-colored legs and a pliable underbill. Like the duck, the wild goose – whichever the species, such as Barnacle, Brent or Chinese – should be eaten within a day or two of being shot. It is best well larded and roasted with a moist stuffing of apples or prunes. An older bird is best stuffed and braised in red wine or cider. Serve wild goose with red cabbage, sour-cream sauce, or any of the tart orange- and endive-based salads that go so well with waterfowl.

WILDFOWL

The mallard
This is the most common variety of wild duck and also the largest – a fat mallard will feed from two to three people.

The widgeon
This is considered superior to the mallard in flavor. One bird will feed one hungry person, or two at a pinch.

The teal
An ornamental duck, tender, and almost too pretty to eat. It will feed one.

Other varieties include the excellent pintail, and the American canvasback, which obligingly feeds on wild celery and tape grass which make its flavor interesting and delicate, lacking any fishy overtones.

Most species of wild duck, however, enjoy a diet of plants growing below the water and so the flavor is, according to their particular biochemical processes, more or less strong, distinctly aquatic and, not to put too fine a point on it, fishy. This can be countered by placing a raw onion inside the bird for an hour or two (remove it before cooking) or by rubbing the bird inside and out with half a lemon dipped in salt; or you may find that it is enough just to spike the gravy with lemon juice and cayenne or Tabasco.

No matter what the species, the duck is preferable to the drake, which tends to be tougher and may therefore need to be marinated. Wild duck should be cooked within 24 hours of killing, unless it is bled so that bacteria do not have the chance to develop. The two small nodules by the tail, which exude a fluid that helps to waterproof the bird, should be removed as they can give the flesh a musky taste.

Leaner and dryer than domestic ducks, all species of wild duck should be well larded and roasted fairly fast on a rack, alternately basted with fresh butter and whisky, red wine or port. They must be served juicy and slightly pink – the longer they cook the tougher they get. The juices that run out when the bird is cut make the best gravy, mixed with orange or lemon juice, red wine, port and Tabasco. Skim the drippings in the roasting pan and taste – if the juices are not bitter, they too can be added to the gravy. Both duck and gravy must be very hot. Serve with homemade potato chips, fried bread crumbs and a sharp salad of orange, celery and watercress. Braised wild duck is good with red cabbage.

QUAIL

In Egypt and around the Mediterranean, particularly in southern Italy and Sicily, these migrating birds, exhausted by their journey to or from North Africa, are easily caught in their millions. There is some evidence that even quail in fine fettle will stand around just waiting to be killed. It is this that has earned one American breed the name fool-quail. Nowadays, since wild quail are scarce and are even protected all the year round in many parts of the world, most of the birds that find their way into kitchens come from quail farms.

Once their feathers have been removed, quail are so small that they are scarcely worth eating. Only if there are at least two apiece, supported by small pieces of fried bread or toast, do they give the impression of being enough. They are best roasted in butter, first on one side, then the other and finally breasts upwards. This keeps the meat moist, what there is of it. Make the gravy with the pan juices and a little Madeira, and if you like add a few tablespoons of cream and some soaked raisins. Or they can be wrapped in vine leaves and roasted, or cooked in a casserole with chopped shallots and garlic, softened in butter. In America, quail is the largest of several small game birds that can be prepared in the same ways.

ORTOLAN, WOODCOCK AND SNIPE

Woodcock and snipe are sometimes cooked with their trail – meaning innards – intact. Due to their habit of excreting during flight they are white and clean inside.

Ortolans
These are the tiniest of the trio. They are almost too small for the piece of toast on which they are served, plainly broiled or, for preference, threaded like pearls on a necklace and cooked on a spit. They can also be wrapped in vine leaves and cooked, tightly packed, in the oven.

Woodcock
Gently dappled and speckled with a brown-leaf light-and-shade pattern, it has a long, distinctive beak. It eats greedily of almost anything it comes across, and as a result of its omnivorous diet of heather, insects, worms and moss it should be a fat little bird with a fair amount of meat for its size. One bird is just the right amount for one person. It is plainly roasted with its head on, complete with beak, and the head is split after cooking to expose the brains, which are considered a delicacy. It is eaten on toast on which the cooked mashed entrails have been spread.

The snipe
This is a smaller bird than the woodcock, with a similar beak, and it is often trussed with its beak through its body. It is cooked like woodcock, but its lesser size has also given it a cooking method of its own: beak threaded through one wing or through the body, it is encased in a hollowed baking

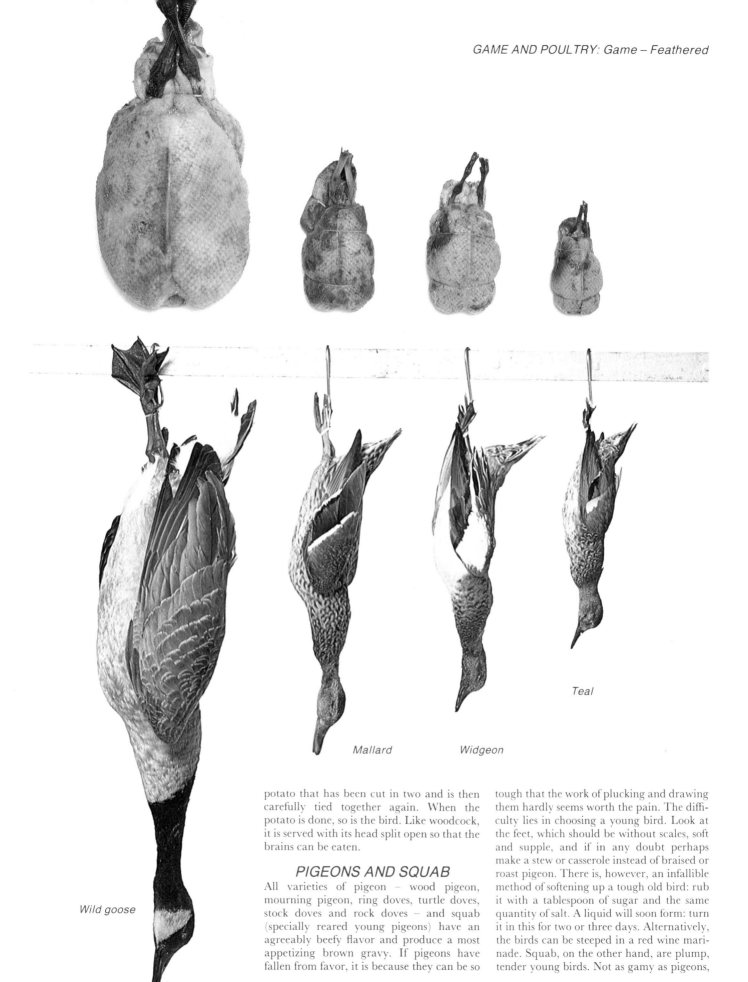

Wild goose

Mallard

Widgeon

Teal

potato that has been cut in two and is then carefully tied together again. When the potato is done, so is the bird. Like woodcock, it is served with its head split open so that the brains can be eaten.

PIGEONS AND SQUAB

All varieties of pigeon – wood pigeon, mourning pigeon, ring doves, turtle doves, stock doves and rock doves – and squab (specially reared young pigeons) have an agreeably beefy flavor and produce a most appetizing brown gravy. If pigeons have fallen from favor, it is because they can be so tough that the work of plucking and drawing them hardly seems worth the pain. The difficulty lies in choosing a young bird. Look at the feet, which should be without scales, soft and supple, and if in any doubt perhaps make a stew or casserole instead of braised or roast pigeon. There is, however, an infallible method of softening up a tough old bird: rub it with a tablespoon of sugar and the same quantity of salt. A liquid will soon form: turn it in this for two or three days. Alternatively, the birds can be steeped in a red wine marinade. Squab, on the other hand, are plump, tender young birds. Not as gamy as pigeons, they can be roasted or braised, and make a useful addition to a game pie.

If you shoot your own pigeons, hang them by the feet to bleed and pluck them while still warm, when the job is much easier. A Malayan recipe recommends that the pigeons be given a final swig of alcohol before their intoxicated and unsuspected despatch. This is thought to be both kinder and taste improving. They are then rubbed with aniseed inside and honey outside and fried in sesame-seed oil. In the Western world, it is usual to serve pigeons with petits pois, braised onions and mushrooms, cabbage and bacon or, for a more gamy dish, with braised red cabbage or lentils.

PARTRIDGES

In Britain, these are the round little birds that explode from the stubble during autumnal country walks. They are always pretty, but are more delicate to eat if they are of the greyish-brown, grey-legged variety. The red-legged partridge is definitely duller. Partridges make the best eating when they are young – about three months old, weighing about 1 lb/450 g, most of which is supplied by the plump breast. Allow one bird per person.

Roast partridge is a great delicacy, while *partridge en Chartreuse* – a pie of partridge, cabbage, sausage, carrots, onions and cloves covered with pastry – is a tremendous dish for a cold winter's day as is a deep-dish pie made with partridge, mushrooms and a suet crust. Use old birds for pies. (Experts can distinguish the old from the young: the older birds have blunt tips to their flight feathers.)

Young partridges require only a little hanging, as their delicate taste should not be overpowered by highness. Clear gravy, homemade potato chips and watercress are all that are needed with roast partridge.

THE GROUSE FAMILY

The flavour of grouse is one of the greatest treats of late summer and early autumn. In the controversy about what makes better eating, partridge or grouse, it is the northern British red grouse, *Lagopus scoticus*, that is being held up for comparison. Its numerous cousins all have merit, but none can match the red grouse, which tastes of game at its gamiest. In America, the ruffed grouse is considered quite choice.

Since young grouse look surprisingly like old ones (except that, as with partridges, there is a difference in the tip to their flight feathers), and you can't get to know very much about grouse just by eating it a few times in a decade, it is best to go to a really expert purveyor of game for these expensive little birds.

For all their gamy taste, grouse are very clean-feeding birds whose diet is heather, berries and small insects, and they are quite easy to cook to perfection. Young birds, born in the year they are eaten, need to be

European quail

Wood snipe

Wood pigeon

Woodcock

wrapped in bacon and roasted in a quick oven for 15 – 20 minutes, until they are pink and slightly underdone. The nicest way to serve them is to sit them on a piece of toast or fried bread with a few straw potatoes and a little watercress. Older birds, while very delicious, take more time to prepare. They are good in game pies and in pâtés and terrines, or braised in red wine and stock with celery, onions and carrots, and button onions added just before the end of their cooking.

The capercaillie

This is the largest of the European grouse tribe. It is almost 3 ft/90 cm long, weighs between 7 and 10 lb/3–4.5 kg and has spectacular plumage of green, black, red and white. It is a northern bird, and owing to its habit of feeding off the tops of young pine trees it tastes distinctly of turpentine, which is not agreeable. Old English recipes variously suggest that to remove the pungent tang the bird should be soaked in milk or vinegar or buried in the ground for 24 hours. A good method of improving a cock bird is to stuff it with raw potatoes, which are discarded after cooking.

In Scandinavia cream plays a great part

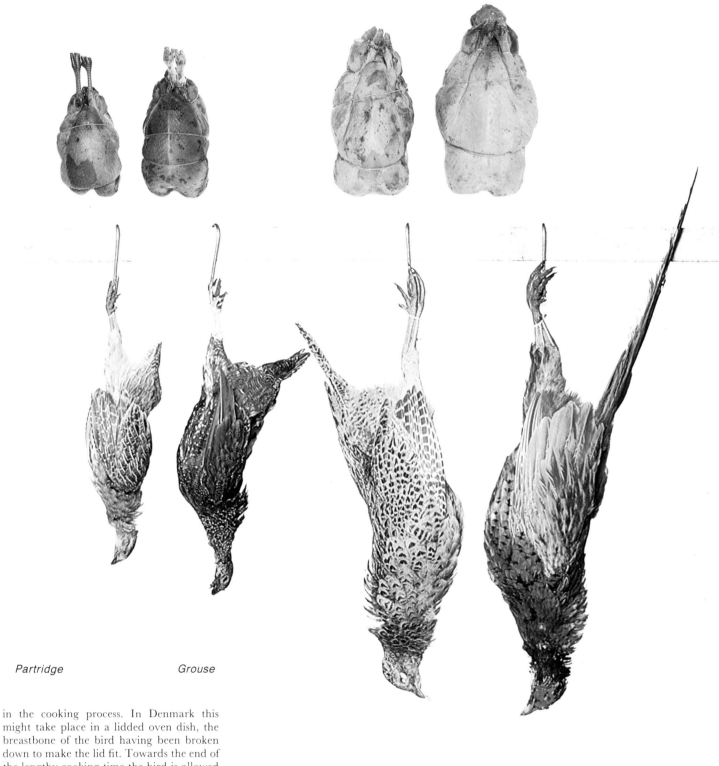

Partridge   Grouse

Hen pheasant

Cock pheasant

in the cooking process. In Denmark this might take place in a lidded oven dish, the breastbone of the bird having been broken down to make the lid fit. Towards the end of the lengthy cooking time the bird is allowed to brown and it is served in its sauce with a sharp cranberry jelly, little gherkins and potatoes. In Norway a creamy, cheesy sauce is poured over the carved bird, which has been roasted in the ordinary way.

The blackcock and the greyhen
The cock will feed three or four people, but the greyhen two at most, for the cock, with his glossy plumage with white bars and his

tail feathers curved like a lyre, is twice as large as his wife. Roasted, both need a good lump of butter in the belly, but blackcock is also casseroled, and made into pies and salmis; in fact, it is treated much like red grouse, although its taste is less delicate.

The ptarmigan

Its size is similar to that of the red grouse, as is its taste, which makes it excellent eating. It is cooked in much the same way as grouse, but in northern Europe, where it is extremely popular, slices of bacon are sometimes inserted under the skin as well as tied over the top. Sour cream goes into the sauce, or there might be a cold sauce of apples cooked in wine, blended with mayonnaise.

PHEASANT

The pheasant stands out like a target among the quietly feathered birds of the autumn landscape, and a target is just what he is, hand reared with loving care to offer sport for countrymen. And who can complain when pheasants make such delicious eating. The cock pheasant is the more handsome, but the hen, although slighter and less gloriously plumaged, is often the plumper, juicier bird. A hen makes a superlative meal for two; a large cock can just feed four.

To choose a pheasant in its plumage, feel the width of the breast to see if it is plump, and see that the legs are smooth and the feet soft. It is easy to tell a young cock by its spurs: rounded and without points in the first year, pointed but still short in the second year.

Make sure the bird is hung to your liking before you cook it, as this improves its succulence and flavor. Without hanging – the time depends on your taste and on the weather – pheasant can taste rather like a dry version of the chicken (to which it is closely related). Since pheasant tends towards dryness in any case, it needs to be wrapped in bacon. It also needs basting with butter, partly to keep it moist, partly to make the skin crisp. Traditionally a young pheasant is served roasted, together with brussels sprouts, braised celeriac, creamed celery or braised endive, and with watercress, clear gravy, fried bread crumbs and faintly clove-scented bread sauce.

A plump pheasant boiled, its skin unbroken, on a bed of celery and served with a celery sauce with the merest dash of lemon juice, has been described as a dish for the gods. Roast pheasant with bitter orange is also good: the juice of a Seville orange is used to baste the bird towards the end of the cooking. Spiced cabbage, even mild sauerkraut, accompanies pheasant in parts of Europe. But it is generally accepted that the natural foods of bird or beast provide the best and most appropriate dressing with which to send it to the table. So cranberries, juniper berries, rowanberries and sweet chestnuts, as well as watercress and celery, play their part in GAME and fowl recipes.

POULTRY

CHICKEN

In the days before intensive farming, when chicken was a rare Sunday treat, young farmyard fowls had to be specially fattened for the table. In France a young fowl would be roasted, an older bird, nicely stuffed and boiled with plenty of vegetables. The backhähndl of Austria (a young roasted rooster) was accompanied by a paprika-sprinkled salad of cucumber cut transparently thin, while in England chicken was always stuffed and served roasted. And then, of course, there is the Jewish mother's panacea for any kind of debilitation from flu to stress – chicken soup made from a fully matured hen.

Today we eat chicken often and in a thousand and one ways. Unlike its ancestors, the battery-bred chicken is fattened so fast and killed so young that it does not have time to develop its full flavor. Sad though this is, a modern chicken responds to being enhanced and improved, and makes a good vehicle for a number of different flavors. Even so, it pays to begin with the best chicken you can find. Free-range birds undoubtedly have the best flavor because of the variety of their diet as they scratch happily for their living, and the fact that they have been able to run about in the sunshine gives them altogether more character. But even among the battery-reared supermarket poultry there are varying degrees of taste.

There is the fresh-chilled chicken, which may or may not be plastic wrapped and has been gutted and stored at just above freezing point. The giblets (not necessarily its own) are found neatly wrapped inside it. You can cook it at once – which one can never do in the case of a frozen chicken – and fresh-chilled chicken has a good texture and plenty of meat on it.

Birds sold by poultry dealers will not be free-range unless specifically advertised as such, and they are sadly hard to come by, especially in cities. The majority will be unfrozen battery birds, complete with innards. Ungutted birds should not be kept for more than seven days, including the time in the store. The poultry dealer will oblige by drawing and trussing the bird for you, and handing you the giblets, which should never be turned down, since they greatly improve the flavor of homemade chicken stock, and can be used in other ways as well.

The plastic-wrapped chicken that has been blast-frozen at a temperature of 0°F/ −18°C or less is usually the cheapest variety that is available. From the seller's point of view, it has the edge over fresh poultry because no skilled labor is needed for the drawing and trussing. Also, provided the bird is stored at the correct temperature it will not deteriorate, and the wrapping film not only helps to preserve its bright appearance but substantially retards weight loss through evaporation.

All this is good news for the trade and is also welcomed by economists and nutritionists, because these birds are a cheap source of energy-giving protein. It is not such good news for the cook because frozen chicken can be rather characterless, needing quite a lot of flavoring and enhancement to make it taste of anything.

When buying frozen chicken, avoid any with freezer burn (they will be dry and tasteless) and also those with noticeable chunks of ice between them and the bottom of their wrappings – these have at some time been partially thawed and refrozen, which is not good for the quality of the flesh. All chickens, fresh-chilled or frozen, are drawn through a bath of water as soon as they have been plucked and drawn. In the case of the fresh-chilled bird, the water has dried off before it reaches your kitchen. In the case of the deep-frozen bird, however, the water drains off only when the chicken is defrosted at home, and the bird ends up in a pool of pink liquid which you have paid for at chicken prices.

Thaw your deep-frozen bird most thoroughly. Not to do so is dangerous, since bacteria develop as the bird is exposed to the heat of the oven and must be killed by thorough cooking. This is impossible if the chicken goes into the pan with a frozen spine (especially if you mean to stuff it), so check not only the meat but also the interior of the chicken before you cook it. Any signs of ice crystals on the inside, or indeed of undue coldness, and the bird is not ready to go into the oven.

Thawing is best done slowly in the refrigerator. The second-best method is to thaw the bird at room temperature in the kitchen. Third comes plunging the bird into cold water. Never give a stiffly frozen chicken a bath of warm water: rapid defrosting spoils the texture of the meat beyond redemption and, whichever recipe you follow, it will come out as dry, stringy chicken in some sort of disguise, the meat having lost all resilience and juiciness. A disappointing end to your efforts.

As soon as you can while it is thawing, remove the wrapped giblets from the chicken so that air can get to the cavity, and never forget to remove the giblet package from any bird before it goes into the oven. This may sound a little basic, but there have been too many surprise stuffings for the advice not to bear repetition.

Squab chickens and Rock Cornish hens

Squab chickens are small, immature birds and are, generally speaking, rather dull, but they can be good split and grilled over charcoal or under fierce heat. Rock Cornish hens are tastier and can be cooked in the same ways, but are best when roasted, perhaps with a wild rice stuffing. Allow one squab chicken or Cornish hen per person.

Poulardes

These are fat, neutered young hens, firm and tender and as prized as capons. The most famous come from Bresse, in France, a district so jealous of its superiority that a true *poularde de Bresse* proclaims its provenance by a metal disc clipped to its wing and is displayed with great pride at the poulterer's or the restaurant.

Capons

These are young neutered roosters fattened on corn, sometimes to an immense girth. Often considered the best chicken available, they are extra succulent because their flesh is marbled with fat, which melts during the cooking process.

A word of warning – the birds may be neutered by hormone pellets implanted in their necks (although in France this method is illegal and caponizing is done by performing a small operation on each bird). The implant method means that by using the neck in cooking you can pass the hormones on to your family, so throw the neck away if you eat capons at all frequently.

Boiling fowl

Once abundant, these are now hard to find, but any of the old recipes that specify boiling fowl can be made at a pinch with a young roasting bird. The boiler is an older bird and therefore a good deal tougher as well as cheaper. But treated to long, gentle simmering it can be made tender and has both light and dark meat like a turkey, each with a pronounced flavor of its own. Useful in pies and salads, it also provides a quantity of very good broth.

Broilers and chicken pieces

Young broilers are the most popular sort available and can be used for most chicken recipes. Allow a 3½–4lb/1.75–2kg broiler to feed 4–6 people.

Of course you can also buy chicken portions in the shape of the legs, or breast and wing, or a mixture of both. Comparatively, these are a little more expensive than a whole chicken but very convenient if you are short of time. Deep fried with lovely crisp golden batter, chicken pieces eaten with corn bread and fried bananas become chicken Maryland. Chicken breasts wrapped around a piece of chilled garlic butter, egg-and-crumbed and deep fried make the delicious chicken Kiev that spurts hot garlic butter into the eater's eye.

TURKEY

Calculate 1lb/450g of dressed weight per person – thus a 20lb/9kg bird will provide 20 helpings as well as seemingly endless supplies of stock and soup.

The bird to look for is a broad, compact one, hen rather than cock, with a fresh looking but not moist skin and a pearly white tint to the flesh rather than purple or blue.

It should have been hung for at least three days, otherwise it will have very little flavor. This makes a fresh turkey your best buy, because although frozen birds can, of course, be quite good, they are sometimes frozen as soon as they have been killed, which means that although they may be juicy the taste may be rather dull.

A frozen turkey takes about 48 hours to thaw. Simply put it in the refrigerator two days before you want it (three days if it is extra large) and let it thaw gradually. Then let it spend a few hours at room temperature just to make certain that it has properly thawed. It won't be cooked in the middle if it hasn't, and domestic birds not cooked through are as dangerous as undercooked pork and much nastier. Once it has thawed, it should be cooked soon. Resist the temptation to prestuff the turkey in order to save time on the day of the dinner, even though there will be so many other traditional bits and pieces to see to. Get the stuffing ready on the eve of the day by all means, but put it inside the bird just before it goes into the oven, as the stuffing may spoil if it sits around inside the bird, even if the stuffed bird is kept in the refrigerator.

GOOSE

Martinmas, on 11 November, is the traditional day for eating goose in northern Europe. It is, presumably, an extended annual punishment meted out to these birds, whose cackling once gave away the farmyard hiding place of the modest St. Martin as he was attempting to evade admiring followers who wanted him to be Pope. (The raucous cry of geese saved the ancient Romans from barbarian invasion – but that has not stopped the Italians from eating goose, richly stuffed with sausage meat, olives and truffles.)

In England goose used to be eaten on Michaelmas. This was not so much because this saint and all his angels had a grudge against geese, but because his day, 29 September, was, like St. Martin's, a fast day – one of so many that people were getting heartily sick of being forced to eat fish. Waterfowl – including geese – didn't count as meat and so could be eaten without offense to God or man. Moreover, both saints' days fell in the season when the geese were getting fat.

When buying a goose for the table, choose a young bird with downy feathers around the legs and a pliable lower beak and breastbone. A well-filled plump breast denotes succulence and value for money. Look for creamy skin with a warm tinge to it, almost pale apricot, without a trace of blue or brown.

A gosling, or green goose, of no more than three months old weighs up to about 5lb/2kg and can hardly help being tender and delicate. At 8–9 months old it becomes a goose (in culinary terms it is never a gander). At

8–9 months the goose, weighing 6–12lb/2.5–5.5kg, is in its prime; with advancing age it becomes both fatter and tougher, needing longer and longer periods of braising or stewing – very delicious, but perhaps not quite the rare treat that goose is usually expected to be.

You will need to trust in the expertise of your supplier in keeping fresh, chilled or frozen birds in the right condition – the goose should be hung for a few days before it is gutted and plucked. If by any chance you have to pluck the goose at home, put it into a large bowl and pour boiling water over it to loosen the feathers, or the job is likely to take you all day.

DUCK

A duck is nobody's best buy: it is a bony creature covered in fat, with a shallow breast. When you come to carve it – and here you may come to blows with the bird before you have finished – you will find that there is not enough breast to go around; but hot or cold, duck has such an excellent flavor, richness and succulence that it is well worth the occasional extravagance.

The very best French ducks are the small Nantais, and the larger Rouen, which is suffocated to retain the blood so that its flesh stays dark, giving it a strong flavor which is something of an acquired taste. The Rouen duck should be cooked within 24 hours of its demise. Roasted very rare and divested of breast, drumsticks and wings, it is this duck which is pressed, together with its lightly cooked giblets, in the great silvery duck presses which are still a feature of elegant French restaurants, to make the juice for the gravy.

The most famous English duck is the Aylesbury and the most popular American variety is the Long Island duckling. This, like the Nantais, the Rouen and the Aylesbury, is a descendant of the Imperial Peking duck, a Chinese snow-white breed of special excellence, which was once reserved for the Emperor alone.

"Duckling" was once, strictly, the term for birds under two months old, but it is now used until the birds are six months or so. Duckling sounds more tender than duck, but it is a mistake to invest in too young a bird as it does not have enough meat on its bones to be worth eating. However, the best eating age and weight varies with the breed. Make sure that the duck's underbill is soft enough to be bent back easily, that the webbing of its feet is pliable and that its breast, when pinched, feels meaty.

As for how many persons a duck will feed, it is hard to say. A wit once observed that the duck was a difficult bird – too much for one, too little for two. However, two people can dine more than well even on a Nantais; and three, or even four if helpings are modest, on an Aylesbury or a Long Island duckling.

Ducks take quite kindly to freezing – their

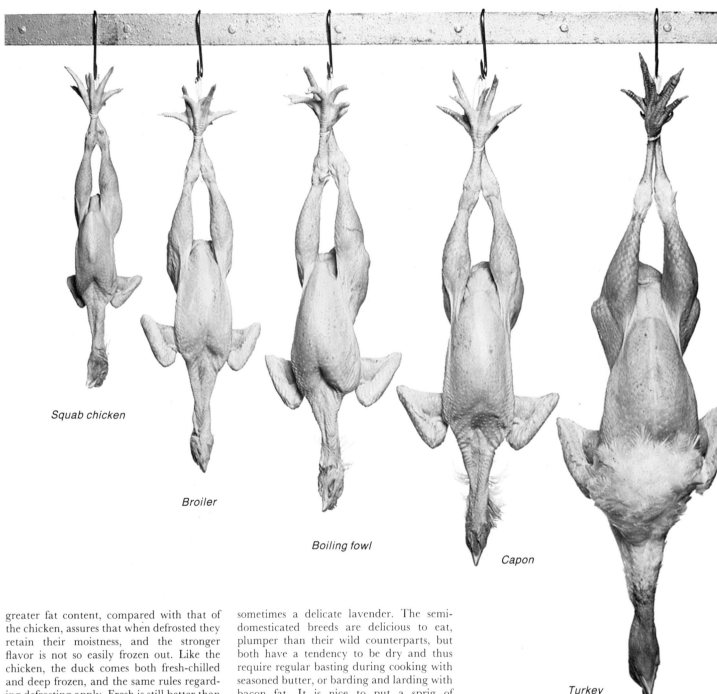

Squab chicken

Broiler

Boiling fowl

Capon

Turkey

greater fat content, compared with that of the chicken, assures that when defrosted they retain their moistness, and the stronger flavor is not so easily frozen out. Like the chicken, the duck comes both fresh-chilled and deep frozen, and the same rules regarding defrosting apply. Fresh is still better than frozen, and free-range better than battery. But unlike the battery chickens, who may never have set foot to ground throughout their lives, battery ducklings may have been allowed to waddle about the yard in their youth, before the fattening up process put an end to exercise.

GUINEA FOWL

This elegantly spotted fowl, of West African ancestry, is an endearing but stupid bird. Looking somewhat like a walking cushion, its feathers are a marvel of pattern, white-spotted on black like old ladies' dresses, or

sometimes a delicate lavender. The semi-domesticated breeds are delicious to eat, plumper than their wild counterparts, but both have a tendency to be dry and thus require regular basting during cooking with seasoned butter, or barding and larding with bacon fat. It is nice to put a sprig of marjoram under the waistcoat of fat if you do not plan to stuff the bird.

Guinea fowl are often seen in European shops wearing the wing feathers – perhaps to distinguish them from young chickens, which they resemble in size. They taste like a slightly gamy chicken and recipes for pheasant, partridge or young roasting chicken will do justice to their delicate flavor.

To be enjoyed at their best, guinea fowl should hang, unbled, in a cool place for one or two days to tenderize the meat. Ask the poultry supplier to pluck it, gut it and truss

it for you. The demand for guinea fowl is not enormous so they are not always available, but they are on the market all year round. In America they are either home-raised or available only in specialty stores.

GIBLETS

The giblets – the neck, heart, gizzard and liver – of most poultry are usually packed inside the body cavity or handed over by the poulterer. Giblets make a wonderful stock for

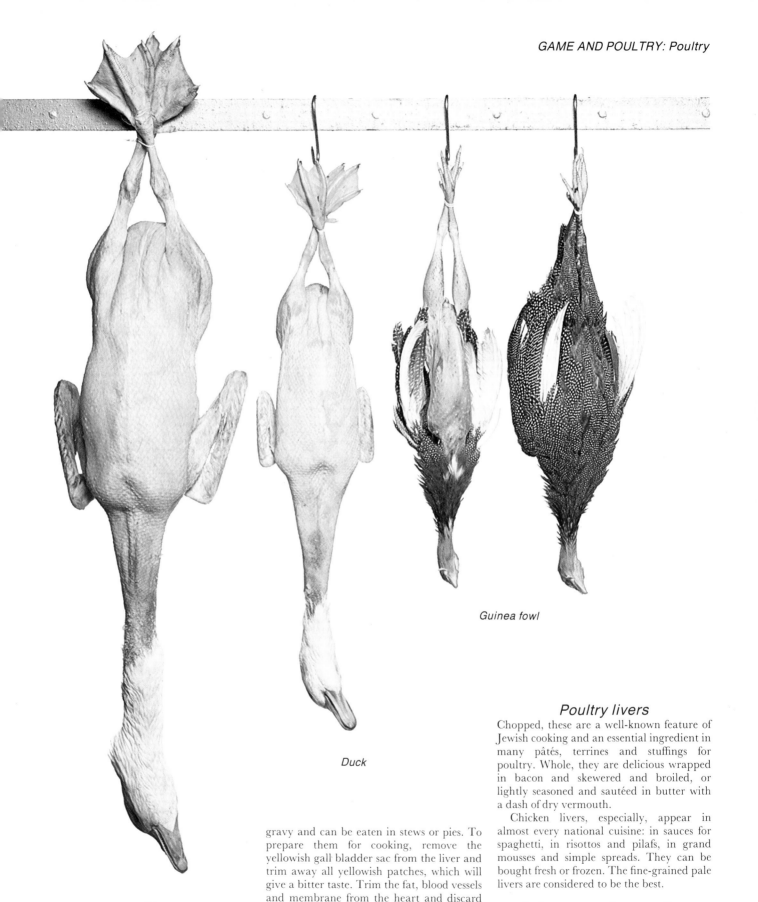

Goose

Duck

Guinea fowl

gravy and can be eaten in stews or pies. To prepare them for cooking, remove the yellowish gall bladder sac from the liver and trim away all yellowish patches, which will give a bitter taste. Trim the fat, blood vessels and membrane from the heart and discard the outer skin and inner sac containing stones and grit from the gizzard. When making a giblet stock, it seems wasteful to boil up the liver, which can be enjoyed in many different ways.

Poultry livers

Chopped, these are a well-known feature of Jewish cooking and an essential ingredient in many pâtés, terrines and stuffings for poultry. Whole, they are delicious wrapped in bacon and skewered and broiled, or lightly seasoned and sautéed in butter with a dash of dry vermouth.

Chicken livers, especially, appear in almost every national cuisine: in sauces for spaghetti, in risottos and pilafs, in grand mousses and simple spreads. They can be bought fresh or frozen. The fine-grained pale livers are considered to be the best.

Foie gras and goose liver

The wit of the English Regency, the Reverend Sydney Smith, defined his idea of heaven as "eating foie gras to the sound of trumpets." Indeed, there can be nothing to compare with the exquisite, pale, fattened liver of the goose, for which the bird is expressly bred, particularly in areas of south-western France.

To make foie gras the geese are force-fed until their livers weigh around 4lb/2kg apiece. The best comes from a breed already known to the ancient Romans. These geese, unlike table geese, have an extra pleat of skin under the breast, which neatly accommodates the enlarged liver. Ducks are also increasingly being bred for foie gras, with the result that fresh foie gras is becoming much more widely available than ever before.

The liver of a goose on a normal diet weighs about 4oz/115g. Soaked in milk it will swell a little and become even more tender. It is good sliced and fried and eaten with rice or with scrambled eggs. Pounded, together with white bread crumbs, marjoram, chopped mushrooms and diced bacon and bound with egg, it is used to stuff the fat skin of the neck, which is then tied at both ends and poached in giblet broth and white wine, or fried in goose drippings. In France, no part of a goose is wasted, and in some country areas even the blood is eaten in the form of little cakes flavored with garlic.

RECIPE SUGGESTIONS

Poulet paysanne

1 chicken weighing 3 lb/1.5 kg
18 small new potatoes, a bit larger than a walnut
¼ lb/115 g mushrooms
2 cloves garlic
½ stick/55 g butter
3 tablespoons peanut oil
salt and freshly ground pepper
1 tablespoon chopped parsley
⅔ cup/1.5 dl chicken stock made with the giblets

SERVES 4–6

Scrape or scrub the potatoes. Slice the mushrooms thinly, and peel and chop the garlic. Cut the chicken into six pieces. In a wide shallow pan, heat half the butter and 2 tablespoons of the oil, and put in the pieces of chicken, side by side. Let them cook gently, uncovered, for about 15 minutes, turning them from time to time until they are golden.

Meanwhile, heat the remaining butter and oil in a smaller pan and add the potatoes, first dried in a cloth. Let them brown, shaking the pan occasionally, and turning them over. When the potatoes are evenly colored, add the sliced mushrooms and mix them in. Let them cook together for a minute or two, then add them together with their butter to the chicken. Season with salt and pepper, cover the pan and simmer gently for about 30 minutes until the chicken is tender and the potatoes are cooked through.

Remove the lid, and sprinkle in the chopped parsley and garlic. Stir around and cook on for a further 3–4 minutes. Remove the pieces of chicken, potatoes and mushrooms to a deep serving dish and keep them hot. Spoon the fat off the cooking juices and pour the chicken stock into the pan. Scrape and stir to dislodge any cooking juices caramelized on the bottom of the pan and allow the liquid to reduce to about half its volume. Pour it over the chicken, and serve very hot.

Goose with apple stuffing

1 goose weighing about 11–12 lb/5–5.5 kg
2 lb/900 g russet or Golden Delicious apples
1 onion
2½ cups/6 dl stock made with goose giblets, or chicken stock
1 glass sweet white wine
1 tablespoon dried sage
1½ tablespoons flour
salt and freshly ground pepper

SERVES 8–10

Preheat the oven to 425°F/220°C.

Salt the goose inside and out, removing any stray quills. Remove the stalks of the apples, core the apples but leave them whole and unpeeled, and fill the goose with them. Sew up or skewer closed the bird's rear cavity and neck flap.

Peel and slice the onion. Cover the bottom of a roasting pan with the stock and white wine. Add the onion and sage, put the goose in the pan, breast downwards, and roast in a fast oven for an hour, basting with the liquid and pricking the skin with a fork to let the fat run out. Then turn the bird over and roast for a further 2 hours at 350°F/180°C, continuing to baste and prod it with a fork, but not too deeply or you will make the juice run out of the meat. When the goose is done, remove it to a hot dish and put it back in the oven while you pour off most of the copious fat from the roasting pan. Add the flour to the juices remaining in the pan, stirring it around until it is cooked. Taste the gravy for seasoning. Add boiling water if it is too concentrated. Strain into a gravy dish.

Serve the goose with this sauce and the apples from the inside of the bird—they will have collapsed into a delicious stuffing.

White devil

12–18 slices cold roast turkey
2 cups/4.5 dl heavy cream
2 tablespoons Worcestershire sauce
2 teaspoons hot mustard
2 tablespoons sherry
generous dash of Tabasco
salt and freshly ground pepper

SERVES 6

Preheat the oven to 350°F/180°C.

Lay the slices of turkey in the bottom of an oval earthenware gratin dish. Mix all the rest of the ingredients in a saucepan and heat to boiling point. Pour the mixture over the turkey and heat in the oven for 20 minutes. If necessary put the dish under a hot grill until brown, glazed and bubbling. Serve with a refreshing salad of lettuce, crisped in the refrigerator, which is excellent for mopping up the juices left on the plate.

Duck with green olives

1 duck weighing 3½–4 lb/1.75–2 kg
2 cups/4.5 dl chicken stock
1 teaspoon tomato paste
bouquet garni of parsley, thyme and a bay leaf
salt and freshly ground pepper
1¾ cups/170 g pitted green olives
2 teaspoons potato flour
½ glass Madeira or dry sherry

SERVES 4

Preheat the oven to 450°F/230°C.

Prick the duck here and there in order to allow the fat to escape during cooking. Put the bird into a casserole and brown it on all sides in the oven for about 15 minutes. Pour off the fat and add the stock, tomato paste, the bouquet garni and a generous seasoning of salt and pepper. Cover the casserole and cook the duck for a further hour and 10 minutes; test to see if it is tender by piercing the thickest part of the thigh with a skewer.

Meanwhile, blanch the olives in a large pan of unsalted boiling water for 5 minutes. Drain them. Take the duck out of the casserole, put it on a heated serving dish and keep it hot. Remove most of the fat from the top of the sauce with a tablespoon and add the olives. Put it over a gentle heat, dissolve the potato flour in the Madeira or sherry and add it to the sauce. Remove the bouquet garni and simmer the sauce over a gentle heat, stirring constantly, until it thickens and coats the back of the spoon.

Taste for seasoning, add salt and pepper if necessary and then pour the sauce over the duck. Serve with plain boiled potatoes.

Pheasant with chestnuts

1 pheasant, plucked and cleaned, and its giblets
2 Spanish onions
2 shallots
6 small carrots
6 thick slices bacon
2 tablespoons/30 g butter
flour for dusting
½ cup red wine
1¼ cups/3 dl stock, made with the pheasant's neck, heart and liver, 1 onion, 2 carrots and a bay leaf
salt and freshly ground pepper
bouquet garni of 1 bay leaf and a sprig each of thyme and parsley
½ lb/225 g chestnuts
1 teaspoon arrowroot

SERVES 2–3

Preheat the oven to 325°F/170°C.

Peel and slice the onions, shallots and carrots. Cut the bacon into little sticks, and fry them in the butter in a flameproof casserole. Dust the pheasant with flour and fry it gently in the same butter on all sides, until it is nicely browned. Remove the pheasant and the pieces of bacon, and fry the vegetables lightly in the fat remaining in the casserole without browning them. Pour in the red wine and let it bubble for a few minutes; return the bacon to the casserole, and put the pheasant on its side on top of the vegetables. Pour on the stock, season with salt and pepper and add the bouquet garni. Cover the pan and put the casserole in a low oven for 30 minutes.

Meanwhile, peel the chestnuts. Put them into the casserole around the pheasant, turn the bird over, and replace the lid. Cook for a further 30 minutes. Remove the pheasant, chestnuts and vegetables with a slotted spoon and keep them hot. Skim the braising juices, tipping the casserole to make it easier. Dissolve the arrowroot in 3 tablespoons of water in a cup and stir it into the juices. Taste for seasoning. Allow to simmer for 5 minutes, stirring from time to time.

Carve the pheasant. Arrange it with the vegetables and chestnuts on a deep serving dish and pour on the lightly thickened sauce.

PREPARING BIRDS – PHEASANT

1 PHEASANT

Hold the legs firmly with one hand and start plucking from the breast area. Pull the feathers down in the direction of growth. Pluck firmly but gently and try to avoid tearing the skin.

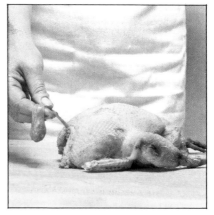

Withdraw the crop from just inside the neck cavity and discard it.

When the body is completely plucked, cut the tough flight feathers from the end of each wing.

Feel inside the neck cavity and detach the entrails from the body. This makes it easier to draw them out from the opposite end.

Turn the bird breast down, cut off the head and slit open the skin encasing the neck.

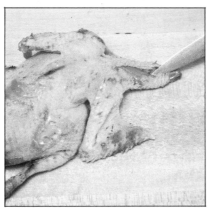

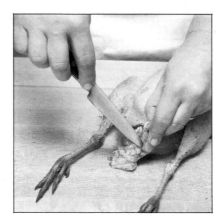

Cut around the rear vent without piercing the intestine, which is attached to the vent and lies just inside.

Open out the neck skin and sever the neck. Reserve this for making gravy.

Pull out the entrails, reserving the liver and heart for making gravy.

PREPARING BIRDS: PHEASANT – DUCK

Run a knife around each leg just below the joint, snap the bone and twist off the foot, pulling with it the stringy tendons.

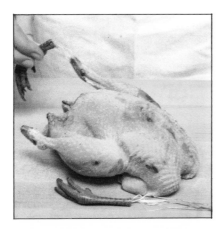

Place the knife between the ball and socket of the thigh joint and twist the knife to sever the thigh bone. Do the same on the other side.

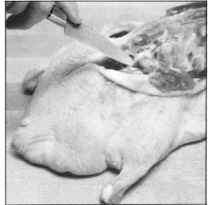

This pheasant is cleaned and trussed ready for roasting, with the liver, heart and neck set aside for making gravy. All poultry and game birds can be plucked and cleaned in the same way. Turkeys should be plucked while still warm, starting with the tough wing feathers.

Slide the knife in the other direction towards the neck until the shoulder bone is well exposed. Free the other shoulder bone in the same way.

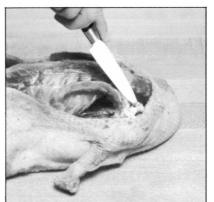

2 DUCK

Lay the duck breast down and with a strong, sharp, short-bladed knife split the skin along the center of the back from neck to parson's nose.

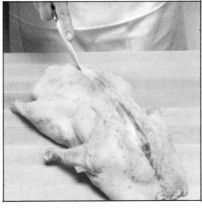

Cut through the wing joints and continue to cut, keeping the bones as free of flesh as possible, until you reach the breastbone.

Cut down each side of the backbone, starting a little below the neck cavity, and peel back the skin and flesh until you encounter the joint of the thigh bone.

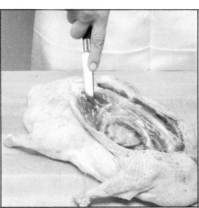

Lift up the bones, cutting away the remnants of flesh. Take care not to puncture the breast.

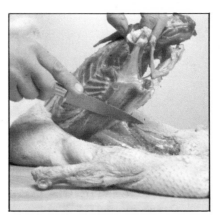

PREPARING BIRDS: DUCK – CHICKEN

Finally, sever the bony framework at the parson's nose, separating it completely from the flesh.

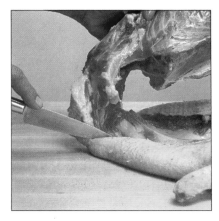

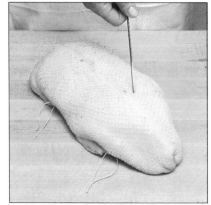

Push the duck into a long, oval shape, truss and then prick the bird all over to allow the fat to run out freely while roasting.

Remove the leg bones from the body, working down each with the knife edge. Start from the inside of the duck and push down on the flesh, keeping the skin as intact as possible.

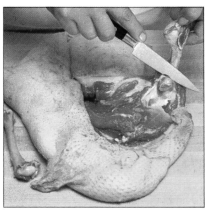

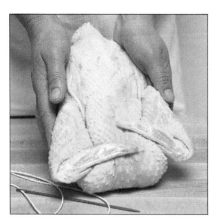

3 CHICKEN

Take a cleaned chicken, stretch the neck flap firmly under the bird and fold back the wing tips to secure the flap in place.

Slip out each wing bone in exactly the same way as the leg bones.

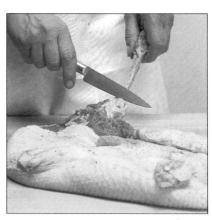

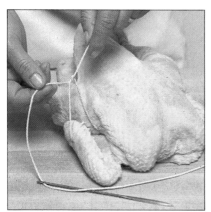

Push a threaded trussing needle right through the body just above the wings. Return it through the body, but this time pierce the wings. Tie and trim the two loose ends of string. Re-thread the trussing needle.

Fill the bird with stuffing of your choice, but do not pack it too tightly or the duck will burst during cooking. Sew up the slit with trussing string.

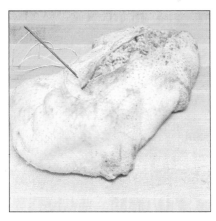

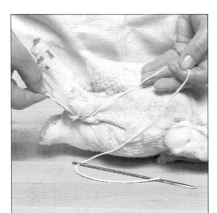

Push the needle through the skin just under the drumstick joint, then through the gristle on either side of the parson's nose and emerge through the skin under the far drumstick. Return the needle through the bird, just to one side of the original path. Tie securely and trim the ends.

PREPARING BIRDS: CHICKEN

4 JOINTING A CHICKEN

With a short, sharp knife cut off each of the chicken's legs at the point where they join the carcass. Do this by forcing the knife blade between the ball and socket joint and slicing down to either side of the parson's nose.

Discard the breastbone and cut each side of the chicken in half.

Slide a large, heavy knife inside the bird and make two cuts, one on either side of the backbone.

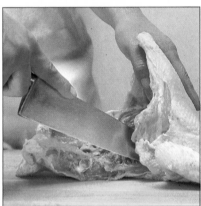

The resulting portions are two legs, two wings and two breasts.

The backbone, which should be as bare of flesh as possible, can now be withdrawn from the body and reserved for making soup or stock.

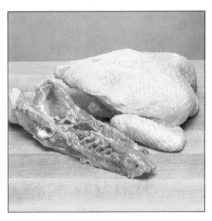

5 STUFFING

Take a breast of chicken, with wing bone attached, and cut off the wing tip at the second joint. Lay the breast skin side down and push a roll of chilled garlic and herb butter under the natural flap of flesh.

Turn the bird over and cut along either side of the breastbone.

Seal the flap closed by pressing the outer edges together, and then roll the breast up from the tip towards the wing bone. Tie with cotton or trussing string to make a neat parcel.

EGGS

For primitive man, with a mind far less tortuous than ours, there was no such thing as a chicken-and-egg dilemma: he recognized the egg as the beginning of life and celebrated it as such.

In the kitchen the hen's egg is celebrated still. Indispensable to the cook and rich in vitamins and minerals, it is one of the most versatile and valuable of foods.

There is a popular misconception in Europe that brown eggs are somehow better than white, whereas in the United States, white are usually preferred. But shell color reflects neither flavor nor nutritional content, merely the breed of the laying bird. The best egg, brown or white, large or small, is one that has been freshly laid by a free-range hen – properties difficult to ascertain in the store or supermarket, where boxes enticingly labelled "farm fresh" may contain factory eggs up to four or five weeks old.

From the time an egg is laid, the membranes weaken and the flavor changes. The white of a fresh egg is thick (making wonderful fried and poached eggs), getting runnier and thinner as time goes by. It is easy enough to tell if an egg is fresh or stale once you get it home. At the rounded end of the egg, between the shell and the membrane, there is a small air chamber, all but invisible when the egg is fresh, increasingly large as the egg gets older and loses moisture through its pores. So one way of assessing freshness is to hold the egg upright against a strong light and examine the size of the air space. Another is to weigh it in your hand: the heavier for its size the better; yet another is to immerse it horizontally in cold water. A perfectly fresh egg will stay put; older eggs will tilt; if more than three weeks old they will float. If the egg rises to a vertical position it is really getting old.

Large eggs are good for breakfast, but when cookbooks specify eggs they generally mean medium-size ones. The average egg used to be a great deal smaller than it is today and was probably laid by bantam hens. These still make the best sitters and are sometimes used for hatching eggs of larger hens bred for laying rather than motherhood. But no bantam, however devoted, can be as efficient as a mechanized battery. "Factory" eggs are no less nutritious, their flavor is standard and good, if rather slight, but they fail to give as much pleasure as eggs from contented hens scratching about for their food in the farmyard. These "free-range" eggs arrive in the stores ready boxed, often with a token bit of down attached, and it is probably a sign of the times that in parts of California the token feather is of hygienic plastic. Eat genuine farm-fresh eggs as soon as possible, especially if they have been cleaned, as washing removes the natural protective film from the shell.

Because eggshells are porous they are

White hen egg *Brown hen egg* *Duck egg* *Goose egg*

Quail egg *Pheasant egg* *Gull egg*

highly susceptible to neighboring smells, which is fine if they are intended for truffle omelets and stored in an egg basket with a truffle, as they are in parts of Périgord, but not such a good thing if their near neighbors are unwrapped, strong-smelling foods such as onions and particularly ripe cheese.

Eggs should be kept in a cool place – not necessarily a refrigerator – standing with the rounded end up to allow the air space to breathe. For cooking, they should be at room temperature – eggs straight from the refrigerator will crack if plunged into boiling water, a cold yolk will not emulsify reliably and cold whites will not whisk well.

COOKING WITH EGGS

A beaten egg will thicken soups, stews and sauces because heat causes the egg to coagulate, thus holding the liquid in suspension. The raw yolk will hold oil or butter in suspension and to this happy fact we owe such good things as mayonnaise and hollandaise sauce. An egg is sticky and so will bind mixtures for croquettes and stuffings or hamburgers. As for food that is to be deep fried, a dip into a beaten egg will not only keep the bread crumbs in place but the film of egg will protect the food from becoming sodden with fat.

The volume of beaten egg white depends on the eggs being at room temperature before you start and the way you whisk them – electric food processors are too fast and produce a dense texture. Big "balloon" wire whisks, while taking a little more time and energy, do produce the desired airy froth.

Apart from omelets and batters, which are cooked briefly over a high heat, eggs respond best to gentle warmth – too high a heat and too long a cooking time makes them leathery.

OTHER EGGS

No other bird has proved anywhere near so obliging as the domestic hen, which lays up to 250 eggs a year, but hens' eggs are by no means the whole story.

Ostrich eggs
One ostrich egg is equal to two dozen hen's eggs but they are rarely sold these days – Queen Victoria once tasted one made into a giant omelet and declared it to be very good.

Duck eggs
These are extremely rich with somewhat gelatinous whites, so although they taste quite good alone they are best in custards, mousses and other puddings.

Goose eggs
Make very good omelets, custards and mousses.

Quail eggs
Can come both fresh and preserved. Fresh, they make a good first course served hard boiled with celery salt.

Gulls' eggs, plovers' eggs and pheasants' eggs are sometimes to be found, but in many countries they are, quite rightly, protected from the unheeding gourmet.

RECIPE SUGGESTION
Egg mayonnaise

4 eggs
1¼ cups/3 dl mayonnaise, made with peanut oil or half peanut, half olive oil
2 tablespoons light cream
sprinkling of cayenne pepper

SERVES 4
Boil the eggs for exactly 12 minutes, then cool them under cold running water and shell them carefully. Cut them in half and put them rounded sides up in an oval dish. Stir the cream into the mayonnaise, to make it more liquid, taste it to make sure it is well flavored and spoon it over the eggs. Sprinkle lightly with cayenne pepper and serve.

DAIRY PRODUCE

The cow is a good friend to mankind, providing us with one of our most complete foods. Milk contains most of the nutrients required by the human body – proteins, vitamins and minerals, especially calcium – and since cows are so generous with their supply, milk and its products are still good value for money.

MILK

Most children and quite a number of adults enjoy drinking milk and it is also used in a variety of ways, including for cooking.

The majority of milk on the market today is pasteurized. Pasteurization involves heating the milk to a point where any potentially dangerous bacilli are killed but the flavor of the milk is not impaired.

Milk should always be heated slowly and cooked at low temperatures. A skin forms on the top when it reaches high temperatures; to avoid it do not boil but scald the milk. That is, remove it from the heat just as it shows a wreath of tiny bubbles around the edge.

Fresh milks

There are three main types of fresh milk, which need to be kept as cool as possible.

Whole milk

This is milk with its natural cream intact and has one of the best flavors of all milk sold.

The creamiest milk usually comes from Jersey and Guernsey cows, but today many farmers are producing good quality milk from Friesians and Holsteins.

Homogenized milk

The cream is still present in homogenized milk, but as the name suggests it has been evenly suspended throughout instead of being allowed to float to the top as in whole milk. Homogenized milk is good for making ice cream as it freezes well.

Skimmed and low-fat milk Skimmed milk is milk that has been divested of its cream. The cream is removed by centrifugal force and the resulting almost fat-free milk is good in low-fat diets, since it contains only 0.1 percent fat. Slightly less watery low fat milk contains 2 percent fat.

Long-life milks

These milks will keep, unopened, for much longer than ordinary pasteurized milks. Once opened, however, or reconstituted, they will keep only as long as fresh milk.

Sterilized milk

This is pasteurized, homogenized and then held at a high temperature until all the bacteria have been destroyed. It will keep unopened for about seven days but has a slightly peculiar taste due to the caramelization of the sugar present in milk, known as lactose.

UHT (Ultra Heat Treated) Milk

First pasteurized, this milk is then treated at a temperature of 270°F/132°C for a single second, which means that the lactose does not caramelize to such an extent that the flavor is impaired. It will keep unopened for several months.

Other milks

Although Western Society drinks mainly cows' milk, there are many other kinds such as sheep's, goats' and water buffaloes' milk.

Both ewes and goats give milk for delicious cheeses such as pecorino, Roquefort and Spanish manchego, while buffaloes' milk is a fine basis for mozzarella.

Soured milk products

It is the presence of living lactic acid bacteria in milk that makes it go sour. This used to be a real problem before pasteurization. Pasteurization, however, kills the lactic acid bacteria and now milk, if left, does not go sour but merely bad, so a souring culture must be introduced in order to achieve soured milk products.

Buttermilk

This used to be a favorite drink of farmers' children. It had a fresh, slightly acid flavor and was made from the liquid left over when butter was made on the farm. It was also used in cooking to activate the bicarbonate of soda that was used as a leavening agent in baking to give a soft, tender quality to cakes and scones. The buttermilk sold today is thicker than the farm variety and is made with a culture.

Yogurt

This is eaten as a dessert and is used extensively as a marinade for meat, in soups and salads, and even in cooked dishes. For the latter it must first be treated to prevent it separating.

Good yogurt is easily made at home with an earthenware bowl or yoghurt maker.

Commercially made yogurts are made by injecting a low-fat or skimmed milk with a culture of *lactobacillus bulgaricus, lactobacillus acidophilus* or *streptococcus thermophilus*. A combination of these strains produces the most acidic yogurts, often considered to have the best flavor.

Although only some yogurts are labelled "live," the only ones that are in fact not live are those that have been sterilized.

CREAM

Creams vary in thickness and richness according to the amount of butterfat present – the thicker the cream the more butterfat it contains and the richer it is.

The thickest cream is for spooning over strawberries, for syllabubs and for filling cakes, éclairs and so on, and is whipped for decorating cakes and puddings. Thin, light creams are ideal for soups and sauces, for pouring over puddings and desserts and for putting into coffee.

Whipping creams are usually used in soufflés, ice creams and mousses. A thin cream will not whip no matter how long you work at it, as there is not enough butterfat to trap the air bubbles, so buy heavy cream.

Whipped cream should be light, airy and about doubled in volume – a balloon or spiral whisk will achieve the best result. A blender is too fast and even a rotary whisk is too fierce. To achieve the right texture the cream, bowl and whisk should all be cold. A spoonful of cold milk or a crushed ice cube added to each $\frac{2}{3}$ cup/1.5 dl of cream as it thickens gives a lighter result, and if you add a little sugar to the cream the whipped result will not separate so easily.

As well as varying in texture cream can be fresh, which is the best for all purposes, sterilized, when it acquires an odd, flat, sweetish flavor, or treated to a version of UHT, when it has a long life but is not the best choice when flavor is important. Fresh cream will keep, refrigerated, for up to four days in summer and seven days in winter. In America some heavy creams will keep for several weeks. Some farms still deliver untreated cream to local stores.

Clotted cream
This is a specialty of the west of England, where great pans filled with milk are heated, cooked and then skimmed of their thick, wrinkled, creamy crust.

Crème fraîche or crème double
This French cream is treated with a special culture that helps it to stay fresh longer and gives it a lively though not exactly sour taste. It is this cream that is required when French recipes call for cream; A tablespoonful of buttermilk added to 2½ cups/6dl of cream – heavy whipping cream is best – and put in a warm place, between 75–85°F/24–29°C, for a few hours will produce the authentic taste.

Soured cream
Light or heavy cream treated with a souring culture is known as soured cream. It is sometimes sold by its Russian name smetana, and in that country it is served on borsch, salads and is used in marinades. Germany, Austria and Scandinavia include it in sauces, which it makes glossy and slightly acid. To make your own sour cream, add a few drops of lemon juice to fresh heavy cream.

BUTTER

Normandy butter, ivory colored and rich, is the most admired, especially the Norman butter of Issigny. Melted, it resembles cream. Spread on bread, its taste is sweet and nutty and its texture firm and smooth. There are no visible beads of water – if butter has a water content of more than 12 percent it will not cream well. When pressed it does not crumble and its aroma is delicate and mild.

For normal everyday use we tend to buy butter by brand name or by price, cheaper butters being the blended ones. Both for eating and cooking it is always better to buy a good-quality butter, since a low-grade butter can have such an overpowering flavor that it quite spoils fresh vegetables and delicate sauces. Buy only a week's supply at a time and take it out of the refrigerator about 15 minutes before using so that it loses its hardness. Rewrap what has not been used before replacing it and keep it well away from strong-smelling foods and soft fruits since butter absorbs these flavors.

Butter can either be salted or unsalted. Salting improves the keeping qualities of butter.

Unsalted butter has a much sweeter taste than salted butter. It makes an excellent table butter and is preferred in cooking.

Butter can be blended with a number of ingredients to make delicious garnishes and fillings for sandwiches.

There are also many types of butter sauces, including beurre blanc, sauce meunière and beurre noir.

The addition of a little oil will prevent butter burning when cooking but will also impair the buttery flavor, so the best butter for frying very delicate foods is clarified butter, from which all the milk solid deposits have been removed. This is the ghee used in India, but only for special occasions – less expensive vegetable ghee is used for everyday cooking. Clarified butter, however, no longer has the fresh taste that makes it so nice on vegetables.

To clarify butter, melt it in a small saucepan and cook it for a few moments over a gentle heat, without browning. When it separates, remove from the heat, allow to settle for 10 minutes and then strain into a bowl through a paper towel moistened with hot water and placed over a sieve. Store in the refrigerator.

Fresh cream butter
This can be salted or unsalted and is also known as sweet cream butter, made from unripened cream. The cream is pasteurized, deodorized and cooled before being placed in ageing tanks for at least 12 hours. Salt, which acts as a preservative, can be added during this time. American, British and New Zealand butters tend to be of this type.

CHEESES

If you want to enjoy cheese at its best, find a good cheese store where the cheeses are kept in good condition and allowed to ripen naturally – not in a refrigerated storeroom or cabinet.

Having found your dealer, buy only one or two types of cheese at a time, taking one generous cheese or piece of cheese in perfect condition, rather than all sorts of bits and pieces. Keep it, if possible, in a cool place such as a cellar, between 50° and 60°F/10° and 15°C, rather than in a refrigerator, with the cut surfaces covered and the crust free to breathe, but protected from flies. If no cool place is available, keep it loosely wrapped (in transparent wrap that allows the passage of air) in a large airtight container in the bottom of the refrigerator. Take the cheese out a good hour before you serve it, to give it time to recover, and do not leave it too long before you eat it.

The serving of cheese varies from country to country. In France it is generally served after the salad, which has then done its job of refreshing the palate, with crusty French bread and good unsalted butter, which sets off the subtlest cheese flavor and will not spoil the most delicate. (Some of the richer Normandy cheeses obviously don't need any butter at all.) The Burgundy or Bordeaux served with the main course is finished off and appreciated with the cheese.

In Britain cheese is either eaten plain and hearty as a whole meal, with a nice hunk of fresh bread, or if it is a serious dinner it is brought to the table at the end of the meal, after the pudding, and is traditionally accompanied by good port. There are usually homemade breads and water biscuits or some other neutral crackers on the table for those who want them, and, again, unsalted butter. A strong cheese may be served with walnuts or celery or perhaps with crisp apples.

When cooking with cheese, it is unwise to use up any old scraps or ends of moldy cheese. The best results are obtained by using the best cheese. a piece of good, mature farmhouse Cheddar will be worth any amount of cheap factory-made block cheese – and, whatever the manufacturers may say,

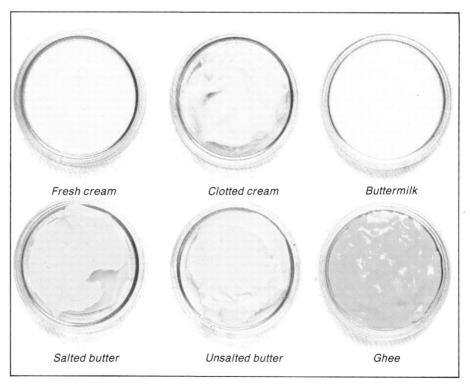

| Fresh cream | Clotted cream | Buttermilk |
| Salted butter | Unsalted butter | Ghee |

it is possible to tell the difference. Another thing to notice is the difference between cheeses made from pasteurized and unpasteurized milk. The unpasteurized cheese will go on developing and maturing because the milk that the cheese was made from was "alive," while pasteurized milk does not have the ability to develop the same subtle flavors and textures.

FRESH CHEESES

These are the simplest of all cheeses. They are made from the curds of soured milk or from milk that has been coagulated with the help of rennet – a curdling substance obtained from the stomachs of unweaned calves. They can also be made from whey, the thin liquid left over from cheese making. The milk used for making fresh cheese has often been skimmed of its fat content, but some fresh "cream" cheeses have a high fat content and make some of the world's most fattening desserts – cheesecake for one.

These cheeses used to be made on country or mountain farms from surplus milk or milk and cream, but are now usually mass produced in factories from pasteurized milk, and sadly in the process have become rather bland. Some fresh cheeses, however, are left to ripen and ferment for weeks or months, during which time they develop a characteristic bloom and an agreeable sharpness.

Curd or cottage cheese
Made from the curds of skimmed milk and therefore having a low fat content, this cheese is popular with people trying to lose weight. The curds are broken into different sizes and cream is sometimes added, in which case it becomes creamed cottage cheese. Its slightly acid taste makes it a refreshing accompaniment to a summer fruit salad. In Germany, where a version known as quark is popular, it is often mixed with fruit purées, while in Provence a similar homemade white cheese is traditionally eaten with tiny new potatoes cooked in their skins. American pot cheese is a cottage cheese made from a large curd with no salt, while Scottish crowdie, also a cottage cheese, is made from fresh sweet milk and butter.

Liptauer or Liptoi
Originally from Hungary, this ripened curd cheese is usually made from goats' or ewes' milk. It has a piquant taste and is delicious when blended with butter, seasoned with salt, paprika and caraway seeds and spread on rye bread.

Mysost and Gjetost
In Norway any cheese which has been made from thickening the whey after it has been separated from the prepared curd is known as Mysost. There are several varieties, but the most popular is Gjetost. It is cooked until it looks like fudge and has a sweet flavor.

Gomost
This Norwegian fresh cheese is made from soured, unsalted milk, and in France is known as Caillebotte. White and creamy, it is sometimes eaten with sugar or mixed with stewed or fresh ripe fruit.

Pultost
This is also a Norwegian curd cheese but is stiffer and harsher than Gomost. It is made from whey or butter-milk and caraway seeds are often added.

Ricotta
Traditionally made from the whey left over from making the Italian ewes'-milk pecorina cheese, this can also be made from the whey of other cheeses. Its dry, bland texture makes it ideal for mixing with fruit and raisins, or it can be eaten – as it is in Rome – with salt, or with cinnamon and suger. It is especially good used with Parmesan, spinach and chard to stuff ravioli.

Fromage blanc
One of the main ingredients of the delicate sauces of *Cuisine Minceur*, this popular French cheese is made from skimmed milk soured with a culture. An acceptable substitute can be made by combining equal parts of cottage cheese and yogurt with a squeeze of lemon juice and then whipping them in a food processor to a fine consistency. It is excellent with fresh raspberries or other berries.

Cream cheese
Rich and creamy, soft and mild, this cheese can be made from whole milk or a combination of whole milk and cream. It is delicious when mixed with chopped raw vegetables or nuts and raisins and is also an essential ingredient of American cheesecakes. In France a vast number of fresh cream cheeses are sold, with varying fat contents: *double crème*, *triple crème* and, when put into heart-shaped molds and drained, *coeur à la crème*, eaten with wild strawberries and powdered sugar.

Fontainebleau
Rarely available outside its native France, this cream cheese is made from a mixture of curd and whipped cream and is usually eaten with sugar. It can be made at home by blending demi-sel or Petit Suisse with whipped cream, but one is unlikely to produce the super-aerated result achieved by commercial manufacturers.

Petit Suisse
French in origin, but called Swiss because a French-employed Swiss dairyman is credited with its invention, this mild, light little cream cheese is delicious with fruit and excellent in any recipe where cream cheese is required.

Demi-sel
Small and square, soft and white, this wrapped cheese is sold under a number of brand names but is especially good when it has been made in Normandy, where it originated. It has a high fat content and, as its name implies, is slightly salted.

Neufchâtel
This whole cows'-milk cheese comes from Normandy. It is either eaten fresh, when it has the first growth of a soft white down and a delicate taste, or allowed to ripen until it is firm and pungent with a warm-colored, bloomy rind. It comes in a variety of shapes.

Mascapone
Made in Lombardy and Tuscany, this cheese is enjoyed all over Italy, where it is sold in muslin bags and eaten with fruit or sugar and cinnamon.

Mozzarella
This rubbery white cheese was originally made from water buffaloes' milk, but now cows' milk is often used; it is sold swimming in its own milk and is springy when fresh. It is served as an hors d'oeuvre in southern Italy, with olive oil and freshly ground pepper, and is ideal for cooking, being a traditional ingredient of pizza. Keep mozzarella fresh for days in a bowl of milky water in the lower part of the refrigerator.

Feta
Crumbly and salty, this is the best known of the white cheeses ripened in brine or salt and known as "pickled" cheeses. It was originally made from ewes' milk by shepherds in the mountain regions near Athens and is popular in Greek cooking, especially crumbled into salads with tomatoes, cucumbers, black olives and olive oil. It can be made less salty by soaking it in milky water.

HARD CHEESES

The word "hard," when applied to cheeses, means that they have been subjected to pressure to make them dense. They will be softer or firmer according to their age.

Hard cheeses develop their various characteristics according to the milk used and the methods by which they are made. The speed of coagulation, the way the curd is cut, and whether the curd is then left or cut again, all affect the taste and texture, as does the treatment the cheese receives during the ripening process.

Some of these cheeses are derivations of more famous originals, but while some remain copies, others have developed a character of their own and deserve to be thought of as cheeses in their own right.

Grana cheeses
The hard, grainy cheeses known collectively as grana are the well-known Italian grating cheeses, familiar to anyone who has ever eaten a plate of pasta or a bowl of minestrone soup. Their slow ageing process and low moisture content give them their long-keeping qualities and their crumbly texture. The young grana cheeses are more delicate and are delicious when broken in chunks and eaten accompanied by white wine.

Parmesan
More correctly, Parmigiano-Reggiano, this, the most famous and expensive of all the granas, is sweet and fragrant. It keeps for years, growing harder and fuller as it ages. When young, it can be eaten at the end of meals; it is an essential ingredient of many of the best and most characteristic northern

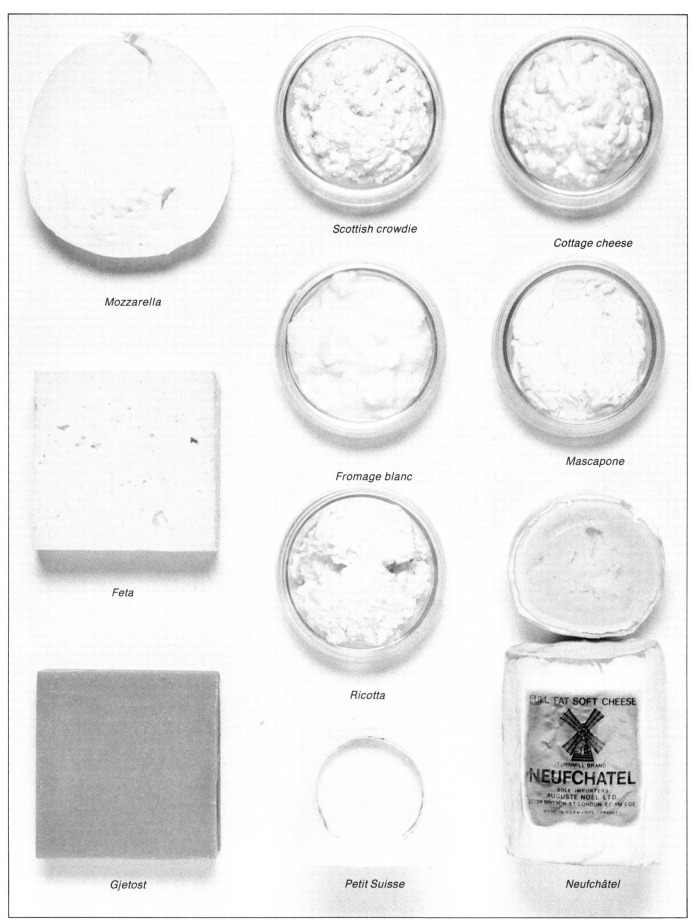

Mozzarella

Scottish crowdie

Cottage cheese

Fromage blanc

Mascapone

Feta

Ricotta

Gjetost

Petit Suisse

FULL FAT SOFT CHEESE

TURNMILL BRAND
NEUFCHATEL
SOLE IMPORTERS
AUGUSTE NOEL LTD.
27/39 BRITTON ST LONDON EC1M 5QE
MADE IN NORMANDY FRANCE

Neufchâtel

Italian dishes, and is grated and then scattered on top of soups and pasta.

When buying Parmesan, the name Parmigiano-Reggiano burned in dots on the rind is proof of authenticity. The cheese should be straw colored and brittle, with pinpoint holes that are scarcely visible but give it a rocky surface. It should never be grey, sweaty or waxy, and should always smell fresh. It is possible to buy ground Parmesan, but it will be a poor substitute for fresh.

Pecorino
This is the name given to grana cheeses made from ewes' milk, which are used in much the same way as Parmesan. A pecorino is round, hard and white, with a yellow crust when mature (except for that made in Siena, which is red). The taste is strong, pungent and salty, and there are many varieties which often go by the names of the districts in which they are made. Pecorino Romano is the original variety and is still considered to be the best.

Grana Padano
This is made in the Po valley and since it is cheaper than true Parmesan is often used in cooking.

Sbrinz
This ancient and splendid Swiss cheese is equal in virtue (although distinct from) Parmesan. Its texture is granular and brittle and it has an uneven surface with pinprick holes. In central Switzerland it is often shaved in thin slivers and served with a glass of wine. It is also ideal for cooking.

Schabzieger
Also known as green cheese, or in America as sapsago, this is a hard, truncated little green cone. Made from skimmed cows' milk, it ferments naturally and is mixed with pulverized blue melilot, or sweet clover, which gives it its green color and characteristic pungent flavor. It smells of coriander or cumin, and is used as a condiment for a variety of dishes.

CHEDDAR-TYPE CHEESES
These are the real grass-root cheeses, made and eaten all over the world and used indiscriminately in recipes that call for cheese.

English Cheddar
No hard cheese has been more widely imitated than English Cheddar, which originated in the small town of Cheddar, in Somerset, and was well established by the sixteenth century. It is a splendid all-purpose cheese, good to eat and to cook with. It has a sweet, full flavor when young and mild, and a sharp nutty flavor (often referred to as "tasty") when mature.

Mature English farmhouse Cheddars, still made on some farms and ripened for months or years, are among the world's greatest cheeses. They compress more than ten times their weight of creamy milk when pressed into a cylindrical form and wrapped in a cloth, which may then be waxed. A

traditional Cheddar weighs about 50–60lb/ 22.5–27kg, while small, whole Cheddars, known as truckles, usually weigh about 14lb/ 6kg. English Cheddar is also made in large blocks, but these do not develop and mature like the traditional aged cheeses.

Small Cheddars of various shapes are made outside England, but may vary widely from the true Cheddar flavor. In New York state, the home of the first Cheddar-cheese factory in America, a number of Cheddars are still made in varying sizes. Wisconsin, Oregon and Vermont are also known for the quality of their Cheddars, but these, and most other Cheddars, like the Australian and New Zealand varieties, are made from pasteurized milk and lack the authentic taste of the English farmhouse variety. Canadian Cheddar, however, which is still sometimes made of unpasteurized milk, may have the

Parmigiano-Reggiano

Pecorino Romano

English Farmhouse Cheddar

Cheshire

Caerphilly

Double Gloucester

characteristic tangy, nutty flavor. Look for Belleville-Brockville Cheddar (in a plain waxed cloth), or Black Diamond (with a black waxed surface).

Cantal
Sometimes called the French Cheddar, Cantal has a smooth texture and, if the truth be told, a duller flavor than Cheddar. It is large, hard and yellow and is made in cylindrical forms, to which it may owe its old name, "fourme de Cantal." Cantal can be good if allowed to mature – it takes as long to ripen as Cheddar.

Cheshire
Usually known as "Chester" abroad, and well liked under this name in France and Italy, this is the oldest of the British cheeses. It is crumbly, nutty and salty and can be red, white or blue. The red, which is dyed with anatto and is a marigold-orange, makes excellent eating as well as first-class soufflés. It is fat and rich, with a special piquancy that is also to be found in the white and blue varieties. The white variety, which is in fact a pale cream, is sharper than the red. It ripens faster but does not keep so well. The blue Cheshire is farmhouse made, and there is also an accidental blue Cheshire, which can start either white or red and is called, rather confusingly, Green Fade.

Gloucester
This hard, robust English cheese originated in Gloucestershire and is now made in Somerset. It used to be made in two sizes – the well-matured double and the thinner and milder single – but only the large Double Gloucester survives. In taste it lies between Cheddar and Cheshire, although there is none of Cheshire's crumble about it. Farmhouse Gloucester, with its natural hard crust, should not be darker than straw colored. It is a good cooking cheese and makes delicious cheese straws.

Caerphilly
One of the mildest, softest, crumbliest and fastest-ripening of the British hard cheeses, this was once known as the Welsh miners' cheese because it was the favorite ingredient of their packed lunch. But the best Caerphilly today is made on Somerset farms. Made of skimmed milk, it is slightly sour and is eaten rather immature. Its melting quality makes it suitable for dishes calling for a mild cheese flavor.

Wensleydale
This is similar to Stilton in shape but smaller. White, moist and flaky, it has a delicately sour buttermilk flavor.

Leicester
The largest English cheese in circumference, Leicester is a rich orange color and shaped like a millstone. It is mild and nutty, moist and flaky, and very different from Cheddar in texture and flavor, since the curd is shredded rather than milled into knobs. It is ideal for cheese sauce.

Sage Derby
Once made for eating at harvest suppers, this farmhouse cheese is a sage-flavored version of plain Derby, which is similar to Cheddar but closer textured and more distinct in flavor. It should be aged for at least nine months and be mottled with natural-looking sage-green streaks, but at its worst it is heavily marbled with a vivid green, is artificial in taste and too waxy in texture to even recall the real thing.

Vermont sage cheese is a similar cheese, spicy and succulent.

Gouda-type cheeses
Firm and fat, these familiar round cheeses become drier and sharper with age. Flavored with cumin or caraway seeds, they are good with rye bread and wine.

Gouda
Made in the town of Gouda, outside Amsterdam, this is the archetypal Dutch cheese. It

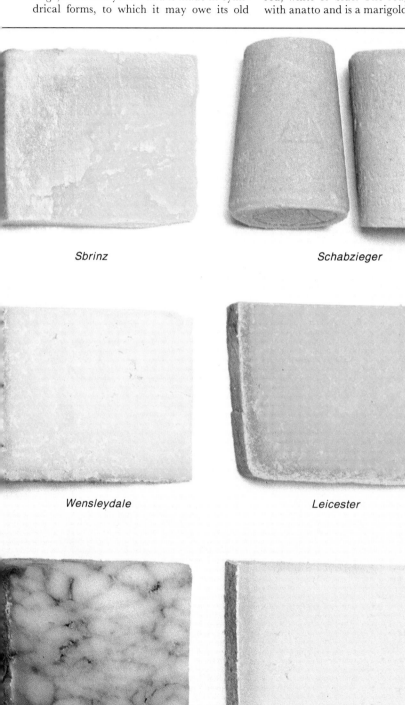

Sbrinz

Schabzieger

Wensleydale

Leicester

Sage Derby

Cantal

is creamy, golden and flattish, with a yellow paraffin-waxed protective skin. A mature Gouda will be more pungent than a youthful one. A black skin indicates that it is seven or more years old, when it becomes known as an Alt Gouda. Gouda étuve has been subjected to a prolonged maturing period or to artificially accelerated ripening. It is a simple eating cheese, which in its native Holland appears for breakfast, and in the kitchen it is fried with potatoes, grated into sauces and melted to make a type of fondue.

Edam
Made from partially skimmed milk, Edam, encased in bright red or yellow livery for the export market, has a lower fat content than Gouda and is less smooth and round flavored. When young it tends to be boring, but once aged and ripened it acquires a rather pleasant mellowness.

Mimolette
This is similar to Edam but bright orange inside, turning a rich red with age. The best Mimolettes are aged for up to two years, look like cannon balls dug up from an Armada wreck and when chipped away at have a glorious rich flavor, but most are young and flabby.

Leyden
Resembling Gouda, this cheese has a sharp, tangy flavor. It is usually flavored with caraway seeds, but varieties with cloves and cumin are also available. It is branded with the crossed keys of the arms of the Dutch city of Leyden.

Gruyère-type cheeses
Reminiscent of alpine meadows, these cheeses range from mild flavored to a rich, full nuttiness. Straw yellow in color, characterized by holes caused by gas forming during ripening, they are the cheeses most popular with French cooks who appreciate their melting qualities, so well suited to the making of gratins and sauces.

Gruyère
This Swiss cheese is made of cows' milk and has a fairly smooth rind. Ivory-yellow with tiny pinprick holes spaced far apart, it should have a waxy rather than a velvety surface. It is a main ingredient of the classic cheese fondue because of its fine melting qualities, and is also often served after a meal with grapes, figs or pears.

Comté
Made in the Franche-Comté, this is a first cousin to Gruyère. The best "fruitiest" cheeses are made in village one-man dairies, or fruitières, to which the village farmers bring their milk, and can be identified by a green oval plaque on the outside of the whole cheese. These cheeses often have almost no holes at all, and are matured in the Franche-Comté itself.

Emmental
This is the famous cheese with the large holes. It comes in huge, shiny golden wheels and its ivory-colored paste is riddled with bubbles, which form during its fermentation and cooling period. It has a sweet flavor that grows fuller with age and is excellent for eating and cooking.

Fontina
Made in the Piedmont area of Italy and also in Switzerland, this is a fat, rich, softish cheese. Experts recommend the Swiss version as a table cheese and the Italian one for cooking. It melts beautifully and is used for Piedmontese fonduta, a fondue served with sliced white truffles.

Appenzell
A Swiss relation of Emmental, washed in a mixture of white wine and brine, this makes a tasty element in a fondue when young. Mature, it is firm but buttery with a rich, sweet flavor.

Jarlsberg
This popular Norwegian cheese is similar to Emmental but milder and more rubbery. Its taste is slightly nutty.

SEMI-HARD CHEESES
These cheeses, some of which resemble Cheddar, are characterized by their firm but elastic feel. They are sometimes soft and tender, but, unlike truly soft cheese, do not become runny as they mature.

Cacciocavallo
Made from cows' milk, this is often smoked. An ivory-white cheese with a golden-yellow to grey rind, it is sold in pairs joined by a string and is usually eaten at the end of a meal. It is one of the pasta filata, or drawn curd cheeses, so named because they are stretched into strands in hot water during their making.

Provolone
There are two main types of Provolone: a pasta filata, or drawn curd cows-milk cheese *dolce*, which is young and usually dull, and *piccante*, sometimes available from good Italian delicatessens, which is sharp, strong and often very salty, but a good cheese. It is sometimes smoked, and is molded by hand into various shapes.

Monterey Jack
The pale California cheese, with small interior holes, comes in various shapes and degrees of softness. When it has a high moisture content and is quite soft, it is often called Jack, while the harder grating varieties are called Monterey.

Colby
This cheese of Wisconsin origin is similar to Cheddar but has a more open texture. It is a soft, mild, bland cheese and does not keep so well as Cheddar.

Tilsit
German in origin, this yellow cheese is pungent with a slight smear to its surface. It is sometimes made with caraway seeds.

Danbo and Samsoe
These firm, nutty cheeses are the national standbys of Denmark, just as Cheddar is the standby of Britain. (Samsoe is named after the island where it is made).

Manchego
Made in Spain, the cheese has a high fat content, can be made from cows' or ewes' milk and is matured for up to three years, sometimes spending a year ripening in olive oil. It may be white or yellow, with or without eyes, and varies widely in taste.

SOFT CHEESES
The characteristic flavour of the creamy white soft cheeses comes fron bacterial growths, which begin at the outer edges of the cheese and move into the center. A ripe cheese will be soft at the center and can be tested by pressing lightly around the middle with the fingers. The bloomy white rinds are also a result of bacterial growth, natural in farm or artisan production, where the mold is established in the ripening premises, or induced in many factory-made cheeses by penicillin sprayed onto the crust. (In cheeses with a russet mold, which have a washed crust, the same applies).

These cheeses are considered ready for eating when they are soft, with a bulge in the middle of the cut surface but no trace of runniness. Any smell of ammonia indicates that the cheese is past its best. Soft cheeses are delicious on French bread. The most famous varieties come from Normandy, which has some of the best pastures producing the richest, creamiest milk in the world (although Normandy farmers say artificial fertilizers are changing the quality of this wonderful milk).

Camembert
A farmhouse Camembert is made from raw milk, while the more common factory-produced Camembert is always made fron pasteurized milk. The best Camemberts are from Normandy, and are made in rounds weighing 8-9 oz/225-255g. Camembert is also available in half moons and in portions, but unfortunately is only reliable if ripened as a whole cheese: proportion and thickness of crust and consistency of the interior are all affected by alteration of size or shape before ripening. A really fine Camembert is never chalky.

Brie
A whole round, flat Brie usually measures 14 in/35.5 cm across and is sold in wedges. The unliquefied part in the center of a ripe Brie is important and is called "the soul of the Brie." Farmhouse Brie, known as Brie de Meaux fermier, is the creamiest variety and has a bouquet that is full and mild. (Nowadays Bries are mainly produced in factories and there are many imitations, but obtain unpasteurized farmhouse Brie from Normandy should you ever get the chance.) The Brie de Melun affiné, a smaller cheese, is one of the finest of all.

Pont-l'Evêque
This cheese is square, soft and fat, with a shiny golden or reddish salty rind and warm farmyard taste. It should always have Pays d'Auge and *lait cru* or, alternatively,

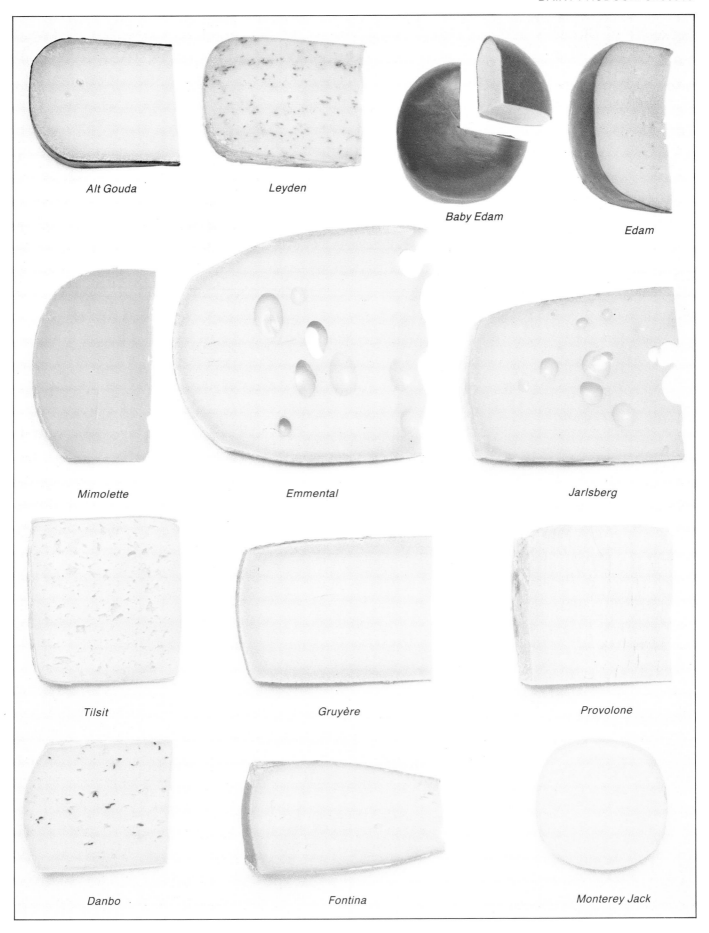

Alt Gouda

Leyden

Baby Edam

Edam

Mimolette

Emmental

Jarlsberg

Tilsit

Gruyère

Provolone

Danbo

Fontina

Monterey Jack

non-pasteurisé stamped somewhere on the wrapping paper or box, proving that it comes from unpasteurized milk.

Livarot

This cheese, still made at its place of origin and elsewhere in the Pays d'Auge, is round, weighs about 1 lb/450 g and is about twice the depth of a Pont l'Evêque. It has a thicker crust and, although it is obviously of the same family, quite a distinct flavor. Traditionally it is bound with five strips of raffia-like leaf or paper.

Vacherin

Usually banded with spruce bark, which not only saves it from collapse but also gives it a faint aroma of resin. Vacherin is a seasonal cheese, made in winter by the Comté-producing farms when there isn't enough milk, or transport is too difficult to produce the Comté they make in summer. Slice it like a Brie with a very sharp knife to cut the bark, as the outside crust is delicious and should not be wasted.

Maroilles

Square and strong smelling, this comes from Flanders and is ripened for up to four months, with much crust-washing. It is

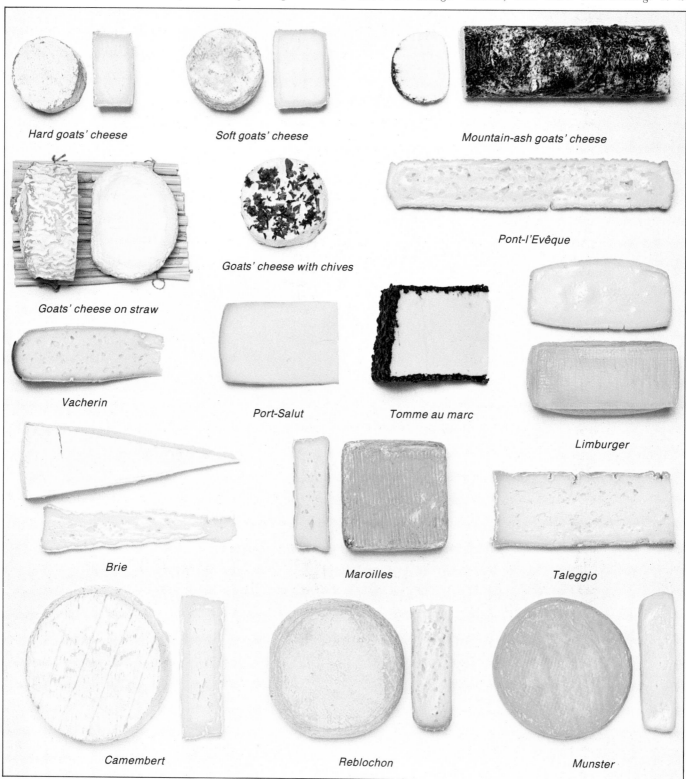

Hard goats' cheese

Soft goats' cheese

Mountain-ash goats' cheese

Goats' cheese on straw

Goats' cheese with chives

Pont-l'Evêque

Vacherin

Port-Salut

Tomme au marc

Limburger

Brie

Maroilles

Taleggio

Camembert

Reblochon

Munster

delicious with a full-bodied wine and is used to make *goyére* and *flamiche*, the cheese pies peculiar to Flanders.

Reblochon
This fine cheese from Savoy is smooth and creamy with a pinkish-gold crust and a strong farmyard flavor.

Port-Salut
Also called Port au Salut – haven of rest – after the Trappist abbey where it was first made, this is a velvety smooth whole-milk cheese, semi-soft or semi-hard, and mildly pungent. One variety is still made by the monks under the name of Fermiers-Réunis at their Champagne dairy from the unpasteurized milk of their cows. Commercial Port-Salut, made by a farmers' cooperative at Entrammes, is a more rubbery and less tasty affair, as is the Bricquebec – a similar cheese made in the monastic dairy.

Taleggio
Made from whole cows' milk, this comes from Lombardy in Italy. It has a smooth pink skin with a straw-colored interior, and is fruity in flavor.

Munster
Originating in the Vosges, this is the national cheese of Alsace. Its paste is firm and its ring red and smooth. It has a pungent smell and flavor, and is traditionally eaten with rye bread, caraway seeds and chopped onions.

Limburger
The cheese may take the form of a log, a corrugated roll or a little disc or blob and has a moist, pale rind and an overpowering smell. It is an acquired taste and should be eaten with robust country bread.

Liederkranz
Rather like a non-odorous Limburger, this gold crusted, tawny cheese is America's best soft cheese.

Bel Paese
This is the trade name for a soft, cream-colored cheese of which there are many local and factory-made variations throughout Italy. It is tender and mild.

Tommes
This is the family name of a large number of rustic cheeses, made of ewes', goats' or cows' milk in almost any shape. The Tommes are from Savoy, all along the southern mountain ranges of France and in the east of Switzerland. Tomme au Marc is coated in fermented grape "marc" – made from the pressed skins and seeds of grapes left over from wine-making, which gives it its characteristic taste, while Tomme de Sovoie has a nutty flavor.

Saint Nectaire
A mountain cheese from the Auvergne, this is a round, flat cheese with a dark rind and a soft, supple but not creamy, straw-colored inside. It has a nice light flavor.

Epoisses
A very smelly cows'-milk cheese from Burgundy, this is cylindrical and reddish on the outside, and soft, oozy and rich inside

with a strong earthy taste. It is traditionally aged in brine and marc.

Soumaintrain
Like Epoisses, this flat, round cheese comes from Burgundy. It is semi-soft with a sticky red-brown crust, a strong smell and an earthy taste.

Chaource
Is one of those small, deep, white, downy, luxurious-looking cheeses that give a fresh note to an otherwise heavy meal. It has a faintly acid, fruity flavor and a velvety rather than creamy texture.

GOATS' CHEESES
There are infinite varieties of goats' cheeses, of which the vast majority are simply described as "chèvres" and have no distinguishing names. They are made on small farms and dairies all over France and throughout the Mediterranean, and are usually known as "frais" or "mi-frais," which means fresh; "affiné," which has been matured and should be velvety, occasionally creamy and fairly soft; and "vieux," which is well aged and varies from soft and creamy to rock hard. They should not be chalky or soapy – this may be a sign that they have been refrigerated.

The flavors of goats' cheeses vary according to the ripening period, the locality and altitude, which have a bearing on the taste and quality of the milk, and the different mold cultures, which affect flavor and texture. But in general goats' cheeses, whether strong or mild, should taste nutty and sweet with a goaty piquancy. Some are flavored with chives or garlic and other fresh herbs, while others are rolled in mountain ash. Some goat cheeses are sold sitting on the straw mat on which they have been drained. These are delicious tasting and have a distinct country flavor.

BLUE CHEESES
Blue cheeses originally started to turn blue by a happy accident. Roquefort, the ancestral blue cheese, was, at first, just a humble curd cheese made of ewes' milk, and had it not been for a lovelorn shepherd who, as legend has it, set off in pursuit of a country girl, leaving his luncheon cheese in a limestone cave, the blue mold might never have happened. However, returning after a week or so of dalliance, the shepherd found that his lunch had changed in texture, color and taste and become "blue." Since that time, the penicillin molds that turn cheese blue have been isolated and identified, and blue cheeses have multiplied. The cheese's paste itself may be firm or creamy, buttery or brittle, and any color from chalk white to deep golden-yellow. The only thing that the paste of a blue cheese should never be is brown and dingy.

Roquefort
The veining of Roquefort, a ewes'-milk cheese, is due to *Penicillium glaucum* – now

better known as *Penicillium roquefortii* – which thrives in the caves high upon the Cambalou plateau. These ancient caves, cool and damp owing to underground springs, are still used for maturing Roquefort. The blue veining is now accelerated by layering the curd with crumbled bread molds, but even so, the ripening process still takes about three months, and the cheese will not be at its best until it is at least six months old.

A Roquefort in its prime is creamy, with green-blue veins. Persillé – parsleyed – is the French term. It is smooth, firm and buttery when cut, but crumbly owing to the mold, which should be evenly distributed. It is strong, with the fine grain and the extra pungency that ewes' milk produces. It should not, however, be salty – although those for export tend to be over-salted as a precaution against spoiling.

Bleu de Corse
Is a cheese made by Corsican shepherds and sent to the Roquefort caves to become blue and to mature. It is similar to Roquefort in taste.

Gorgonzola
Once exclusive to the Italian village of that name, the cheese is now produced all over the lush plain of Lombardy. The squat, cylindrical cheeses, made of cows' milk, are no longer matured in the local caves but in the great maturing houses in the district. *Penicillium mycelium* accounts for the streaking. Although Gorgonzola is often described as an early copy of Roquefort, it is softer, milder, creamier and less salty. It should have very little rind, being wrapped in foil, and should be rather smooth and blue-grey. The cheese should be springy to the touch. It may smell a little musty, but should never be overpowering. Other Italian blues include the creamy factory-made Dolcelatte and Mountain Gorgonzola, which is smaller than a true Gorgonzola.

Pipo Crème
This cylindrical cheese was first produced as a counter-attraction to Gorgonzola but has a quite distinct character.

Danish Blue
Similar to Roquefort but is made with cows' milk, this cheese can be cylindrical, rectangular or square, and is white with blue veins. It has a high fat content and the saltiness inevitable in this type of cheese.

Bresse Bleu
A French cheese similar to Gorgonzola, this soft blue cheese comes from the Bresse region, which also produces a more stodgy blue called, confusingly, Bleu de Bresse, another stodgy one called France Bresse, and most recently Belle Bressane, with a hole in the middle.

Torta di Gordenza
Also marketed as Gorgonzola con Mascapone, this is a cheese made from layers of piquant Gorgonzola and fresh Mascapone – a delicious combination, like fresh clotted cream.

Bleu de Causses

This is a cheese of high quality, somewhat similar to Roquefort, coming from the same region and having the same mold, but made with cows' milk.

Fourme d'Ambert

A naturally blued cows'-milk cheese, this is from the Auvergne. It is exceptional in being almost the only non-English blue cheese to have a hard crust, which is grey flecked with yellow and red. It comes in cylinders weighing about 3 lb/1.5 kg and is sharp and strong.

Stilton

One of the very few English foods to be admired by the French, this is a highly protected cheese made only in Derbyshire, Leicestershire and parts of Nottinghamshire. Although a noble cheese, Stilton is a comparative latecomer and in fact was never made at Stilton, but it was there, at the Bell Inn in the eighteenth century, that it was first served. It should be a creamy ivory color with greenish-blue veining throughout. The paste should be open textured, velvety and never dry, hard or salty.

Stilton is served with a white napkin wrapped around it, and should be stored wrapped in cloth. Should the cheese become dry in spite of this, it helps to moisten the cloth and to leave it until the dampness restores the cheese's proper consistency.

Blue Wensleydale

Among the other English blue cheeses is Blue Wensleydale (now made in Derbyshire). Claimed by its admirers to be even better than Stilton, it should be creamier, sweeter and nuttier, but is nowadays not as soft as it should be.

Dorset Blue

Is a hard white cheese with bright blue veining. It is made of skimmed milk, which makes it agreeably sharp.

RECIPE SUGGESTIONS

Swiss fondue

1¼ lb/565 g Emmental or Emmental and Gruyère mixed, grated
2 cloves garlic
1 glass dry white wine
1 teaspoon flour, preferably potato flour
freshly ground black pepper
pinch of nutmeg
1 small glass kirsch
1 drop corn oil
plenty of French bread cut in quarters lengthwise and then cut in 1 in/2.5 cm cubes

SERVES 6

Peel and crush a clove of garlic and rub the chafing dish with it. Pour the wine into the dish and add the remaining clove of garlic, peeled. Heat the wine gently and add the grated cheese, sprinkled with the teaspoon of potato flour to ensure a smooth finish. Stir with a wooden spoon and add a little more wine if it seems too thick. When the cheese has melted to a cream, add a pinch of pepper, the nut-meg and the kirsch with the corn oil in it.

Carry the dish to the table and place it over a gentle burner. When the fondue begins to bubble, the guests can start dipping their bread into it on the end of their forks. Twist the forks around to prevent the cheese dropping off in long strings. When the bottom starts to make a crust, those who like it can scrape this up with their spoons. Turn the heat down to prevent it burning.

Special fondue sets include long-handled forks, a stoneware or enamelled iron chafing dish to hold the cheese and a little burner to keep the cheese hot and bubbling. If you don't have one of these, you might improvise with a candle warmer. Traditionally white wine is drunk with fondue, or hot, unsweetened tea as an aid to digestion—never cold water.

Toasted blue cheese

½ lb/225 g Stilton or other blue cheese
4 thick slices very fresh white or dark bread, crusts removed (walnut bread is delicious)
butter for spreading
1 large teaspoon hot mustard
freshly ground pepper
2 teaspoons red wine or ale (optional)

SERVES 4

Heat the broiler.

Make 4 rounds of thick, tender toast, butter them well, spread with mustard and season with pepper. Place them in an ovenproof dish. Slice the cheese thinly and distribute it over the toast. If you like, sprinkle the cheese with red wine or ale. Place under a moderate broiler until the cheese has melted and is piping hot. Serve at once.

The old-fashioned Welsh way of serving this dish was to put a layer of cold roast beef, spread with mustard and horseradish, under Stilton cheese and to sprinkle, or rather saturate, the cheese with ale and shallot vinegar, which sounds like heavy eating but must have been delicious.

Stilton soufflé

5 oz/140 g Stilton or other blue cheese
½ stick/55 g butter
6 tablespoons/45 g flour
1¼ cups/3 dl milk
pinch of salt
cayenne pepper
4 eggs and 1 extra egg white

SERVES 4

Preheat the oven to 400°F/200°C.

Melt the butter in a saucepan. Stir in the flour and let it cook gently for a minute or two, then add the milk gradually, stirring gently until you have a smooth, thick sauce. Let it cook over a low heat for several minutes, stirring frequently to prevent it sticking to the bottom of the pan.

Crumble the Stilton into the sauce and let it melt. Stilton is often quite salty so taste the sauce before adding salt. Season quite highly with cayenne pepper and allow to cool slightly. Separate the eggs and beat the yolks into the sauce one at a time.

Butter a 2 quart/1.75 liter soufflé dish. Whisk the egg whites until they hold their shape and stand up stiffly on the end of the whisk. Stir a tablespoon of beaten egg white into the sauce to make it a little lighter, then fold the mixture thoroughly into the rest of the egg whites. Spoon the mixture lightly into the soufflé dish and cook for 20–25 minutes until well risen but still moist. Serve immediately.

Gorgonzola

Stilton

Danish Blue

Mozzarella in carrozza

6 oz/170 g Mozzarella cheese, in 4 slices
8 slices white bread, crusts removed
8 anchovy fillets (optional)
3 eggs
salt
oil for frying

SERVES 4

Cut each slice of cheese and each slice of bread in half. Make eight sandwiches with the bread and cheese, and you can add an anchovy fillet to each. Beat the eggs in a bowl with a pinch of salt. Heat the oil. Dip each sandwich into the beaten egg, immerse in the hot oil and fry until golden, turning them over as they fry so that they brown on both sides. Drain on a paper towel and sprinkle with salt. Serve very hot.

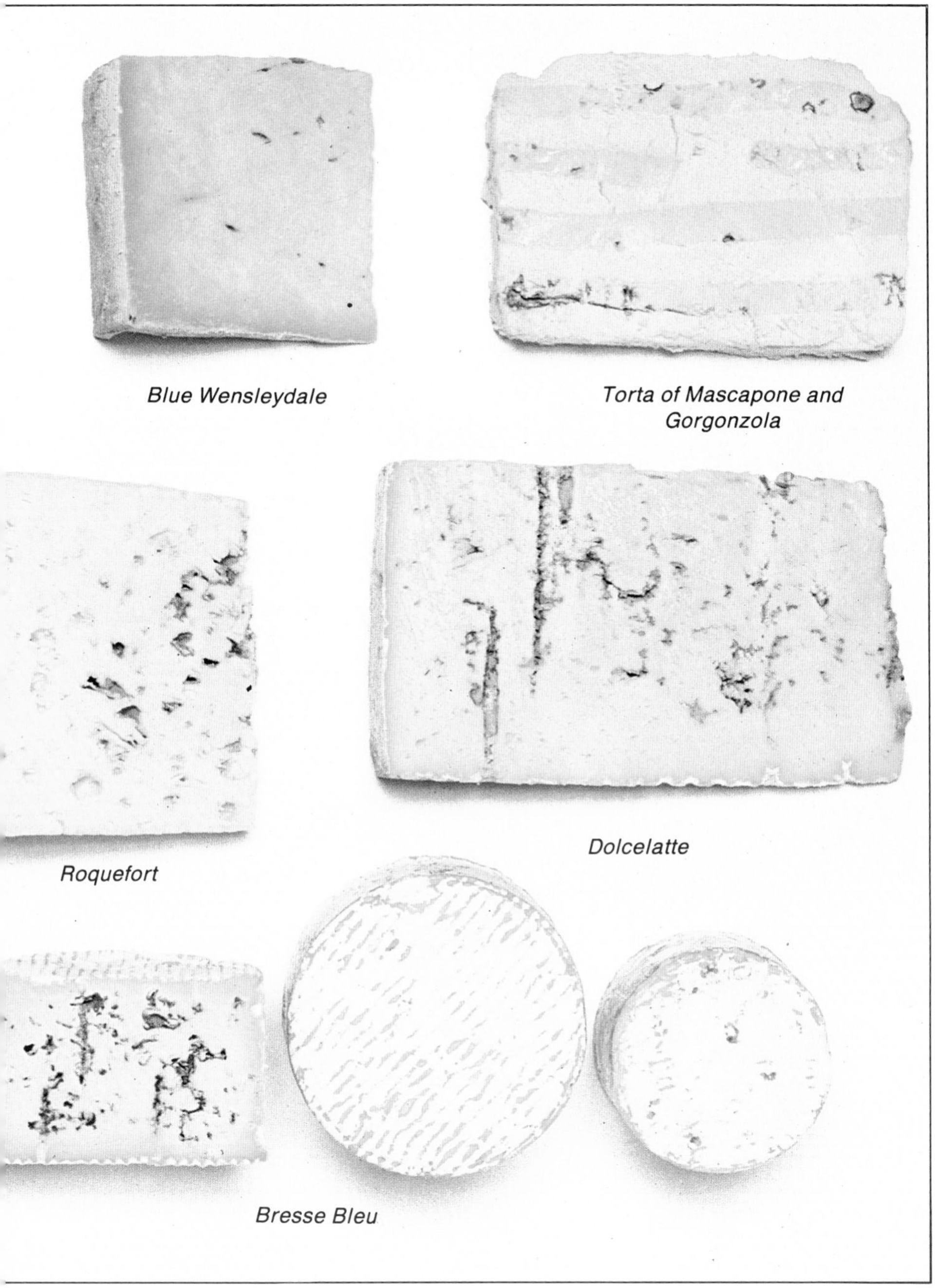

Blue Wensleydale

Torta of Mascapone and Gorgonzola

Roquefort

Dolcelatte

Bresse Bleu

Cheese straws

¼ lb/115 g Cheddar cheese, finely grated
puff pastry made with 2 cups/115 g flour
1 teaspoon curry powder

MAKES 20

Preheat the oven to 375°F/190°C.

Roll out the pastry fairly thinly into a square. Scatter half of the square lavishly with the cheese and season with half the curry powder. Fold the other half of the pastry over the top and roll out lightly. Scatter with the rest of the cheese and curry powder, fold and roll again and cut in strips. Twist the strips and bake for 15–20 minutes until well risen and golden brown. Serve hot.

This is a good way of using up any trimmings of puff pastry left from making pies.

Croque monsieur

¼ lb/115 g Emmental cheese, in 4 slices
8 thinly cut slices light white bread
butter for spreading
4 thin slices best ham

SERVES 4

Heat the broiler.

Butter the bread, cover 4 of the slices with ham, then cover the ham with a layer of cheese. Make sandwiches by covering with the remaining pieces of bread and toast both sides under a hot broiler.

ALTERNATIVE: *fry the sandwiches on both sides until golden, in a mixture of oil and butter. Croque monsieur makes a splendid quick lunch or supper.*

Cauliflower au gratin

1 large cauliflower, broken into flowerets
½ stick/55 g butter
¼ cup/30 g flour
2 cups/4.5 dl milk
½ cup/1.5 dl light cream
¾ cup/85 g Emmental, Gruyère or Parmesan, freshly grated
salt and freshly ground pepper
½ cup/55 g fresh white bread crumbs

SERVES 4–6

Cook the cauliflower in boiling salted water for 8–10 minutes, drain and keep hot. Make a good mornay sauce with half the butter, the flour, milk, cream and most of the cheese—it should be fairly thin but creamy. Season with salt and pepper. Heat the broiler.

Fry the bread crumbs, sprinkled with a little salt, in the remaining butter until they are nicely browned and crisp. Add the cauliflower, mix it around until every piece is coated with the fried bread crumbs, and put it all in a gratin dish. Pour the sauce around the cauliflower, sprinkle with the rest of the cheese and brown under the broiler.

Celery and Parmesan salad

1 head fresh celery
½ cup/55 g fresh softish Parmesan in a piece
4 tablespoons olive oil
juice of ½ lemon (optional)
salt and freshly ground pepper

SERVES 6

Wash the celery and cut it into fine crescents. Slice the Parmesan into the thinnest possible flakes—if they are very large, break them up a bit. Mix the celery and Parmesan in a bowl, dress with olive oil only, or with olive oil and a squeeze of lemon juice. Season lightly with salt, add plenty of pepper and serve as a separate course after roast veal or pork, or as an hors d'oeuvre.

Cheesecake

for the crust:
1½ cups/225 g graham cracker crumbs
1 stick/115 g butter, melted
¼ teaspoon each nutmeg and cinnamon
3 tablespoons/45 g sugar

for the filling:
½ lb/225 g cream cheese
2 tablespoons sour cream or heavy cream
2 tablespoons sugar, vanilla sugar if possible
2 eggs
juice of ½ lemon
⅓ cup/55 g sultanas

SERVES 4–6

Pound the graham cracker crumbs to powder and mix with the melted butter, spices and sugar. Line a well-buttered 8 in/20 cm spring-sided pan by patting this mixture over the bottom and up the sides into a firm layer. Chill in the refrigerator until the butter is set. Preheat the oven to 350°F/180°C.

Beat the cream cheese, add the sour or heavy cream and the sugar, then the eggs one at a time, beating continually. Finally add the lemon juice and sultanas. Pour the mixture into the firm crust and bake for 20 minutes.

Allow to cool and then chill for 1–2 hours in the refrigerator before carefully removing the cheesecake from the pan.

COOKING FATS AND OILS

Every cook in the world uses fat or oil of some kind as a cooking medium. In cool northern regions the fats from grass- and grain-fed animals are traditionally used, while in the hot Mediterranean countries, where the blessed olive tree grows, olive oil is the essential ingredient. Other regions may use goose fat or pork fat, mustard seed oil or grapeseed oil, sesame oil or walnut oil, each giving its distinctive flavor to the local dishes. The Chinese use peanut oil which is often flavored with fresh ginger.

Corn oil

Olive oil

Greek olive oil

Virgin olive oil

Today, the limitations of climate count for far less than they used to and we can obtain and cook with almost any medium we choose. But the flavor of food depends very much on what fat or oil is used, and a good cook will always try to use the right medium for the right dish in order to keep the flavor as authentic as possible.

Unfortunately, the amount of fat, whether animal or vegetable, in our Western diets has come under major criticism from doctors and nutritionists. Not only do we get our chief source of energy from fats that are an "invisible" part of most foods, but we are all too likely to load up on rich fats in the form of butter, lard and oils. While vegetable fats, unlike the traditionally suspect animal fats, contain no cholesterol, the cook should use either type only as part of a well-balanced diet that includes plenty of fibrous, non-fatty foods such as vegetables and fruit.

FATS

To the cook, fats are for the most part of animal origin and are either purchased, or collected at home from a roasting joint and then left to solidify. It is this quality of solidifying naturally that distinguishes fats from oils. However, vegetable oils can now be solidified by various chemical processes, so we have solid blocks of vegetable fats at our disposal as well as animal fats, and very often margarines and shortenings are a blend of the two.

Margarines

All margarines are based on fats and oils, and most contain skimmed milk or whey. Many contain animal fats together with fish and vegetable oils, unless the label specifically reads "edible vegetable oils" as opposed to simply "edible oils."

The taste and texture of margarine differ slightly according to brand but, with the exception of the all-important flavor, its characteristics in the kitchen are somewhat similar to those of butter, except that it is not particularly suitable for frying since it splutters and burns easily. Soft margarines are too soft to be rubbed into flour, so when making pastry with this type of fat mix the margarine, water and only a third of the flour at the start. Gradually add the rest of the flour until you have a smooth ball of dough which can then be kneaded and rolled out as usual.

Low-fat spreads, which usually appear on supermarket shelves, alongside margarines, are designed simply for spreading and cannot be satisfactorily used for cooking.

Suet

Is the firm, white fat surrounding beef or lambs kidneys. If you are shredding suet, a little flour sprinkled over the suet will keep it from getting too sticky. Beef suet has a wide range of uses. It goes into sweet puddings such as Christmas pudding and jam roly-poly, and into savory ones like steak-and-kidney and steak-and-mushroom puddings. A good suet crust, made with self-rising flour and mixed with a light hand, is one of the most satisfying of winter foods.

Lard

Lard is usually light and clean tasting and is used mainly for frying and for baking, where its creaming properties are appreciated.

The best lards are those rendered from the stomach (leaf) fat of the bacon pig and fat that lies directly under the skin of the back. Lard made from other pig fat has a stronger taste and is the lard most widely sold; add a sprig or two of rosemary to the melted fat to overcome any porky taste when frying potatoes and other delicate foods.

Caul fat

After the fat has been removed to make fine quality leaf lard, a very thin membrane of fat that surrounds the stomach is separated to become the delicious and delicate caul fat, or lace fat. This fat with its lace-like appearance is sold in large white sheets in French, German and Chinese shops. It needs to be soaked in warm water until it softens and becomes pliable for wrapping around sausages and chopped meats as in French charcuterie, while the English use it to enclose fresh faggots. In Chinese cooking, caul fat is used to envelop poultry before it is deep fried or baked. The fat provides a basting layer, melts into nothing and leaves behind a delicate, delicious golden brown crust.

Fatback

This is the fat from the loin of the pig. When cut thinly and beaten into long pieces it is used primarily for larding dry meats – veal and game birds. The pieces are tied over the birds like a waistcoat and baste the flesh during cooking. Cut into strips called lardons, they can be inserted with a special needle into the flesh of dry meat to keep it succulent while it cooks.

It is also used for lining terrines for pâtés and for rendering lard at home.

Drippings

Drippings from different kinds of meat should not be mixed. Beef drippings can be

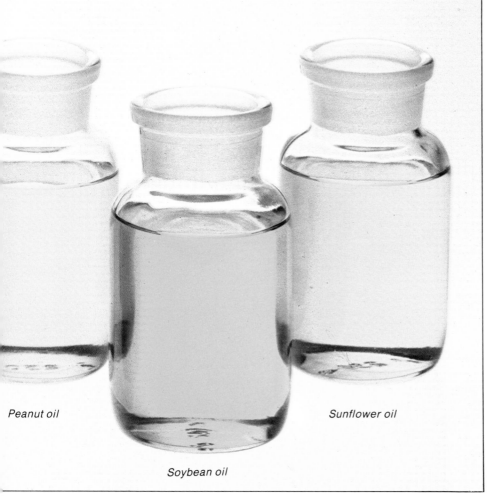

Peanut oil

Soybean oil

Sunflower oil

used to fry the meat for beef stews; pork drippings can be used for any savory dish. Chicken fat, when rendered, is fine and delicate and is much used in Jewish cooking, where it replaces lard. Use the fat from geese or ducks for poultry dishes and fried potatoes, or eat it on hot toast. Lamb drippings smell and taste rather unpleasant and are not used very much.

Shortenings

All hard fats are shortenings, meaning that they are capable of producing a crumbly "short" crust (the greater the amount of fat in the mixture, the greater the shortening effect). However it is the white cooking fats that are neither pure lard nor drippings that have claimed the name.

White cooking fats may be made of blended vegetable oils or a mixture of vegetable and animal fats or fish oils. In taste they are bland, in texture light and fluffy. When using white fat for frying, break it into small pieces so that it all heats up at the same rate. If you use shortening for making pastry, look for a variety that has been aerated or whipped. This will certainly make creaming and rubbing in easier, but remember that it is totally flavorless and will not contribute one iota towards the flavor of a pie or tart.

OILS

Unlike fats, oils are liquid at room temperature. They perform the same functions as fat in shallow and deep frying, but oils can be reused as long as they are not overheated and are carefully strained after each use.

When frying, oils should be heated slowly to the correct temperature. Underheating causes too much oil to be absorbed by the food and overheating is dangerous. A simple rule is to wait for a blue haze to rise from the oil but never allow it to smoke. Test the temperature of the oil with a thermometer: it should be around 320°F/160°C for meat and up to 360°F/180°C for French fries and other vegetables. Poultry and fish come in between. Or fry a small cube of day-old bread in the heated oil: if the bread turns golden and crisp in one minute, the temperature is roughly right.

The object of deep frying is to seal the surface of the food; the pieces to be fried should be as nearly as possible of uniform size so that they cook evenly.

There are a great many oils in the world. To start with – and this goes a long way to help one make a sensible choice – there is the distinction between oils that are unrefined and refined.

Unrefined oils are those that have simply been cold pressed and then left to mellow for a few months before being bottled. They tend to be cloudy but come to the customer in full possession of their natural flavor and color. Often called cold-pressed oils, they are more expensive than refined.

Refined oils have been extracted by pressure under heat. They are then degummed, neutralized, heated and blanched, "winterized" to keep them from going cloudy, deodorized by an injection of steam and finally given artificial preservatives to make up for those that they have lost in the processing.

Olive oil

Indispensable for pasta, salads and many Mediterranean recipes, olive oil, the finest of all oils, varies in character from country to country. Generally speaking, Spanish olive oil has a strong flavor, Greek a heavy texture, Provençal a fruity and Italian a nutty taste. The best from any country is virgin oil from the first cold pressing.

Virgin oil is usually a greenish color – often helped by putting a few leaves into the press – but may also be golden yellow. It is best for salads and for mayonnaise, where its beautiful, fruity flavor can be most appreciated.

Subsequent pressings produce olive oil with a blander and less characterful taste and a paler color. Use these less expensive grades for cooking. When used for shallow-frying vegetables, olive oil imparts a glorious mellow flavor particularly complementary to Mediterranean cooking, and it is essential for making ratatouille and cold vegetable dishes.

Peanut oil

Known also as groundnut oil, arachide oil, *huile d'arachides* and arachis oil, this is the favorite cooking oil of those French chefs who do not cling to olive oil.

Peanut oil is used for salads and mayonnaise when a delicate flavor is wanted, although extra seasoning, lemon juice or vinegar may be required.

Corn oil

This is one of the most economical oils for shallow and deep frying, having one of the highest smoke points. Unrefined, it has a strong taste of maize about it. Refined, it is practically tasteless when cold, but surprisingly produces a strong and not very agreeable smell during frying.

Sesame oil

There are various types of sesame oil. The

Grapeseed oil

Sesame oil

Chinese sesame oil

thicker and browner the oil, the more aromatic it is – the Chinese use this dark oil, made from toasted sesame seeds, more for seasoning than for frying, as it burns easily.

The pale yellowish oil that appears in many Indian and Middle-Eastern dishes is quite different from the brown; it is odorless and light textured.

Sunflower oil

Sunflower oil is light, mild and thinly textured.

Excellent for cooking with and good for using with more expensive oils when making delicate salad dressings, it is the best oil for all recipes where a fairly neutral oil is required.

Safflower oil

This oil, so often confused with sunflower oil, is made from the safflower, a pretty thistle-like plant with orange, red or yellow flowers. Usually a deep golden color safflower oil is found refined in supermarkets and unrefined in health food stores. It is very light and used in the same way as sunflower oil. It is also the oil most recommended for use in the low-cholesterol diets of heart patients.

Mustard seed oil

Although mustard seed oil has a distinctive smell and taste when cold, most of this is driven off when the oil is heated. This oil is used in parts of India as an alternative to ghee. It is also used in Kashmiri curries and as a preservative in pickles.

Rapeseed oil

This oil, also known as colza, is widely used in Mediterranean countries and the East for frying and salads.

Soybean oil

More oil is produced from soybean than from any other plant and most of it goes into the blending of oils, cooking fats and margarines.

Grapeseed oil

This light, aromatic oil is a by-product of the wine industry and is popular in France and Italy.

Used in salads and for gentle frying, this oil comes into its own as the best cooking medium for fondue bourguignonne.

Walnut oil

Cold pressed from dried walnuts, strong, with a deliciously nutty flavor, this is an unusual salad oil.

Walnut oil does not keep well and should be bought in small quantities.

Almond oil

When almond kernels are pressed they produce a clear, pale yellow oil. Oil obtained from the bitter almond is used to make sweet almond oil. When further processed this oil becomes oil of bitter almonds.

Wheat germ oil

Extracted by cold pressing, this pleasant, nutty-tasting oil is mainly taken by the spoonful as a vitamin E supplement.

Vegetable oils

The most economical oils on the market are the highly refined pale golden oils that are a blend of various vegetable products. They have a high smoke point, little taste and are good for frying.

Walnut oil

Almond oil

Wheatgerm oil

Safflower oil

GRAINS, BREADS
AND THICKENING AGENTS

Besides yielding flour for our daily bread, grains are the staple foods of a great many countries. The porridge of Scotland, the polenta of Italy, the couscous of North Africa, the kasha of Russia and countless other grain dishes are all basically the same thing: the local grain, in one form or another, cooked in boiling water until swollen and tender and then eaten plain or with whatever else makes up the national diet.

GRAINS

WHEAT

One of the first cereals ever to be cultivated, wheat has become the most valuable of all food grains, widely used in all its stages from whole and unadulterated to finely milled and sifted. When "flour" is called for in modern recipes it is invariably wheaten flour that is meant. Broadly speaking, the wheat flours can be divided into those made from the high-gluten, hard or strong wheats grown in hot, dry areas and used for bread and pasta, and the soft-grained or weak varieties grown in temperate places, suitable for cakes, cookies and general use.

Whole wheat grain
To eat it as a grain, soak it over night before cooking and then boil it in plenty of water for about two hours. Eat it in the same way as rice with meat, fish or vegetables, or mixed into a salad.

Cracked or kibbled wheat
This is simply the whole wheat grain cracked between rollers. It is eaten in the same way as whole wheat but takes only about 20 minutes to cook.

Burghul or bulgur
Is cracked wheat that has been hulled and parboiled. Eat it in place of rice, or in the Lebanese salad called *tabbouleh*, for which burghul is mixed with chopped onions, parsley and mint.

Bran
This is a by-product of the refining processes of the whole wheat grain and can be bought in health food stores and some supermarkets.

Wheat germ
The heart of the wheat grain, is often extracted or destroyed during wheat refining processes. It can be bought toasted from

supermarkets and raw from health food stores. The raw variety should be kept in the refrigerator, since the oil in the germ quickly goes rancid. Sprinkle it on breakfast cereals or mix it with yogurt.

Semolina
When wheat grain is first milled it is separated into bran, wheat germ and endosperm. The first millings of the floury yellow endosperm are known as semolina and can be found in Italian specialty stores.

When medium-ground, semolina is quite widely used in making desserts. The finest ground semolina is used to make one kind of Italian gnocchi. Semolina made from hard durum wheat is used commercially to make pasta, but it is unsuitable for home pasta making. (To make your own pasta use a good, unbleached, plain flour.) Flour-coated semolina grains make couscous, part of the excellent North African dish of the same name.

Farina
Similar to semolina, this well-known breakfast cereal can be used as a substitute in recipes calling for semolina.

Whole grain or graham flour
This consists of the whole of the wheat grain. Stone-ground flour has a better flavor than roller milled since the slow grinding of the stones doesn't overheat and destroy the vitamins in the wheat germ. It makes a dense loaf with the warm earthy taste of the wheat. Stone-ground flour doesn't keep as well as roller milled so buy only a month's supply at once; keep in a cool place.

Whole wheat flours
These are actually flours from which some of the bran and germ have been removed, leaving behind between 80 and 90 percent of the grain. The resulting flour is lighter in texture than whole grain flour and so produces a less

dense dough. Loaves made from whole wheat flour rise well, have a smooth crust and still retain some of the sweet nutty taste of the wheat. The name whole wheat is often applied to whole grain flour.

All-purpose flour
In the United States, this general-purpose flour is milled and refined from a blend of hard and soft wheats. It contains virtually none of the grain's bran and germ but is required by law to be "enriched," which means that some of the lost nutrients are restored during processing. As its name suggests, it is suitable for all types of cooking from bread to sponge cakes.

Cake flour
This is the refined and bleached product of soft wheat. Soft wheat flours produce only a small amount of gluten and so give a light, short texture in baking. Its fine silky consistency is particularly good for producing even-textured cakes.

Self-rising flour
Is a plain, soft flour mixed with baking powder and salt and is best used within two or three months. Use if for making cakes and in any recipe that calls for the addition of baking powder.

Strong plain white flour
Familiar in Britain, this is usually a blend of soft and hard wheats. This type of flour is suitable for all yeast baking and produces excellent loaves, buns and pizza dough.

CORN

Second in importance only to wheat, there are countless varieties of corn – some hard, some soft, some creamy, some golden, some red, some purple.

Hominy
An American Indian name for hulled and dried white corn. It can be bought either dry

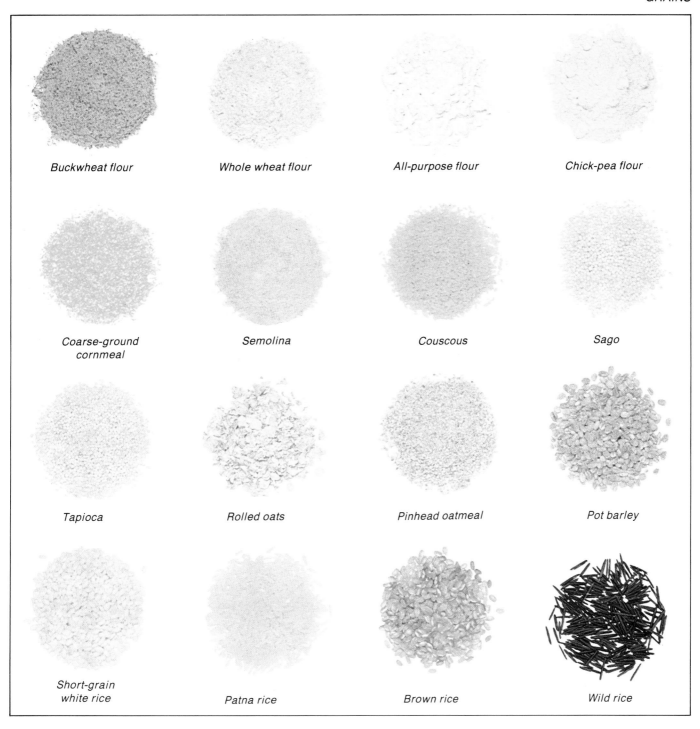

Buckwheat flour   Whole wheat flour   All-purpose flour   Chick-pea flour

Coarse-ground cornmeal   Semolina   Couscous   Sago

Tapioca   Rolled oats   Pinhead oatmeal   Pot barley

Short-grain white rice   Patna rice   Brown rice   Wild rice

or ready-cooked in cans. Hominy is also available ground and is then known as hominy grits. Coarse-ground hominy grits cooked in milk and served with butter and syrup or with gravy is a traditional breakfast dish in the southern states of America.

Cornmeal, maize meal, polenta
These are made from ground white or yellow corn and are available in coarse and medium grinds. The best cornmeal is ground by the old millstone method, but it does not keep as well as cornmeal ground by more modern processes.

In the United States there are a number of simple cornmeal dishes such as griddled jonnycakes and deep-fried hushpuppies. In the southern states corn bread is served hot with fried chicken or ham or with syrup.

In the south of France, cornmeal is mixed with wheat flour to make rough, flattish loaves, while the traditional northern Italian dish of polenta is made by boiling coarse-ground, yellow cornmeal until it becomes a stiff porridge. This is then shaped and sliced and eaten steamed, broiled or fried. The tortillas of Central America are made from *masa harina* – a fine cornmeal ground from white corn which is soaked in limewater.

Masa harina can be bought as a wet dough, or dehydrated.

Cornstarch, cornflour
The white heart of the corn kernel is ground to a silken powder. Used primarily as a thickening agent, it can be added to cakes, shortbread and cookies to give a fine-textured result. A little cornstarch added to an egg custard will stop if from curdling.

OATS

These are among the most nutritious of all cereals. Being rich in oils they soon become rancid, so do not buy more oat products than you can use in about three weeks and keep them in a cool place.

Oatmeal

Is available in three grades, pinhead or coarse, medium and fine. The coarser the meal, the longer it will take to cook. Medium oatmeal is traditionally used to make porridge. It is also used to give bulk to sausages and haggis, and can be added to wheat flour when making bread. Pinhead oatmeal is good in thick soups and stews. Fine oatmeal is used in baking oatcakes, scones and cookies. Fine-grade meal is also used for oatmeal pancakes and is good for flouring Scottish herrings before they go into the frying pan.

Rolled oats, oat flakes, porridge oats

These are oats which have been steamed and flattened between rollers, a process which makes them quicker to cook. Porridge takes only ten minutes to make when using rolled oats. They are also used to make English flapjacks – sticky, chewy, teatime cookies. Uncooked rolled or toasted oats are the main ingredient of the Swiss breakfast cereal muesli.

RYE

This strong-flavoured, hardy grain has a tough kernel which if bought whole, needs to be cracked with a rolling pin and then soaked before being cooked.

Whole rye kernels

These kernels must be boiled until tender and can be added to stews or mixed with rice.

Rye flour

This flour makes a rather heavy, distinctive loaf and is widely used in bread making in many parts of Europe. Coarsely ground whole rye flour goes into pumpernickel. Finer ground flour is used for black bread; light-colored rye breads are made with rye flour and wheat flour mixed.

BARLEY

Although more widely used for brewing than eating, barley has a pleasant nutty taste and can be cooked in a variety of ways.

Pot or Scotch barley

This is the whole grain with only the outer husk removed. It requires overnight steeping and several hours' cooking.

Pearl barley

A polished grain that is more widely available than pot barley and will cook to tenderness in about 1½ hours. It is traditionally used in Scotch broth.

Barley meal and barley flour

The first is ground pot barley, the second is ground pearl barley. Both can be added to wheat flour when making bread.

RICE

At least a third of mankind eats rice as its staple food. There is an enormous number of varieties, each with its own special properties, and it is important to choose the right variety of rice for the right dish.

Brown rice

This is any rice that has been hulled but has not lost its bran. To the regret of dieticians, polished white rice is usually preferred to brown rice which contains more nutrients, particularly vitamin B, a deficiency of which causes beriberi. It takes rather longer to cook than the white variety and is much improved by being soaked first. Boil for 40 – 45 minutes in plenty of salted water. Brown rice is available in short, medium and long grains. Long and medium grains are best eaten as a vegetable, or as a basis for a pilaf. Short grains are delicious in puddings. You may need to cook less brown rice as it is rather more filling than its polished, white counterparts.

Patna rice

This has a long, milk-white grain. It can either be cooked in plenty of salted boiling water for up to 15 minutes or until just tender, or as for basmati rice. The center of each grain, when cooked, should have a slight resistance but no hint of chalkiness. Patna, cooked to perfection, produces a beautiful mound of separate grains, good for pilafs, salads, stuffings and all dishes where the rice is served dry.

Converted rice

For those who cannot wait the 15 minutes or so that long-grain white rice takes to cook, there is a more expensive fast-cooking variety. This is steam treated and more nutritious than one might think because it is processed before it is hulled, and so has the chance to absorb the bran's nutrients before this is discarded.

Basmati rice

Available from Asian food stores, this is a superior long-grain rice. It is slightly more expensive than patna but its better flavor and consistency is well worth the extra cost. Before cooking, it sometimes needs to be carefully picked over for any bits of grit and husk and should then be washed thoroughly under running water to remove excess starch.

Basmati consistently produces good results if cooked in the following way: add one part rice to three parts cold salted water, bring to boiling point, stir, cover the pan and turn down the heat until the water is barely simmering. After 12–15 minutes the rice will have absorbed all the water and, when forked up, the grains will be beautifully dry and separate. It is ideal for pilaus and as a filling and soothing foil for highly spiced Indian dishes.

Carolina rice and Java rice

These are not to be confused with the American brand name Carolina rice, the "extra long-grain rice", but are shortish versions of long-grain species. When cooked, the grains swell enormously without disintegrating. They are very suitable for milk puddings, whether baked in the oven until caramel colored and brown on top as in England, or cooked plain on top of the stove and served with sugar and cinnamon as in Germany, or blended with whipped cream and layered with black cherries as is traditional in Switzerland. These types of rice are also suitable for making molds and stuffings.

Italian Piedmontese rice, Arborio rice

These are Italian risotto rices and have short, round grains that are either white or pale yellow. Their special asset is that their grains can absorb a great deal of liquid over a long period without becoming soft. This, and their distinctive flavor, makes them ideal for risottos and any dish such as paella or jambalaya.

Wild rice

Is the seed of an aquatic grass related to the rice family, which grows in the United States. It is hard to find and prohibitively expensive but has a rare, distinctive, nutty flavour not be be missed if you are really interested in food.

Ground rice

Can be purchased loose or, more usually, packaged. Cook with milk for a fine-textured dessert or add it to a shortcake mixture for extra crunchiness.

Rice flour

Is polished rice very finely ground to a silky consistency. A little rice flour can go into a walnut or hazelnut cake of the type that uses no flour, only grated nuts, and is a useful thickener for dishes that are to be deep frozen as it will prevent the mixture separating when heated.

BUCKWHEAT

Also known as saracen corn or beechwheat, buckwheat grows in great quantities in northeast Europe. Buckwheat is the correct flour to use for Russian blini – small speckled, yeast-risen pancakes that are eaten with caviar. It is also used to make crêpes.

MILLET AND SORGHUM

These are closely related and are invariably sold shelled as the husk is extremely hard. Their greatest characteristic is that they swell enormously – at least five parts water are needed to one part millet or sorghum. Both have a blandish, slightly nutty taste. They are best cooked and eaten like rice. Millet and sorghum flours produce flattish breads.

SAGO AND TAPIOCA

The starch obtained from the stem of the southeast Asian sago palm, sago is usually exported in pearled form. It is most commonly made into sweet milk puddings, which are thought to be easily digestible and so are fed to children and the elderly.

Tapioca

Prepared from the tuberous roots of the tropical cassava or manioc shrub, tapioca is as tasteless and starchy as sago and comes both pearled and powdered.

THICKENERS

All starchy meals and flours will, in the presence of heat and moisture, act as thickeners. Finer flours, before being added to the pan, must first be blended to a lump-free paste with a little of the cooking liquid or with some butter, to make a roux or beurre manié.

As an alternative to plain all-purpose flour, try using something a little more robust such as fine-ground cornmeal or whole wheat, sorghum, barley or chick-pea flour. These will add flavor and color as well as body to soups. Chick-pea flour, also called gram flour or besan, also makes a very good batter and is used to make *pakoras*, spicy little Indian fritters.

Fécule is the general French name for starchy powders used in cooking. It is usually associated with potato flour. The other very fine, quick-thickening flours such as cornstarch, arrowroot, tapioca flour and rice flour are all virtually tasteless. They have double the thickening power of flour, turn translucent when cooked and are suitable for thickening delicate chicken or game dishes and sauces to accompany sweetbreads. Arrowroot and potato flour are particularly suitable for thickening fruit sauces because they turn completely clear when cooked, and arrowroot has the added feature of being ideal for cooking at low temperatures.

YEAST AND BAKING POWDERS

When buying flour for baking you will probably also need a leavening agent such as yeast for bread, pizza dough and buns, and baking powder for scones and cakes.

Compressed or fresh yeast
Is a pale beige, pastry substance which should be solid but able to crumble easily and should have a clean, sweet, fruity smell. Look for it in health food stores, the refrigerated section of supermarkets and at small bakeries.

Dried granular or active dry yeast
Dried yeast has been freeze dried and so will keep for several months if stored in a cool, dry place, but it needs a warmer liquid than fresh yeast in which to dissolve.

Brewer's yeast
The brewer's yeast sold for home brewing is too bitter, for baking purposes.

Debittered brewer's yeast
Found in health food stores, has no leavening properties but is high in vitamin B. It should be treated as a nutritional additive to mix into drinks and sprinkle over foods.

Baking powder
This combines acid and alkaline substances that act together when in contact with mois-

ture to create air bubbles which expand during baking to give a fine, delicate-textured result. When adding the milk or water to a baking powder and flour mixture, work quickly so that the resulting carbon dioxide does not have a chance of escaping. Double acting or SAS baking powder, widely available in America, is easier to use because the chemicals spring into full action only when they are exposed to the heat of the oven.

Bicarbonate of soda and cream of tartar
You can make your own baking powder by mixing these in the proportion of one teaspoon of soda to two of cream of tartar for every cup of flour. Bicarbonate of soda, the alkalin, will work alone if used in a recipe in which there is an acid ingredient such as the sour milk in soda bread. A little cream of tartar helps increase the volume and stability of whisked egg whites.

Salt of hartshorn
Chemically imitated these days with ammonium carbonate, it is used in Scandinavian countries as a baking powder to produce light, crisp cookies.

BREADS

The qualities of the plain white loaf are, of course, proper for such things as croûtons, melba toast and English bread sauce, but there is a host of other breads.

French bread
This is most often seen in long sticks or *baguettes*, has a hard, crisp crust and a wide-holed crumb. When made in the authentic French manner it will only keep a few hours, but it is bread at its very best.

Malt loaf
A dark, moist, sweet bread enriched with syrup and malt extract, often comes wrapped and may contain raisins.

Light rye bread
Rye bread is popular for sandwiches, particularly in the United States.

Dark rye bread, pumpernickel and vollkornbrot
A dark rye loaf with its hard, thick crust keeps fresh for a week or more, while pumpernickel and vollkornbrot lose their moisture quickly and keep best wrapped in foil.

Bagels
These ring-shaped rolls are boiled before baking and are a Jewish specialty, very good with cream cheese, smoked salmon or jam.

Croissants
These soft doughy crescents that are an essential part of the French breakfast, are made of a rich dough of milk and flour liberally interleaved with butter.

Brioches
These rich, featherlight little loaves are made from a dough of milk, water, eggs and butter. Eat warm with butter and jam or hollowed out and stuffed with mushrooms

English muffins
Muffins popular in the United States for breakfast or brunch, are pulled or "forked" apart and toasted.

Crumpets
Crumpets should be first toasted and eaten piping hot and dripping with butter.

Baps
These soft, floury breakfast rolls from Scotland, are eaten straight from the oven, split and spread with butter.

Pita bread
Eaten hot, they are sometimes cut in half and filled with broiled lamb and salad. They are always eaten plain with Greek meals.

Pizza
A flattish but yeast-leavened Italian bread, it is best eaten hot and cut in triangles to accompany a main course.

Tortilla
This Mexican unleavened bread is made with *masa harina* or with whole wheat flour. Corn tortillas are fried and filled to make *tacos*, or simply fried until crisp to make *tostadas*.

Chapati
Indian unleavened bread made from *atta* – chapatis are eaten hot with curries and other Indian dishes.

Puri
This is a deep-fried, air-filled chapati.

Paratha
Is a shallow-fried, butter-enriched variety of chapati.

Naan
Tear-drop shaped, this rich, leavened variation on the chapati is traditionally slapped on the side of a charcoal tandoori oven to cook.

CRISP BREADS

There is a huge array of crisp breads on the market, ranging from rusks to water biscuits.

Scandinavian crisp breads
Are generally made from whole rye and are popular as a slimming aid, as rye is the most filling cereal and so gives one a feeling of satisfaction with fewer calories.

Matzo
This Jewish wheaten crisp bread, similar to water biscuits, is traditionally eaten during Passover. Eat as bread, especially with cheese and spreads. It is completely unsalted.

Poppadoms
These wafer-thin Indian chips are available plain or spiced and need only to be broiled or deep fried for a few seconds.

Pretzels
They are usually crisp but some varieties are soft in the middle. Best served with drinks or cheese; the soft ones are good with spicy mustard.

Bread sticks
Known also by the Italian name, *grissini*, are long, thin sticks of bread with a fine texture, baked and dried until crisp or accompanying an Italian meal instead of rolls. Eat with drinks or with an Italian meal.

RECIPE SUGGESTIONS

Malt loaf

2 cups/225 g all-purpose flour	
4 cups/450 g stone-ground whole wheat flour	
2 cakes fresh yeast	
large pinch of salt	
¼ lb/115 g raisins	
½ stick/55 g butter, melted	
3 tablespoons malt extract	
1 tablespoon molasses	
sugar and milk for glazing	

MAKES 2 MEDIUM-SIZE LOAVES

Cream the yeast with a little warm water and leave it in a warm place to froth up. Mix the flour, salt and raisins in a large warmed bowl, make a well in the center and pour in the creamed yeast. Add the butter, malt, molasses and a scant 2 cups/4.5 dl warm water, kneading to make a somewhat slack dough.

Cover with a sheet of oiled plastic wrap and allow to rise for 2 hours or until the dough has doubled in size. Cut the mixture into two pieces, then form into loaves by kneading each piece of dough into a ball, then flattening the ball into a thick disc. Roll up the disc, tuck the two ends of the roll underneath and drop into a greased loaf pan. Press down well, shaping the top so that it is nicely rounded, cover, and allow to rise for 45 minutes until puffy. Preheat the oven to 375°F/190°C.

Bake the loaves for 50 minutes or longer, turning the pans round halfway through and covering the loaves with foil if they start to look too black. Boil a little sugar and milk together and glaze the loaves with the mixture 5 minutes before the end of the cooking time.

Children love this excellent tea bread.

Crumbs, croûtons, toasts

Fresh bread crumbs: cut thick slices of white bread, remove the crusts, cut the slices into cubes and reduce them to crumbs in a food processor. Alternatively, you can use a grater, but this is a much slower process.

Dried bread crumbs: put all your leftover ends of bread in a very low oven until dry, golden and biscuity. Wrap the dried pieces in a clean cloth and pound them with a rolling pin, using a rolling motion once they begin to break down. Sieve the resulting crumbs—any lingering bits and pieces should be pounded again.

Croûtons: cut crustless slices of white bread into small neat cubes and fry them in a mixture of hot butter and oil, tossing them frequently, until they are an even golden brown. Remove them with a slotted spoon and drain them on kitchen paper. Croûtons can be reheated in a low oven.

Melba toast: toast slices of white bread, with their crusts on, and when brown on both sides, slice each piece horizontally in half. Scrape away the soft untoasted inside, cut off the crusts and dry the wafer-thin pieces for a few minutes in a low oven until they begin to curl and brown. Serve with hors d'oeuvre, caviar, pâté.

Pain perdu soak slices of white or dark bread in beaten egg, shallow fry in butter until brown on both sides and serve hot, sprinkled with sugar and cinnamon, or with a spoonful of maple syrup and crisp slices of bacon.

Pain perdu is also known as French toast and makes an excellent breakfast dish.

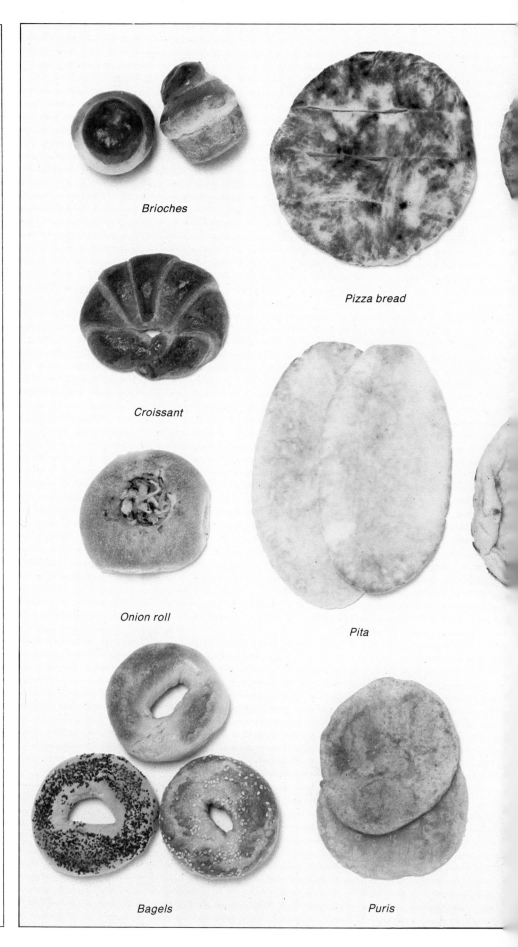

Brioches

Pizza bread

Croissant

Onion roll

Pita

Bagels

Puris

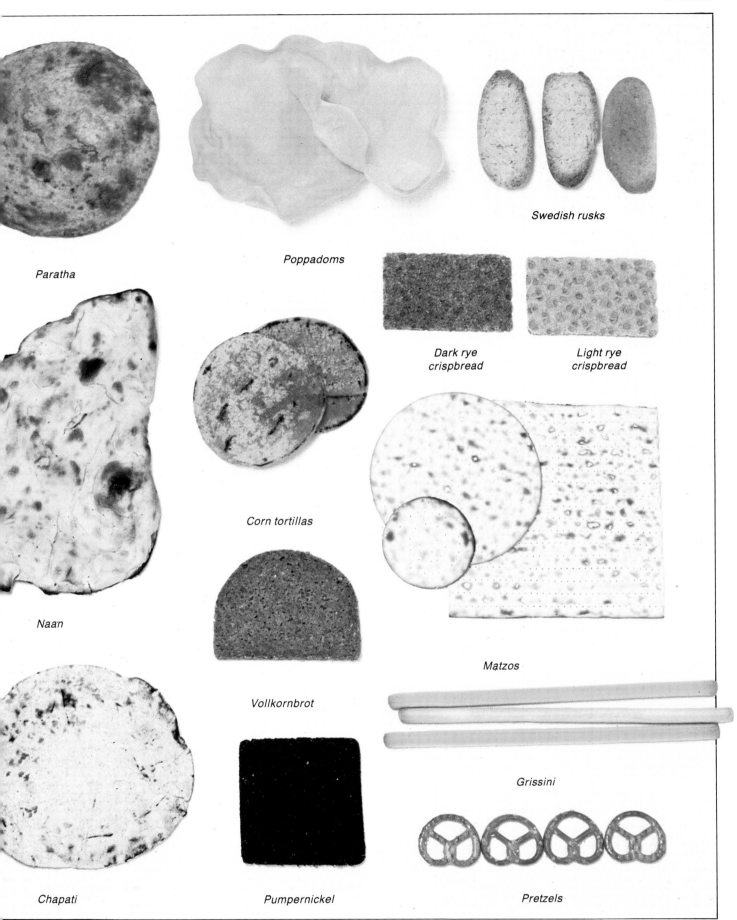

Paratha

Poppadoms

Swedish rusks

Dark rye
crispbread

Light rye
crispbread

Naan

Corn tortillas

Vollkornbrot

Matzos

Chapati

Pumpernickel

Grissini

Pretzels

PASTA AND NOODLES

Pasta of one kind or another is the main part of most Italians' daily diet. Six hundred or so pasta shapes are made in Italy, from spaghetti, the traditional pasta of Naples and the best known of all, to the miniature pastas which are usually served in beef or chicken broth and come in any form you can think of – stars, crescent moons, rings and even hats, boots and motor cars. In China and Japan also noodles and stuffed pasta dumplings have been an important part of the classic cuisine for several thousands of years.

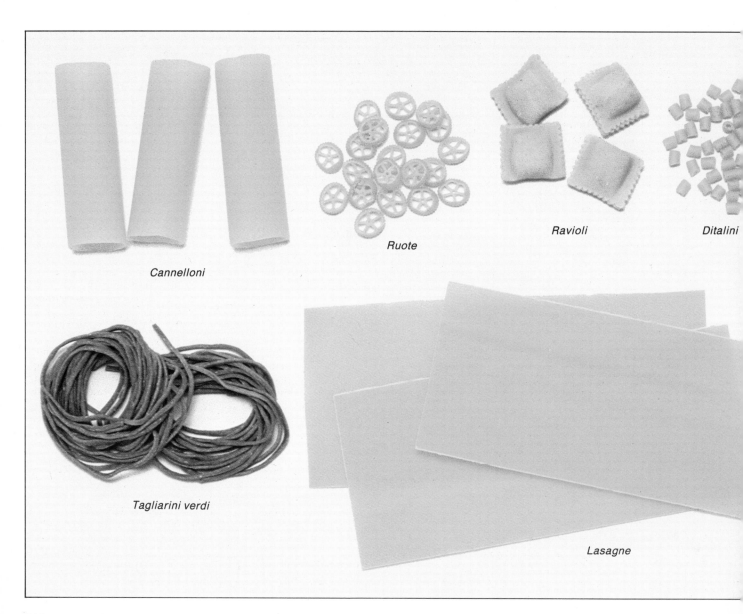

Cannelloni

Ruote

Ravioli

Ditalini

Tagliarini verdi

Lasagne

PASTA

Records show that the Chinese were eating pasta as long ago as the Shang dynasty, some 3,500 years ago, and it was long believed, rather romantically, that Marco Polo brought pasta to Italy from the court of Kubla Khan. But Etruscan murals in Tuscany show all the kitchen equipment needed for pasta making, from the kind of wooden table still used to roll it on (so far laminated plastics have not replaced it) to the fluted wheel with which to cut pappardelle, lasagne and ravioli. Even without the murals the story had been put in doubt by the estate of a military man who died in the thirteenth century, leaving among his effects a precious chest of *maccheroni*.

Whatever its origins, the Neapolitans have always been Italy's most serious pasta eaters and Naples and the surrounding area have long been regarded as the center of the dried pasta industry. Certainly the best flour for pasta making, made from the extra hard wheat *Amber durum*, comes from the hot, dry south. This absorbs the minimum of water as it cooks. The warm, dry windy climate means, too, that spaghetti can be dried in the open air, swathed like curtains over long canes that are supported on tall stands – although with industrialization, modern factories have taken the place of the old traditional family enterprises.

When buying dried pasta look for that made in southern Italy, especially the Abruzzi, and make sure it is a clear yellow color without any chalky greyish tinge. Thinner pastas should be translucent when held up to the light, with the exception of dried egg pastas, which should be a sunny bright yellow.

Most pastas can generally be described as long or short; round, tubular or flat; smooth or ridged; solid or hollow. An attempt to classify their shapes by name, however, is a problem, since one shape can have several different names and sizes. The north of Italy insists on one appellation, the south another, and even different regions quite close together cannot reach agreement. Miniature pastas, or *pastina*, which come in every shape you can think of from stars to motorcars to apple seeds, are in a category of their own. They can be made from fresh or dried egg pasta or plain dried pasta (without eggs) and are generally cooked and served *in brodo* – in chicken or beef broth.

The long, round, solid pastas that are coiled around the fork, such as vermicelli, spaghetti and spaghettini, are generally eaten dry (*asciutta*) with oil or butter, a tomato-based sauce or a seafood sauce. Meat sauces, with the exception of *ragú bolognese*, are not generally eaten with these as they do not cling to the pasta well. Short, hollow pastas such as conchigliette, elbow macaroni or penne are the ones to serve with meat as the pieces catch easily in the hollows and curves of the pasta.

The larger short, hollow pastas such as cannelloni and manicotti are usually boiled and then stuffed with cheese or meat before baking. Macaroni and rigatoni are sometimes boiled and then baked in a sauce in the oven, perhaps as part of a molded shape called *timballi* which is among the oldest of all pasta dishes. Two egg pastas, lasagne and tagliatelle, can also be baked in this way, as can farfalle, conchiglie, ruote and lumachine.

Serve cream sauces with short, ridged, hollow pastas, since these catch the cream and do not slip off the fork. Tagliatelle and other flat fresh pastas are generally eaten with rich meat or vegetable sauces, and the same fresh pasta dough is used to make stuffed pastas such as ravioli, anolini, tortelloni, tortellini, conchiglie and lumachine.

Having said all this, of course, one can eat any pasta with any sauce and have a perfectly good meal.

Spaghetti

This is the best known of all pastas and always comes in long, straight bundles. It is marketed in a number of widths that go under such names as cappellini, spaghettini, vermicelli, vermicelloni and thin or thick spaghetti. The thicker ones are better with rich sauces while the thinner ones are better with plainer sauces.

Spaghetti has long been the traditional pasta of Naples and the traditional way of eating it is still *alla napoletana* – first turned in oil and then topped with a ladleful of tomato sauce. Naples also eats its spaghetti *all' aglio e olio* – pasta bathed in olive oil and mixed with sautéed garlic. Grated grana cheese such as Parmesan or pecorino is served with all spaghetti except those with seafood additions such as *spaghetti alla vongole*. This is made with tiny clams and is another Neapolitan specialty, although it is, of course, much enjoyed all over Italy.

Macaroni

It is not known how the idea of making the tubular pasta called macaroni or *maccheroni* started. But the most likely theory is that someone wrapped a piece of rolled-out pasta around a filling, leaving the ends open.

Macaroni comes in an ever greater range of sizes than spaghetti. Apart from the long variety, with bore holes that can be measured in millimeters, there are also those that can be measured in centimeters, culminating in cannelloni, but these are despised by purists as too modern an invention, designed solely to make filling our pasta easier. However, we ought to be grateful that we are not obliged, as was the composer Rossini, to fill our macaroni with the aid of a silver syringe. He is said to have used this for filling tubes of pasta with foie gras, for which he had a well-known passion.

Apart from cannelloni there are ribbed rigatoni, mafalde, zite, penne – cut like quills – and elbow macaroni – the curved, short lengths of macaroni used in baked pasta dishes and, of course, for the ubiquitous macaroni and cheese.

Macaroni used to be virtually the only pasta known and loved by English-speaking countries. Called macrow, it had been eaten at the court of Richard II of England. It fell into decline, but was rediscovered by eighteenth-century Englishmen in the Italian part of their grand tours and taken back to Britain. Soon macaroni and cheese became an important high-tea dish, and it is still eaten at home by many British as well as American families.

Egg pasta

In northern Italy housewives traditionally made egg pasta or *pasta all'uovo* daily at home with eggs and flour. Emilia-Romagna, the area with the richest farming land in Italy, was renowned for its beautiful hand-made pasta, and young women from that region

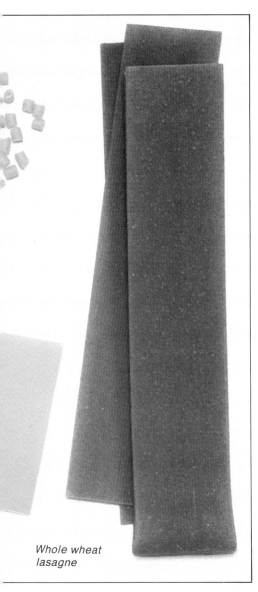

Whole wheat lasagne

were keenly courted by young men and their mothers for their pasta-making skills. Egg pastas are richer and lighter than ordinary pastas.

Pasta making is a craft and to see an expert rolling out a golden circle of dough, as thin as fine suede, to the size of a small tablecloth is a wonderful experience. In Bologna, the gastronomic center of Emilia-Romagna, you can watch it being made in a shop window. It is then turned into tortellini – little stuffed, folded-over pasta triangles – at lightning speed in front of your eyes.

Fresh pasta can be made at home, when it becomes known as *pasta casalinga*, either by hand or with a pasta machine, but perfectionists say that the former is better since the machine squeezes the pasta and tends to give it a slippery surface that does not hold the sauce so well.

In fact a great deal of the *pasta all'uovo* now eaten in Italy and elsewhere is made in factories, where by law it must contain five eggs in each kilo of flour. It is sold in nests or in skeins that loosen when boiled. Buy it wrapped in cellophane or loose, if you can; boxed pasta is more expensive, the size of the box often bears little relation to the contents, and it is impossible to see if the brittle pasta inside is whole or broken.

The best-known egg pasta is tagliatelle, or – as it is called in Rome – fettucine: those golden strands that were supposed to have been inspired by the long blonde hair of Lucretia Borgia. In Bologna and Parma and all the other places of gastronomic pilgrimage with which northern Italy abounds, the tagliarini (thin tagliatelle) is still normally freshly rolled out every day.

Tagliatelle is, of course, not only eaten *alla bolognese*, even in Bologna, but also *in bianco*, mixed with plenty of melted butter, freshly grated Parmesan and cream, or *al burro*, with the cream left out. Bologna also eats its tagliatelle mixed with strips of delicious sautéed pancetta and grated Parmesan.

Green pasta

Lasagne verdi and tagliatelle verdi prove that spinach has a special affinity with pasta. Both are colored by a small amount of spinach purée that is worked into the dough. **Lasagne** can be bought in long, wide, flat strips or in curly pieces which do not stick together as easily as flat pieces when boiling. It can also be bought as squares which are easier to fit into a baking dish. In Bologna strips of green lasagne or the narrower lasagnette are alternately layered with uncolored strips and with Bolognese sauce and rich creamy béchamel sauce. This dish is baked in the oven and emerges, glazed here and there with deep golden flecks, as *lasagne al forno*.

Tagliatelle Tuscany and Umbria make a pretty mixture of yellow and green tagliatelle or tagliolini, which is called *paglia e fieno*, meaning straw and hay. It is eaten with melted butter and cream and sprinkled as usual with Parmesan.

Whole wheat and buckwheat pasta

Although Venice has always had its thick whole wheat spaghetti called *bigoli*, it is not common throughout Italy. There are, however, some relative newcomers in the health food stores, such as the buckwheat and whole wheat pastas.

Whole wheat lasagne and macaroni and buckwheat spaghetti are some examples. These have a nutty flavor and are richer in vitamins and minerals than the traditional pale pastas. They take longer to cook as they contain five times as much fiber as pale pasta. The Italian whole wheat pastas are, on the whole, lighter than those made elsewhere.

Whole wheat and buckwheat noodles also feature in Japanese cooking and are often eaten cold as a late afternoon snack.

Stuffed pasta

Pasta stuffed with a large variety of finely ground fillings is eaten throughout Italy. Parmesan cheese and mortadella sausage with pork and veal, diced or pounded and mixed with minced turkey breasts, provide the traditional stuffing for tortellini and tortelloni. These are the coiled half-moons which are the famous Bolognese version of ravioli and are by custom eaten on Christmas Eve and for big celebrations. Perugia, in Tuscany, on these occasions eats cappelletti, or little hats, whose stuffing includes finely ground veal and sweetbreads or brains. The hollowed shells called conchiglie or the larger conchigloni and even lumache can also be stuffed.

Throughout the length and breadth of Italy ravioli with delicious spinach, beet leaf or chard fillings are to be found. The chopped leaves are mixed with soft white cheese such as ricotta and with Parmesan or pecorino, bound with egg and flavored with a touch of nutmeg or garlic depending on the local taste.

Soup pasta

If the dough and the basic shape of pasta *asciutta* are fairly consistent – allowing for a thousand and one small regional variations – the same cannot be said of soup pastas. The range is vast and includes anellini and stelline, which are used for serving *in brodo*, while the larger varieties such as farfalline, conchigliette and ditaline are used for making hearty soups such as minestrone or *pasta e fagioli*.

Italy garnishes its soups with tiny car radiators, cogs and wheels, with flying saucers, hats, boots, letters and numerals, all made of pasta. The more traditional shapes include grains of rice and melon seeds, twisted bow ties, butterflies, stars, crescent moons, seashells of every description, rings, hoops, elbow macaroni and noodles which

plain buckwheat
Spaghetti

Lasagne verdi

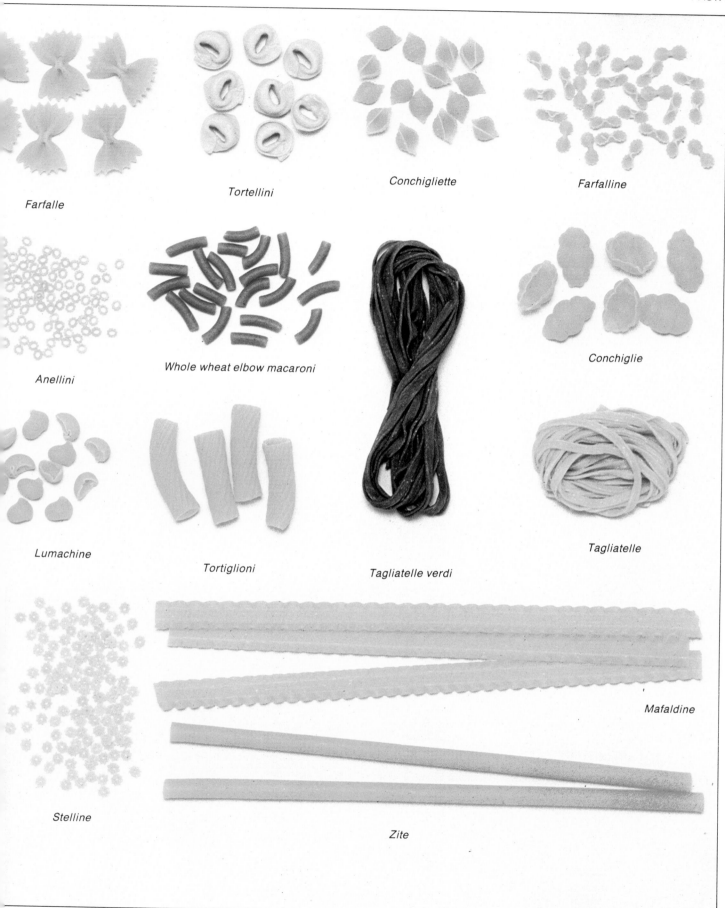

Farfalle

Tortellini

Conchigliette

Farfalline

Anellini

Whole wheat elbow macaroni

Conchiglie

Lumachine

Tortiglioni

Tagliatelle verdi

Tagliatelle

Stelline

Zite

Mafaldine

are as thin as matchsticks.

These garnishes are sometimes cooked separately and added to the soup just before serving, as they tend to shed a bit of starch, which can make a clear broth cloudy.

GNOCCHI

In Italy, gnocchi are eaten in the same way as pasta and at the same point in the meal, but they are not strictly speaking pasta. There are several local variations and they can be made from ricotta cheese and spinach, or semolina, or mashed potato or potato flour. They are usually poached in boiling salted water until cooked, when they rise to the surface. They are then served with a variety of sauces. Gnocchi are generally made fresh, the semolina variety being extremely easy to make.

NUDELS, NOUILLES AND DUMPLINGS

In the German-speaking countries, which are supposed to have introduced nudels into Italy in the Middle Ages, flat nudels have been consistently eaten for centuries. They are often baked with raisins and sweetened lemon-flavored curd cheese and served as a pudding. In Alsace they are known as nouilles and are prepared in countless savory and delicious ways. *Coq au vin*, for example, is often accompanied by nouilles, which are always better when fresh.

In Alsace we also find the ancestral dumpling known as noque, while farther south it appears under the name of nockerln. By whatever name, it is a pasta dumpling and can be eaten with a variety of sauces.

CHINESE NOODLES

Wheat flour, rice flour, arrowroot or pea starch are the main ingredients of Chinese noodles. They come in a variety of thicknesses and shapes, can be used interchangeably and are often tied in bundles or coiled into square packages. The majority, however, are long, as this is thought to symbolize and encourage long life.

Although most Chinese buy their noodles, some do make their own. Fresh noodles are obtainable from Chinese supermarkets and taste best when they are first parboiled and then steamed in a colander over boiling water. Once boiled or steamed, Chinese noodles become part of more elaborate preparations that often involve several cooking methods for one dish.

Soup noodles

These are traditionally served in broth with a topping of finely cut meat or seafood and bright, fresh-looking vegetables. The cooked noodles are put into the bottom of the bowl, the hot broth is poured over them, then come the vegetables, previously stir-fried

Fresh rice noodles

Soup vermicelli

Arrowroot vermicelli

Wonton wrappers

Wheat noodles

Cellophane noodles

with the meat or seafood, as the garnish.

In the north of China, where wheat is the primary grain, wheat noodles, with or without egg, are used. Egg noodles are often sold in little nests while pure wheat noodles may be packaged like Italian spaghetti as well as in square-shaped nests. In the southern districts of China, where paddy fields abound, rice noodles are used. These range from square packets of coiled rice sticks to the thin thread-like rice vermicelli that comes tied in bundles. White arrowroot vermicelli is also available.

Fried noodles

Crispy fried noodles, known as chow mein, are a Cantonese specialty, and since most Chinese restaurants in the West are Cantonese these are perhaps the best known of all noodle dishes. They can either be flattened in a frying pan with plenty of seasoned oil and then turned like a pancake, or they can be fried gently with leftover vegetables and meat from a noodle and soup dish.

Pea starch noodles can also be used if a crisp garnish is all that is required.

Sauced noodles

In the West, where Chinese thickeners such as lotus root flour are not readily available, sauced noodles or lu mein are usually served in sauces thickened with cornstarch. Since texture is just as important to the Chinese as taste, a crunchy element is often introduced to these sauces with matchstick slivers of bamboo shoots or crisp stalks of scallions and leeks. Protein is provided by adding meat such as chicken, shelled shrimps or oysters. Lu mein dishes are usually served at birthday celebrations.

Pea starch noodles, also known as transparent or cellophane noodles, are never served in their own right but are generally used in lu mein dishes. Since they absorb liquid at the rate of four times their weight they are ideal. They are usually cooked as part of the savory dish and then the entire dish is served with rice.

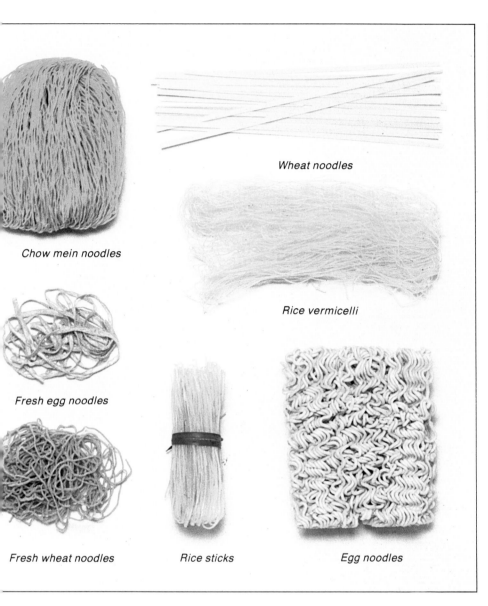

Chow mein noodles

Wheat noodles

Rice vermicelli

Fresh egg noodles

Fresh wheat noodles

Rice sticks

Egg noodles

DUMPLINGS

Chinese dumplings or wontons are similar to the Italian ravioli. The delicate ingredients, finely ground and variously flavored, are wrapped in squares of fine noodle dough. They may be purchased in Chinese supermarkets, but can be made at home in the same way as fresh pasta. Boiled or steamed they are often served floating in a clear broth.

One of the prettiest dishes available in a Chinese restaurant arrives at the table as a towering pagoda of baskets. Each one fits into the other and contains bite-size packages of dumplings called dim sum. These contain pork, shrimp or other meat or fish fillings and are ideal for a light lunch.

JAPANESE NOODLES

There are four main types of Japanese noodle, all of which play an important part in the national cuisine. Soba are thin, brownish noodles made from buckwheat flour.

They are used in soups and sometimes served cold with a garnish. Harusame are equivalent to the Chinese pea starch noodles and can be deep fried, or soaked and then cooked in various dishes. Somen are very fine white noodles – you can substitute vermicelli if somen are not available. Udon are made from white flour and are more substantial.

RECIPE SUGGESTIONS
Tagliatelle alla panna

¾ lb/340 g dried tagliatelle, or sufficient freshly made tagliatelle for 4
4–5 tablespoons heavy cream
3 tablespoons/45 g butter
salt and freshly ground pepper
grating of nutmeg
¼ lb/115 g raw or cooked ham, thinly cut
freshly grated Parmesan

SERVES 4

Bring a large pan of salted water to the boil and cook the tagliatelle until just *al dente*. Meanwhile put the cream and butter into a large saucepan, season with salt, pepper and grated nutmeg and heat through. Cut the ham into tiny, delicate strips.

When the pasta is cooked, drain it well and put it in with the cream and butter mixture, turning it over until well coated. Add the ham, stir it and cook over a gentle heat for 2 minutes.

Serve in a large dish accompanied by freshly grated Parmesan. This recipe is extremely rapid and simple to make and is quite extraordinarily good.
ALTERNATIVE: *add a tablespoon of meat glaze or consommé to the cream and butter mixture. The brown jelly that can be separated from cold beef drippings is perfect for this and helps to prevent the sauce from becoming too bland.*

Spaghetti alla rustica

1 lb/450 g spaghetti
2 cloves garlic
6 tablespoons olive oil
1 can anchovy fillets in oil
2 teaspoons oregano
salt and freshly ground pepper
2–3 tablespoons coarsely chopped parsley
freshly grated Parmesan

SERVES 4

Peel and crush the garlic and fry in the oil in a small saucepan. When the garlic has browned and smells nutty, remove it and turn the heat down as far as it will go. Chop the anchovies, add them to the oil and let them melt down to a mush. Add the oregano.
Cook the spaghetti in a large pan of boiling, well-salted water until it is *al dente* – this is particularly important for this type of spaghetti dish, which does not have a thick disguising sauce. Put the drained spaghetti into a heated dish, stir in the anchovies and olive oil, season and sprinkle with the parsley. Serve with plenty of Parmesan – this is a particularly fine way of eating spaghetti.

Bucatini alla marchigiana

¾ lb/340 g bucatini (ribbed elbow macaroni)
1 small onion
1 stick celery
1 carrot
2 tablespoons olive oil or 1 tablespoon/15 g lard
3 oz/85 g ham, cut in little strips
1 small glass red wine
1 lb/450 g ripe tomatoes or a 1 lb/450 g can of tomatoes
2 tablespoons tomato paste
pinch each of marjoram and thyme
salt and freshly ground pepper
¾ cup/85 g freshly grated Parmesan

SERVES 4

Peel the onion and then chop all the vegetables, except the tomatoes, together finely to make a battuto (a mixture of chopped vegetables). Brown them in a saucepan in the oil or lard.
Add the ham and stir it around for a few minutes. Add the wine and let it reduce until it has almost evaporated. Chop the tomatoes and add them to the pan with the tomato paste, herbs and seasoning and bring to the boil. Turn down the heat and simmer for half an hour.
Drop the macaroni into a large pan of boiling salted water and cook for 15 minutes or until just tender. Drain, put into a heated bowl, mix in 3 or 4 tablespoons of Parmesan and stir in half the sauce. Serve the remaining sauce and cheese separately.

DRIED PEAS AND BEANS

The dried seeds of podded plants were first popular as a food many thousands of years ago. In Egypt, the pyramids have been found to contain little mounds of dried beans – not only to sustain departed pharaohs on their journey to the next world but also because Egyptians believed beans to be particularly helpful in conveying the soul to heaven. After centuries of neglect by European chefs, peas and beans are again in fashion. They are recognized as a good source of protein and a satisfying food which can make an excellent substitute for meat.

Although thousands of species of beans and peas, botanically known as Leguminosae, now exist, they have many common characteristics. Flavor and mealiness may vary, but all have a straightforward earthy taste and satisfying sturdy quality. All are a rich source of protein and, being a healthy and body-building form of food, make a very sound substitute for meat, especially when combined with cereals. Hence their label "poor man's meat."

A popular misconception is that dried peas and beans have an indefinite shelf life. In fact, they should not be stored longer than a year for they harden with age and become difficult to cook. There are two methods of preparing them, both of which help to clean and tenderize them. The most common method is soaking, to which all dried peas and beans respond, preferably in soft water. The dried peas and beans that are prepared for supermarkets are sure to be clean and may not need to be soaked: the label should tell you. The alternative to soaking, useful when you are short of time, is to put them into a pan of cold, unsalted water, bring them to the boil, then simmer them for five minutes. Cover the pan, remove it from the heat and allow the peas or beans to cool. Then cook them in whatever way the recipe calls for.

All these vegetables should be cooked in soft water – a pinch of bicarbonate of soda will soften hard water – and simmered rather than rapidly boiled. Unless very fresh, they require lengthy cooking. They should be salted towards the end of cooking – if salted at the outset, the skins will split and the insides will harden. A little fat in with the cooking water – salt pork, bacon or oil – improves the texture of all dried peas and beans. When bought canned rather than loose or packaged, they are already cooked and only need heating.

HARICOT BEANS

The word haricot covers the botanical species of beans *Phaseolus*. It derives from medieval times when dried beans were used chiefly to go into a pot containing a *haricot* or *halicot* of meat – haricot meaning simply that the meat was cut in chunks for stewing. When English and French cook books specify haricots, what is meant are white beans, smooth and oval rather than kidney shaped. In the United States they are known, sensibly enough, as white beans.

Soissons
These are generally considered the finest haricot beans. They originated in northern France, but are used to greatest effect in the famous regional dish *cassoulet*, from Toulouse, cooked with preserved goose, mutton and sausage.

Flageolets
In a semi-dried state, flageolets, are an important ingredient in another classic French dish, *gigot d'agneau*. Usually, however, they are found only dried, either green or white. The green are the more interesting, having a delicate flavor and a lovely color.

Cannellini
These Italian haricots are slightly fatter than the English or French ones and popular in Tuscany in soups and in dishes such as *tonno e fagioli* – served cold with tuna fish in a garlicky vinaigrette.

Navy beans or Yankee beans
At one time, these small round beans were served by the US Navy, hence their name. They are very popular in the United States, particularly for making Boston baked beans.

Pea beans
These are sought out by discerning New Englanders for authentic Boston baked beans, but they are used interchangeably with navy beans in canning.

Brown Dutch beans
Used also to make Boston baked beans, brown Dutch beans are available in England as well as the United States.

LIMA BEANS

Also known as butter beans, these can be large or small. Although, when fresh, they are highly prized, especially in America, the large dried bean easily becomes mushy when cooked and so is best when used in soups and purées. When recipes for other dishes call for either haricot or butter beans, it is the smaller bean that should be used.

RED KIDNEY BEANS

Best known outside Mexico for their part in chili con carne – which is not, as it happens, a true Mexican dish – red kidney beans are a staple in Central America and are the beans that, with black beans, were cooked by the Central American Indians in their earthenware pots (still much the best receptacle for baked beans, which should never be decanted before serving). After the introduction of lard from Spain, beans were often mashed, formed into a stiff paste and then fried to become *frijoles refritos* – still one of the most popular ways of eating beans in Mexico. In this form they may be used as an accompaniment to a main dish, or as a filling for *tacos*, *tostadas* and *tamales*, those crisply fried corncakes which are popular far beyond the borders of Mexico itself. Red kidney beans also appear in many dishes in New Orleans.

BLACK BEANS

As well as being used interchangeably with red kidney and pinto beans to make *frijoles refritos*, black beans, with their glistening black skins and creamy flesh, are the staple of many soups and stews in South and Central America. There they are often baked with ham or other cured pork and flavored with garlic, cumin and much chili pepper. In the southern states of the United States, black bean soup is a great favorite. The beans are cooked with a ham bone or hock, blended to the consistency of a heavy sauce and served with slices of hard-boiled egg and lemon floating on top.

BORLOTTI BEANS AND PINTO BEANS

Both these beans are often mottled in color. The pink-splotched pinto bean grows freely all over Latin America and, like the borlotti bean from Italy, is an ingredient in many regional stews and is often mixed with rice. The borlotti bean is also mixed with pasta to make the soup *pasta e fagioli*.

BLACK-EYED PEAS

These white peas with their characteristic black splotch came to Europe and America from Africa, brought over in the seventeenth century by the slave traders. The bean thrives in warm climates and has become a favorite food crop in the southern United States, where it is eaten fresh as well as dried. It is often served with pork and corn bread, and is the essential ingredient in a traditional southern dish called Hoppin' John – a mixture of peas, brown rice, bacon and plenty of oil.

FAVA BEANS

Sometimes known as broad beans, these are the strongly flavored beans that form the basis of the Egyptian *ta'amia* or falafel: deep-fried little patties made with soaked and pounded raw beans and flavored with garlic, onions, cumin, coriander and parsley. Most often used in their fresh green state, as in the rib-sticking *fabada* from northern Spain – a mixture of beans, cured meats, sausage and plenty of garlic – they become brown when dried.

FULL MEDAMES OR EGYPTIAN BROWN BEANS

Also known as the field bean in England, these small, brown, nobbly beans are grown in southeast Asia and Egypt, where they are a staple food. There the beans are usually sprinkled with garlic and parsley, with oil and seasonings passed around separately. They also make a filling for an Arabian bread to become a sort of meatless hamburger, eaten with tomato and onion salad. They are also good when served in a tomato sauce, but they do require lengthy soaking and cooking.

CHICK-PEAS

The botanical name for this pea (which is, strictly speaking, not a pea at all) is *Cicer arietinum* because of its alleged resemblance to the skull of a ram, although to those of us with a less discerning eye it looks more like the kernel of a small hazelnut.

The flavor of chick-peas vaguely recalls that of roasted nuts and they are eaten with drinks in Greece. Large ones are a better buy than small ones as they do not need such long soaking. However, they will still sometimes need as much as 10 hours' soaking and 5–6 hours of gentle simmering to become completely tender.

Once cooked, *ceci*, as they are called in Italy, are very good dressed simply with oil and eaten as a salad. The Italians also make chick-pea soup and mix them with pasta – a dish known as thunder and lightning. In France, where chick-peas are called *pois chiches*, they are stewed in good stock with herbs to make *pois chiches en estouffade*, and also used in soups and as a garnish. In Spain, *garbanzos* form the basis of *olla podrida* (which means rotten pot) and in Portugal they are combined with spinach and eaten with bacalhau – dried salted cod – and other dishes. In the Middle East chick-peas are combined with tahina paste, lemon and garlic to make the delicious spread, hummus, and Israel uses them for its version of falafel, which is so widely eaten that is has almost become the national dish. They are a common ingredient of couscous and are also mixed with beef and vegetables to make a rich and filling Israeli dish called Defeene or Daphna. They are an important crop in India, where they are often cooked with garlic and chili peppers and turned in aromatics before being fried with herbs and spices in clarified butter.

SPLIT PEAS

Although there are still some dingy grey dried peas to be had, most are now sold skinned, split and bright green or golden yellow. Thick yellow pea soup – *ärter med flask* – is the traditional Thursday evening dish in Sweden, keeping alive the memory of the unpopular King Eric XIV whose last supper on earth, on a Thursday, consisted of this very dish. His brother had contrived to slip a dash of arsenic into this humble food, which would hardly have crossed royal lips had Eric not been imprisoned at the time by his eventual successor.

Green split peas form the basis of a traditional English dish, pease pudding, which is usually eaten in slices with gammon. Although an egg is sometimes beaten into the mushy pea mixture to make it creamier still, it is one of the characteristics of split peas, yellow or green, that they turn into a purée by themselves and do not have to be mashed.

LENTILS

Red, brown and green lentils have all the virtues of dried peas and beans, and the additional one of needing less cooking time, particularly split lentils. The small red split lentil, originally a native of India, needs no soaking and becomes tender within about 20 minutes' cooking, quickly turning into a mush if overcooked. The brown lentil, also known as the German lentil, and the green lentil of France, *lentille de Puy*, take a little longer to cook.

Lentils make excellent purées and soups. In Germany they sometimes accompany roast duck, while in France lentils cooked with garlic and flavored with a squeeze of lemon joice are eaten with a *petit salé* – hot salt pork.

DHALS

These are not a particular type of bean but the Hindi word for dried beans and peas, and most packages labelled dhal in the West will contain split varieties such as chick-peas, lentils and the pigeon-pea, which is known as the tur dhal. They are not soaked but are cooked for 40–45 minutes and served spiced as a thick purée, or are mashed to make thick soups. Another of the dhals, the urd dhal, is often ground and becomes the basis of the poppadom, without which no curry would be complete.

MUNG BEANS

These beans, called green gram or golden gram, can of course be cooked in the usual way, but they tend to become rather sticky. They are now chiefly used, like alfalfa seeds and soybeans, for sprouting.

SOYBEANS

The soybean is the most nutritious of all beans and the most easily digested. Better known for its products than for the bean itself, it is one of the few known sources of complete protein. It has been periodically rediscovered by the West, but was first brought to Europe in the eighteenth century, when it confounded scientists with its amazing qualities and is still the subject of considerable research.

But while the West has only recently started knitting soybeans into steaks and processing it into cheese, the Chinese have for thousands of years called them "the meat of the earth," and have used soybean curds – a bland substance known as *tofu*, which soaks up other flavors – as a substitute for meat, fish and chicken. The extracted "milk" is used in cooking many vegetable dishes, soy sauce is used for flavoring and a dark paste made from the bean is sweetened and used in desserts in the manner of jam.

Of the thousand or so known varieties, two soybeans are chiefly cultivated – one sort for commercial purposes, the other to be eaten both fresh (when young) and dried, in which case they are prepared and cooked just like other dried beans.

ADZUKI BEANS

The adzuki bean, also known as the asuki bean and the aduki bean, is one of the most delicious and also one of the more expensive of the dried beans.

A native of Japan, it is small and red with a curious keel-shaped ridge. It is a fairly recent arrival in the West and is found mainly in health food stores. It is cooked in exactly the same ways as other dried beans, both in Japan and abroad, but since it is very much sweeter than most other beans its flour is also much used for cakes and pastries in Japan, and the crushed bean is made into puddings and ice cream by the Chinese. It is one of the most easily disgestible of all the dried beans.

RECIPE SUGGESTION

Boston baked beans

¾ cup/340 g navy or pea beans, soaked overnight
¼ lb/115 g salt pork, or slab bacon, rind removed
2 tablespoons/30 g butter
1 onion
2 tablespoons molasses
2 tablespoons tomato paste
1 tablespoon hot mustard
1 teaspoon cider vinegar
salt

SERVES 4

Put the beans into a large saucepan and cover with fresh cold water, which should come 1 in/2.5 cm above the level of the beans. Simmer for about an hour, until tender. To see if they are cooked, take out a spoonful of beans, pour off the liquid and blow lightly on the beans. The outer skin will curl if they are ready. Drain them, reserving the cooking liquid, and put them in a special bean pot or, if you do not have a bean pot, a heavy, deep casserole. Preheat the oven to 300°F/160°C.

Cut the pork or bacon into thickish slices. Melt the butter in a frying pan and fry the slices on both sides. Transfer them to the casserole or bean pot, together with their fat, and half bury them in the beans.

Peel the onion and push it into the middle of the beans. Mix the cooking liquid from the beans with the molasses, tomato paste, mustard, vinegar and a teaspoon of salt and pour it all over the beans. Cover the pot and bake in a very slow oven for 2–3 hours, adding more water if necessary. Remove the lid for the last 30 minutes to brown the top.

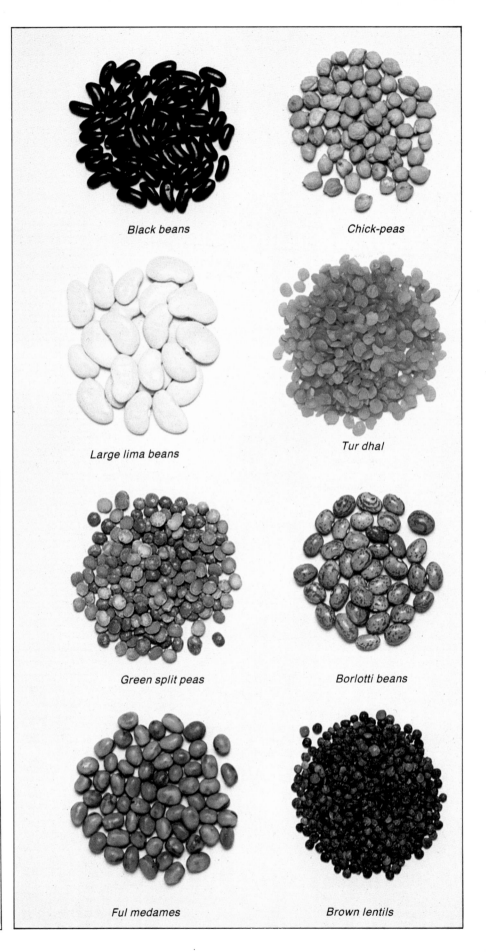

Black beans

Chick-peas

Large lima beans

Tur dhal

Green split peas

Borlotti beans

Ful medames

Brown lentils

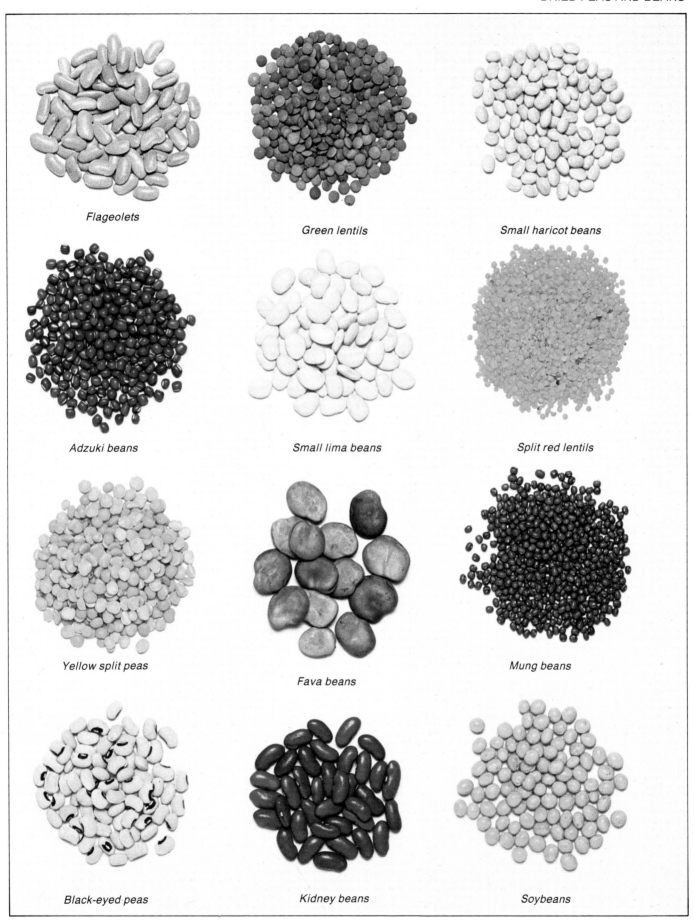

Flageolets

Green lentils

Small haricot beans

Adzuki beans

Small lima beans

Split red lentils

Yellow split peas

Fava beans

Mung beans

Black-eyed peas

Kidney beans

Soybeans

VEGETABLES

The term vegetables covers a wide range of plants which are eaten cooked or uncooked. With some it is the leafy heads which are eaten, with others it is the shoots and stalks; yet others are prized for their roots and tubers. Added to these are the fruits which need strong sun to ripen them, from the humble tomato to the exotic avocado and egg plant.

SALAD

Exactly at what point of the meal to serve a green salad is a matter of taste. Sometimes it is eaten as a first course in the United States. It is more usual to eat it with or after the main course: immediately following, as in France and England; or at the same time.

Green salads should not meet their dressings until they are on the point of being served, since once dressed they rapidly become limp. Some people prefer to mix the dressing at the table, while Italians simply pour olive oil and then vinegar onto the salad.

To make sure that your green salad vegetables are fresh and good, see that the leaves look vigorous and show no sign of brown. Inspect the cut parts: they should be sound, neither blackened nor soggy.

A salad plant in good condition will stay fresh in the refrigerator if it is wrapped in a plastic bag to retard the evaporation of its moisture. Should it have wilted, it can be refreshed by being plunged into water, shaken dry and put into a large covered pan, or in the refrigerator in a plastic bag or wrapped in a damp dish towel.

Salad leaves should be washed and dried – either by absorbing the moisture with a clean dish towel or by getting rid of it in a salad shaker. The leaves should be torn rather than cut, to avoid bruising. For such dishes as seafood cocktail, which require shredded lettuce, a knife has to be used, but only just before the greenery is needed since it wilts so quickly after being cut.

Apart from being used in salads, lettuces and other leafy plants can be cooked. The less substantial the leaf, the faster if collapses. For braising, choose small plump lettuces and cut them in half or braise them whole.

ROUND OR CABBAGE LETTUCES

These vary greatly in size and crispness but have in common their general round shape. Although there are many varieties of cabbage lettuce, ranging from soft to very crisp, there are three main types.

Butterheads

A particularly melting butterhead, Bibb, is prized in the United States. Another, Continuity, is grown in England and sports leaves with a reddish tinge to them. It is often sold by name as a special delicacy. Butterheads tend to be floppy, a characteristic which is by no means a defect as long as the loose leaves are fresh.

Icebergs

Whereas there is not much joy in eating a tired and wilting butterhead, these hearty lettuces, when fading on the outside, may still be full of vitality in the middle. Icebergs, such as Webb's Wonderful, are by far the crispest lettuces – they are also called Crispheads and are often sold without their aureole of outer leaves, looking like tightly wrapped heads of cabbage.

Looseheads

These are cabbage lettuces which have no heart at all. Instead of the leaves, which are often crinkled, becoming more tightly packed towards the centre, they all splay outwards from the middle.

ROMAINE OR COS LETTUCE

Far more elongated in shape than round cabbage lettuces is the romaine or cos lettuce. Tall and large with a nutty flavor to its vigorous leaves, it has a beautifully crisp and tender heart.

CHINESE CABBAGE OR CHINESE LEAVES

A wide variety of these are grown in China, and they frequently end up in large wooden barrels, coarsely chopped and pickled in brine. They are often used for dishes that need a piquancy or bite to them.

The Chinese *pe-tsai* resembles a large, pale romaine lettuce and is crisp and delicate with a faint cabbage flavor. Its crinkly inner leaves are best in salads, while the outer leaves, once divested of their tough ribs, can be braised, stir-fried, simmered, or treated like ordinary cabbages.

Less familiar is the Chinese *bok-choy*. It looks more like spinach, and indeed is also known as Chinese mustard spinach. The large coarse leaves radiate loosely from the stalk. This variety is often used for pickling by the Chinese since the leaves taste somewhat harsh.

CORN SALAD OR LAMB'S LETTUCE

This is what you are served when you order a dish of *mâche* in France. The spoonshaped leaves grow in dark green rosettes, which are difficult to wash since they harbor sand. It is more substantial than lettuce and has a nutty taste which blends particularly well with the sweetness of beets for an excellent winter salad.

CHICORY, ENDIVE AND ESCAROLE

Wild chicory

Has pretty blue flowers and is the ancestor of varieties that are now grown primarily for their roots, which are roasted and ground to make a coffee substitute. Its leaves have a bitter taste and are sometimes mixed with other salad leaves.

Belgian endive or witloof

This is the best known of the cultivated chicories. It is blanched by being grown in the dark or under peat, and with its tightly furled leaves it resembles a fat white cigar. A yellowish frill bands the juicy white parts, which are in fact the broad, succulent center ribs of an underdeveloped leaf. Sliced across or with the leaves separated, it makes a fresh and interesting salad.

What little bitterness there is in Belgian endive tends to come to the fore when it is cooked, so it is usually blanched in a little stock and a few drops of lemon juice before being braised.

Radiccio or ciccorio

There are several types of this chicory introduced from Italy. Looking like miniature colored lettuces, the plants can be either deep ruby-red, cream splashed with a fine wine-red, or marbled pink when they have been grown in the dark. When they have not

Butterhead lettuce

Continuity lettuce

Webb's Wonderful lettuce

Curly endive

Loosehead lettuce

Iceberg lettuce

Romaine lettuce

Chinese cabbage

Belgian endive

Radiccio

been carefully shaded they look green or dark copper colored and less pretty. It is its beauty that recommends radiccio: it tastes much like a lettuce, but with more bitterness and has somewhat tougher ribs.

Curly or frizzy endive and escarole

The curly-leaved endive and the broad-leaved escarole are more robust than the lettuce tribe. Although by nature they are bitter, they become less so when the jagged rosettes are shielded from the light and blanched to a succulent pale golden-green. Look for these in winter – they have much more character than most hothouse-reared winter lettuces. Curly endive looks like a pale greenish-white mop, and escarole has broad crinkled strap-shaped leaves with a rather leathery texture.

Prepare curly endive and escarole as you would a lettuce, but with a more highly flavored dressing; use them to give texture to a salad made of more delicate leaves or on their own. A few walnuts with perhaps some strips of bacon make a good addition, and this is the salad to eat with Roquefort dressing.

Escarole is often called by its variety name, Batavia, while the different names used for curly endive must stem from its Latin name, *Chicorium endiva* – in France it is known as *chicorée frisée,* and in the United States it is called chicory as frequently as it is known as curly endive.

CRESSES

Watercress

Dark green, bunched sprigs of watercress make a beautiful garnish for broiled kidneys, chops and game, and little sprigs enhance both the taste and look of a green or an orange salad. A watercress sauce is an excellent and pretty complement for fish. When buying watercress, the rule is the darker and the larger the leaves, the better. Use it soon after purchase, keeping it meanwhile in the refrigerator in a plastic bag or, better still, in a cool place in water, like a bouquet in a jam jar or, even better, completely submerged in a bowl.

Mustard and cress

The tiny embryonic leaves of mustard and salad or garden cress are usually found in the thinnest and most delicate sandwiches and as a garnish sprinkled over salads. What you are most likely to buy growing in little boxes is simply cress, the smaller of the two.

RADISHES

As a family, these roots belong to the mustard tribe, which, considering their hot pungency, is not surprising. In shape and color they range from little scarlet or white globes to long red and white types such as the Icicle radish. There is even a black radish, which has ice-white flesh.

Pungency varies not only according to type but also according to the soil in which the plants are grown. The red and white

Corn salad

Scarlet Globe radish

type tends to be the mildest and goes by the name of French Breakfast radish. The most pungent of the pure white radishes is the type offered in Bavarian beer halls to encourage thirst.

Except in the East, where radishes are eaten as a fully fledged vegetable, they mostly provide an appetizer. They are simply dipped in salt and eaten with crusty French bread and butter, or themselves buttered. In Italy thin white slices of radish with their pretty red edges are scattered over green salads.

Winter radishes

This term is applied to those large varieties with compact, firm flesh. They are cooked or can be grated into salads.

Daikon, or mouli

This is the winter radish from the Far East, the birthplace of radishes. Long, white, cylindrical and enormous, it can be pickled, or grated and mixed with grated ginger roots to make a sauce for fried vegetables, and features in tempura dishes.

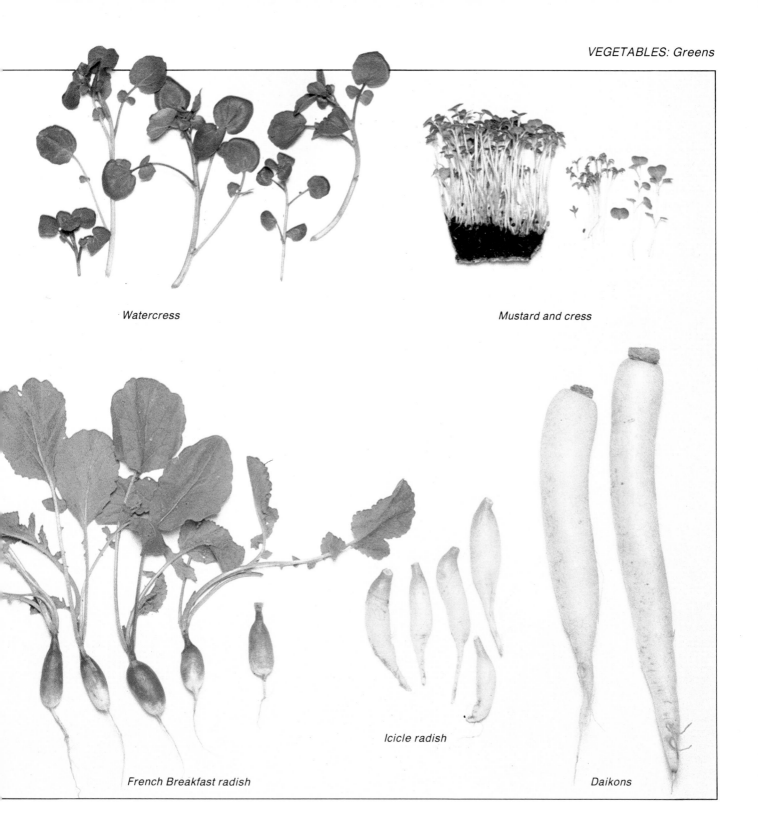

Watercress

Mustard and cress

French Breakfast radish

Icicle radish

Daikons

GREENS

SPINACH

The long cultivation of spinach over thousands of years ago, has resulted in succulent leaves of a beautiful green, which may be small and rounded – the best for salads – or larger and more pointed.

Since spinach greatly reduces in volume when cooked, you need to allow ½ lb/225g for each person. It is customary to remove the stalks and, if they are coarse, the midribs from each leaf. The spinach should then be well washed in several changes of water to remove the grit which it often contains. It should be cooked on a low flame, pan uncovered, with only the water that clings to the leaves. As the lower layer softens, stir the spinach and continue in this way until all the leaves have wilted down. It must be very well drained as it tends to exude water after it is cooked.

As an accompanying vegetable it can be served simply with masses of butter, or in a mornay sauce, or as a purée with cream.

In Italy there are dozens of lovely spinach recipes: spinach is eaten in soufflés, frittatas and dumplings; mixed with ricotta, Parmesan and nutmeg to make a filling for stuffed pasta; and used to make fresh green pasta, which looks so pretty with a cream or tomato sauce. No wonder that spinach garnish goes under the Italian name of *alla fiorentina*.

Spinach can also be eaten raw: delicious salads can be made with small, fresh spinach leaves garnished with pieces of crisply fried bacon and hard-boiled eggs, tossed in a garlic-laden vinaigrette.

There are also some wild plants that are reminiscent of spinach in flavor, two of them so close to spinach in taste that they are sometimes cultivated.

New Zealand spinach
A fleshy leaved plant discovered by Sir Joseph Banks, botanist on Captain Cook's *Endeavour*, who brought it back to Europe. It is still grown outside its native land, flourishing where excessive heat and lack of water would prevent true spinach growing well. Somewhat tougher than true spinach, it is often sold in local French markets, where it is called *tetragon*.

Malabar spinach
This thrives in tropical Asia and in tropical parts of America. The large, bright, shiny leaves have a distinctive but good taste, and are treated in the same way as spinach. In China it is cultivated for its fleshy berries, which yield a dye that has been used by women as a rouge and by high-ranking officials for sealing documents.

CABBAGE GREENS
Any member of the cabbage family which does not form a proper head becomes simply "greens," also known as spring or winter greens in England and collards in the United States. All greens should be very fresh and need to be bought in generous quantities, since they reduce in volume when cooked. They should be cheap enough to allow any woody stems, coarse midribs or damaged leaves to be ruthlessly discarded. See that the midribs are crisp and snappy.

Collards (spring and winter greens)
These are the Cinderellas of the vegetable world, but, like Cinderella, they are good and can be quite splendid when properly dressed. The leaves are particularly tender and delicate when cooked, and are excellent for sustaining dishes such as New England's "mess o'greens," which usually contains salt pork and is much like the southern United States' dish called "pot likker," always eaten with corn bread to sop up the broth.

Kale and curly kale
Of the two, curly kale is the better known and certainly the better tasting. Kale, with its smooth, greyish-green leaves, is less succulent than other greens but is good when stir-fried.

Curly kale has crimped leaves, like giant

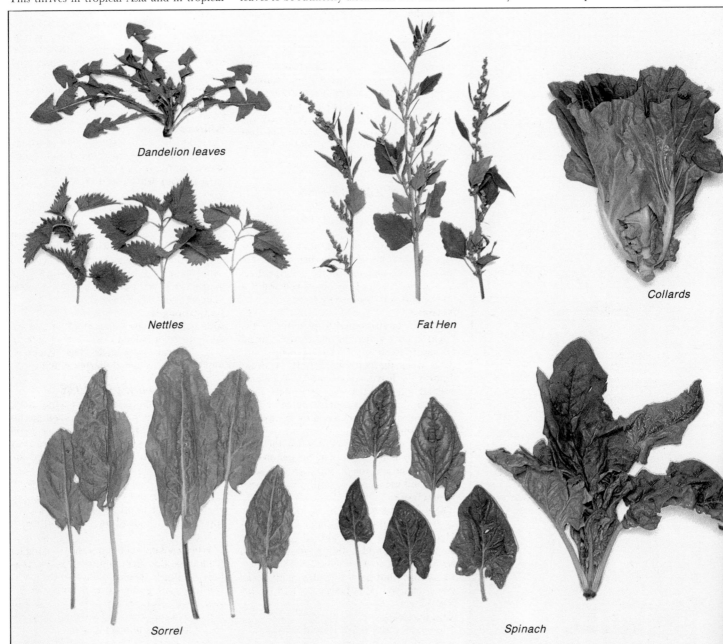

Dandelion leaves

Nettles

Fat Hen

Collards

Sorrel

Spinach

parsley. There are many varieties some of which are grown as ornamental plants. The edible ones taste rather like collards but stronger and can be used for all cabbage recipes.

BEET GREENS OR SPINACH BEET

Beets are not only cultivated for their excellent red roots but also specially for their leaves.

Beet greens are grown extensively in eastern districts of France where, together with Swiss chard, they are known as *blettes* and are used interchangeably with both Swiss chard and seakale beet. They are often mixed with sorrel to counteract the latter's acidity, being themselves extremely mild. When cooked, they are used like spinach.

Curly kale

Beet greens

SORREL, DANDELIONS AND PURSLANE

Sorrel
Of all the different types of sorrel, it is the cultivated French variety that is best for eating, adding an acid, lemony note to salads, soups, purées, sauces and omelets. Because sorrel, even more than spinach, is rich in oxalic acid, it should be eaten in moderation.

Dandelions
Weed though they may be, dandelions are certainly useful. The roots can be used as a caffeine-free coffee substitute and the leaves make excellent salads.

You can remove most of the bitterness from wild dandelions by placing a plate or tile over a patch of young plants, but the juiciest, least bitter dandelions are those grown from a packet of seed. Blanch them before they start to produce flower buds and pick them young.

Purslane
In America and in England purslane is discarded as a weed by most people. The French are more astute and consider purslane – known as *pourpier* in France – to be a salad plant worth cultivating. The succulent leaves can also be boiled, and are good when briskly fried in butter and then cooked in an omelet. In the Middle East, it is an important ingredient in *fattoush* – a salad mixture eaten with pita bread.

WILD GREENS

There are still many edible green-leaved plants growing wild and free which, if nothing else, can be regarded as survival food. Make sure, though, that you know exactly what you are gathering. If you are uncertain of what the plants look like, take sketches with you of the plants you want to find so that you can identify them.

Nettles
Northern countries used to prize the nettle, but it is now something most people avoid because of its sting (which completely disappears when the nettle is cooked). In Scandinavia the leaves were boiled like spinach. Ireland combined nettles and oats in a broth. Italians still eat nettle purée or soup in the spring as it is supposed to be excellent for cleansing the blood.

Nettles should be picked when they are only about a finger-length high; later on they comes bitter and tough. Remember to wear gloves and use scissors to snip off the leaves.

Goosefoots
The two best-known members of this family are the delightfully named Good King Henry and Fat Hen, both of which were staples in antiquity but have now been superseded by spinach. Fat Hen tastes much like spinach but is considerably milder. The leaves of Good King Henry are also treated like spinach.

Chickweed
Cooked in butter with chopped onion, this goes well with rich meats.

BRASSICAS

CABBAGES

When buying cabbages, no matter what kind, look not only at the leaves, which should be sound and unblemished, but also at the cut trunk. This should be neither dry and split nor woody and slimy. Those with wilted outer leaves or a puffy appearance should be avoided.

The firmer the cabbage, the longer it will keep.

Green cabbages
Early green cabbages are a deeper green and more loosely packed than the later ones, often with pointed heads. Buy them in the spring, checking that the leaves – frequently curly at the edges – are fresh and crisp. Even the outer leaves should be tender.

The later green cabbages are altogether tougher, but have solid hearts. They include the crimped variety, called the Savoy cabbage, which is particularly tender and mild flavored and needs less cooking than other varieties. The Savoy's head is firm and is a beautiful green with a touch of blue; it stands up well to frosty weather.

White cabbages
These are in fact the very palest of green, almost white, and are sometimes called Dutch cabbages. Like red cabbages, they have smooth leaves, and should be quite hard and firm.

The simplest way of cooking a green or white cabbage, is to boil it, after removing the core and thickest stalks, and washing it in a bowl of cold water with a tablespoon of salt. Cut into quarters or shreds, it needs no more than 8-10 minutes to cook – the moment it starts to sink it is ready – and it should be cooked uncovered.

Red cabbages
Although these have magenta or dark purple skins, the color fades during cooking unless a little vinegar is added. The flavor is improved by the added sharpness, too.

CAULIFLOWERS

Modern cauliflowers can be enormous, although a strain no larger than golf balls is being grown for the freezer. A type of cauliflower grown in Sardinia and southern Italy is purple, but turns green when cooked unless it is carefully steamed.

A fresh head of cauliflower will have a compact cluster of creamy white flowerets, or curds and feel heavy for its size. Loose or spreading flowerets mean the cauliflower is overmature.

When cooking cauliflower, start testing for tenderness after five minutes or so by carefully sticking a skewer into a side stalk, and continue testing until there is little, but still some, resistance. A whole head in boiling water cooks in about 25 minutes; flowerets take about eight minutes and will cook more evenly. Flowerets of raw cauliflower make a good cocktail party dip, and cold cooked flowerets in a mustardy vinaigrette dressing make a delicious salad.

BROCCOLI

Broccoli of whatever kind is best boiled briefly so that it still preserves some crispness, and it can be used for all cauliflower recipes.

Purple sprouting broccoli

In Sicily broccoli is cooked in the oven with anchovies and onions. In the rest of Italy it is often parboiled and finished off with oil and garlic in the frying pan, and perhaps eaten with pasta.

Althouth less succulent than Calabrese, purple sprouting broccoli is a very fine vegetable. Its stalks are usually cooked whole with the small loose flowerbuds and served drenched in butter. There are also white and green sprouting broccoli and these are treated in the same way. The flavor of all is excellent but they must be picked young or they become stringy and tough. Purple sprouting broccoli turns green on being cooked; the others keep their original color.

Cauliflower

Purple cauliflower

Calabrese

Savoy cabbage

Green cabbage

Calabrese broccoli

This beautiful bluish-green broccoli keeps its color when it is cooked. The large flower-heads sit on succulent spikes, and one of the tests for freshness is to see that the spike snaps cleanly: however, one's eye can also tell one whether they are juicy and stiff. Avoid flow-erets that show the least sign of turning yellow.

BRUSSELS SPROUTS

Brussels sprouts grow at the intersection of leaf and stalk on a tall plant that much resembles the old wild cabbage. They have a delicate nutty taste, especially when they are small. Cooked until tender but not too soft, they are an excellent vegetable.

The ideal size for brussels sprouts is just a little larger than hazelnuts. These, however, are more expensive than the ordinary medium-size ones. Do not waste much time before using them – they soon turn yellow. Look for compact green heads and uniform size so that they will cook evenly. They need to be washed, trimmed of any yellowing leaves, and to be cooked in fast-boiling well-salted water without a lid so that they preserve their good green color.

STALKS & SHOOTS
FLORENCE FENNEL

Looking like a short, bulbous celery plant, Florence fennel, also called sweet fennel or finocchio, is a close relation of the herb, and the same feathery leaves can be seen emerging from its fat overlapping stalks. Like the herb, it tastes of anise and its leaves can be used to flavor court bouillons for fish dishes. Southern Italians eat it raw, dressed in oil or with an aïoli sauce, and it makes a very good addition to a green salad.

When braising fennel, allow one head per person, trim away the stalks and string it as you would celery, and halve or quarter it. Choose fat round bulbs in preference to long flat ones. Buy fennel as fresh as possible; it should be white with a greenish cast – any yellowness is a sign of age. It will keep crisp in a plastic bag in the refrigerator.

ASPARAGUS

Although there are many species of asparagus, from the thorny ones of Spain to the shiny ones of the Far East, asparagus is always something of a luxury because its season is so short. There are also many differences in the way it is raised: French asparagus is cut near the crown when the top part has emerged above the soil; English and American asparagus is allowed to grow above the ground, which gives it its green color all the way down the stalk; Dutch and German ivory-tipped asparagus is always grown under mounds of soil, which helps to blanch it, and it is cut as soon as the tips begin to show.

Whatever the color, the thick varieties of asparagus are the ones which are most prized. Those of Argenteuil, with their white stalks showing a purple tinge towards the top and their pointed green and purple heads, are considered to be the very best, certainly in France, but this does not stop England and America from believing their asparagus to have a superior flavor. In fact each of the great asparagus-growing areas – Argenteuil, Candes, Fribourg, Schwetzingen, Bassano and Norfolk and many parts of the United States – tends to prefer its own asparagus, because although asparagus travels well it starts to lose flavor from the moment it is cut; it is a revelation to eat asparagus fresh from the garden, cut and cooked within the hour or even sooner.

Thick or thin, the tips are the best part and this is the part to inspect when buying asparagus. The tips should be tightly furled with the scales close together, and none of them discolored or moist. Loose asparagus, which is sometimes thin and often short, and may be sold as "grass" or "sprue" asparagus, is usually well worth having.

The difficulty encountered in cooking asparagus arises from the fact that the tips, being much more tender than the stalks,

Purple
sprouting
broccoli

Brussels
sprouts

White cabbage

Red cabbage

cook more quickly and may break off when you transfer the asparagus to the serving dish. The answer is to cook asparagus in an asparagus kettle, a special pan with a rack, but failing this, cook them tied together in bundles in a wide pan, in which case it is extremely important not to overcook them or boil them too fast, otherwise the tips will become damaged.

To prepare the asparagus, wash it well, cut off the hard ends and pare the lower part of the stalks with a knife or potato peeler, then tie the asparagus into two or three bundles. Bring a deep saucepan of well-salted water to the boil, lower the bundles into it so that the stalks are in water and the tips in the steam, and return to the boil as rapidly as possible. Cover with a loose dome of foil to help retain the steam and boil for 15 – 18 minutes, until the lower parts of the stalks are easily pierced with tip of a knife. Don't overcook them – they should be just tender when pierced and will go rather slimy if boiled for too long.

Save the asparagus water and a few token asparagus for making soup. Serve the rest, carefully drained, and slightly less than hot. In Britain, thick asparagus is always served as a separate course, usually at the beginning of the meal, occasionally at the end, and it is always best eaten with the fingers, the delicate tips first.

Served warm, thick asparagus is good with melted or whipped butter or hollandaise, or with mousseline sauce, or *à la flamande* with halved hard-boiled eggs and noisette butter served separately. Served *à la polonaise*, the noisette butter – butter heated in a pan until it is a pale hazelnut color – is poured over the tips that have been sprinkled with finely chopped hard-boiled eggs.

In Italy, asparagus is eaten with Parmesan and butter over the tips, melted for a moment under a broiler. If served cold, mayonnaise or vinaigrette are the usual accompaniments. As asparagus contains a certain amount of sulfur it spoils the taste of wine, so save this for other courses:

Thin asparagus makes a good vegetable dish and goes well with delicate, light kinds of meat: veal, brains, sweetbreads, chicken breasts, slices of turkey or rosy boiled ham, thinly sliced. Broken asparagus can also go into quiches or omelets. In restaurant dishes, the presence of asparagus tips is indicated by the words *à la princesse*, but in all but the very best establishments these tips will most likely be the limp canned variety as opposed to fresh specimens.

CELERY

This can be white, which means that it has been blanched during cultivation or is the self-blanching kind that is naturally golden-white, or it can be green. The white varieties are usually more tender and less bitter than those that are green.

Celery is usually sold neatly packaged in

Florence fennel

Asparagus

Green celery

White celery

Globe artichoke

Seakale beet

Swiss chard

transparent wrap and already washed, ready for use. The stalks should be thick and crisp, the leaves green and full of vitality and the base sound. When the leaves and the outer stalks are missing (which you can see when examining the base), the celery is not likely to be very fresh, but limp celery can be revived by wrapping it in moist paper and standing it in a jar of water. Raw celery sticks are often served with cheese in a tall pitcher with their decorative leaves intact, but the coarse outer strings should be removed first by cutting partway through the stalk bases and pulling off the attached strings down the length of the stalks.

Raw celery is excellent with cheese and, chopped, it is a good mixed with cream cheese and in sandwich fillings. Celery also goes into poultry stuffings and sauces, and can be stewed with butter and lemon juice as an accompaniment to game. It is delicious par-boiled, stuffed and served *au gratin,* and is equally good when braised plain, or *à la grecque,* when it is eaten cold.

SEA KALE

Highly popular in earlier times, although less often seen now, this frail, pale vegetable grows wild in English coastal districts, forcing its stalks up through piled up sand so that they emerge perfectly white. Cultivated sea kale is cut when its leaves are no more than a yellow frill edged with purple, and is boiled in seawater, or in salted water by those who are distant from the shore. The juicy but delicate stems are sometimes found in the stores wrapped in dark blue tissue paper, for once they are exposed to the light they very soon lose both their pallor and their flavor.

Sea kale should be boiled for about 18 – 20 minutes to become tender, or it can be par-boiled and then braised. Plain boiled in little bunches, it makes, like asparagus, a course of its own, and is served with the same sauces as asparagus. It is also good raw, like celery, with cheese.

SWISS CHARD AND SEAKALE BEET

No relation to the seakale of coastal areas, these varieties of beets are grown primarily for their pale, wide midribs. Their green leaves can also be prepared like spinach or beet greens (whose stalks are not big enough to be cooked separately).

The large, silvery Swiss chard, also known as silver seakale beet, has a delicate flavor and, like the smaller seakale beet, is extremely succulent when boiled or steamed. Both can be served *au graitin* or simply dressed with melted butter.

CARDOONS

A relation of the globe artichoke, the cardoon is cultivated for its leaf stalks and has a flavor that faintly resembles the artichoke. Left to itself, it produces a smaller, spikier head than the artichoke, which can be picked and eaten in exactly the same way, but what comes into the stores are the bottom ends of the plant, looking like overgrown grey-green celery. Like celery, cardoons are earthed up to blanch the stalks, which gives them their delicate texture and delicious flavor.

To prepare them, trim off the skin, which is fibrous and prickly at the ridges, blanch them in boiling water and then cook them for about 30 minutes in acidulated water – like artichokes, cardoons discolor easily when cooked. Serve them with a béchamel or cheese sause, or *alla piedmontese* – dipped in a sauce of anchovies, oil and garlic – or simply eat them with melted butter.

BAMBOO SHOOTS AND PALM HEARTS

Edible young bamboo shoots – and not all bamboos are edible – are bought fresh in the Far East and, stripped of their tough brown outer skins, the insides are eaten. Their texture is similar to celery and their taste to a globe artichoke.

The canned variety is the most readily available kind outside the Far East and needs no peeling, but it should be rinsed before use because it is preserved in brine. Chopped bamboo shoots can be used in a number of stir-fried vegetable and meat dishes, and as a garnish for clear chicken broth. They can also be served with any of the sauces that are suitable for asparagus.

Fresh palm hearts, which are the buds of cabbage palm trees, need to be blanched before being cooked to get rid of their bitter flavor. They can then be simmered in wine, perhaps, or braised. When hot, they are eaten with any of the sauces suitable for asparagus; cold, they need a vinaigrette dressing. They are also good in mixed salads. Hot or cold, they are usually served cut in half lengthwise.

GLOBE ARTICHOKES

Although not strictly a stalk, shoot or bud, the globe artichoke is usually considered in the same group as delicacies such as asparagus. While some of its flavor lies in the fat base of each of its leaves, the best part – the heart, or *fond* – lies deep within its center.

When you buy artichokes – they can be green or purplish – make sure they still have a good bloom on their leaves and that the centers have not unduly darkened, ready to burst into great purple thistle-like flower heads. They don't keep well and should be used at once, but if you must keep them, place their stalks – they are usually sold with about 4in/10cm of stalk – into water.

To prepare them for cooking, twist off the stalks, which will also remove some of the tougher fibres from the base. Then, with a stainless-steel knife, cut the globe flush so that it won't wobble on the plate when it is served and rub the cut surface with lemon to prevent it turning black. If the leaves are very spiky, cut them into a pretty V shape. Wash the artichoke and then boil it in acidulated water in a non-oxidizing pan, perhaps with a piece of lemon tied to its base. Test for readiness by tugging at a leaf: when it comes away and is tender, the artichoke is done and ready to be drained upside down on a rack.

One of the best ways of eating globe artichokes is simply to take each leaf in the fingers and dip the fleshy part in turn into melted butter or into vinaigrette or hollandaise. Then draw it through the teeth, eating the fleshy part and putting the remains of the leaf onto your plate. When you come towards the end of the vegetable, and the tiny pale leaves seem to be arranged in the form of a little pointed hat, grasp it tightly at its top and pull off the whole rosette. Pull away and discard the prickly straw-like choke, which may come away with one tug or need a bit of scraping, and eat the heart, which is slightly pitted, with a knife and fork.

It is possible to remove the choke before cooking, to form little cups. This is usually done in good restaurants, where instead of a simple butter or vinaigrette dressing you may be offered various sauces such as puréed shallots reduced in wine. The hearts can also be stuffed, perhaps with a béchamel enriched with egg yolks and Parmesan. They are usually parboiled before they are stuffed, and then go into the oven, surrounded by vegetables and anointed with oil or butter, until the stuffing is cooked. For delicate dishes or when artichoke hearts are required as a garnish, remove the green leaves, keeping the firm white-green part.

Among the many ways of preparing artichokes, the Italians have produced the most inventive. They simmer large globes in broth or wine, or in wine with oil, tomatoes and garlic, and fry small, tender ones in oil; sometimes they blanch them and then dip them in batter before deep frying them. As elsewhere, they are also eaten cold.

PEAS, BEANS AND CORN

From the moment they are picked, peas, beans and sweet corn start converting their sugar into starch. Because this process subtly alters both their taste and texture, it is freshness just as much as youth that matters and they should be chosen carefully and eaten the very day they are bought. Freezing, however, arrests these changes, which is why frozen peas, beans and sweet corn retain their sweetness and melting consistency so well.

PEAS

Once inordinately expensive and considered a green luxury, peas have become one of the best loved of all vegetables and endless varieties have been developed, especially in

England where the climate suits them to perfection.

Snow peas

Snow peas, also known as mangetout and sugar peas, are, as their French name suggests, eaten pods and all. There are many varieties, all bred with the minimum of thin, tough membrane that lines the pod of the common green pea, so both the large, flat snow pea pod with immature seeds and the smaller, darker kind make tender eating, provided they are very young. If they have threads at the sides, these should be removed in the kitchen during topping and tailing.

Snow peas taste best when they are briefly boiled, in plenty of well-salted water; the salt helps them retain their color. When cooked, they should still have a little bite to them, and they are best served perfectly plain with enough butter to coat each pod. Very young snow peas are good in salads, and all snow peas are excellent when they are stir-fried.

Asparagus peas

These are not a relation of the asparagus but of the cow pea, and in fact not a true pea at all, are rarely seen these days. They have winged pods which, like the snow pea, are eaten as well as the seed, but they are only good when they are very young and 2 in/5 cm long or less.

Garden peas and petits pois

Contrary to popular belief, petits pois are not small because they are immature but are a dwarf variety. These are the peas canned in vast quantities by the French and Belgians, and they are excellent: tiny, dull green and very sweet, quite unlike most other canned peas, especially the fat, ugly canned peas sold in Britain, swimming in green dye. These are best avoided altogether.

Gardeners make a distinction between two types of garden pea: the larger marrowfat, which is wrinkled when dried, and the varieties that remain smooth when dried. The former is much sweeter and is the one most often frozen.

The reason for the disappearance of many varieties of green peas is, of course, the ubiquitous frozen pea; more expensive to be sure, but a great timesaver. And by the time peas bought in their pods have been shelled, the actual price difference does become blurred.

Shelled peas respond to all sorts of treatment: in England they are liked best plain, boiled and bathed in butter, but some cooks like to add a small sprig of fresh mint. In Italy peas are often mixed with fine shreds of raw ham, or with rice, in which case the dish becomes *risi e bisi*. In the countries where vegetables are habitually served in a light coating of béchamel sauce peas, too, are given this treatment. They are often mixed with carrots, *à la flamande*.

Petits pois à la française are peas cooked in a lettuce-lined saucepan with a little sugar, some tiny silver onions, a lump of butter and only as much water as clings to the lettuce leaves after washing. Cooked in this way, the peas turn a delicate yellowish color and have a most delicious flavor; even peas on the mealy side become melting and young tasting. Really solid older peas are best for fresh green-pea soup or purées.

POLE BEANS

This is a group of beans, eaten for their pods, which came to market in colors ranging from deep green and purple to pale yellow. The two main types are the French or green beans, and the runner or pole beans.

Of the French beans there are dozens of varieties. Snap or string beans, a fairly fat, fleshy variety, should snap in half juicily if they are fresh. The highly prized haricot vert is slim and delicate and should be eaten very young and when no larger than the prong of a carving fork. The yellow wax-bean is also a French bean and is somewhat mild in taste.

Runner beans have long, rough and usually stringy pods, although stringless varieties are available. As their name suggests they are a type of climbing bean, as are the delicious purple-podded beans, which have stringless purple pods, but turn the normal green when they are cooked.

PREPARING GLOBE ARTICHOKE HEARTS

1 SNAP

Snap off the stalk, drawing with it the fibers from the heart.

3 SLICE

Slice off the top of the artichoke so that the pink tips of the choke are just visible.

2 TRIM

Trim the stem end with a stainless-steel knife, just exposing the white base, and trim away all the tough outer leaves. Have a lemon handy to rub on the exposed parts to prevent them discoloring.

4 SCOOP

Scoop out the prickly choke with a sharp-sided stainless-steel teaspoon until you are left with a pale empty cup-like heart. Put this immediately into a bowl of water, acidulated with lemon juice.

Whatever the type, podded beans should be crisp and bright – avoid buying wilted ones or overly mature beans with tough-looking pods. They all need topping and tailing, and some types still need de-stringing. Test for stringiness by keeping the top or tail end just attached to the pod and drawing it downwards: if a portion of stout thread comes away, careful de-stringing is indicated.

All podded beans are cooked in the same way. Too often they are overcooked, but they should be plunged into well-salted, rapidly boiling water and cooked until just *al dente*. Once drained, they can be tossed in butter until they glisten, or French beans can be served in a sauce containing shallots, or cream and butter with chives, or bathed in a tomato paste with a touch of onion.

FAVA BEANS AND LIMA BEANS

In their first youth, neither fava beans nor lima beans strictly require shelling, but the pods are nearly always discarded to reveal large, flattish seeds.

Fava beans

These are also known as broad beans or Windsor beans; these are the original Old World bean, much appreciated in Italy and Spain. These large, lumpy beans with their furry lined pods should be shelled immediately before going into the pot, unless they

are very young, in which case they need only to be topped and tailed and can then be cut up, cooked and eaten pods and all.

Lima beans

Named after the capital of Peru, these are most familiar in America in their shelled and frozen state, but are at their best when they can be bought fresh and in their shells. They appear in the American Indian dish succotash, which also includes sweet corn, and are known in the southern American states as butter beans. There are two types of lima bean – the baby Sievas, pale in color, and the larger Fordhooks.

For a plain dish of fava beans or lima beans, plunge them into rapidly boiling water and cook until just tender, but not a moment longer. They are also delicious with cooked ham or bacon. Elderly beans need skinning after they are cooked.

OKRA

These curved and pointed seed pods came originally from Africa, but travelled to America and feature a great deal in Creole cooking. The flavor resembles that of eggplant but the texture is mucilaginous, and this is what gives the body to the Creole stews and gumbos to which okra is added.

Crossbreeding has produced a range of colors and surfaces, but the slim green octagonal okra is the one usually sold in the West. Look for crisp pods and avoid any that are shrivelled or bruised. To cook okra whole, trim off the tip and the cap, but be sure not to expose the seeds and sticky juices

inside or the okra will split and lose shape during cooking. Cooked in boiling salted water until just tender, they can be served with a tomato sauce or simply tossed in butter.

BEAN SPROUTS

The sprouts that can be bought in plastic bags and are the main ingredient of chop suey have usually been sprouted from mung beans or soybeans. Look for crisp, pale sprouts; even a hint of exuding brown juice means that they are past their prime. Mild flavored, they add a crunchy texture to salads, or they can be stir-fried briefly over high heat and seasoned with soy sauce and scallions. Serve them immediately or they will lose their crunch. Keep sprouts in a plastic bag or box in the refrigerator while they are waiting to be used.

CORN

One of the delights of late summer is the appearance on the market of fresh, tender young sweet corn. The husks should be clean and green, the silk tassels bright and golden brown with no sign of dampness or matting, the kernels plump, well filled and milky, with no space between the rows. Avoid cobs with immature white kernels or older large ones that look tough and dry.

With fresh sweet corn, time is of the essence – the briefer the span between picking and eating, the sweeter and more tender the corn will be. But if you can't use it immediately then keep it in plastic bags in

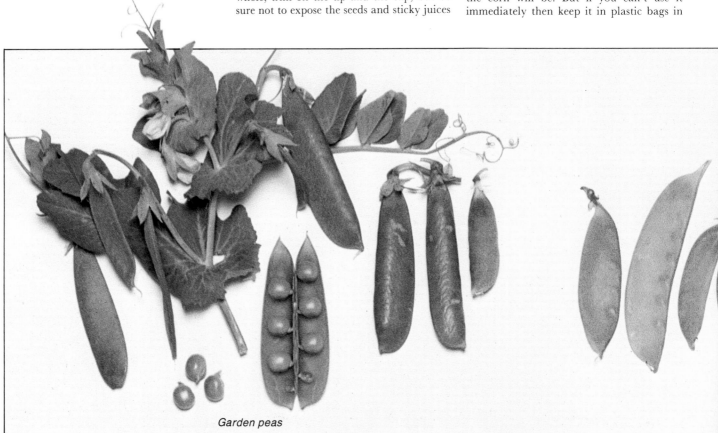

Garden peas

the refrigerator for two or three days. Allow corn plenty of space – if the cobs are piled on top of each other, this tends to generate warmth and "cook" the corn.

To cook corn on the cob, strip away the green packaging and silk tassel and plunge into briskly boiling water or milk and water. A little sugar can be added for extra sweetness – especially for the corn sold in Europe, which is never quite as sweet and tender as American corn.

Serve with plenty of butter, salt and freshly ground pepper, and large napkins.

THE ONION FAMILY

Being both flavoring agent and vegetable in its own right, the onion is something that no kitchen can ever be without.

GREEN OR FRESH ONIONS

These are eaten fresh in salads, but can also be cooked. There are two types of green onions, so called because of the green leaves that form above the white part.

Scallions or spring onions

These may be slim and tiny, like miniature leeks, except that their leaves are tubular, or they may have been lifted from the soil after small silvery bulbs have formed just above the roots. They taste mild, and both the white bottoms and the green tops are used as lively additions to salads. When cooked they are added to some dishes in which other onions would be too strong.

Welsh onions or Japanese bunching onions

If you find scallions mentioned in Chinese or Japanese recipes, these are the onions you should use, if you can get them – they are not widely known in the West and certainly not in Wales, despite their name. The difference between scallions and Welsh onions is that the bulbs, or enlargements, of the Welsh onions are covered with dry outer coats. They grow in a cluster and can be used early in the year as scallions, then as fresh bulb onions.

Globe or dry-skinned onions

It is a good idea to try to buy globe onions in assorted sizes, or to choose smaller rather than larger specimens as, once cut, they do not keep well. To keep back the tears when peeling an onion, try skinning it under running water.

Chopping an onion into dice can be quite a fast business if efficiently tackled. Peel the onion but do not cut off the root end. Halve the onion through the root and lay the half onion cut side down. Slice down into narrow strips from tip end to root end, but do not let the strips fall apart. Now, holding the half onion together, cut strips lengthwise, at right angles to the first cuts, remove the root end and the onion will fall into dice.

Globe onions come in all sizes from pearly button onions to coppery spheres as large as a grapefruit, and in a variety of shapes: oval, round, slender and flat. All come to a peak at the top.

Yellow onions

These are so called although their outer skin is golden brown rather than yellow, are considered to be the most pungent of all the globe onions. Look for sound specimens, dry, with no trace of moisture at the base or the neck and with no growth of light greenery at the top – a sign that they have begun to sprout again at the expense of the soundness of their core.

Spanish onions

These large, flattened, brown or pale copper-colored onions are generally inclined to be milder and sweeter than the yellow variety. Their size makes them particularly suitable for stuffing and baking.

Italian onions

These are large, relatively mild and distinguished by their deep red skin and the red-tinged layers below the skin. They can be used for the same purposes as Spanish onions and are good to eat raw.

White or silver onions

These relatively mild little onions have shimmery silver skins, They are about the size of a walnut and are best either added to stews or served in a cream sauce. Very tiny white onions are called pearl or cocktail onions and are sold in jars.

SHALLOTS

These slender, pear-shaped bulbs with long necks and skins that range from grey to copper are intense in taste without being unduly pungent. They grow singly or in clusters and are more seasonal than onions,

Early snow peas   *Late snow peas*

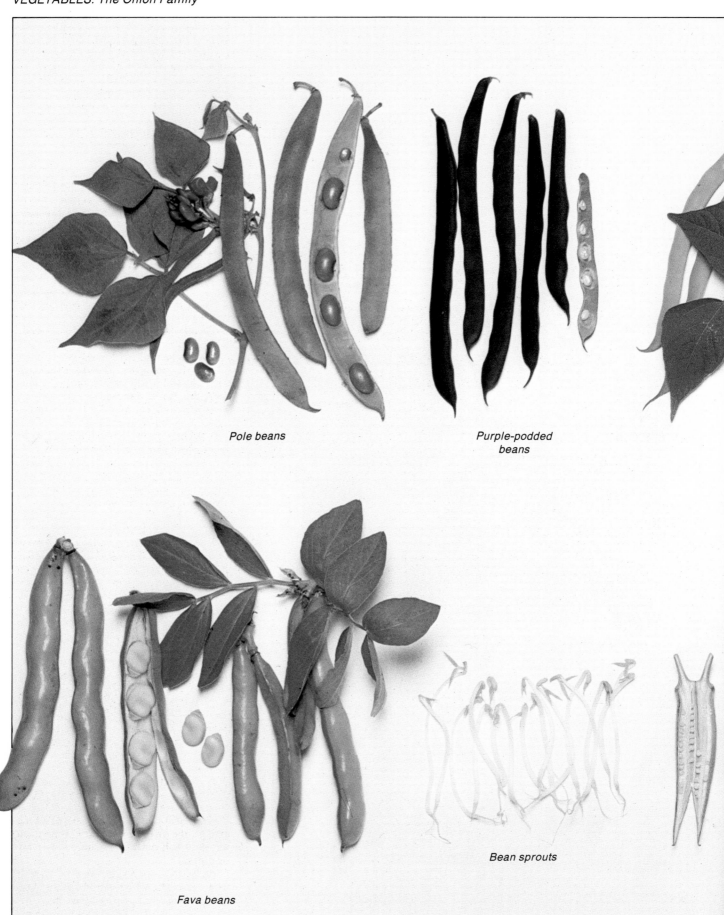

Pole beans

Purple-podded
beans

Bean sprouts

Fava beans

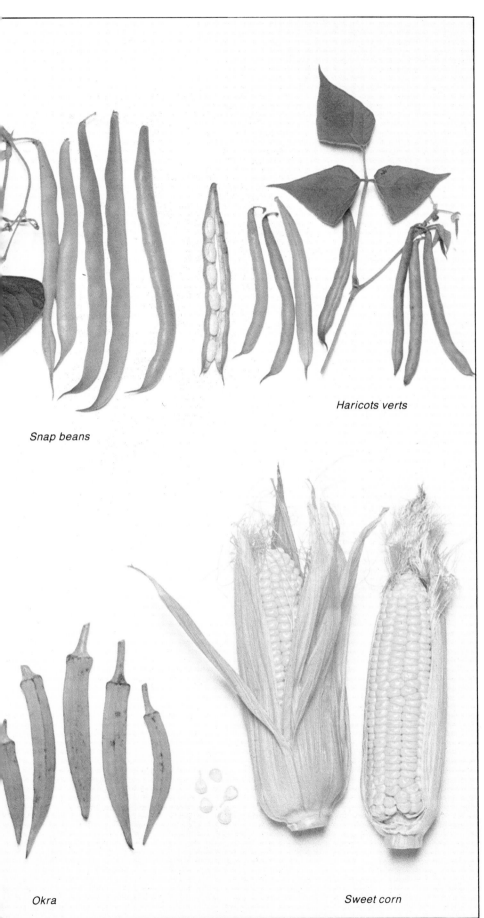

Haricots verts

Snap beans

Okra

Sweet corn

since they do not keep as well. The crisp layers of their flesh are finely textured, and since shallots taste sweet and delicate they are mostly used for flavoring.

When recipes specify shallots, they should be used. On the other hand, it is sometimes perfectly in order, although extravagant, to use shallots instead of onion. The exception comes when browning is involved – this makes shallots taste a little bitter.

GARLIC

Garlic grows in a cluster of pointed bulbs, called cloves, from a single base. Many people are prejudiced against garlic because it lingers on the breath, but it is said that vast quantities of garlic eaten at a single sitting will not have much effect on the breath. It is certainly true that a slowly cooked dish using a great deal of garlic tastes much sweeter and far less garlicky than something like a salad with raw peeled and bruised garlic in the dressing.

When buying garlic, look for fat, round, hard bulbs.

Most garlic is allowed to dry off: it keeps well in a dry airy place. Too much moisture in the air, and it will start sprouting in due course: too much warmth, and the interior cloves turn to black dust – but this takes a matter of months rather than weeks.

To prepare garlic, carefully skin as many cloves as you plan to use. Whether you chop them in the ordinary way, mash them with salt under the point of a knife, or crush them in a garlic press, the finer the result, the more of the pungent oils are released.

LEEKS

With their flat leaves arranged in chevron formation, leeks are more delicate in taste than onions. They are excellent simmered in butter, stewed in red wine, or lightly browned and then cooked in a tomato sauce.

If they have a drawback, it is that they can be rather a bore to clean. There is no problem when recipes call for chopped leeks, when it is a case of chopping first – after pulling off the outer membrane and trimming the wilted part of the greenery – and cleaning later. This is best done by placing the chopped leeks in a colander set in a bowl and running cold water over them until all the grit has settled at the bottom of the bowl. But when recipes call for sliced leeks, it is necessary to loosen the leaves gently so that the water can run right into the furled vegetable. Only the outside dirt has been removed by the growers; in the kitchen it is usually a question of making little slits with the point of a knife in appropriate places and of rinsing until all the grit has gone, or cutting them almost in half down the middle if they are very gritty.

When you buy leeks, examine them at both ends. The white part should be firm and unblemished; the green part fresh and lively, since it it useful for soups or stock.

Avoid leeks which are sold trimmed as they are probably rather old.

ROOTS AND TUBERS

POTATOES

Potatoes are one of the world's most important food crops; easy to grow, cheap to buy, simple to cook and tremendously filling.

Different types of potatoes, round, oval or kidney shaped, pink, red or white, do have very different qualities, and a well-informed supplier will be able to tell you which variety is which. There are floury or mealy potatoes, ideal for mashing and baking, but annoying if you want to boil them whole as they tend to fall apart in the water. They are also useless for making French fries. Waxy potatoes are very firm fleshed and not at all good for mashing, as they become glutinous, but they make excellent potato salads, lovely boiled potatoes, and excellent pommes dauphinoise, when the potatoes are cooked in slices that are supposed to remain whole.

There are also all-purpose potatoes, whose texture is described as firm. These can be used for almost anything, except perhaps potato salads. They don't disintegrate, can be made into French fries and are good for baking. But they don't always have the best flavor, so try different varieties.

Spanish onions

Yellow globe onions

Leeks

Pickling onions

Shallots

As well as different varieties there are, of course, new and old potatoes. Potatoes which are called new or early are simply those dug early in the season while they are still small and sweet. Old potatoes, or maincrop, are lifted when they are mature and fully grown, and have converted their sugar into starch. These can be stored through the winter and until the beginning of the next season when the new potatoes reappear.

Buying and storing potatoes

New potatoes should be small and faintly translucent under a coating of slightly damp loam; if the skin is a little ragged and so tender that you can pull it off in strips, so much the better – this shows that the potatoes are fresh and will be easy to scrape. New potatoes do not keep particularly well, becoming more difficult to scrape (in which case scrub them and cook them in their skins). They also lose their flavor after a few days, so buy them in small quantities and keep them in a cool, dark place.

Old potatoes are more amenable and can be stored in a cool, dark, dry place for months on end. Choose dry potatoes with some earth on them, free of sprouts and without the green patches that appear when potatoes are exposed to light – these contain poisonous alkaloids. If they do have green parts, cut them off. Avoid potatoes that have scaly or rotting patches and, if buying washed potatoes in bags, avoid those that look damp or show signs of condensation as you may find that they have an unpleasant, moldy flavor.

Potatoes for boiling

The very best dish in the world is probably new potatoes boiled and served with a good deal of melted butter and a sprinkling of coarse salt. For perfection, choose walnut-sized potatoes, scrape or scrub them and drop them into already boiling salted water. Bring them back to the boil, and after about 10 minutes of gentle boiling start testing frequently with a kitchen needle or skewer. Drain as soon as they are tender. A small sprig of fresh mint added to the water heightens the flavor.

For a delicate, somewhat earthy flavor, old potatoes can be scrubbed and boiled in their skins – this conserves the vitamins, too – and then peeled while they are still hot, unless you want to be rustic and serve them with skins on.

Otherwise, old potatoes should be peeled as thinly as possible, as many of the vitamins are concentrated just under the skin. If they are not to be cooked immediately they must be put straight into a bowl of water or they will dry out, and some varieties will discolor on contact with air, but don't soak them too long as this can also lead to a loss of vitamins.

When ready to cook them, put them in a pan of salted cold water, bring them to the boil and then cook them fairly gently – fast boiling causes them to bump against each other, which breaks them up. When they are just tender, drain them thoroughly and return them to the pan. Let them steam for a minute, then drop in a few nuts of butter and turn the potatoes over gently until they are well coated.

Potatoes for sautéing

The dry, firm texture of yellow-fleshed maincrop potatoes makes them ideal for sautéing. Cut them up and drop them into boiling, well-salted water for about five minutes before frying them, or fry them raw, drying them in a cloth before putting them into the hot fat.

Potatoes can also be grated before they are sautéed. Rösti, the Swiss national dish, is usually made with potatoes that have been boiled the previous day and kept overnight, traditionally in the snow but the refrigerator will do, to dry them out a little. They are then grated and fried gently in butter, formed into a pancake and inverted on to a plate with the golden crust uppermost.

Potatoes for frying

Whether you call deep-fried potato sticks French fries or chips, choose firm, dry potatoes. The yellow-fleshed varieties are best, although whites are also good. These are also the potatoes to use for croquettes, game chips, gaufrettes – waffle-cut game chips – matchsticks, ribbons, potato puffs and all the many other varieties of fried potatoes.

When frying raw sliced or chipped potatoes, they should be soaked in cold water for at least an hour to rid them of their surface starch, otherwise the pieces will stick together when fried. Dry them well, since hot fat foams up over wet potatoes and could easily bubble over.

Potatoes for roasting

Most maincrop varieties are fine for roasting, but small potatoes should be avoided because roasting tends to dry them out, and new potatoes do not roast well. Potatoes roast better if they are first boiled in well-salted water for about five minutes, drained and then returned to the pan to dry off over a low heat, uncovered, for a minute or two.

Potatoes for mashing

Dry, floury, "old" potatoes are ideal for mashing. Peel and boil them until they are very tender, drain them well and then mash them thoroughly before adding any liquid, which should be hot for best results. Add butter at the end, beat thoroughly and taste for seasoning – they always need more salt. In France, meat juices are sometimes added to mashed potatoes instead of milk.

Potatoes for baking

Dry, floury potatoes such as the long, white-skinned varieties are ideal for baking. They have a white, creamy flesh and are usually large or medium size, which is what is needed for baking. So-called russet potatoes are also good. Baked potatoes are extremely health giving since there is no loss of goodness or flavor into water that is then thrown away.

They are also a wonderful vehicle for toppings such as cheese or sour cream.

Potatoes for salads

The classic potato salad is plainly boiled and sliced waxy potatoes mixed with a simple vinaigrette while they are still hot. A little more dressing is added just before serving. Another version is mixed first with a little dressing while still warm, and then with some good, creamy homemade mayonnaise when cool. Celery, freshly cooked French beans or dill are good additions to fresh potato salad. Serve it with frankfurters or salt herrings – its bland flavor is an excellent foil.

Garlic

Scallions

SWEET POTATOES

The tuberous roots of a tropical vine, sweet potatoes have a taste of faintly scented artichoke. The small or medium-size ones are best; they should be firm and well shaped. Avoid cracks and damp patches.

Sweet potatoes are an important ingredient in Creole cookery and are eaten fried, whipped up into purées or soufflés and as an accompaniment to sugar-cured Virginia ham. In the southern United States they are often boiled and mashed with nutmeg, or made into a sweet-potato pie. Candied, they are a traditional accompaniment for a Thanksgiving turkey, and in Australia they are parboiled and roasted with pork.

YAMS

Yams belong to a family of climbing plants that flourish in South and Central America and the West Indies. They come in a large number of shapes and sizes and the flesh is white or yellow, with a texture similar to potatoes. In North America, where true yams are not cultivated, orange-fleshed sweet potatoes with brownish skins are known as yams. The true yam, however, is much sweeter and moister than the sweet potato, although both are usually prepared in much the same ways, boiled and served with butter, nutmeg and other spices as well as apples, oranges and nuts. Like sweet potatoes, they are delicious when fried.

CARROTS

These range from slim little slips, pale apricot in color and no longer than a little finger, to long, stout cylinders, light orange to the ·deep color of nectarines.

Young carrots, tender and melting, have a most delicate flavor. Washed and simply thrown into boiling water for no more than seven minutes, then tossed in butter and sprinkled with parsley, they are one of the celebratory dishes of early summer. Parboiled and glazed in a stout pan with butter and possibly a little sugar to emphasize their natural sweetness, they become one of the garnishes of haute cuisine.

When young carrots are boiled in their skins, then drained and rubbed in a towel, the skin will slip off quite easily and in this way the smooth, transparent inner skin, beneath which the vitamins lie, is retained.

Mature carrots are the great standby for hearty winter dishes. They accompany boiled beef and dumplings and it is to them, together with onions, celery and leeks, that good warming broths owe their flavor – but don't put in too many or the broth will

Old, or maincrop, all-purpose whites

Old, or maincrop, all-purpose yellows

Waxy maincrop for boiling

Waxy salad potatoes

Yam

become so sweet that people will think there is sugar in it. They are also used to make the excellent carrot soup, potage de Crécy.

The stubby, bright, almost translucent carrots of uniform size usually found in supermarkets are bred more for the convenience of the seller than the buyer, because they travel well. Although their flavor is a little elusive they are delicious eaten raw and make a good dish on their own, either as carrots Vichy – sliced and cooked in Vichy water and spinkled with parsley – or simply served with butter and parsley. Their main advantage is that they stay crisp for longer during cooking.

Buying and storing carrots
Avoid specimens that are rubbery, blemished or cracked with age. The green discloration sometimes seen at the top of certain carrots denotes immaturity but does not diminish their flavor. If storing carrots in the vegetable compartment of the refrigerator, take them out of their plastic wrapping. Outside the refrigerator, they should be kept in a cool, airy place to preserve their crispness.

PARSNIPS
Related to the carrot, parsnips are almost as sweet but blander. They are delicious in soups and stews, and there are many old country recipes for parsnip flans and puddings which make good use of their sweetness. Sweet parsnip dishes are part of the English country tradition, as is parsnip wine. Boiled parsnips mixed with mayonnaise were once served as mock lobster.

Available from early autumn until spring, parsnips are at their best in midwinter, especially when their ivory skin has been touched by frost. They can be bought washed, or with traces of soil still clinging to them, in which case they keep better. Those with brown patches or those that look wizened or dry should be avoided, but parsnips with "fangs" and blemishes can be cheap buys and as good and as nutritious as perfect specimens.

Store parsnips in a cool place such as an airy larder or the crisper compartment of the refrigerator.

SALSIFY
Black-skinned salsify, which has snowy white flesh, is known as scorzonera; white salsify is also called the oyster plant because its taste is supposedly reminiscent of oysters. In fact, the flavor of both has a nodding acquaintance with that of asparagus; it is just as delicate and therefore at its best when simply boiled or poached and served with a good knob of butter, or perhaps a creamy white sauce made of a roux moistened with the cooking liquid and a dash of cream.

Salsify is neither easy to peel nor to clean, so it best boiled in its skin and peeled afterwards, or skinned thinly with a swivelling potato peeler and plunged immediately into a saucepan containing a "blanc" – water to which a tablespoon of flour has been added (vegetables cooked in a blanc will keep their color). The white stalks should then be cooled and gently reheated with a little butter. As they are water retaining, they will neither fry nor burn providing the pan has a well-fitting lid.

When buying salsify, choose those with a topknot of fresh-looking leaves, avoiding any that look sad or shrivelled, or buy canned salsify, since this is one of the few vegetables that lends itself really well to the canning process.

CELERIAC
The edible root of a certain kind of celery, celeriac is not a neat-looking vegetable and needs to be peeled with a sharp knife. Under its brown exterior the flesh is pale, but discolors when exposed to the air so should be plunged immediately into a bowl of acidulated water. Cooked, its texture is similar to that of a potato, but less smooth and with more bite to it. Celeriac is a great standby; soups and broths are often improved by a slight celery flavor and it is in season when celery perhaps is not. Boiled and diced, celeriac is delicious in potato salads, and in Germany it is served with diced apples, potatoes and beets in a herring salad. Puréed, it is excellent with game.

BEETS
Globe shaped or long and pointed, beets come in bunches with edible greenery at the top when young, loose and trimmed of leaves when mature. When buying raw beets make sure that their whiskers are intact and that

Sweet potatoes

New, or early, potatoes for boiling

they have at least 2in/5cm of stalk at the top – if they are too closely trimmed they will bleed, meaning that they will give up their color to the cooking water and be no more than pale shadows of themselves when they are cooked. For the same reason, beets are never peeled before they are cooked.

When making borsch, the ruby-colored Russian soup that is as good iced as it is hot, make use of the beets' tendency to bleed and don't worry about keeping the skin intact. It is a good idea, though, to cook one or two specimens whole to add at the end, cut into julienne strips, to bring their fine dark red color to the soup.

To prepare sliced beets as a vegetable dish, sauté them gently, moistening them with wine vinegar to set the brilliant colour and give them a perfect flavor. The greenery attached to young beets can be cooked and tastes like spinach.

Beets are not always red but also golden and white; they may taste the same and are sometimes served with hare and venison, but they are rather disappointing to look at after the glorious red ones.

If buying beets already cooked, make sure the skins are still moist. It is best to buy them on the day they have been boiled, while they are still warm and steaming. (Avoid like the plague those that have already been steeped in vinegar – they are violent and indigestible.) In France beets are cooked in the oven or in the ashes of a wood fire, which gives them a charred skin and a smoky flavor.

RUTABAGAS AND TURNIPS

Both these roots are, in fact, members of the cabbage family and so closely related that it is not surprising to find their names sometimes used interchangeably. To add to the confusion, rutabagas are also called swedes, while in Scotland they are known as neeps and are considered to be turnips, and they are also sometimes called Swedish turnips. Rutabagas, however, with their pale, dense flesh, grown to immense sizes without impairment to taste or texture, while white-fleshed turnips coarsen if they are allowed to become larger than tennis balls. They should be heavy with no spongy patches, worm holes or large blemishes. Specimens that have grown side roots should be avoided.

Rutabagas

These make a delicious winter dish when mashed alone and are the essential ingredient for "mashed neeps," a Scottish dish served with haggis, in which the rutabagas are mashed with potatoes and butter.

Baby turnips

Globe shaped, conical or flattened, baby turnips are as different from maincrop turnips as new potatoes are from old. They should not be peeled before cooking, but rubbed afterwards: the skin comes off easily and beneath it lies their flavor and goodness. Although it seems a pity to do more to any young vegetable than to boil it for a few minutes, glazed baby turnips are delicous and the classic accompaniment to roast duck. Their fresh greenery can be cooked in the same way as collards.

Mature turnips

They may have a purplish tinge on their nether regions and are peeled before roasting or boiling.

KOHLRABI

White, pale green or purple, kohlrabi is a member of the brassica family but is bred for its bulbous stem; it looks like a horizontally ridged turnip and is at its best when young and small, since it becomes coarse and fibrous as it grows larger. The leaves, which grow in stalks from the spaced-out ridges, can be used in the same way as young turnip tops, but are usually removed before they are marketed. The skin can be peeled easily with a kitchen knife to expose the pale green flesh below. Tiny kohlrabi can be cooked whole, but the larger ones need to be sliced.

JERUSALEM ARTICHOKES

These knobbly tubers are neither artichokes nor do they come from the Holy City, but from the New World. Like the sunflowers to which they are related, they were christened girasole – from whence "Jerusalem" – because their yellow flowers tend to turn towards the sun.

Jerusalem artichokes are at their best in the late autumn and winter. When buying them, look for neat specimens with the minimum of knobs. Their skin is brownish, like that of potatoes but more delicate, and the white flesh must not be exposed to the air as it quickly turns a grey-purple color. When boiling artichokes, add a squeeze of lemon juice to the water – this will prevent them turning color, especially if you plan to make the delicious white soup, sometimes called Palestine soup.

RECIPE SUGGESTION
Jerusalem artichokes

2 lb/900 g Jerusalem artichokes
2 tablespoons/30 g butter
salt and freshly ground pepper
5 cups/1 liter chicken stock or water
2 tablespoons chopped parsley
$\frac{2}{3}$ cup/1.5 dl heavy cream
grating of nutmeg
squeeze of lemon juice

SERVES 4

Peel the artichokes and slice them thinly, a little thicker than a coin. Melt the butter in a large heavy frying pan and put in the artichokes. Season with salt and pepper and cook gently for 5–6 minutes until each slice is well coated in butter. Add enough stock or water to come just to the top of the artichokes and simmer, uncovered, until just tender. Add the parsley and the cream and continue to cook gently until the artichokes are bathed in a creamy sauce. Taste and add salt, pepper, nutmeg and a squeeze of lemon juice. Serve hot with game or roast pork.

Carrots

Jerusalem artichokes

Turnips

Beets

Kohlrabi

Parsnips

Black salsify

Celeriac

Rutabagas

RECIPE SUGGESTIONS

Céleri rémoulade

1 lb/450 g celeriac—2 heads

for the sauce:
1 generous teaspoon Dijon mustard
1 egg yolk
generous ⅔ cup/1.5 dl peanut or sunflower oil
squeeze of lemon juice
salt and freshly ground pepper
2–3 tablespoons light cream

SERVES 4

Make the sauce in exactly the same way as you make mayonnaise, mixing the mustard and egg yolk together vigorously with a pinch of salt before starting to add the oil. Stir in the cream at the end and taste for seasoning.

Peel the celeriac and grate it coarsely, either on the wavy blade of a mandoline or on a grater. Drop the shreds into a bowl of water acidulated with lemon juice as you grate them, to keep them nice and white. Bring a saucepan of salted water to a vigorous boil. Drop in the grated celeriac and drain it immediately in a colander, splashing it with cold water to cool it down. This short blanching keeps the celeriac white but some prefer it raw. When it has drained thoroughly and is completely cold, mix it with the mayonnaise and serve the same day, either as a dish on its own or as part of an hors d'oeuvre.

Mashed rutabaga

1 rutabaga
2 potatoes
2 tablespoons/30 g butter
3–4 tablespoons heavy cream
salt and freshly ground pepper

SERVES 4

Peel the rutabaga and potatoes and cut them into chunks. Put them in a saucepan of cold salted water, bring to the boil and boil until completely tender. Drain the vegetables in a colander, mash them and then make a fine purée by sieving them through the medium blade of a food mill or using a food processor. Return the purée to the cleaned saucepan and beat in the butter and cream; season with salt and plenty of pepper. Serve very hot.

Ratatouille

scant ⅔ cup/1.5 dl olive oil
2 lb/900 g tomatoes
salt and freshly ground pepper
2 pinches sugar (optional)
2–3 onions
3 cloves garlic
2 red or green sweet peppers
1 lb/450 g zucchini
1 large eggplant

SERVES 6

Heat half the olive oil in a small pan. Skin and chop the tomatoes and simmer them in the oil with a seasoning of salt, pepper and, if they are not very ripe and sweet, 2 good pinches of sugar, for 10–15 minutes.

Meanwhile, peel the onions and slice them downwards, fairly coarsely. Peel and slice the garlic, cut the peppers in strips or squares, discarding the core and seeds, and cut the zucchini into ¼ in/5 mm slices or quarter them lengthwise. Finally, cut the eggplant into slices and quarter each slice. Heat the remaining oil in a heavy-bottomed pan, throw in the onions and garlic and fry gently. When the onions are soft, throw in the peppers, then the zucchini and finally the slices of eggplant. Add salt and pepper and continue to cook slowly.

When the vegetables are shining and beginning to soften, add the tomatoes, which will have collapsed to a fairly moist sauce. Gently stir the vegetables around at all stages of cooking this dish, otherwise they will cook unevenly and stick to the bottom of the pan. When all the vegetables are soft and tender, the ratatouille is done. It reheats very well.

Ratatouille comes from the south of France where the dish varies from a delicate mixture of lightly cooked vegetables to a really dark brown stew, floating with oil and exhaling garlic. Ideally it should be rich and moist with different vegetables just distinguishable in a smooth, aromatic tomato sauce. Frying the vegetables and tomatoes separately, as here, helps them to remain intact.

Sweet pepper salad

2 red, yellow, or green sweet peppers
2–3 tablespoons olive oil
salt

SERVES 2–4 AS AN HORS D'OEUVRE OR SALAD

Heat the broiler.

Remove the stalks from the peppers with a small sharp knife, pulling out the cores with them, and shake out any loose seeds. Put the peppers whole under the hot broiler and let them blister and blacken, turning them frequently so that they become black all over. Take them from under the broiler and wrap them in a clean cloth and leave them to cool. When cooled in this way, the peppers will be perfectly easy to skin.

The broiling makes them sweet and mellow.

Cut them into large 1 in/2.5 cm wide strips and lay them all facing the same way on a rough plate—this is simple food and does not need smart serving. Pour the oil over the peppers, sprinkle with salt, turn the pieces over in this dressing and serve lukewarm or cold.

ALTERNATIVE: *add some lemon juice to the dressing.*

Stuffed tomatoes

6 large tomatoes
1 large clove garlic
8 green olives
6 anchovy fillets
½ cup/55 g fresh white bread crumbs
½ stick/55 g butter, melted
1 teaspoon chopped basil or marjoram
salt

SERVES 4–6

Preheat the oven to 325°F/170°C.

Cut the tomatoes in half across the middle, scoop out the insides and discard the seeds. Peel and chop the garlic and chop the olives and anchovies.

To make the stuffing, mix together the tomato flesh, garlic, olives, anchovies and bread crumbs, moisten the mixture with the melted butter and add the basil or marjoram and a little salt. Stuff the mixture into the tomato halves, put them in an oiled roasting pan and bake in the top of the oven for 40 minutes until tender.

Serve on their own as an hors d'oeuvre or with a simple salad as a delicious lunch.

VEGETABLE-FRUITS

PEPPERS (CAPSICUMS)

Peppers may be mild, sweet, hot or unbearably fiery, but they are all members of the Capsicum family. The large Capsicums are known as sweet peppers, bell or bullnose peppers, and may be red, yellow or green. There are fiery types, but generally only the mild varieties are sold.

Chili peppers are the hot peppers that add heat rather than flavor to a dish, although some of them are quite mild. They can be green, red, yellow or black, and in general the smaller the pepper the hotter it is. When testing them for heat, simply touch a piece of the broken flesh to your tongue.

Most peppers are green to begin with, ripening to red and finally becoming red-brown when dried, although some peppers turn a pale yellow when ripe or a deep mahogany color. Peppers that are sold half ripe – part red and part green – will never ripen to full red but will simply shrivel.

Sweet peppers

Bought fresh, large sweet peppers are quite light in weight. Red peppers are sweeter than the green ones, and the yellow ones are closer in flavor to red peppers than green.

Capsicum means box, and the fleshy walls of sweet peppers contain no more than a few ribs and a cluster of seeds. These should all be discarded to the last flat seed, which even in the mildest pepper can occasionally be bitingly hot. The empty boxes can then be filled with any number of stuffings, then put side by side in a baking pan and slowly cooked in oil.

As well as being stuffed, sweet peppers can be cut into strips and used in a variety of dishes. Sweet peppers are also sometimes combined with chili peppers, as in rouille – the bright orange, fiery sauce that floats in the centre of a bowl of bouillabaisse.

Chili peppers

These should look fresh and bright – dullness is a sure sign of overmaturity – with no brown patches or black spots.

With chili peppers, not only the seeds but the box itself is pungent, and except in Central America, notably Mexico, people wisely use them sparingly.

Capsicum irritates the skin and especially the eyes, so keep your hands – even after washing – away from your eyes for an hour after you have prepared chili peppers, and rinse the peppers in cold water, not hot, or the irritating fumes may rise into your face. To prepare the peppers, pull off their stems and break each one in half, all under cold running water. Chili peppers soaked for a while in cold salted water will be less hot, and they can also be blistered under the broiler to give them a lovely smokey flavor.

Canned chili peppers should be washed to remove the brine in which they have been preserved. They may be already sliced or diced, or they may need seeding like fresh ones. Dried peppers, torn into small pieces, can be used as they are to season simple Mediterranean dishes, or they can be steeped in water first. For a much milder flavor, put them into a pan of cold water, bring slowly to the boil and then drain.

Chili experts, of course, can distinguish between the flavors of the various peppers, but non-experts tend to differentiate only between the hot and the unbearable. The cayenne chili peppers are not one particular type but a group of peppers, always hot and used for making chili pastes and sauces. Serrano chili peppers are extremely hot, while ancho peppers, looking like small sweet peppers, are quite sweet and only faintly hot.

TOMATOES

Ripened to a marvellous blazing red in the sun, tomatoes are one of the cook's most essential provisions. Ideally, one should have tomatoes in the larder at all times, both fresh and in cans.

There is no better salad than a tomato salad, preferably scattered with fresh basil leaves, which have a great affinity with tomatoes. The Italians often add slices of mozzarella, a bland cheese that goes well with tomatoes. To dress it, a good sun-ripened tomato only needs olive oil, since it provides its own astringency. But a duller one needs vinaigrette. Tomatoes should never be allowed to sit about in their dressing, which will turn them soggy.

Buying and storing tomatoes

The best tomatoes are those that have been allowed to ripen slowly on the vine, developing their flavor in the warm sun.

Buy bright red tomatoes for immediate

PREPARATION

1 CELERIAC

Peel off the rough skin and root parts with a sharp knife or potato peeler.

Slice thinly and then cut into delicate julienne strips.

Alternatively, celeriac can be grated. If it begins to turn brown, put it into a bowl of acidulated water.

2 KOHLRABI

Trim away any leaves. The young sprouting leaves can be cooked in the same way as spinach. The kohlrabi shown here is a green one; there is also a purple variety.

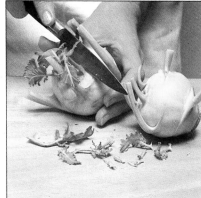

Cut off all the stalks, and the fibrous part where the stem has been cut.

Peel the kohlrabi thickly or, if you prefer, leave the peeling until the vegetable is cooked.

use; for use in the near future, choose a paler pink color – after a day or two in a cool spot they will be a vivid red. If tomatoes have been picked when green but after reaching maturity, they are called "mature green" and will redden well if kept in a drawer or in a brown paper bag (they will ripen faster with a red tomato keeping them company, exuding its ethylene gas, which is responsible for the color change). Tomatoes picked when green and unripe will never turn red and are best used for making pickles and chutneys.

The large, ridged tomatoes, deep red or orange and green and often quite misshapen, tend to be the best, with rather fewer seeds than the smaller, more ordinary globe tomatoes, grown to uniform size and often with very little flavor. The cherry tomatoes or Tom Thumbs, can be used whole in salads, while the richly flavored Italian plum tomatoes, with relatively small seed clusters and pulp that is inclined to be dry, are best for sauces and purées. Fleshy tomatoes are best for sandwiches because there is less liquid to turn the bread soggy. Slice them across rather than downward.

Golden-yellow tomatoes are like red tomatoes in every aspect except color, and make a pretty salad when mixed with the reds or on their own.

Cooking with tomatoes

The traditional tomato dishes include tomato soup, tomatoes with various stuffings, and fragrant tomatoes *provençale*. *A la provençale* invariably means the presence of tomatoes in a dish, and just as Provençal cookery relies on tomatoes, so does Italian cookery.

Many recipes require tomatoes that have been *concasséed* – skinned, seeded and roughly chopped. In the case of Italian plum tomatoes the skin usually comes off perfectly easily, but globe tomatoes need a quick dip in boiling water first. To seed tomatoes, cut them in half crosswise and squeeze them in the palm of your hand over a bowl, giving a little shake as you do so. You can sieve the contents of the bowl and use the seedless liquid as stock.

EGGPLANT

These can be long and slim or as fat as zeppelins, with glossy purple or almost black skins, or plump ivory-white ovals, but they all have the same slightly acrid taste. The difference lies in their consistency: the plump ones, marginally juicier, are the ones to use for such dishes as moussaka; the long slim ones, being rather dryer, are best for frying.

When buying eggplant, those that feel heavy for their size are likely to have the smallest seed channels because their flesh will have filled out. They should have smooth, unblemished skins with no rough, spongy patches or brown spots.

It is a good idea to salt eggplant before cooking to sweat out some of the moisture

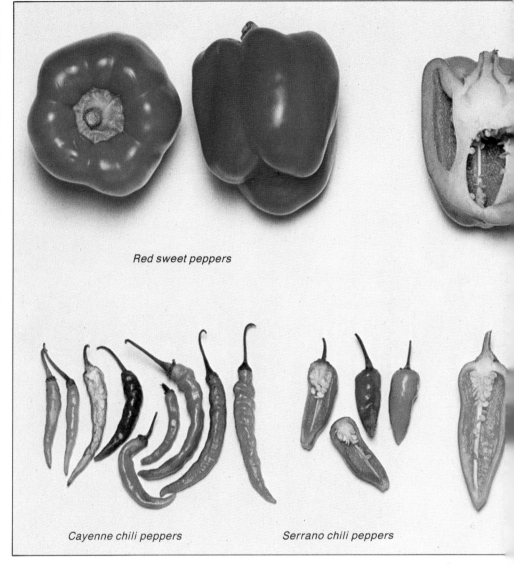

Red sweet peppers

Cayenne chili peppers   *Serrano chili peppers*

and possible bitterness, although the slim ones do not really need this treatment. To salt them, cut them into thin slices, sprinkle with fine salt and allow them to drain in a colander for about half an hour, then rinse them and pat them dry.

It is not usual to peel eggplant because the skin contributes to their flavor and color, and in dishes such as stuffed eggplant it prevents them disintegrating. But in dishes that involve mashed eggplant, such as "poor man's caviar," the traditional way of peeling them is to roast them in their skins over a fire or under a broiler until they blister, and then to scoop out the flesh, which will have acquired a delicious smoky taste.

Eggplant may be halved and stuffed, or filled from the stem end after the seeds and a portion of the flesh have been removed to make room for the stuffing. They look very beautiful if they are first peeled in strips so that white flesh and purple skin make handsome stripes around the outside.

Whether eaten hot or cold, *à la grecque* or in batter, eggplant are always first fried in

hot olive oil; if you fry them fast they do not become so oil laden.

AVOCADOS

The avocado pear is, strictly speaking, a fruit, but is used mainly as a vegetable because its flavor is bland, mild and nutty.

There are two main types of avocado: those that appear in the summer and those that appear in the winter. The summer variety, with a rough, pebbly skin that is green when unripe and purple-black when ripe, has gold-yellow flesh. The winter ones are more pear shaped, with smooth green skin and pale green to yellow flesh. With the winter avocados, skin color is no indication of ripeness, and the test for this is to apply gentle pressure at the thin end: if there is some give, the avocado is ready.

It is best to purée avocado shortly before it is to be eaten because it turns a dirty brown color when exposed to the air. So does the flesh of a cut avocado, so either halve it just before serving or rub the cut surfaces with lemon.

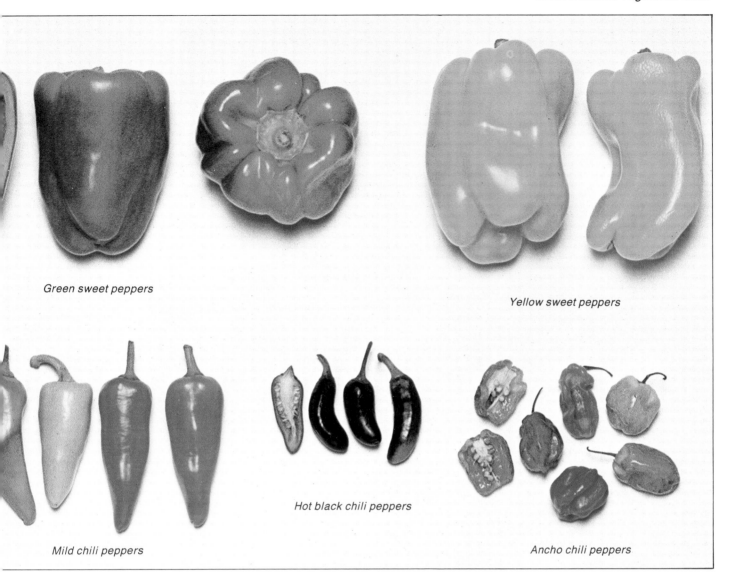

Green sweet peppers

Yellow sweet peppers

Mild chili peppers

Hot black chili peppers

Ancho chili peppers

OLIVES

Whether olives are green or black (which may in fact be brown or purple) is not a matter of type but of timing: olives picked young are still hard and pale green; black olives have had time to ripen and darken on the tree and have developed more of their oil. They are soaked in an alkaline solution and exposed to the air to develop their characteristic black color.

Green olives are treated rather differently, first steeped in an alkaline solution and then put into tightly sealed barrels of brine and left for up to 12 months to develop their olive green, smooth succulence. Olives destined for the oil presses are allowed to ripen fully; some of these looking a little shrivelled and quite small, are also cured in salt and eaten, and can be the best of all.

Among the many olives on the market, the most common are the big, green, solid, Spanish ones, called Queens, which are slightly acid and which connoisseurs like to dip in olive oil before eating, and the small, succulent Manzanillas.

Olives are preserved in a number of ways. The black ones range from those preserved in oil with herbs to those in brine. There are also cracked olives – green olives pickled with garlic, spices or herbs – and the pitted, pressed green olives packed with chili peppers, which are very fine.

Besides the best-known green and black olives, there are also the pale or dark brown ones found in Italy and Cyprus, and the straw-colored California olives which some people prefer above all others.

If you buy too many olives and do not use them all at once, store them in the refrigerator, or better still in the larder, in a jar of olive oil or in a mixture of water, oil and vinegar.

RECIPE SUGGESTION

Guacamole

3 ripe avocados
juice of 1 lime
1 tomato
4–6 green chili peppers
1 scallion (optional)
⅓ cup/0.75 dl olive oil
salt and freshly ground pepper
dash of Tabasco (optional)

SERVES 6–8

Remove the flesh from the avocados and mash it together with the lime juice, mixing well. Skin and chop the tomato. Chop the chili peppers and scallion finely and pound them to a paste using a pestle and mortar or food processor.

Add the mashed avocados and the tomato. Slowly incorporate as much of the olive oil as you can, drop by drop, whisking with a fork or blending in the food processor. Add salt and pepper and a little Tabasco. Chill briefly and serve with toast.

Guacamole should taste both hot and cool at the same time.

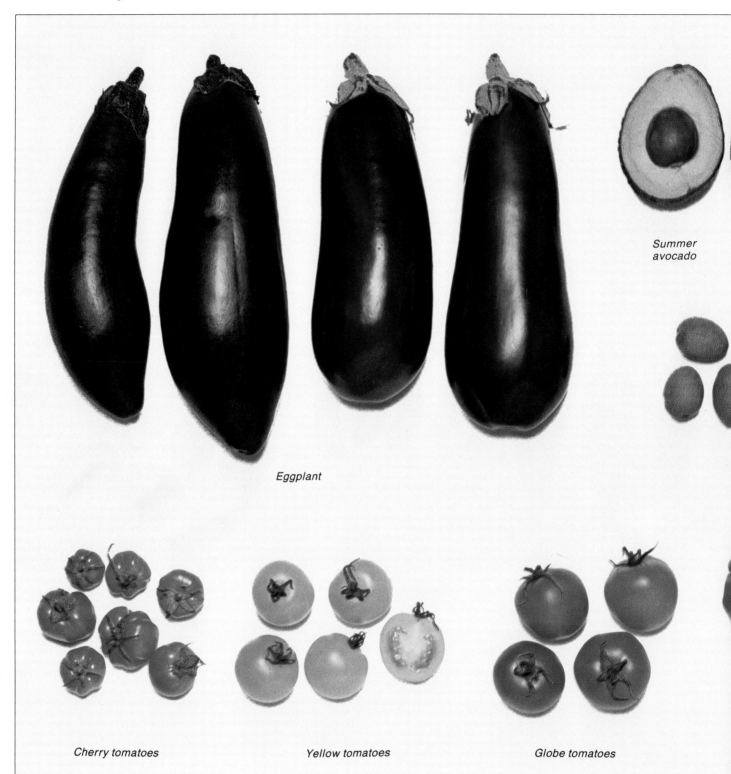

Eggplant

Summer
avocado

Cherry tomatoes

Yellow tomatoes

Globe tomatoes

Winter avocados

Green olives   *Black olives*

Large ridge tomatoes   *Plum tomatoes*

CUCUMBERS AND GHERKINS

Before cucumbers had the bitterness bred out of them they were invariably peeled and salted and drained. This is no longer necessary, unless you want to make a delicate Austrian or French cucumber salad, for which salting and draining are essential. Otherwise, cucumber salads are likely to consist of slices cut transparently thin on a mandoline and dressed with sour cream or vinaigrette, or, in the Hungarian version, of little dice dressed with yoghurt and chives and sprinkled with paprika. Cucumbers are also interesting cooked and served hot.

Small ridge cucumbers have plentiful seeds and smooth, dark green skins (their name comes from the way they are grown on ridges). If ridge cucumbers have been waxed, as they often are in the United States, they need to be peeled before they are used. Unwaxed and unpeeled, they are the cucumbers that are brined, or pickled with a head of dill.

The long, clear green cucumber (known in America as the English cucumber) has fewer seeds and an exceedingly thin skin and is often sold in a tight plastic jacket to keep it fresh. Largest is the Zeppelin, firm and juicy, that turns a pale yellow when fully ripe. The apple or lemon cucumber, almost round and with crisp, juicy flesh and tough yellowish skin, should always be peeled.

Cucumbers are best when they are young and tender and look as if they are bursting with juice. They can be stored in the refrigerator for about a week at most, but do not like very low temperatures.

Gherkins, covered in warts, are usually found pickled in unsweetened vinegar and are eaten with cold meats, with hot *boeuf bouilli*, or chopped and incorporated in sauces such as tartare sauce.

SQUASHES AND PUMPKINS

These belong to the climbing family known as Cucurbitas, together with melons and cucumbers and the decorative autumn gourds. Some are soft skinned and for eating when young and tender, which is why they are often known as summer squashes; others are best when they have been allowed to mature slowly to develop hard, sweet flesh.

Soft-skinned or summer squashes

These should be cooked as soon as possible after they have been picked.

Zucchini

These are infinitely superior to the larger squashes. with a much more interesting and delicate taste. There is hardly any work involved in their preparation: just give them a little wash, and then leave tiny ones whole and cut larger ones into circles or slice them lengthwise into halves or quarters. Give them a very few minutes' boiling, steaming or frying, add some herbs such as basil or parsley, with perhaps a dash of cream, or a quantity of butter or olive oil, and an extremely good vegetable dish is ready to eat. But don't keep it waiting, because the vegetable continues to soften even after it has been taken off the heat.

Zucchini are excellent fried in oil, either plain or in batter, and their big golden flowers are also sometimes stuffed and deep fried in a crisp batter. They form part of an Italian *fritto misto* in which there may also be apples, artichoke hearts, eggplant, brains, or veal cut into little strips as beef is for *boeuf stroganoff*.

Straightnecks, crooknecks and cocozelles

Much like small zucchini in flavor and texture, these can be used in the same ways. The crookneck has bumpy yellow skin and curves at the neck; the cocozelle looks like a large zucchini, but its pale skin is striped with green.

Vegetable marrows

Grown to enormous size, these peculiarly English squashes are not very delicate as a vegetable and, to some tastes at least, are even less acceptable transformed into jam.

Boiled into a watery mush, medium-size specimens can be equally disappointing, but started off with a little butter and chopped onion and steamed in their own juice, and sprinkled with a handful of chopped parsley, they can be fresh looking and delicious, especially when tomatoes are added.

A parboiled or blanched marrow or large zucchini, halved and hollowed out, makes a good vehicle for a ground beef and onion stuffing bound with an egg, or a rice and meat stuffing, but both need lively flavoring because the flesh itself is bland.

Vegetable spaghettis

These stubby yellow squashes are grown with particular attention to the squash's tendency to produce stringy flesh and are eaten, with sauce, just like spaghetti, and wrapped around a fork. They are always boiled, the end pierced so that the heat reaches the interior, and are served cut in half lengthwise. Pass a tomato sauce separately. They are also good eaten simply with butter and grated cheese.

Patty pans

Usually creamy in color, although they also come in shades of yellow and green, these taste rather like zucchini. They are best up to 4 in/10 cm across, when the skin is soft and the interior tender, and their scalloped shape need not be spoiled by slicing. Boil them and then cut off the tops, scoop out the seeds and fill the hollow with melted butter, and eat them with a spoon.

Chayotes

Small and pear shaped, these squashes have a large single seed, which in very young chayotes is edible. They feature in Central and South American cooking, where besides being used as a vegetable they are candied, filled with nuts and raisins and eaten as a dessert.

Chinese hairy melon, or wax gourd

Looking like a large torpedo, this can be bought in Chinese supermarkets. When young it is covered with a silky fuzz, which is easily washed off by running the hand over the skin under cold running water. In maturity it is usually coated with wax, which also washes off. It has a slight bitterness but is excellent stir-fried.

Pumpkins and winter squashes

With bright autumn-colored or green skins, these have flesh that is firm and floury.

Winter squashes

A favorite winter vegetable in America, these include the Acorn squash, which can be green or orange or a combination of the two; the Butternut, looking like a huge, pale orange peanut, and the smooth-skinned Buttercup, which swells to a turban shape towards the blossom end; the bumpy skinned Turban squashes and the large, warty Hubbards, often sold in wedges. Look for firm, unbruised specimens, or wedges that show no signs of softening around the edges.

Peeled, cut into pieces and boiled for about 20 minutes, squash can be served mashed with butter, salt and pepper or a little orange juice. The smaller squashes can be left unpeeled, halved and baked in the oven for about 30 minutes with butter and brown sugar or maple syrup.

Calabaza squash

Often sold in wedges to display its golden-orange flesh, this West Indian variety features in Caribbean soups; otherwise it can be used for any hard-skinned squash or pumpkin recipe.

Pumpkins

Best known and best liked are the handsome golden field pumpkins that go into American pumpkin pie, pumpkin soup and pumpkin bread, and are carved into smiling, gap-toothed faces for Hallowe'en.

The earliest pumpkin pies were not the familiar spiced golden ones now eaten at Thanksgiving. For the Pilgrim Fathers, pumpkin pie was simply a pumpkin with its head sawn off and its seeds removed, with the cavity filled with milk, spices and honey and baked until tender.

Nowadays, because of the business of baking, straining, seeding, scraping and puréeing the pumpkin, many people use canned purée – one of the few foods that can be better canned than fresh. For pumpkin soup, which looks so pretty served in a hollowed-out shell, canned purée can also be used, but for baked and fried pumpkin you need fresh ones.

English pumpkins are much softer fleshed, and because they cook so readily into a mush they are best used for pumpkin soup, or they can be combined with potatoes or root vegetables to give them a little extra body when used in vegetable dishes.

Gherkins

Cucumbers

Large zucchini

English cucumbers

Zeppelin cucumber

Small acorn squash

Zucchini

Yellow straight-necked squash

Small butternut squash

RECIPE SUGGESTIONS

Pumpkin soup

1 pumpkin or slice of pumpkin, weighing about 1 lb/450 g
2 large leeks
1¼–2 cups/3–4.5 dl milk
5 cups/1 liter chicken stock
2 sprigs fresh basil or ¼ teaspoon dried basil
pinch of grated nutmeg
salt and freshly ground pepper
2 tablespoons/30 g butter
2–3 tablespoons heavy cream

SERVES 4

Trim and wash the leeks, reserving the green tops, and finely slice the white part. Remove the seeds and pith from the pumpkin, cut the flesh away from the skin and chop it into cubes. Put the sliced white leek and the cubed pumpkin into a saucepan with a few tablespoons of water, just enough to cover the bottom of the pan. Put it over a gentle heat and allow the vegetables to soften and melt to a mush. Stir from time to time to make sure they do not stick to the pan. When they are tender, purée them either in a food mill, using the medium blade, or in a food processor.

Return the mixture to the cleaned pan and add the milk, stock, basil, nutmeg and salt and pepper. Finely slice about half a teacupful of the green leek tops, cutting them into rings. Melt the butter in a small saucepan, add the green rings of leek tops and sweat until just tender.

Stir the leek tops and the cream into the soup just before serving.

If you are making this to serve in a pumpkin shell, double the quantities.

Pumpkin pie

shortcrust pastry made with 1½ cups/170 g flour
1½ lb/700 g pumpkin
6 tablespoons/85 g sugar, preferably superfine
¼ teaspoon ground allspice
1 teaspoon ground ginger
3 eggs
⅔ cup/1.5 dl creamy milk or light cream
¼ teaspoon ground nutmeg

SERVES 4

Line an 8 in/20 cm pie dish with the pastry and bake it blind.

Peel the pumpkin, cut it in cubes and put the pieces in a large shallow saucepan or sauté pan with 3 tablespoons of water. Cook gently, stirring from time to time, until the liquid starts to run out of the pumpkin. Let it soften over a low heat for about 40 minutes, stirring occasionally. The liquid should run out quite liberally. When the pumpkin is soft and translucent, put it in a wire sieve and drain. Preheat the oven to 375°F/190°C.

Purée the drained pumpkin with the fine blade of a food mill, a blender or a food processor, then add the sugar, allspice and ginger, the eggs and the milk or cream and blend to a creamy purée. Put the mixture into the prepared piecrust, sprinkle the top with nutmeg and bake for an hour. Cover with foil, loosely, if the pastry becomes too brown.

Squash provençale

1 lb/450 g summer squash
1 onion
2 cloves garlic
2 tablespoons olive oil
¼ stick/55 g butter
1½ lb/700 g ripe tomatoes
3–4 sprigs thyme
1 tablespoon chopped parsley
salt and freshly ground pepper
1 teaspoon sugar

SERVES 4

Peel and chop the onion and garlic and sauté them in the oil and half the butter. Skin and chop the tomatoes and add them to the onion and garlic with the thyme, parsley, salt, pepper and sugar. Simmer to a thickish sauce. Meanwhile, cut the marrow into rectangular pieces, 2 x 1 in/5 x 2.5 cm, removing the seeds. Drop the pieces into boiling salted water, cook until just tender and drain well. Heat the broiler.

Mix the cooked squash into the sauce and pour the whole glorious mixture into a large oval gratin dish. Dot the top with the remaining butter and put under a fierce broiler until brown and bubbling. This really glorifies a common squash.

Vegetable marrow

Patty pans

Vegetable spaghetti

English pumpkin

Calabaza squash

American pumpkin

Stuffed zucchini

2 lb/900 g zucchini
1¼ cups/3 dl thick béchamel sauce
¼ cup/55 g Parmesan, freshly grated
2 oz/55 g prosciutto crudo or cooked ham, sliced thinly
and cut into ¼ in/1 cm squares, about ¼ cup
salt and freshly ground pepper
pinch of grated nutmeg (optional)

SERVES 4

Cut the zucchini in half lengthwise and scoop out the seeds with a teaspoon. Drop the halved zucchini into boiling salted water and let them cook for about 8–10 minutes. Drain very thoroughly in a colander.

Preheat the oven to 425°F/220°C.

Make a thick béchamel sauce, stir in most of the Parmesan and all the ham. Taste for seasoning, add a little nutmeg if you like and allow to bubble for 15 minutes. Put the drained zucchini into an earthenware gratin dish and then, using a spoon, fill them with the mixture. Bake for 15 minutes.

Heat the broiler.

Sprinkle the stuffed zucchini with the remaining cheese and brown quickly under the broiler.

Serve as an appetizing hors d'oeuvre or a very light summer lunch.

They are eaten, in Italy, before a beef steak or a baked fish. (The only other vegetables would be in the form of a mixed salad of lettuce, little leaves of rocket and a few finely sliced rounds of radish.)

MUSHROOMS
AND OTHER FUNGI

In many countries the mushroom forage is an autumn treat, with whole families combing the ground for the 80 or so edible species of fungi which are either sold in the local markets, dried, or enjoyed fresh as a luxurious addition to the normal diet. It is important to remember, however, that for the amateur picker the business of mushrooming is fraught with risk. Some mushrooms are indigestible; a few are lethal.

WILD MUSHROOMS

Cep (*Boletus edulis*)
A strong, meaty, bun-shaped fungus known to the French as *cèpe*, to the Germans as *steinpilze* and to the Italians as *porcini*, it is smooth and shiny and with the texture of fine kid gloves. Unlike many other wild mushrooms, it does not collapse in cooking but keeps its texture. Except when using ceps in soup, however, it is advisable to draw off some of their ample water content by stewing them gently for a few minutes in oil or butter. After draining, the liquor is saved for future use and the ceps can be cooked in fresh oil or butter.

Dried ceps need soaking in warm water for about half an hour, and the liquid as well as the ceps is used to flavor the dish. When dried they are used almost like stock cubes.

Chanterelle (*Cantharellus cibarius*)
The frilly, trumpet-shaped chanterelle, common in woodlands in summer and autumn, is quite unlike any other edible mushroom and there are many varieties. Most are bright yellow and have an odor reminiscent of apricots and a delicate flavor. Like most mushrooms they do not improve with immersion in water, but whereas many can simply be wiped with a damp cloth, the chanterelle is harder to clean because of the grit or sand trapped in the pleated gills. The best method is to run cold water over them, and then shake then dry.

Somewhat rubbery in texture, chanterelles take a long time to cook. They should be started off gently, like ceps, and left to exude their liquid, which is better replaced with butter rather than oil. Treat dried chanterelles to a soaking in lukewarm water for 20 to 30 minutes before cooking.

Morel (*Morchella esculenta*)
The handsome morel is the first mushroom of the year, appearing in spring. It is as delicate as a natural sponge and varies in color from pale beige to dark brownish-black and has a meaty flavor.

Cut in half and carefully washed and dried, morels can be put into a casserole dish with a little butter. Sauté for a few minutes and then add a squeeze of lemon juice. Stir around a few times, add salt and pepper, cover the pan and simmer for up to an hour, adding a little stock from time to time. When the mushrooms are tender, thicken the juice with egg yolk, season and serve hot with toast.

Retaining a good flavor, dried morels are best soaked for ten minutes and then pressed dry before they are added to soups or stews; or they can be softened in butter, sprinkled with flour and then enriched with cream, and seasoned with salt and pepper.

Horn of plenty (*Craterellus cornucopoides*)
This is a very good mushroom although it has a rather unprepossessing appearance, being trumpet shaped, somewhat ragged and almost black. Sometimes called the trumpet mushroom, it is eaten sautéed in butter and goes into stews and soups.

Oyster mushroom (*Pleurotus ostreatus*)
These ear-like grey or greyish-brown "bracket" mushrooms grow in clumps on deciduous trees. They need careful cooking as they may be tough, but have an excellent flavor. Cook them in butter with parsley and garlic or coat with egg and crumbs and deep fry until golden.

Shaggy cap, shaggy ink cap
(*Coprinus comatus*)
These singular and graceful mushrooms grow in groups in rich pastures. They push up like white folded umbrellas and this is the time to eat them. As they age they blacken, become bell shaped and finally dissolve into a pool of black ink. Cook young shaggy caps as soon as possible after picking, either baking them in cream or sautéing them gently in butter.

Their close relative *Coprinus atramentarius*, which is similar but grey and without scales, is also edible, but do not drink alcohol if eating it, as the combination could make you sick.

CULTIVATED MUSHROOMS

Cultivated mushrooms are available all year round, there is no waste – they don't need peeling – and they are utterly safe. Most common is the champignon, cultivated relative of the field and horse mushrooms, which is sold in three grades: button, cup, and open or flat.

Button mushrooms
Small and succulent, they are slighly weaker in flavor than the more mature grades. Remaining pale, they are useful for white, creamy sauces and also for salads.

Cup mushrooms
The kind where the membrane is just breaking to expose the gills, can be kept pale if rubbed with a cut lemon, or if a few drops of lemon juice or white wine are added to the cooking liquor.

Open or flat mushrooms
These most resemble their wild cousins and are almost as penetrating in taste. Fully mature, these are the kind to eat broiled with bacon. They can be used in dark soups or casseroles, but are troublesome cooked with chicken, for example, as they turn it an unattractive grey. It is best to buy mushrooms a few at a time and often. Button mushrooms become cups even in the refrigerator, and their flesh soon starts to shrivel. To limit evaporation they can be wrapped in plastic or foil.

CHINESE DRIED MUSHROOMS

Dark-colored Chinese mushrooms (the kind served in Chinese restaurants) must be soaked for at least half an hour to revive the meaty texture; the tough stems are discarded. Also available in Chinese supermarkets is the stemless type known as cloud ears, used for texture rather than flavor.

TRUFFLES

One of the rarest and certainly the most expensive of all fungi, the black Périgord truffle (*Tuber malanosporum*) is the most sought-after of the truffle species.

With its rich, mold-like flavor, a little of the black truffle goes a long way. The classic dish *truffe sous cendre* – truffle wrapped in bacon fat or pastry, baked and served with a bottle of St. Emilion – is rated by gourmets as the experience of a lifetime. Unfortunately, truffles found in pâtés often have no flavor at all and are probably canned.

Used more liberally and with less reverence, the white truffle of Piedmont is larger, stronger in flavor and almost as expensive as its Périgord cousin. While the latter is invariably eaten cooked, the Italians use their white truffle raw, grating it in showers over risottos and salads. One of the great Florentine specialties is a delicate little bridge roll which contains a paste of raw white truffle, Parmesan and butter.

RECIPE SUGGESTION
Mushroom risotto

1¼ cups/170 g Italian rice	
1 oz/30 g dried ceps	
½ lb/225 g button mushrooms	
2 cloves garlic	
3 tablespoons olive oil	
¼ stick/55 g butter	
2 tablespoons chopped parsley	
1 glass dry white wine	
1¼ cups/3 dl chicken stock	
¼ cup/30 g freshly grated Parmesan	
salt and freshly ground pepper	

SERVES 4

Soak the ceps for half an hour in 2 cups/4.5 dl of hot water. Squeeze them dry, keeping the liquid to use when cooking the rice.

Slice the fresh mushrooms, and peel and chop the garlic. Heat the oil and half the butter in a large frying pan and fry the ceps and sliced fresh mushrooms, together with the garlic and chopped parsley. When the mushrooms have exuded some of their juice, add the rice and fry it for a minute or so, stirring it around until it becomes slightly transparent. Add the white wine and let it bubble until it has almost all evaporated, then add a ladleful of the stock and stir the rice until the liquid is almost all absorbed and becoming creamy. Keep adding first the stock and then the liquid in which the ceps were soaked, leaving a little at the bottom of the bowl as there may be some grit in it left over from the ceps.

When all the liquid has been absorbed and the rice is tender and bathed in a creamy sauce, stir in the grated cheese and a good knob of butter. Taste for seasoning, add a little salt and freshly ground pepper if necessary, and serve.

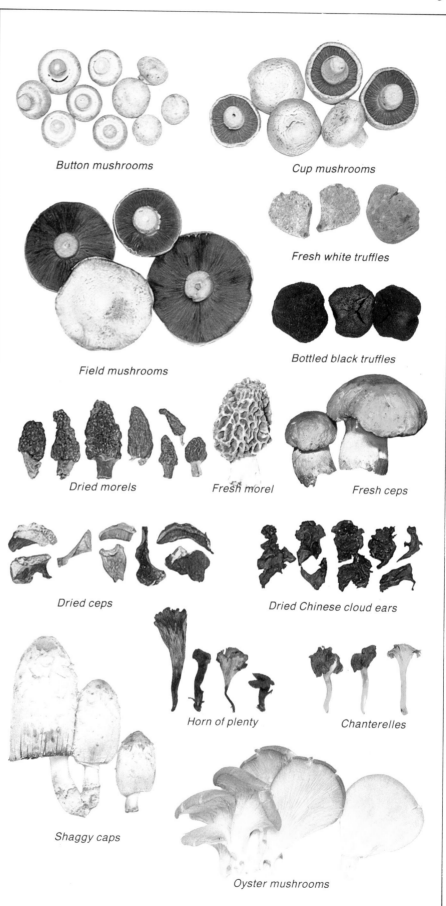

Button mushrooms

Cup mushrooms

Fresh white truffles

Field mushrooms

Bottled black truffles

Dried morels

Fresh morel

Fresh ceps

Dried ceps

Dried Chinese cloud ears

Horn of plenty

Chanterelles

Shaggy caps

Oyster mushrooms

FRUIT

Fruit can add a rich variety of flavors, textures and color to any meal. Apples and pears available throughout the year; citrus fruits which covers everything from golden oranges to dark green ugli fruit. Soft downy peaches and juicy red cherries. Succulent raspberries and strawberries. Tropical and Mediterranean fruits like lychees, guavas, fresh figs and dates. Melons and grapes from the vine and lastly, dried fruits which prolong the flavor of summer.

Golden Delicious

Laxton's Superb

Granny Smith

Orleans Reinette

APPLES

Apples and pears, although frequently bracketed as if they were almost one and the same fruit, could scarcely be more different.

Today, unfortunately, the choice and variety of apples is getting smaller and smaller; although there are several thousand different apples cultivated in gardens and nurseries, very few find their way into commercial orchards, where the fruit grown must keep well and be tough, disease resistant and good at travelling. Of the 7,000 varieties known in the United States only 50 are seriously marketed, while the British are limited almost entirely to Cox's, Granny Smiths and Golden Delicious, with Red Delicious and Bramleys as runners-up.

It is sad that this is the case, since there are so many aromatic old-fashioned apples that are worth growing. So hunt through the countryside in the autumn and you may find interesting varieties for sale that are worth trying. Apples sold as windfalls are also good buys and are perfect for cooking, since unripe apples have plenty of acid, essential to the flavor of apple pies, tarts and crumbles. The best eating apples are those that retain some of their acidity even in their final sweetness, and have a mellow flavor and a firm, juicy texture. The eating apples known as reinettes, with their red-flushed golden skins, are especially good.

Buying and storing apples

While obviously one should avoid apples with bruises and soft spots, do not be put off by dull, rough, brown patches on sound apples. This is called russeting and in the case of apples that go by the name of russets will extend over the whole surface. Russets are splendid with cheese, and cook well.

Those buying for the trade test for ripeness by grasping apples around the middle and applying gentle pressure: if the skin wrinkles slightly the apples are at the peak of perfection. But it takes a bold shopper to emulate this practice in a store or market. Fragrance is important when testing for ripeness and the fruit should be firm.

Apples are the most common, the most easy-going and the most useful of all fruits, both to eat casually at any time of the day and to cook with – there are more apple puddings than any other sort. Pears on the other hand are a fragile luxury – large, aesthetically pleasing and opulent, they make a grand ending to a grand meal, and speak to the diner of sunny orchards and of careful harvesting and marketing.

Apples continue to ripen after they have been picked. If they are to be stored they should be spread out so that they are not touching each other. If you want to buy apples in quantitiy, at one of the pick-your-own orchards for example, keep them on racks or in special fiber apple trays in a cool, dry, dark place. A cool loft is the ideal place to store apples.

Cooking with apples

Selecting the right apples for cooking is important if you do not want your pies to end up watery or your baked apples to collapse in a frothy mess all over the oven. Some apples, such as America's favorite eating apple, the Red Delicious, are too tender for cooking and lack the acidity that gives

Worcester Pearmain

Crispin

Cox's Orange Pippin

Egremont Russet

Red Delicious

McIntosh

apple dishes their delicious flavour. The hard, crisp apples such as the popular Granny Smith or some of the russets will require longer cooking than the softer-fleshed ones.

Apple purées

When making these, choose crisp, juicy apples with plenty of acid – adding sugar towards the end of cooking time – as these will quickly turn to a froth. Tart apples give a sweet-acid taste that is delicious with pork, pheasant or goose.

Cooking apple slices

Many of the dishes involving apples, such as tarts, turnovers and fritters, depend on apples retaining their shape. Sugar and/or butter added at the beginning of the cooking helps to prevent them from disintegrating. Europe's favorite reinettes and russets, noted for their unique subtle flavor, are excellent for cooking. These are the apples that French cooks use when making *tartes aux pommes* – with their neat rings of apple slices nicely browned on the upper edges. The Golden Delicious, one of the most popular and common of today's apples, retains its shape well, but lacks the flavor of the reinettes and russets, so cook it with cinnamon and plenty of butter and sugar.

Stewing apples

When stewing apples use the same varieties as you would use for pies and tarts. To vary the flavor you can add cloves, cinnamon, or perhaps coriander seeds and grated lemon rind. Rum or Calvados and butter are also good with stewed apples. Some savory stews such as Persia's *khoresh* involve apples with cinnamon and onions. In West Germany apples are stewed, sprinkled with bread crumbs and gently fried, and then served with ham.

Baking apples

These are cored with an apple corer and the cavity filled with sugar, butter and perhaps almonds, blackberries or raisins. They are then baked, possibly basted or flamed with Calvados or brandy, and served with thick cream. The best apples for baking are the large ones. Run your knife around the circumference of the apple (to prevent the skin from splitting before you stuff them and put them in the baking pan. Thick-skinned varieties such as Rome Beauty are ideal, since their skins are less likely to burst. The harder the apple, the longer it will take to bake: it is done when the top is frothy and seeping with juice.

Fried apples

A classic accompaniment to fried or broiled *boudin noir* is peeled, sliced apples fried golden in butter. They are also very good with pheasant.

Raw apple slices

These when added to salads give a crisp, crunchy texture – the famous Waldorf salad of celery, apples and walnuts tossed in mayonnaise is especially good. A squeeze of lemon juice will prevent the slices from turning brown. Any crisp, sharp eating apple will make a good salad.

CRABAPPLES, QUINCES AND MEDLARS

These three fruits, like the apple are related to the rose family and used to be called the fruits of Merrie England.

Crabapples

Roasted and still hot, the crabapples that "hissed in the bowl" in the hot spiced ale punches of Shakespeare's day were most likely the small, sour apples that still grow wild or in gardens and are the ancestors of all our modern apple varieties. These beautiful tiny fruits, which can be yellow, red or green, are no longer eaten (except by birds) because they are generally not worth the bother, being mostly core and often very sour. They do, however, make a lovely clear, golden-pink jelly, which is excellent on bread and butter and with Petit Suisse. The larger crabapples are slightly sweeter and grow from the seeds of cultivated apples that have become wild. They have a crisp, tart flavor.

Quinces

These came originally from Portugal, where they are called marmelos, and until they were supplanted by oranges they were the fruit from which marmalade was made. Yellow-gold and aromatic, they are a pleasing sight on the kitchen table in autumn and are usually used to make jellies, jams and cheeses, but a slice or two added to an apple pie or tart gives these dishes a delicious scent and flavor. Quinces can also be boiled down with sugar to a thick paste, which is then dried and eaten as a dessert.

Medlars

These are never found in stores, but are sometimes seen growing wild on roadsides. They look like open cups of a warm golden brown and resemble a large rose hip insofar as each is crowned with a five-tailed calyx. Since they do not ripen on the tree they need to be well on the way to being rotten, or "bletted," before they are edible. In the past this was done by laying the fruit in straw or packing it in bran, except in the warm south where medlars ripen in the normal way. The ripe state is easily recognizable, as the unripe fruit is rock hard. Once bletted, medlars are usually baked, or made into a slightly bitter jam or jelly, or the flesh is scraped out of the cup and eaten with sugar and cream. The taste and texture are slightly reminiscent of marzipan.

PEARS

This fruit, which can be so delicious, is more temperamental than the apple. It has an unpleasant habit of becoming mealy from the core outwards, a state described by fruiterers as "sleepiness," and it does not keep so well as the apple.

Pears come in almost as great a variety as

Rome Beauty   *Bramley's Seedling*

apples. Europe has about 5,000 named varieties and America about 1,000, but as with apples only a small proportion reach the market. Three shapes predominate: the ordinary pear shape, the long-necked shape called calabash, and the oval, almost round shape. Colors, too, vary a great deal, from a soft blurred brown to bright green with dark brown, grey-black or green flecks, to golden with a handsome red-gold flush.

The Comice pear
Doyenné de Comice, is considered to be one of the best pears. It has a perfect balance of sweetness and acidity, a certain spiciness, and its juicy, sweet flesh is buttery – meaning that it is melting and not grainy. Large and greenish-yellow, it has a red blush where it has been exposed to the sun. Its thick, shiny skin is stippled with tiny grey spots and fawn patches.

Williams' Bon Chrétien
This pear is usually known as the Williams or Bartlett pear, due to the fact that it was propagated by an English grower called Williams and introduced to America by an American called Bartlett. It has a sweet, musky flavor and a smooth skin that turns from dark green to yellow as it ripens: eat it when its speckles are still surrounded by a tiny halo of green on an otherwise golden skin. These superb pears are unfortunately bad travellers and extremely perishable.

Packham's Triumph
This descendant of the Bartlett or Williams pear looks somewhat like its distinguished ancestor but is not nearly so delicate. It keeps well and is therefore exported in great numbers from Australia, where it is grown in profusion.

The Conference pear
A favorite English pear, this was so called when it won the top prize at a fruit grower's conference for its fine, tender, melting flesh and delicious flavor. It is slim, calabash shaped, stippled with fawn and grey russet-

ing and turns pale yellow when ripe. Kept in controlled cold storage by the trade, it is ripened and released as the market demands, so although it is an early pear it may be found later on in the season.

Beurré Hardy, Beurré Bosc
A number of pear varieties with the French word for butter in their names are characterized by their creamy, melting quality. The Beurré Bosc, so named in honor of a former director of the Jardin des Plantes in Paris, who propagated it, is also known as the Emperor Alexander as a compliment to the nineteenth-century Czar. It has a calabash shape and a fine brown russeting.

Juicier than the Beurré Bosc, the Beurré Hardy takes its name from a nineteenth-century Belgian and is a plumper pear. Both pears in their youth have enough juice for delicious eating and they are also absolutely

NAME	APPEARANCE	FLESH	TYPE
Cox's Orange Pippin	small, round, greenish-yellow tinged with red russeting	crisp, juicy, firm, sweet, some acidity	reinette
Orleans Reinette	small, flat, golden tinged with crimson russeting	crisp, juicy, firm, some acidity	reinette
Egremont Russet	medium, round with brown-orange russeting	soft, very sweet, some acidity	russet
Laxton's Superb	medium, round, greenish-yellow flushed with red	juicy, firm, sweet, some acidity	russet
Golden Delicious	large, conical, green, ripening to yellow	tender, very sweet, no acidity when ripe	all purpose
Rome Beauty	large, elongated, thick skinned, shiny red	crisp, firm, juicy, slightly tart	eating only
Granny Smith	medium to large, conical, green with small, whitish flecks	crisp, juicy, mild but acid	green crisp
Crispin	medium to large, yellow-green	crisp, juicy, mild but acid	green crisp
Bramley's Seedling	extra large, irregular, green flushed with red	crisp, juicy acid	tart green
Red Delicious	large, elongated, thick skinned, shiny red	juicy, very tender, no acidity	eating only
Worcester Pearmain	medium, conical, firm, two-tone red and green	crisp, juicy, sweet, slightly tart	all purpose
McIntosh	small to medium, round, firm, two-tone red and green	crisp, juicy, slightly tart	all purpose

excellent when they are stewed.

Bonne Louise de Longueval and d'Avranches

This pear named after its grower and the place of its birth in Normandy, is now also known as Louise Bonne de Jersey and in German-speaking countries as gute Louise von Avranches. Good it certainly is, and well known not only in its native country but wherever French pears are exported. Smooth skinned, with the merest speckle of russeting, Louise tends to be greenish on the shaded side and yellow washed with pink on the side ripened in the sun. It can be stored without loss of flavor and is an excellent dessert pear.

Seckel, or seckle

This was discovered growing wild in America by an eighteenth-century trapper. It is small, long necked and very popular since it is so sweet, juicy and spicy.

Clapp's Large

A yellow pear with some russeting and occasionally faintly red cheeks, this is a popular American variety.

Passe crassane

This fat, juicy, rounded Italian pear has a lovely flavour and makes an excellent dessert pear. It keeps well and is known as the queen of winter pears.

Buying pears

Pears for eating or cooking should always be sound. Test for ripeness near the stem end, where there should be more than a little give, and at the blossom end, where there should be no oozing softness, since this usually indicates trouble within. Pears are at their best for a very short time, and although they can be left to mature for a little while they must be inspected frequently.

Cooking with pears

Most pears are eating pears, although some are juicier than others. All pears, however, can also be poached in wine or light syrup, and well-flavored eaters such as Bartlett are in fact best for such dishes as pear sherbet and Poires Belle Hélène, the dish in which pears are served on a bed of vanilla ice cream and covered with a hot chocolate sauce.

Cooking pears, which may be sold as such, are harder and less perfumed than the eaters. Poached in vanilla-flavored syrup, they make good compotes and can also be cooked in spiced red wine, in the process of which they become dyed, as the Tudors said, to "a fine oriental red." In Italy they are baked in Marsala, the cavity of each half-pear stuffed with a mixture of ground almonds and crystallized fruit. They can also be made into a relish with lemon juice and ginger or with horseradish, mustard seeds and black pepper, or they can be preserved or picked with sugar, cinnamon and white wine vinegar. Cooked "brown" with butter and sugar, they used to be served hot with game in Germany. They are still served cold there,

poached in lemon juice with cranberries.

Around the North Sea pears also go into main dishes: Frieslanders boil them with green beans, potatoes and beef, while in Hamburg they are cooked with beans and bacon or with salt meat. Boiled potatoes mixed with pears and a dash of vinegar are also sometimes served in northern Europe, while in the *nouvelle cuisine* a purée of pears and spinach can accompany roast duck.

CITRUS

The beautiful citrus fruits all have one thing in common: they ripen while they are still on the tree. Once they have been picked they stop developing and will not get sweeter or improve their flavor. But most of them travel well and remain in good condition for many weeks in the right environment, and only gradually lose weight and pliancy as their juices and oils lose freshness.

Natural untreated citrus fruits are also subject to regreening. This does not necessarily mean that they are unripe but is simply a matter of temperature; the chlorophyll in ripe fruit fades as the thermometer drops and revives as it rises again. Inside the skin the fruit remains unaffected, but since green patches are unattractive on citrus fruit that should by rights be orange or lemon-

Large crabapples

Quinces

Comice pears

yellow, they are often treated with ethylene gas, which fades the chlorophyll, making them more acceptable to the consumer. When buying citrus fruits, choose those that feel heavy for their size as this means plenty of juice. The fruit should be sound with no sign of bruising, damp patches or soft spots.

CITRONS

These fruits are the elders of the citrus tribe. They are large with a thick corrugated skin and resemble large avocados. Since their pulp is too bitter to eat, they are now mostly grown to make the most translucently green, beautiful candied peel, which is used in fruit cakes.

ORANGES

There are three main varieties of oranges: the smooth, thin-skinned sweet oranges such as the Valencias and blood oranges, that range from bright gold to blood red and are full of juice; the larger, rougher, thick-skinned seedless navel oranges that have the best flavor and are easy to peel; and the bitter oranges, also known as Seville or Bigarade oranges, that are used for making the best marmalade.

Invented in Scotland, orange marmalade owes its origins to a boatload of Portuguese oranges which arrived in Dundee in the eighteenth century and unexpectedly turned

out to be extremely bitter. Bitter oranges still come onto the market in their short New Year season and marmalade making is about the only occasion on which we boil oranges to good purpose.

For the most part, however, we like our oranges fresh. In Trinidad they are sold in the street, halved and sprinkled with salt. Orange juice, freshly squeezed and served with ice, used to be standard refreshment in many countries. In Sicily, a paradise for oranges, the juice is drunk not so much as an appetizer but as a final bonne-bouche after a meal, especially the glorious tomato-red juice of blood oranges, which is particularly sweet and full of flavor.

Crabapples

Medlars

Bartlett pears

Conference pears

When making orange juice, thin-skinned oranges such as the virtually seedless Valencias are the best buy. This is not so much because navel oranges lack juice but because their imposing size makes them more expensive, and since their skins have a thick padding of pith a lot of what we pay for is thrown away. The navel orange, which can be peeled neatly and is also virtually seedless, is the best to eat as a dessert.

MANDARINS AND TANGERINES

These and their many cultivars such as clementines and satsumas are the smaller members of the citrus family and their names are sometimes used interchangeably. All are distinguished by having skin that does not cling to the fruit and flesh that separates easily into segments. They are known as various mandarin cultivars to the botanist but to the shopper as different types of tangerines. Those of North African descent, grown in Tangiers with loose-fitting skins and perfumed juice, are responsible for the name tangerine. Canned segments, however, are sold as mandarins.

Clementines
Clementines are thought by some to be mandarins crossed with the Algerian wild orange, but are generally recognized as a variety of tangerine. They are usually tiny with a very good flavor – children are particularly fond of them.

Satsumas
These are the tangerines grown and exported from Japan and Cyprus. They can be quite sour and are very refreshing.

Ortaniques, kings, tangors and murcotts
These along with many other small hybrids, are related to both tangerines and oranges and are often found growing on the same tree, which shows how easily they cross with each other. They are sweet, spicy dessert fruits and are easy to peel.

KUMQUATS

These originated in Japan and have recently been cast from the citrus family by botanists although they continue to look and taste like tiny oranges. They are usually eaten with their skin and are often sold in glass jars, unpeeled and preserved in heavy syrup.

GRAPEFRUIT

These large familiar globes that are either yellow, when they are called white, or rosy, when they are called pink, are desendants of the pomelo, a citrus plant carried from Polynesia to the West Indies in the seventeenth century by an English sea captain. A modern variety of this fruit, pink fleshed and with the merest trace of bitterness, is still marketed under its original name.

The grapefruit is more popular in America than anywhere else. It is primarily a breakfast fruit but often starts meals in the shape of cocktails, or in the half shell with the segments precut. It ends meals in mousses and sherbets and in between turns up in salads mixed with avocado, or with oranges and mint and served on beds of lettuce.

TANGELOS AND UGLIS

Tangelos are a cross between tangerines and grapefruits. They are loose skinned and often stamped "color added' when marketed, since their skin does not color well naturally. The minneola variety is particularly juicy and easy to peel.

The same fruit is also marketed under the name of ugli fruit or, as it is called in Jamaica, hoogli fruit. No cosmetic treatment is applied to it in this guise and its extraordinary bumpy, mottled skin remains greenish-yellow. The light orange flesh is sweet and juicy and delicately flavored with a flower-like perfume.

LEMONS

Rich in vitamin C, these most indispensable of fruits can be large or small, with a smooth, thin skin or a thick knobbly one. For culinary purposes such as puddings and sherbets, lemon butters, lemon soups, frothy sauces and for the wedges served with fish and shellfish, and with iced tea, it is better to use smooth-skinned lemons, which have more juice.

Choose specimens that are truly lemon-yellow. Butter-yellow lemons may have lost some of their acidity in ripening, and lemons that look dull and do not have a moist-looking sheen may be dry and "ricy," meaning that the almost invisible little sacs containing the juice have turned grainy through evaporation.

Lemons owe much of their flavor and aroma to the oil in the outer part of their skin, which is known as the zest. When serving lemon quarters they should be cut lengthwise so that when squeezed the juice will be directed downwards onto the food. Lemon juice should be added whenever possible to dishes after they are cooked, to avoid loss of vitamin C, which disappears when it is heated.

Apart from flavoring, lemon juice has certain other qualities. A teaspoonful of lemon juice added to every cup of water will help prevent fruit breaking up or losing its shape while it is stewing. A few squeezes of juice will help poached eggs and boiled rice to keep their color, and a few drops will acidulate water sufficiently to prevent the discoloration of vegetables such as sweet potatoes and Jerusalem artichokes. It can be used instead of vinegar in salad dressings, and since it helps to counteract the richness of foods it can aid digestion when used with fried foods.

LIMES

These can be pale or dark green and have a tart greenish pulp; if their skins are yellowish this usually means that their tang has gone. The West Indian or Mexican lime, which features so much in Creole cooking, is sharp and aromatic, as are the larger Tahitian limes of which the Persian and the Bearss are two types. The Key limes of Florida have a delicious sharpness and are used to make Key lime pie.

Limes are the most perishable of all the citrus fruits. They can be used for the same

Kumquats

Limes

Lemons

Tangerines

Satsumas

purposes as lemons and their juice, pale when fresh but often with added green color when commercially extracted, goes into daiquiris and margheritas.

STONE

Although hothouse peaches can be found almost all the year round, there is still something wonderfully seasonal about stone fruits. Their year begins with the first cherries and ends with the last of the plums, with outdoor peaches, greengage and damson plums, nectarines and apricots in between. All are closely related members of the Prunus family and when talked about collectively are known as drupes.

CHERRIES

Firmly fleshed or melting, deepest lip-staining black or the palest cream tinged with a rosy blush, cherries come in hundreds of varieties and are generally classified by their growers as sweet or sour. There is also a third type, which is a mixture of sweet and sour, known as Dukes or Royales. Usually black or transparent red, these are all-purpose cherries and can be both eaten and cooked in a variety of ways.

The wild sweet cherry known as the maz-

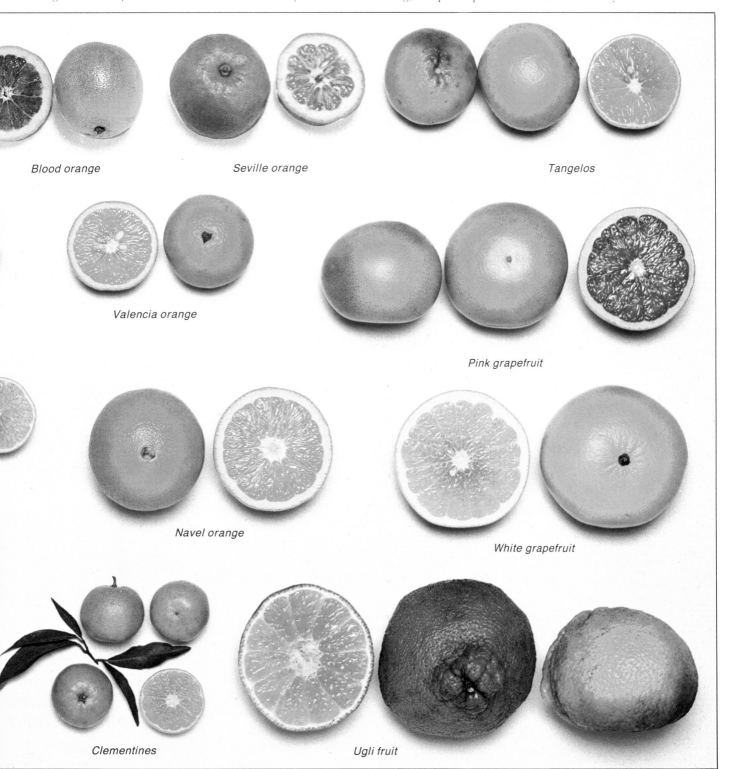

Blood orange

Seville orange

Tangelos

Valencia orange

Pink grapefruit

Navel orange

White grapefruit

Clementines

Ugli fruit

zard is the ancestor of all our varieties.

Sweet cherries

Sweet cherries used to be neatly divided into the hard, crisp bigarreaus and the soft, sweet cherries known as guignes in France, or geans in England. Now, however, with the appearance of many hybrids, the distinction has become blurred.

Among the most delicious of the bigarreaus are the Napoleons, or Naps – big, crisp and golden with a red cheek. They are also known as Royal Annes, and in nineteenth-century England were for a time called Wellingtons. This politically inspired name, however, did not catch on, and to restore the balance England named a dark red cherry the Waterloo. A favorite American cherry, the Bing, is also a bigarreau – large, heart shaped, deep red to almost black, with firm, sweet flesh.

Another red-black cherry that is tender and has an excellent flavor is the Black Tartarian, a type of guigne. It is said to have made its way to Europe from the Caucasus, the seed probably carried by birds. Early Rivers, another of the guigne type of cherry, is a prolific variety with red to deep red flesh.

Sweet, juicy black guignes are used to make the delicious dessert clafoutis, which comes from the Dordogne region of France, while in Kent, England's cherry-orchard county, a similar dish goes by the name of battered cherries. The same juicy type of cherries also go into the exquisite Swiss black cherry jam, slippery and shiny and full of whole cherries. The cheaper versions with chopped-up cherry pulp trying to pass off as the real thing are best avoided.

Sour cherries

If the word sweet is sometimes used too optimistically as far as cherries are concerned, sour is almost an understatement. The dark, short-stemmed, juicy morellos, or griottes as they are known in France, are so acid that they are almost impossible to eat. They are small and round and deep red to almost black. The famous Black Forest cherry cake called schwarzwälder kirschtorte is authentically made with morellos grown in the Black Forest region, and with kirschwasser, the Black Forest version of cherry brandy. Amarelle cherries such as the Montmorency, brighter in color and with pale, clear juice, are so sour that they are not usually eaten uncooked.

Sour cherries go into translucent jams, into pickles to eat with game, pork and poultry, and into liqueurs and cherry brandies. Duck Montmorency, now something of a cliché, requires cherries for its fruity, winy sauce, although they do not necessarily have to be the sour Montmorency cherries of France; any acid red cherries will do. And cherries set alight in a brandy sauce and poured over vanilla ice cream make Cherries Jubilee. Morello cherries are often preserved in jars and make excellent tarts and pies.

Maraschino cherries

The sweet, sticky liqueur maraschino is made from a small, wild Dalmatian cherry called damasca, or marasca, but maraschino cherries, which were originally preserved by being steeped in the liqueur, are now more likely to be cherries that have been bleached and then steeped in syrup flavored with oil of bitter almonds.

Buying and storing cherries

Look for brightly colored fruit; whether heart shaped or spherical, the plump ones are always best. The fruit should be clean and glossy, with unbroken skins and stalks that are fresh and green. Ripe cherries are perishable, but will keep for a few days in the refrigerator; wash then just before they are to be eaten.

Cooking with cherries

Prepare cherries for cooking by pushing out the stones with a cherry pitter or hooking them out with the U-bend of a bobby pin or paper clips. If you try to squeeze the pits out, too much juice is lost.

Canned cherries lack firmness and flavor and are best used in sweet dishes, although they still won't be very good. It is best to avoid them if possible.

PLUMS

No other fruit, said Pliny, has been so cleverly crossed, and since he wrote this some 2,000 years ago, the growers have not been idle. Some plums are grown primarily to be eaten fresh, although many, like the greengages, are equally delicious cooked.

Dessert plums

These are usually larger and juicier than cooking plums, with a higher sugar content.

Gages

Of all the plums, none is more sweetly perfumed than the greengage, known in France as the reine-claude after Francis I's queen. Round and firm fleshed, the old greengage with its rose-flushed cheek is still grown, although there are now other varieties such as the Black Diamond and the juicy Jefferson. There are also many golden descendants of the old French "transparent gage," large and translucent, with the delicious honeyed flesh that is characteristic of all the gages.

The Santa Rosa and Burbank

These are pleasantly tart plums grown largely in California, where the climate suits their warm temperament. Derivatives of the wild Asiatic plum, they are often referred to as Japanese plums, although in fact they were grown originally in China.

The Gaviota

This is one of the newer varieties, grown to giant proportions; it is sweet and juicy and ruby-colored right through to the pit.

The Victoria

Golden red and pink bloomed, the Victoria is one of the most prolific of plums. Oval shaped with golden flesh, it is a favorite in

PREPARING CITRUS FRUIT

PEELING

Using a serrated knife, cut a slice from the top of the fruit to expose the flesh. Peel the fruit in the same way as you would an apple, cutting just beneath the pith.

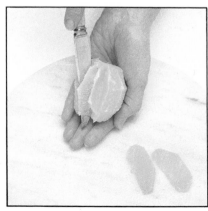

SEGMENTING

Hold the fruit in one hand and cut out each segment, freeing it from its protective membrane as you cut. The resulting segments should be completely free of membrane and pith. This method is suitable for all citrus fruits.

the kitchen and an excellent dessert plum.

Cooking plums

These are usually the smaller, drier, sharp-flavoured plums that retain enough acidity to make them delicious when cooked.

Sloes and bullaces

Dark and mouth drying, the sloe is the wild European plum that grows on spiky hedges and is used for making sloe gin. The bullace, larger than the sloe, is less acid and can be stewed, jellied or preserved.

Damsons

These have a lovely acidity even when ripe and are used for jams, pies and desserts, and in England for damson cheese, an old country confection made of sieved fruit and plenty of sugar, which is potted and aged before it is ready to eat. It also used to be dried in slabs, decorated with almonds and served with a dousing of port as a dessert. Damson cheese is a close relation to the more pliable "mus," the cheese made from Zwetschen, which used to be frequently eaten, especially in Germany.

Zwetschen

Quetschen or, in the Slavonic languages, slivy, are small, dark blue plums with a heavy bloom. They thrive in central Europe, where slivovitz is made, and in Germany and in Alsace, where they are used to make quetsch – a fruit brandy that is clear and potent.

Cherry plums

Cherry plums, also called myrobalans, are very small, with red or yellow skins and yellow flesh. They are soft and juicy and are excellent stewed or made into jams.

Beach plums

These grow wild in the United States, especially around Cape Cod, where the dark purple fruits grow in large clusters and are keenly gathered and made into beach-plum jelly.

Buying and storing plums

When buying plums make sure that they are firm and free from damage. They should be stored in a cool place, but not for too long; ripened plums do not keep for more than two or three days. If you buy them already ripe, they need to be eaten as soon as possible as they will quickly go bad.

Cooking with plums

All dark plums and some of the lighter varieties such as the small golden-yellow Mirabelle, have bitter skins which make a delicious contrast to the sweetness of their flesh when cooked. They can be used to make jams and jellies which are transparently luminous when freshly cooked, but darken with overcooking and ageing. These are the plums, too, that are used to make a delicious sweet-sour sauce that can be served with meat and with the crêpes that sometimes accompany Peking duck.

In Austria plums, fresh or dried, go into the middle of lovely deep-fried little dumplings that are rolled in sugar mixed with grated chocolate, and also go into strudels. Throughout Germany the plum season means Pflaumenkuchen – plums riding on a yeast-based dough that absorbs the juice of the fruit. In Britain, however, many recipes such as plum duff or plum pudding do not require plums at all, the word being used to mean raisins.

PEACHES

The flesh of peaches ranges from almost silvery white to deep gold – the white-fleshed peaches being tender and juicy, the yellow ones slightly coarser but often very good. With some peaches the flesh clings to the stone, hence clingstone peaches, while with freestone varieties the flesh comes away easily and cleanly. In Europe this distinction seems not to weigh so heavily on the shopper, although it is always a shame when too much of the flesh – rightly described as voluptuous – refuses to part in any way from the stone.

Known as *Prunus persica*, the peach reached Greece from its native China via Persia, and Rome and the rest of Europe via Greece. It arrived in America by way of stones carried by Columbus, and the American soil and climate suited the peach tree so well that it spread faster than the settlers. But it is Georgia, especially, which is often known as the peach state. The freestone Belle of Georgia, crimson cheeked, its creamy flesh delicately marbled and its stone sitting in a carmine-tinted pit, comes from seed sent directly from China at the end of the nineteenth century. Elberta, another favourite Georgian, has juicy yellow flesh, firm but tender. It is equally popular fresh or canned, but while canned peaches in heavy syrup are nice enough, they differ almost more than any other fruit from their fresh counterparts: perhaps it is because canned peaches are cooked in a heavily sweetened syrup, for even the sweetest fresh peach never has a cloying quality.

Buying and storing peaches

Large peaches command the highest price but are not always the most delicately flavored. (The native peach of China, venerated ancestor of all the peach trees in the world, bears fruit that is relatively small with a large stone, yet its flavor is said to be unsurpassed by one of our hybrids.)

Peaches are a fragile fruit and should be handled very gently. They should feel firm with a little give; greenish fruit should be avoided as it will never ripen at home. Store ripe peaches in the refrigerator, but those that are still a little too firm are best kept at room temperature.

Cooking with peaches

Spiced or pickled peaches are excellent with ham, and some people eat them in salads, but it is as puddings or desserts that they come into real use. Peach sherbets and ice creams are both delicate and subtle, and there are scores of coupes and sundaes made with peaches, the most famous of which must undoubtedly be Peach Melba. Invented by Escoffier for a late diner, Dame Nellie Melba, the opera singer, this involves a ripe fresh peach gently poached in syrup, with vanilla ice cream and whipped fresh cream, and crushed fresh raspberries for the sauce. In France, peaches and raspberries make an exquisite fruit dessert.

NECTARINES

One of the most beautiful of all fruits, with rosy cheeks like blushing girls, nectarines are smooth skinned like plums and are very like ripe plums in texture, but taste of peach, although they are a little sharper and more scented. They can be used in all the same ways as peaches, but are usually devoured, messily, as a dessert fruit – much juicier than peaches, they are rarely skinned as their skin is much thinner. Called brugnons in France, they are eaten there in vast quantities in July and August. They are grown in California and are widely marketed throughout America.

APRICOTS

Even in the days when fresh fruit was regarded with suspicion, apricots were generally accepted as wholesome food. Known as *Prunus armeniaca* because the Romans obtained them from the Far East via Armenia, they span the spectrum of gentle orangey tones from the very pale to the very rich. Depth of color, however is not necessarily an indication of flavor; it merely means that some varieties have more carotene then others and are richer in vitamin A. The dark apricot called Moorpark is always sweet and delicious.

The flesh of apricots, unlike that of peaches and nectarines, is dry and mealy, which makes them ideal for cooking as well as for eating fresh because they will not turn into a mush, thereby ruining your pastry or whatever else.

Buying and storing apricots

An apricot picked before its time does not sweeten, it only matures a little, so test for ripeness by pressing the fruit between two fingers; it should feel soft. Ripe fruit will keep in the refrigerator for a few days. Unripe, they will keep for longer, and if they are too hard and sour to be eaten fresh, they can be cooked and made into tarts, or pickled in vinegar with cloves for an excellent relish which is delicious when eaten with cold pork or ham.

Cooking with apricots

In France large, fresh apricots make the most mouthwatering flans and tarts, arranged on light flaky pastry, and a compote of apricots, sometimes flavored with Madeira, is served

Apricots

Gaviota plums

Burbank plums

Peaches

Royal Anne cherries

Nectarines

Black Tartarian cherries

Santa Rosa plums

Cherry plums

Early Rivers cherries

Bottled morello cherries

hot on crisp, golden croûtons. Austria's knoedels, or apricot dumplings, are made from fresh skinned apricots individually wrapped in thin pastry, and then poached and eaten with hot melted butter, suger and cinnamon. And brandied apricots are delicious, the fruit poached with suger and put up with brandy in equal quantity to the syrup.

BERRIES

The real feasting begins in the high season and it is then that most berries taste best, simply dredged with sugar and eaten with creamy milk, cream or possibly sprinkled with wine.

There are usually at least two weeks each summer when a great number of berries are available simultaneously. This is the time to make summer desserts or to offer great bowls of mixed berries, sugared well beforehand so that they yield some of their juice. Later in the season, when the smaller berries (which are delicious but cheaper) arrive, it is time to think about making jams, jellies and syrups.

When buying berries it is important to look not only at the top of the little box in which they are likely to be packed but also at the underside. Bad staining or wetness underneath suggests squashed, sad fruit below, which will soon go moldy. If you go fruit picking at a farm – every year more of them open their gates to the public – take plenty of small shallow containers so that your harvest remains in good condition.

Berries, whether bought or picked, are fragile and perishable, so the sooner you eat them the better. If they must be stored, put them in a darkish, airy place, spreading them out well so that furry casualites do not infect the neighbors. No berries, except perhaps the harder ones that come in the autumn, thrive in the refrigerator, for although it is cold and dark, it is too humid, and also the highly scented berries such as raspberries and strawberries tend to permeate other foods, particularly butter, with their smell.

STRAWBERRIES

Best loved among the soft fruits, strawberries conjure up all the well-being of summer. In England they are built into the summer way of life – tea at Wimbledon and Henley and garden parties at Buckingham Palace traditionally include what a sixteenth-century writer described as "strawberries swimming in the cream."

Somewhat surprisingly, perhaps, the ancestor of the cultivated strawberries we delight in these days was American, introduced to Europe from Virginia by early colonists. It was smaller than today's prize specimen, but a positive giant compared with the indigenous fragrant wood strawberries (*fraises des bois*) that had long been transplanted into gardens and regarded as a

cure for all ills. Alpine strawberries (*fraises des alpes*) have slightly larger fruits and some are completely white in color.

Nowadays new varieties of strawberries are regularly introduced and old ones discarded for a number of reasons.

Do not be put off by the lighter berries or those that have paler tips, but make sure that the strawberries are plump and glossy. They should be bought with their green frills intact, and if washing them, do it immediately before hulling. Hulled strawberries yield their juice when sugared. Only in jam making should strawberries be cooked at all. Even when making strawberry sauce to go with ice creams or sherbets, simply liquidize the fresh fruit with sugar and perhaps a little lemon juice.

RASPBERRIES

These beautiful, velvety berries from which the liqueur crème de framboises is made are at their best when a deep garnet red. Black raspberries taste much like the red ones, as do the white ones, which do not often find their way onto the market. Raspberries are always sold hulled, which makes them fragile and particularly vulnerable to crushing.

The flavor of raspberries is intense and their presence will be apparent even if only a handful is mixed with some other fruit, or the juice of a few is mixed with the juice of, say, red currants, for the Scandinavian dessert called rødgrød.

Raspberry juice is much loved in Germany and Scandinavia as a refreshing drink. It also often appears at table to be poured over rice puddings, blancmanges and flummeries. And in Berlin when you order a *weisse mit Schuss* in a beerhall, you will be served a goblet containing a fizzy drink made from pale ale, raspberry syrup and soda. Finally among the raspberry-flavored liquids is raspberry vinegar, which is made by steeping crushed berries in wine vinegar.

A few non-sweet dishes are improved by the addition of raspberries. The Scots stuff grouse and blackcock with the wild raspberries that grow in abundance in the hedges. It is in desserts, however, that raspberries come into their own, either served quite plain with a dollop of whipped cream, crushed in fresh sherbets or puréed with a little sugar and served as a sauce.

BLACKBERRIES AND DEWBERRIES

From the shopper's point of view, the distinction between these two berries is purely academic. From the picker's point of view, these relations of the raspberry are distinguished by their growing habits: upright plants are thought of as blackberry bushes, trailing ones as dewberries.

Although blackberries are generally larger than dewberries, and shiny while dewberries are dull, sometimes with a white bloom, their names are used interchangeably in many

Victoria plums

Greengage plums

Damson plums

Sloes

Bullaces

places. Neither their taste nor their properties differ and both are exceptionally rich in vitamin C. Both remain sour for a long time after turning black and are only fully ripe when they are soft to the touch.

The plant grows freely and English hedges tend to be black with berries from September to November. During these weeks pickers are out in full force and kitchens are filled with the aroma of the berries, which, besides preserves, are also made into wine, syrup and any number of desserts. Like raspberries, blackberries can also be eaten with sugar and cream, but this is a success only when

they are ripe and fresh since, once off the brambles, wild blackberries lose their flavor fast.

Cultivated blackberries are more stable and keep their taste longer. They are always sold with their core but without their green stalks. They, too, make lovely pies, tarts, fools and crumbles.

LOGANBERRIES, YOUNGBERRIES AND BOYSENBERRIES

Whether in an attempt to improve the humble blackberry or to make the raspberry

more robust, Messrs. Logan, Young and Boysen in turn did us a great service in crossbreeding. America's youngberries and boysenberries are used for the same purpose as loganberries, which are more familiar in Europe. All can be made into cooked and uncooked desserts and preserves using any recipe in which raspberries are called for.

The loganberry, basically a cross between a blackberry and a raspberry, is more acid than the blackberry but less intensely flavored than the raspberry. It is purple with a delicate bloom, almost conical in shape and has no troublesome seeds. It needs plenty of sugar if it is to be eaten raw.

THE YOUNGBERRY

The youngberry, the result of crossing a dewberry with a raspberry, looks like an elongated blackberry and tastes rather like a loganberry.

THE BOYSENBERRY

The boysenberry is a cross between a youngberry and a raspberry and has a similar taste to the latter. The size of this fruit causes amazement to those unfamiliar with this fairly recent breed, as it is twice or even three times the size of its ancestors.

CLOUDBERRIES AND MULBERRIES

The cloudberry

This is the raspberry's slow-ripening, cold-weather cousin. It has been found as far north as the Arctic Circle and grows in Siberia, Canada, cold districts of northern America and in Scandinavia, where it forms the basis of many fruit desserts and soups. Fully ripe, it is orange, tinged with red where it catches the sun, and resembles a golden mulberry. Its taste is reminiscent of apples with honey and in Canada it is called the baked-apple berry.

The mulberry

The mulberry, although it is not botanically related to the raspberry members of the Rubus tribe, is used in much the same way.

GOOSEBERRIES

These can be golden, green or red globes, translucent or opaque, covered in whiskers or smooth, and there is one variety that is milky white. They are the only berries among the soft fruits that make the most delicious dishes when they are unripe.

Cook them, topped and tailed, into a purée with a little water over the lowest heat, using sugar to taste. They are always sour and require some sweetening even when making the classic sauce for mackerel, to which a little fennel is sometimes added. For pies and crumbles, gooseberries are also best when they are slightly immature. A cream-colored sprig of elderflowers laid on top of the fruit is a traditional British addition; it scents the gooseberries and makes them taste a little like muscat grapes.

CURRANTS

Red currants, white currants and black currants are, like gooseberries, of the Rubus tribe, but here the similarity ends. They hang like tiny translucent grapes in little bunches on the bush, and the longer they hang, the sweeter they become.

Red currants

There are those who love eating fresh red currants, raked off their stalks with a fork and covered with sugar and milk. Others prefer them in a berry mixture, or bathed in a real vanilla custard to mitigate the acid.

They are delicious with melon and an essential ingredient of summer pudding.

Best loved of all red currant preparations, however, is the red currant jelly. Transform it, with the addition of port, orange juice and peel, into sweet-sharp Cumberland sauce to serve with ham and game.

White currants

These are less acid than their red counterparts and can be eaten just as they are, their thin, almost transparent skins liberally dusted with sugar.

Black currants

These, too, make lovely jams and jellies but are rarely eaten fresh, except by those who like acid-tasting berries. Black currants are rich in vitamin C and a tisane made of their leaves is often taken as a health-giving drink.

BLUEBERRIES AND BILBERRIES

These berries, borne by shrubs found on acid soils and in peaty districts wherever heather grows, come from different species of the same genus and are used for similar purposes. Both have a silvery bloom that intensifies their blueness. They can be small or large depending on the soil, although blueberries are usually larger than bilberries, especially the blue cultivars that are widely grown in America.

CRANBERRIES

In northern Europe where these berries are plentiful they traditionally go into the sharp fruit relish that accompanies venison and roast game birds. With the advent of red currants, cranberries fell out of favour in Britain. America, however, reintroduced the larger, redder cranberry, much eaten as a sauce with turkey at Thanksgiving, and they are still traditional in Britain at Christmas.

When buying cranberries, make sure that they are bright, dry, plump and unshrivelled. They will keep unwashed in the refrigerator for up to two weeks.

ELDERBERRIES, ROWANBERRIES, ROSE HIPS

Elderberries

Elderberries growing black and shiny in flat clusters, are a good addition to blackberry puddings and ripen at about the same time. On their own they may be a little sickly, but the syrup, made of the berries, can add a delicious flavor to apple pies all winter long. Sprigs of the cream-colored flower heads can be dipped in batter and eaten as fritters.

Rowanberries

These are the fruit of the mountain ash, which in autumn is a mass of decorative orange-scarlet berries. They are delicious when made into a bittersweet jelly and served with venison or lamb.

Rose hips

Rose hips, the scarlet ovals that appear in the hedges when the wild roses have blown,

or the flat squat fruits of the Rugosa roses, are the essential ingredients of rose hip syrup, the well-known repository of vitamin C. They also make a delicate, health-giving jelly.

Care must always be taken to strain out the sharp, prickly hairs that surround the abundant seeds in each hip, so after steeping the ground hips in boiling water, pass the liquid at least twice through double cheese-cloth or jelly bags.

RHUBARB

Odd man out in the world of fruit, rhubarb is used for the same type of dishes that also call for gooseberries, apples and plums. It is probably best known in pies and crumbles – in fact, it used to be known as the pie plant – and its tart taste combines well with blander, sweeter fruits. When buying rhubarb, look for stalks that are crisp and firm. Use them as soon as possible as they are very perishable, or keep them in the refrigerator until ready to cook them.

Forced rhubarb stalks with their delicate texture need only the briefest of cooking as they soften so quickly. Tougher maincrop rhubarb takes longer and both need quantities of sugar. If very acid, a teaspoon of red currant jelly added to the cooking water often helps. Rhubarb is usually sold with its leaves as these prevent it wilting, but they must be discarded before cooking as they contain toxic amounts of oxalic acid.

RECIPE SUGGESTION

Strawberry ice cream

3¼ cups/450 g ripe strawberries
3 egg yolks
½–¾ cup/140–170 g sugar, superfine if possible
⅔ cup/1.5 dl milk
⅔ cup/1.5 dl heavy cream

SERVES 4–6

Put the egg yolks and ½ cup/140 g sugar in a bowl and whisk them together with either an electric beater or a hand whisk until the mixture becomes light and pale. Set the bowl aside.

Heat the milk and cream to just below boiling point and pour it in a thin stream into the egg and sugar mixture, beating all the time. Transfer the mixture to the top of a double boiler and thicken over hot water on a gentle heat, stirring from time to time, until you have a nice thick custard that smoothly coats the back of the spoon. Allow to stand until it becomes completely cool.

Hull the strawberries and purée them in a food processor or put them through the medium blade of a food mill. When the custard is cool, fold in the strawberry purée, taste the mixture and add more sugar if necessary. Ice cream tastes less sweet after freezing, so the mixture should be fairly sweet when it goes into the freezer. Transfer it to an ice cream maker or freezer tray and freeze. If you don't have an ice cream maker, blend the mixture once or twice in a food processor as it sets to prevent the formation of large ice crystals.

RECIPE SUGGESTIONS

Rhubarb and raisin pie

2 lb/900 g rhubarb
¼ cup/55 g raisins soaked in a little red wine
shortcrust pastry made with 1½ cups/170 g flour
2 teaspoons flour
6 tablespoons/85 g sugar
a little creamy milk

SERVES 6
Preheat the oven to 425°F/220°C.
Trim and wash the rhubarb and cut into 1 in/2.5 cm pieces. Line a pie plate with half the pastry, put in the rhubarb and sprinkle with the flour and most of the sugar. Spread the raisins over the top and pour the red wine over them. Cover with the rest of the pastry and decorate with oblique cuts. Brush with the creamy milk, sprinkle with the remaining sugar and bake for 12–15 minutes, then lower the temperature to 350°F/180°C and bake for a further 20–25 minutes, covering loosely with foil if the pastry looks as if it might otherwise become too brown.
Serve this excellent pie hot with fresh cream.

Raspberries and peaches

3 cups/340 g raspberries
3 peaches
sugar to taste, preferably superfine
juice of ¼ lemon

SERVES 4
Put the raspberries in a bowl, sprinkle them with plenty of the sugar and put them in the refrigerator for 2–3 hours, until their juice has run into the sugar.
Dip the peaches in boiling water, skin them, cut them away from their stones in thin slices and arrange them over and around the raspberries. Squeeze the lemon juice over the top and sprinkle with more sugar. Put them back in the refrigerator to chill for an hour or two. Serve the fruit plain, without cream.
This is a delicate dessert with a pleasant sharpness.

Blackberry and apple pie

2¼ cups/450 g fresh plump blackberries
3 cooking apples
6 tablespoons/85 g granulated or light brown sugar
3 cloves
shortcrust pastry made with 1½ cups/170 g flour
1 egg yolk beaten with ¼ teaspoon water, or a little water and a sprinkling of sugar

SERVES 6
Preheat the oven to 425°F/220°C.
Pick over and wash the blackberries and peel, core and slice the apples. Put a pie funnel in the middle of a pie dish, put in the fruit in layers, sprinkling the sugar over the layers as you go. Drop in the cloves. Cover the top with pastry, decorating it with leftover pieces, and then glaze the pie with the egg-wash, brushed on with a pastry brush. If you prefer, you can leave off the egg-wash and brush the pie with water and sprinkle it with a little sugar instead.
Bake the pie for 12–15 minutes, then turn the heat down to 350°F/180°C and bake for a further half an hour. If the top of the pie is becoming too brown, cover it loosely with foil.
Serve the pie hot with plenty of fresh cream.

Raspberries

White raspberries

Loganberries

Blackberries

Black currants

Red currants

Cranberries

Blueberries

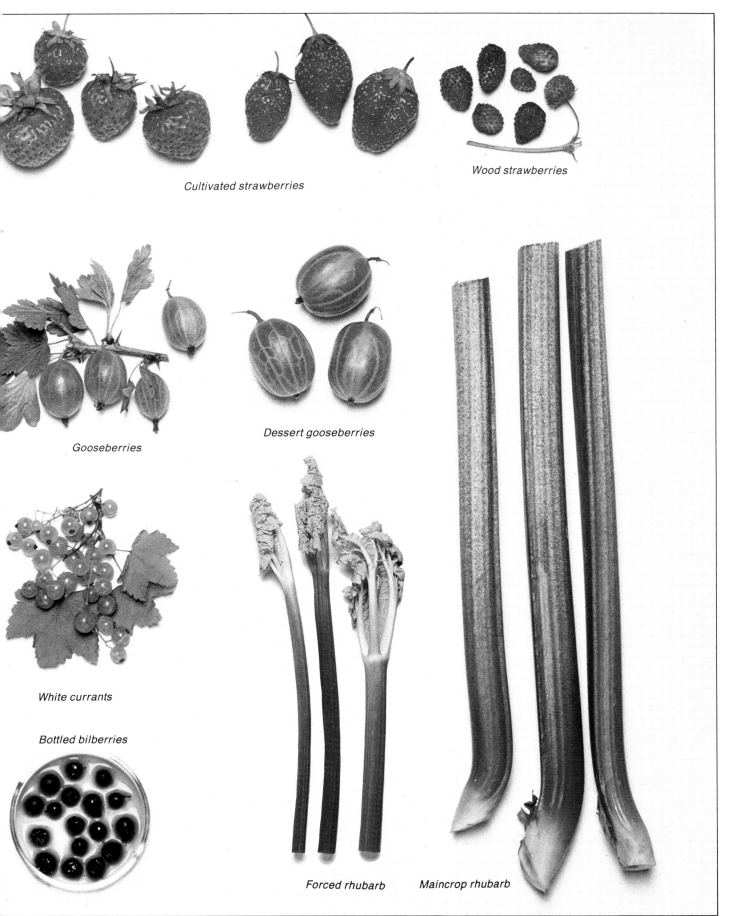

Cultivated strawberries

Wood strawberries

Gooseberries

Dessert gooseberries

White currants

Bottled bilberries

Forced rhubarb

Maincrop rhubarb

RECIPE SUGGESTIONS

Summer pudding

4 cups/450 g raspberries and 2 cups/225 g red currants and 2 cups/225 g black currants or blueberries

1¾ cups/400 g sugar

1 small loaf white bread

SERVES 4–6

Cook the raspberries as lightly as possible with ¾ cup/170 g of the sugar, and the red and black currants in separate pans with ½ cup/115 g of sugar each. Try not to stir the fruit, nor to let it become too mushy. You need some juice but not too much. (These fruits cook very quickly and masses of juice floods out.) A teaspoon of water in the bottom of each pan before it is put on the heat prevents burning and sticking.

Cut the loaf of bread lengthwise into large slices, remove the crusts and use these large slices to line a 5 cup/1 liter pudding bowl, cutting them to size and leaving no gaps. Put in a layer of currants, then a thick layer of raspberries, more currants and then fill with raspberries. Do not add much juice—this should be put in a jar in the refrigerator.

Cover the top with more bread and put a weighted plate on top. Allow to stand for 24 hours. The bread should all be pink. If there are white patches, add more juice. Turn out and serve with the juice and with cream. This is a prince among puddings.

Gooseberry jam

2 cups/450 g sugar for every 1 pint/450 g gooseberries

Top and tail the gooseberries. Put them in a preserving pan with ⅔ cup/1.5 dl of water for every 1 lb/450 g of fruit and bring to the boil. Let the fruit soften for about 15 minutes over a low heat, then add the sugar, stirring to dissolve it before the liquid returns to the boil. Let it boil steadily and rather fast for 10 minutes.

Gooseberry jam, because it gets very thick, has a tendency to burn. To avoid this, stir it with a wooden spoon while it boils, or stand the preserving pan on an asbestos pad.

By the time it has boiled 11–12 minutes—depending on the quantity of gooseberries—it should have reached setting point. Skim quickly and carefully, pour into heated clean jars and cover immediately.

Gooseberry jam has a particularly beautiful color.

Black currant jam

2½ quarts/2 kg black currants

8 cups/2 kg sugar

MAKES 7–8 QUARTS/3–3.5 KG

With a fork, pick the stalks from the currants and remove any green fruit. Put the currants in a preserving pan with 1 cup/225 g of the sugar and 2½ cups/6 dl of water, bring slowly to the boil and simmer for 10–15 minutes. Add the remaining sugar and stir until it has dissolved before starting the simmering again, then simmer for 15 minutes or until the jam sets firmly. Skim well, stir, pour into heated clean jars and cover.

This makes a soft and thick jam. So often black currant jam is hard, or has little chewy currants that feel disagreeable between the teeth, but simmering before the bulk of the sugar goes in softens the fruit completely.

GRAPES

The main role of grapes, of course, is to provide us with "God's choicest gift to man" – wine. The grape contains all that is necessary for making wine: it has yeast in its bloom, natural sugar to feed the yeast, tannin in the skin and seeds, and natural acids to help provide the right environment for the yeast to make alcohol.

MUSCATS

These are to be seen in the stores almost all the year round sometimes swaddled in tissue paper to protect their yeasty bloom, or hanging in full glory in store windows. They may be translucent green with a golden tinge, in which case they are known as white muscats, or a deep blue (known as black muscats), or from scarlet to purple (the red muscats). They are all large, with the richly perfumed flesh that makes muscat wines so distinctive, and they all have seeds.

White muscats

These include the amber, oval-shaped Muscat of Alexandria, with a bloom that rubs off all too easily unless carefully handled; the prized Golden Chasselas, green with an amber tinge which means that it has developed its full flavor; and the fleshy green Almeria, of Spanish stock.

Black muscats

Among these are the delicately flavored Gros Colmar; the large, round Royal with its heavy bloom, very juicy and sweet; Ribier, oval shaped and sweetly perfumed, with a vine-like flavor; and Black Alicante, oval, firm, not as sweet as the Royal but very juicy.

Red muscats

These range from the Cardinal, scarlet and crisp and delightfully aromatic, to the Flame Tokay, a lovely deep red, and Emperor, red or purple, firm and bland.

SWEETWATERS

Sweet and juicy, as their name implies, and with thin skins, the sweetwaters include the sturdy Black Hamburgh; a cutting of this type, planted at Hampton Court in 1769, flourishes there still.

SEEDLESS GRAPES

These have much less tannin than the varieties with seeds, and make the best canned grapes, since tannin tends to alter the flavor of the grapes in the canning process. Sweet, juicy and green, with smallish fruit, varieties such as Thompson Seedless and the smaller Sultana are among the most abundant grape varieties in the world, enjoyed both fresh and dried.

LABRUSCAS AND MUSCADINES

The *labrusca* – not to be confused with Lambrusco, the sparkling red wine of Lombardy – is the native American vine that thrives in the colder climate of the eastern United States, where more tender varieties of grape refuse to grow. With tough skins that slip easily off the flesh, labruscas such as the round, blue-black Concord are rich in pectin and ideal for making grape juice and grape jelly. Delaware, small and a lovely pale rose-red, has a juicy, sweet flesh, and Catawba is red-purple and sweet.

Muscadines such as the large, bronze, sweet-fleshed Scuppernong are grown mainly in the southern states of America and have a rich, spicy flavor.

Buying grapes

Although some grapes have ceased to be seasonal, and are either issued from storage as the market demands or from the greenhouse where they are nurtured all the year round, the end of summer is the traditional grape season. A few stores have taken to naming the grapes on sale, but most sell them unlabelled and few stores offer such a profusion of varieties as to put the shopper in a quandary.

When buying grapes, make sure that the red or black kinds have lost any tinge of green, and that white ones have a tone of amber about them. The stems of both kinds should be fresh looking but show at least a few brown patches, with the exception of Emperor grapes whose stems should be woody-brown all over.

From the trade's point of view the perfect

Emperor grapes

bunch consists of grapes that are uniform in size, who no lurking tiny ones, and all of them firmly attached to their stalks. From the consumer's viewpoint, bunches with a tendency to shedding are often the sweetest, as anyone can testify who has bought local grapes from a huge mound in an open market, through a haze of wasps, and come away with straggly bunches and loose grapes, and found them perfectly delicious and more aromatic than the cosseted sort. But if perfect fruit is desired, it should be plump with no sign of wrinkling in the skin and no brown patches. Avoid bunches with little or no bloom, which shows they have been handled too much, or with any small, shrivelled grapes; these are sour.

Storing grapes

Grapes will keep in good condition for about three weeks in the refrigerator, wrapped in perforated plastic wrap, or for two weeks in a cool larder. But since part of the pleasure of grapes is their appearance, it seems a pity to banish them from sight. A fine bunch in a glass bowl or a basket makes a perfect centerpiece for the dining table; silver epergnes loaded with hothouse grapes were a frequent table decoration at grand Victorian dinners, and talented Victorians would set a bunch of grapes complete with a few leaves and tendrils in a mold of white wine gelatine as an edible showpiece.

Serving grapes

Grapes are usually served at the end of a meal, either alone or with one of the soft cheeses from Normandy or perhaps the hard cheeses from Switzerland, where grapes are a frequent accompaniment to cheese. In Italy you may be offered your grapes in a huge bowl of ice water, with a few floating ice cubes – chilling makes grapes extra refreshing, but room temperature bring out their flavor better.

In the kitchen, grapes are used to make sherbets, jam, jelly and juice, and can also be frosted with egg white and sugar. A Calabrian specialty is a small pastry turnover filled with rum-flavored grape jam, together with walnuts and grated chocolate. In France, grape juice is sometimes boiled until it is syrupy, and then boiled again with sliced apples, quinces, pears or lemons until it is sticky: such fruit is called *raisiné*.

Sole becomes sole Véronique when the rolled, poached fillets in a light white wine sauce are garnished with white muscat grapes. Muscat grapes are good, too, with duck foie gras, sometimes served hot, and pheasant and guinea fowl are sometimes stuffed with peeled, seeded grapes.

Some types of grape slip easily out of their skins, but others may need to be dipped in scalding water for a minute or so. Seeding, too, is simplicity itself if the grapes are first halved. If you want to keep them intact, use the U-bend of a new hairpin or paperclip to extract the seeds.

If you like salads with fresh fruit, try grapes in a mixture of apple and watercress, dressed with oil and lemon. Grapes and cottage cheese also combine well. Make fruit salads prettier with the addition of black grapes, seeded but not peeled, even though the skins of black grapes may be tougher than those of the white varieties. To preserve black or muscat grapes in brandy, prick each grape to make sure that it does not shrivel and then seal the grapes in equal parts of alcohol and sugar. Turn the jar once or twice during the week of maceration. After that, the fruit is ready to eat, poured over ice cream, or the strained brandy can be used in puddings or served in little glasses to accompany the grapes.

Gros Colmar grapes

Muscat of Alexandria grapes

Sultana grapes

MELON

A melon is a luxurious thing. Beautiful and intricately patterned on the outside, a ripe melon no larger than an orange can fill a large room with its fragrance. Inside, cool and full of juice, it offers to quench your thirst and provide you with a delicate sensation rather like eating snow. "There is," say the Arabs, "a blessing in melons. He who fills his belly with melons fills it with light."

Sweet melons, ribbed and encrusted with lacy patterns, were brought to Spain by the Moors, who had in turn received them from Persia or from the depths of Africa – both the Middle East and Africa claim to be the home of this honey-sweet fruit, described as "the masterpiece of Apollo" and celebrated for being as beneficial as the sun itself. Melons appeared in France towards the end of the fifteenth century, to extravagant praise, and were eaten in astonishing quantities by royalty. Served in pyramids and mountains, "as if it were necessary to eat to the point of suffocation, and as if everyone in the company ought to eat a dozen," they were washed down with draughts of muscat wine.

At that time, of course, sweet melons were no larger than oranges, but over the centuries they have been cultivated and improved in both their size and variety.

MUSKMELONS

It is most likely that the muskmelon, or "nutmeg" melon as it is sometimes known, was the kind eaten by the Ancients, who served it with a sprinkling of powdered musk to accentuate the flavor.

Muskmelons are recognized by their distinctive raised netting, which may be coarse like crochet work or fine like lace. This is why they are also called "embroidered" melons in France and "netted" melons in Britain and America. They may be sharply segmented or grooved, with a green or yellow-orange skin, and the flesh ranges from green to salmon-pink.

Americans know their most famous melon of this type as cantaloupe, which is a misnomer. The true cantaloupe melon is not grown commercially in the United States.

CANTALOUPES

These are among the most aromatic types of melon. The rind is ribbed and warty and the flesh is usually a pale orange, rich and juicy. The French prefer to grow this type, especially the Charentais with its deep orange, faintly scented flesh, although new, similar hybrids are always being introduced. The delicate, pale yellow-fleshed Ogen melon from Israel is a small smooth-skinned cantaloupe hybrid.

WINTER MELONS

These are smooth or shallowly ribbed and less aromatic than the muskmelons. The principal varieties include the onion-shaped

Ogen melon

Honeydew melon

Charentais melon

Muskmelon

Casaba with its thick golden-yellow skin and creamy-white to golden flesh; the Cranshaw with green-gold skin and aromatic golden-salmon flesh; and the ubiquitous pale green or yellow honeydew melon with delicate green flesh.

Buying sweet melons

Whatever type of melon you buy, there are a few sound rules to follow. Choose firm, plump melons with clean scars at the stem ends (a roughness here indicates they were picked before they were fully ripe). Netted melons should have no bald patches – this is a sign that the melon suffered a check during its development. Reject any fruits that are soft, scarred or show moist bruises on the skin. It is a bad sign, too, if the stem has started to rot, but light cracking at the stem end is a sign of ripeness. If you press them gently at the blossom end, the cantaloupes and the honeydew winter melons should feel slightly elastic to the touch.

If you are able to shake the melon before buying it and you hear a sloshing sound, the fruit is too ripe and may have started to deteriorate. All melons should feel heavy for their size and – most important – ripe melons should have a pleasant, sweet melon scent about them.

Storing melons

A cool, airy place is best for storing all types of melons – warmer if you suspect that your melon is not quite ripe. When you think that it is ready to eat, and if you do not want it to scent everything in your refrigerator, put your melon to chill in a tightly closed plastic bag before cutting it.

Serving melons

Although the most scented varieties are nicest plain for dessert, melon can be served in salads with leaves of fresh mint and an oil and lemon dressing; with oranges and watercress; or with finely chopped celery, onions, olives and mayonnaise. This mixture may sound strange, but it rests on an old tradition: a seventeenth-century list of "sallet" herbs includes the melon, and ideas for eating it with salt and pepper.

Ground ginger sometimes mixed with sugar has taken the place of pepper – which had ousted powdered musk – as the melon's usual condiment. Plain sugar is often served for the sweet-toothed because even the sweetest melon will be enhanced by a fine dusting of sugar, but the British way of pouring port or other fortified wines into the cavity of a melon is a mistake since it ruins both. Melon slices, resting on the rind from which they have been separated with a sharp knife, beside thin, translucent slices of raw ham – prosciutto – is as delicious a meal-starter as one could hope for. The French used to offer melons only as an hors d'oeuvre; usually chilled, halved cantaloupes sitting in a bowl of crushed ice, but some-

Sugar Baby watermelon

Tiger watermelon

times, in the case of larger light-fleshed varieties, in wedges, the flesh already cut and resting on the rind in a sawtooth arrangement.

These days, melons have rightly taken a place in the dessert course and are to be met in fruit salads, filled with an assortment of fresh fruit, diced and mixed with grapes or red currants, or as melon sherbet or melon ice cream, made with orange and lemon juice and served, if possible, with wild strawberries. The best melons, of course, really need no dressing up, but a cool and refreshing sweet melon salad can be made with an assortment of melon balls or cubes – orange, white, green and scarlet – sugared and chilled: a feast for the eye and an opportunity for the palate to distinguish between the slightly different flavors of the fruits.

WATERMELONS
The watermelon – which Mark Twain called "the food that angels eat" – is a different proposition. Much larger than the sweet melons, and oblong or round in shape, it is an entirely different species and originated in tropical Africa.

Small round watermelons from 6 – 10 lb/ 2.5 – 4.5 kg, with sweet red flesh and pitch-black seeds, may have deep green rinds with a bloom, such as the Sugar Baby, or they may be striped on a light green background, such as the appropriately named Tiger. But the favorites at family picnics are the large spherical or oblong watermelons, often sold in wedges. These usually have a much paler flesh than the smaller varieties because of their higher water content.

When buying a watermelon, it should have a bloom on its skin and the spot where it rested on the ground should be amber colored, not white or green. It should sound hollow when tapped. If you buy your melon by the piece avoid pieces with visible fibers: the flesh should not have any hard white streaks in it.

Watermelon is usually eaten in slices or as part of a fruit dessert.

TROPICAL AND MEDITERRANEAN

BANANAS
There are many varieties of this perfectly packaged fruit. Cooking bananas, called plantains, tend to be starchier and less sweet than the eating variety and are often used before they ripen. Bananas for the table are picked while they are still hard and green and may not be quite ripe when they reach the market. They will, however, ripen quickly at room temperature, turning first yellow, then spotted when they are ready for eating, and finally black when they can still be used to make banana bread. Buy them in

the bunch rather than loose since the skin of loose bananas may well be ripped at the top, thus exposing the flesh.

Bananas, are most enjoyed in their fresh state. Sliced, they form part of many savory dishes, including curries and Creole rice. In fruit mixtures their slightly scented taste and smooth texture complement juicy or crisp fruits such as oranges and apples. Raw or fried, they also make a perfect dessert.

PINEAPPLES
A whole pineapple on the table is a truly luxurious sight. Fresh pineapples form part of many main courses in their native tropical habitat, where they are plentiful and cheap, and it is in the tropics that the idea of serving them hot as an accompaniment to poultry, pork chops and ham originated.

When buying a pineapple it should be fully ripe and fragrant. If the stalk end is moldy or discolored, the fruit bruised or the leaves wilting, the pineapple is not at its best. A pineapple will continue to ripen after it is picked and one that is almost ripe will ripen completely at home.

MANGOES
These beautiful fruits, shaped like large eggs, may be as big as melons or as small as apples. The vivid pinky-golden flesh of ripe mangoes is smooth and fiberless with a taste that has been compared to that of peaches, apricots, melons and pineapples.

When buying mangoes make sure that they are just soft and have a good perfume. If they are completely green they will not ripen properly, and those with large black areas tend to be overripe.

PAPAYAS AND PAWPAWS
The papaya's skin is green to golden, its flesh orangey and its seeds black and shiny. It usually comes onto the market when it is ripening and is sweet and subtly flavored. When buying papayas make sure that they are firm, unblemished except for their speckles and just turning yellow, then allow them to ripen at home.

Like a squash, the unripe papaya may be served stuffed or baked with butter, or it may be added to salads or simply pickled. South American Indians wrap its leaves, freshly plucked, around tough meat to act as a tenderizer, as the plant contains a powerful enzyme that breaks down protein. The ripe papaya is distinctive in fruit salads, pies and sherbets and can also be served simply sprinkled with lemon or lime juice, or sugar or ginger.

The papaya is sometimes called pawpaw, as is another fruit which is similar to look at but is in fact related to the custard-apple.

GUAVAS
Pink fleshed and sweet, these can be as small as a walnut or as large as an apple. They can be served puréed or baked, or eaten fresh

---

RECIPE SUGGESTIONS

Impromptu fruit salad

1 kiwi fruit
2 oranges
1 large slice very red watermelon
2 ripe peaches
juice of 1 lemon
1 tablespoon/15 g sugar, preferably superfine
a few black grapes
scant 2 cups/225 g strawberries

SERVES 4
Peel the kiwi fruit and slice it thinly. Peel and segment the oranges with a sharp knife. Cut the flesh from the watermelon and slice it into 8 thin slices. Dip the peaches in boiling water, peel them carefully, cut into halves and remove the stones, then slice them and sprinkle with lemon juice and sugar. Halve the grapes and remove their seeds, and hull the strawberries.
Divide the fruits between four plates, placing them in groups and arranging them prettily, so that the colors are delicately balanced. Serve chilled.
ALTERNATIVES: *any pretty fruits such as figs, pears, cantaloupe or other melons, mulberries, loganberries and wild strawberries may be included in this salad, depending on what is in season. If you like, you can serve sieved raspberries, sweetened with sugar, as a sauce to go with these fruits.*

Melon sherbet

2 cantaloupes or small honeydew melons weighing about 1 lb/450 g each
juice of 2 lemons
⅔ cup/225 g confectioners' sugar

SERVES 4
Cut the melons in half through the middle and scoop out the soft flesh with a sharp tablespoon discarding all the seeds and fibers from the middle. Keep the rinds on one side. Put the melon flesh in a food processor together with the lemon juice and the confectioners' sugar and blend to a smooth purée. Spoon into an ice cream maker or a freezer tray and freeze. Turn out into the food processor again, blend to a light, smooth slush and pile it into the melon rinds before refreezing.
Served in their shells, these sherbets should be all covered in frost and look very pretty.

with sugar and cream, and they also go well with other fruit such as pineapples or bananas. They are best known, however, for their jelly, which is served with meat or game as an alternative to the usual red currant jelly.

POMEGRANATES

This beautifully shaped fruit, golden outside and filled with crimson beads, each with its central seed, is an intricate construction.

To admire its crimson glory at its best, cut the fruit in half or in segments, slicing through the leather-like, pink-flushed skin. Although the juicy pulp surrounding each of the seeds is beautifully refreshing and aromatic it is rather tiresome to eat.

PERSIMMONS

Unripe persimmons can be astringent so do not shun wrinkled fruit – by this stage the acidity will have disappeared. The fruit does, however, stay glossy and plump when they have been plucked early and artificially matured. Provided they are ripe and soft, with cap and stem intact, their tough skin can be cut downwards and peeled back and the jelly can then be eaten like pulp.

KIWI FRUIT

The brown furry skin covering this egg-shaped fruit hides glistening translucent green flesh with decorative edible black seeds. Once known as the carambola, Chinese and Coromandel gooseberry, it is now best known by the name of New Zealand's national bird, the kiwi.

PASSION FRUIT

The fruit of some species of the passion-flower is also called granadilla and calabesh in the West Indies. It is the size and shape of an egg with a purple-brown hard skin that becomes crinkly as the fruit gradually ripens.

CUSTARD APPLES

These are the fleshy, round or elongated, thick-skinned fruit of the large family of *Anona* trees of the American tropics. There is the apple-shaped cherimoya, and the llama, whose taste has been compared to that of a banana and pineapple. The soncoya is similar but larger, and the sweet-sop is green with flesh that is soft, sweet, aromatic and custard flavored. The sour-sop is green, heart shaped and more acid, with a taste similar to that of a black currant.

LOQUATS

Also known as Japanese medlars, loquats are the size of crabapples but more conical. Although thirst-quenching, they do not have much flavor when raw and are principally used to make jams, jellies and sauces.

Prickly pears

Lychees

Pomegranate

Guavas

Plantains

Papaya

Green bananas

Cape gooseberries

CAPE GOOSEBERRIES

Native to tropical America, these acid-sweet, pleasant, small fruits of the shrub *Physalis peruviana* are encased in papery balloons shaped like Chinese lanterns. Golden when ripe, the berries can be eaten in the fingers or coated with fondant and served with *petits fours*, but are chiefly used to make the most delicious jellies and jams.

LYCHEES AND RAMBUTANS

Lychees or litchis are perhaps best known when served in syrup after a Chinese meal. They appear as translucent half-moons without their knobbly shells and bright red or brown glossy stones.

A rambutan has a hairier shell than a lychee but is used for similar purposes in southeast Asia. Both fruits can be bought in the West, but should be avoided if they look shrivelled, since this means that their pulp is turning black and their delicate flavor will be lost.

PRICKLY PEARS

These are the fruit of a cactus called the tuna and are sometimes known as cactus pears or Indian figs. They are pear shaped, vary in color from green to rosy and are covered with sharp prickles.

When buying prickly pears make sure that they are reasonably bright in color and firm, but not too hard. They are mild flavored and sweet and are usually eaten raw. The fruit should be slit lengthwise and the prickly skin will come off easily. The flesh can then be eaten with sugar and cream or sprinkled with lemon juice.

MANGOSTEENS

These delicate purple fruits with their shiny skin and white, soft, acid-sweet flesh segmented like that of an orange are very popular in southeast Asia. Their taste is refreshing and similar to that of a pineapple.

FIGS

These are perhaps the most sensual of all fruits with their bloomy, bursting skins and luscious flesh. Ancient Greeks thought figs so health giving that they formed part of the athletes' diet for the original Olympic games, and so delicious that poets and philosophers sang their praises. White, green, brown or purple, they are always beautiful and when cut open reveal their pulpy flesh, deep purple, red or pink, embedded with tiny seeds.

The entire fruit is edible and in Italy, where the Sicilian figs are most prized, they are served with prosciutto or as a dessert. In France the purple, white-fleshed Barbillone and many other varieties are also served as a dessert. All are good especially when eaten fresh and ripe. Being perishable, they will not keep for longer than three days in the refrigerator, but should not be served chilled since the cold tends to numb their flavor.

DATES

In their fresh state, dates have a shiny brown skin that sadly promises more juice than the flesh actually delivers. Even the plumpest date has a warm, fudge-like consistency. When buying fresh dates make sure that you pick out fat, smooth-skinned and non-sticky specimens.

DRIED AND CANDIED FRUIT

Dried fruits such as "datyes, figges and great raysings" have been valued in Europe since they were imported in the thirteenth century from the Levant, to sit in the larder alongside domestic "prunellas, apricocks and pippins." There were also dried pears (a special delicacy) and the dried cherries and berries that the medieval housewife would put by in due season. This dried fruit went into a number of what now seem curious dishes. The taste was for the sweet-savory – the sort of dish still found in countries that were once part of the great Ottoman Empire. In Turkey, Iran, Arabia and North Africa, traditional cookery still allies lamb with prunes, apricots and almonds, honey and spices. Chicken is still simmered with prunes, or with quinces, dates or raisins.

RAISINS

The large, sweet raisins made from muscat grapes and called muscatels used to be the kings of the tribe. Now, similiar giants are produced in other places in the world, especially California. It is these that are eaten as a dessert fruit; they used to appear in the stores at Christmastime, but are now available, seedless or complete with seeds, all the year round and are useful in cooking when making pilaus, sauces for quail and hare and in stuffings. Smaller raisins are sold loose and in packs for cake making. Raisins also come packed together with peanuts, shelled hazelnuts and almonds. This once inexpensive mixture is known as Studenten Futter in Germany, because the sugar content of the raisins and the protein content of the nuts quickly revives the energy of poor scholars while they pore over their books.

CURRANTS AND SULTANAS

The currant comes from the small black seedless grape that is a native of the slopes around Corinth in Greece, while sultanas, also known as golden raisins, are made from the seedless white grapes once grown only in the neighborhood of biblical Smyrna. Although both varieties have long been produced elsewhere, the old names have stuck.

In some parts of the world, currants and sultanas are still sun-dried, without the help of chemical treatments. In other centers, science gives nature a helping hand and the

Mangoes

Passion fruit

Bananas

Persimmon

Kiwi fruit

fruit is artificially dried. But welcome the fact that your currants and sultanas, which you can buy separately or mixed and with the addition of finely chopped peel, are likely to have been already washed and tumbledried.

CANDIED PEEL

The delicate green variety is the candied, aromatic skin of the citron – a large, scented, extremely thick-skinned cousin of the lemon. It is citron peel that decorates the top of a traditional Madeira cake.

Orange peel – sometimes sold mixed with citron – and lemon peel can both be bought in large pieces. If you buy peel in a large slice, you will find that it has more flavor than the "cut" peel, not only because there has been less chance for its essential oils to evaporate but also because only the fattest, juiciest peels are sent to market in their entirety. Peel is perfectly easy to cut into neat dice yourself. If the pieces are very sticky, separate them with a dusting of flour and use that much less flour in your recipe. Store peel in airtight jars or it becomes tough and difficult to cut.

DRIED FIGS

The yellow figs of Smyrna were traditionally the most highly prized, and these are now extensively grown elsewhere, together with many other varieties. Although figs pack and travel well, blocks of squashed figs can have a depressing look; so if you mean to enjoy figs with dessert wine after a winter dinner, look for those whose plump, cushion shapes are still discernible. In Provence, a dessert offered at New Year and known as *mendiants*, or "the four mendicants," is a mixture of figs, raisins, hazelnuts and almonds, their colors recalling the habits worn by the four Roman Catholic mendicant Orders.

DRIED BANANAS

Often called "banana figs," dried bananas are quite unconnected with figs and don't have the fig's laxative properties. They are, however, used in the same way as dried figs. Look for them in health food stores.

DATES

Only the stickiest, juiciest dates – "candy that grows on trees" – are sent into the world from their native Arabia, Iran and North Africa, and of them all the Tunisian date, the Deglet Noor, "date of the light," is considered the finest.

These are the dates that have been left on their palm trees to sweeten and mature in the sun, and are then packed in boxes with desert scenes on the lid. You used to find them packed "on the stem," but now the stem is often made of plastic, although the top layer of dates is still "arranged." The bottom layer, however, looks more higgledy-piggledy, so if you buy your dates for both eating and for adding to dishes, dig down to

Pineapple

Fresh figs   *Fresh dates*

the bottom ones to use in cookery. If you plan to stuff dates with nuts or marzipan, making *petit fours* sitting in frilled paper cases to be offered after dinner, you would, of course, use the handsomest dates you can find. Inexpensive pressed blocks of dates are perfectly adequate for cakes.

PRUNES

Until the nineteenth century, prunes were far more popular than plums. Traditionally eaten with game, goose and pork, prunes can also be cooked with red cabbage and are used in the United States to make delicate whips, soufflés, molds and ice creams. The drying process makes prunes good keepers and nothing is easier than to reconstitute their plumpness by soaking them overnight.

The finest prunes are from the red and purple plums of Agen and from those of Tours, the orchard of France. It is these varieties that are grown in California and have made the Santa Clara Valley the center of the excellent American prune industry. Some of the French maintain that the flesh of a California plum is less delicate than that of their native produce, but then in France, plum drying has developed into a fine art. The Perdrigon plum, for instance, is not simply dried. It may be either skinned, pitted, exposed to the sun and flattened to become a *pistole*, or it may be scalded in its entirety and slowly dried in the shade to become a *brignole* or *pruneau fleuri*. This is plumper and less wrinkled than the humble grocery prune and somewhat resembles the Karlsbad plum, a glamorous prune with a blue sheen, tasting strongly of fruit, that is on sale around Christmastime packed in handsome wooden boxes.

DRIED PEACHES, PEARS AND APRICOTS

Dried peaches and pears are most delicious eaten raw: their taste is delicate and does not always survive cooking.

On the tart side even when ripe, dried apricots keep a good deal of their original flavor. Of all the dried fruits, they are the least sickly-sweet. Soaked and cooked, they can be used to make a sharp, fragrant purée, good for puddings, sauces and jam making. Roughly chopped, they can go into pilafs; soaked, they make a good stuffing for lamb and poultry.

Apricots from health food stores are most likely to be sun-dried. Supermarket packaged apricots may have been assisted in drying by sulfur dioxide – the label will reveal the process. Some delicatessens stock commercially "sugar-cured" apricots – tender, chewy fruit which tastes strongly of itself and doesn't need soaking. Apricot paste, a sweetmeat much appreciated in Arabian countries, where it is called *kemreddine*, "moon of religion," can be found in the more exotic stores.

DRIED APPLES

These can be reminiscent of faintly scented rings of chamois leather; only by shopping around, particularly at health food stores, can you find dried apples actually tasting of fruit.

Apple rings have only come into fashion during the last century or so. Before that, and before apple-drying became a commercial operation, there were several methods for drying apples whole – all of them considerably more trouble than to simply core, peel and slice apples, soak them for a few minutes in salted water to prevent discoloration, and thread them onto string looped around the ceiling, where air can circulate around them, until the rings are thoroughly dried.

In whatever way apples have been dried, they have many uses. Applesauce for pork can be made from dried apples that have been soaked and then cooked in plenty of water in a closed pot in the oven. Chopped and mixed with currants and sultanas they usefully stretch a cake mixture. If you use dried apples as a compote, stew them slowly with cinnamon or cloves and add a dash of lemon juice for tartness. If you make your own muesli, you can add chopped dried apple together with the raisins. Indeed, dried apples with any other dried fruit and every type of nut make nourishing winter fruit salads – much nicer if you add fresh oranges and bananas to the mixture.

CHERRIES

Cherries for cakes are candied and glazed with a heavy syrup to aid their preservation. This accounts for their extreme stickiness, and makes it advisable to wash and dry them or steam them for 5–10 minutes in a sieve placed over a pan of boiling water and then dry them, before adding them to a cake mixture. Without this precaution, they are too heavy to float and may sink to the bottom of the cake. A dusting of flour helps to keep them separate and suspended. No need, of course, to wash those cherries you use for decoration – for this, their charm depends on their glistening lusciousness. Beware of "cherries" that are not cherries at all but a cheap and nasty jelly-like substitute, flavored and colored to look like cherries.

CRYSTALLIZED FRUIT AND FLOWERS

Strictly speaking, crystallized fruit is candied fruit with a coating of granulated sugar.

Dates

Dried figs

Dried apple rings

Dried apricots

Dried pears

Glacé refers to the glossy coating of sugar syrup found, for instance, on cherries, pineapple rings and whole candied fruit such as oranges, clementines and figs. The terms, however, have become almost interchangeable.

Angelica, used for decorating cakes, is quite easy to candy yourself. If you have the plant growing in your garden, gather the stalks in midsummer. Blanch them and peel off the outer skin, and boil the inner stems, with a few vine leaves to keep them a bright green, in a syrup made of $\frac{2}{3}$ cup/1.5 dl water and 1 cup/225 g sugar. When the stems are soft and transparent, let them cool and then soak in the syrup for two weeks. Dry the sticks in a cool oven. The same system works for all sorts of small fruit, or chunks or segments of larger fruit.

To crystallize violets, cowslips, primroses or rose petals, you need a light hand. Make a syrup of confectioners' sugar and water, letting it boil until it crisps when dropped into cold water. Draw it off the heat, drop petals or flower heads into it for a minute (in the case of violets, you can dip a little posy at a time) and dry them in a sieve, sprinkling them with more sugar. Sift off the surplus sugar and the flowers are ready to use.

RECIPE SUGGESTIONS

Bread and butter pudding

6 slices well-buttered bread—white, raisin or currant loaf—with the crusts cut off
handful of raisins or sultanas
2 eggs
$1\frac{1}{2}$ tablespoons sugar
large pinch of cinnamon
generous $1\frac{1}{4}$ cups/3 dl creamy milk

SERVES 4

Lay the bread in layers, buttered side up, in a buttered pie dish, sprinkling the fruit between the slices. Beat together the eggs, 1 tablespoon of the sugar and the cinnamon, then beat in the milk. Pour over the bread and leave to soak for an hour.
Preheat the oven to 275°F/140°C.
Just before putting the pudding in the oven, sprinkle it with the remaining sugar and bake for 1–$1\frac{1}{2}$ hours (at the bottom of the oven if you are cooking something else).

Mincemeat

$1\frac{1}{3}$ cups/225 g each of currants, raisins and sultanas
$\frac{1}{3}$ cup/55 g blanched almonds
$\frac{3}{4}$ cup/115 g candied peel
1 carrot
6 firm hard green apples
1 lemon
2 cups/225 g shredded suet
scant $1\frac{1}{4}$ cups/225 g dark brown sugar
1 teaspoon ground cinnamon and ground cloves, mixed
good grating of nutmeg
$\frac{1}{2}$ teaspoon ground mace
1 glass each of whisky and sherry

MAKES 3–4 QUARTS/1.5–2 KG

Chop the currants, raisins, almonds and the candied peel. Wash, scrape and grate the carrot coarsely. Peel, core and chop the apples finely, wash the lemon, grate its rind and squeeze the juice.
Mix all the ingredients except the whisky and sherry in a large bowl and keep covered in the kitchen for three days, stirring daily. Add the alcohol, pack into clean jars and cover. Store in a cool, dry place.
This mincemeat will keep for about two months.

Dundee cake

$1\frac{1}{2}$ cups/170 g flour
salt
1 teaspoon mixed spices
$1\frac{1}{2}$ sticks/170 g butter
generous $\frac{3}{4}$ cup/170 g brown sugar
4 eggs
$\frac{2}{3}$ cup/115 g blanched almonds and 1 cup/115 ground almonds
$\frac{3}{4}$ cup/115 g each glacé cherries and chopped candied peel
$1\frac{1}{3}$ cups/225 g each of currants, sultanas and raisins

Preheat the oven to 325°F/170°C.
Mix the flour, a pinch of salt and the mixed spices and sieve them together. Cream the butter and sugar, beat the eggs and add the flour and eggs alternately to the creamed mixture, beating before each addition. Cut all but about 8 of the blanched almonds into slivers. Add the slivered almonds, ground almonds, cherries and candied peel to the mixture. Shake the currants, sultanas and raisins in a little extra flour and stir them in.
Turn the mixture into a lined, greased 8 in/20 cm cake pan, decorate the top with a star of whole almonds, and bake for $2\frac{1}{2}$–3 hours, covering the top lightly with foil about halfway through. Test with the point of a skewer: if it comes out clean the cake is cooked. Allow to cool in the pan.

Glögg

5 cups/1 liter red wine
$1\frac{1}{4}$ cups/6 dl muscatel
$\frac{2}{3}$ cup/115 g raisins
3 strips orange peel
5 cloves
5 cardamom pods
1 cinnamon stick
2 tablespoons brown sugar
$\frac{2}{3}$ cup/1.5 dl akvavit
$\frac{1}{3}$ cup/55 g blanched almonds

SERVES 6–10

Put the red wine, muscatel, raisins, orange peel, slightly bruised spices and sugar into a large earthenware bowl and allow to stand overnight—this draws the flavor out of the spices.
Put the mixture into a large heavy pan or preserving pan and bring it to boiling point. Add all but one tablespoon of the akvavit and the almonds. Just before serving the glögg, heat the remaining akvavit, pour it over the top and light it. Serve immediately in mugs or tumblers, giving each person a spoon with which to eat the raisins and almonds.

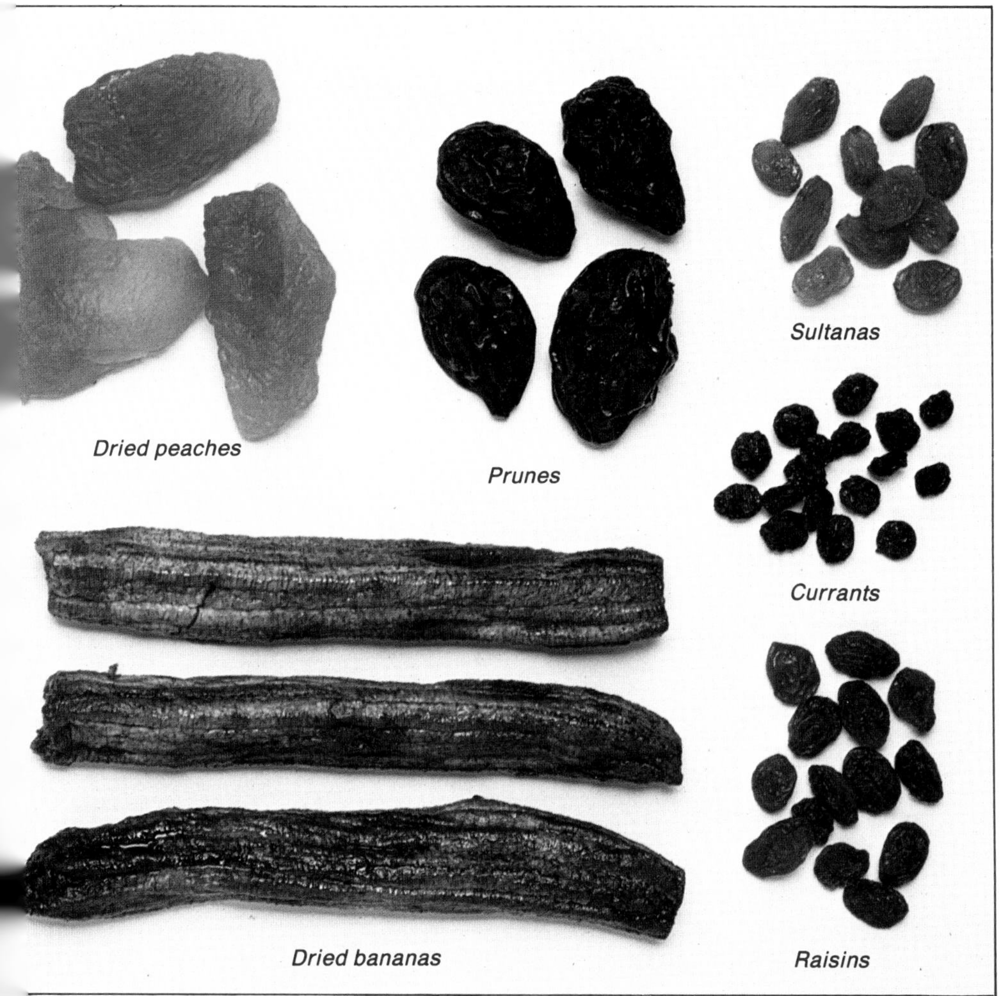

Dried peaches · Prunes · Sultanas · Currants · Dried bananas · Raisins

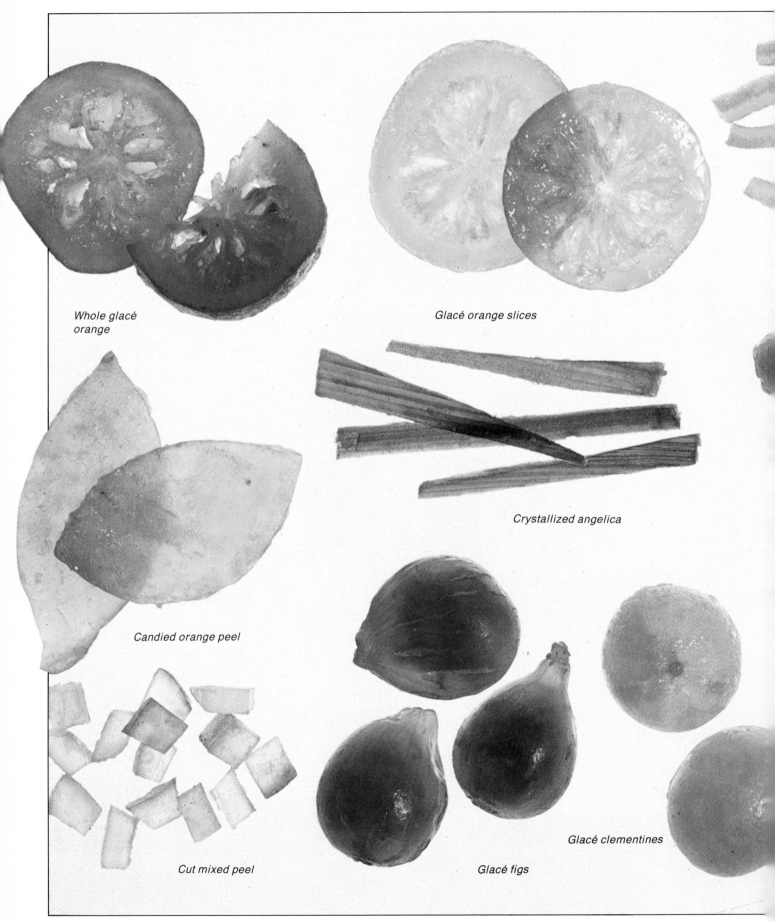

Whole glacé orange

Glacé orange slices

Candied orange peel

Crystallized angelica

Cut mixed peel

Glacé figs

Glacé clementines

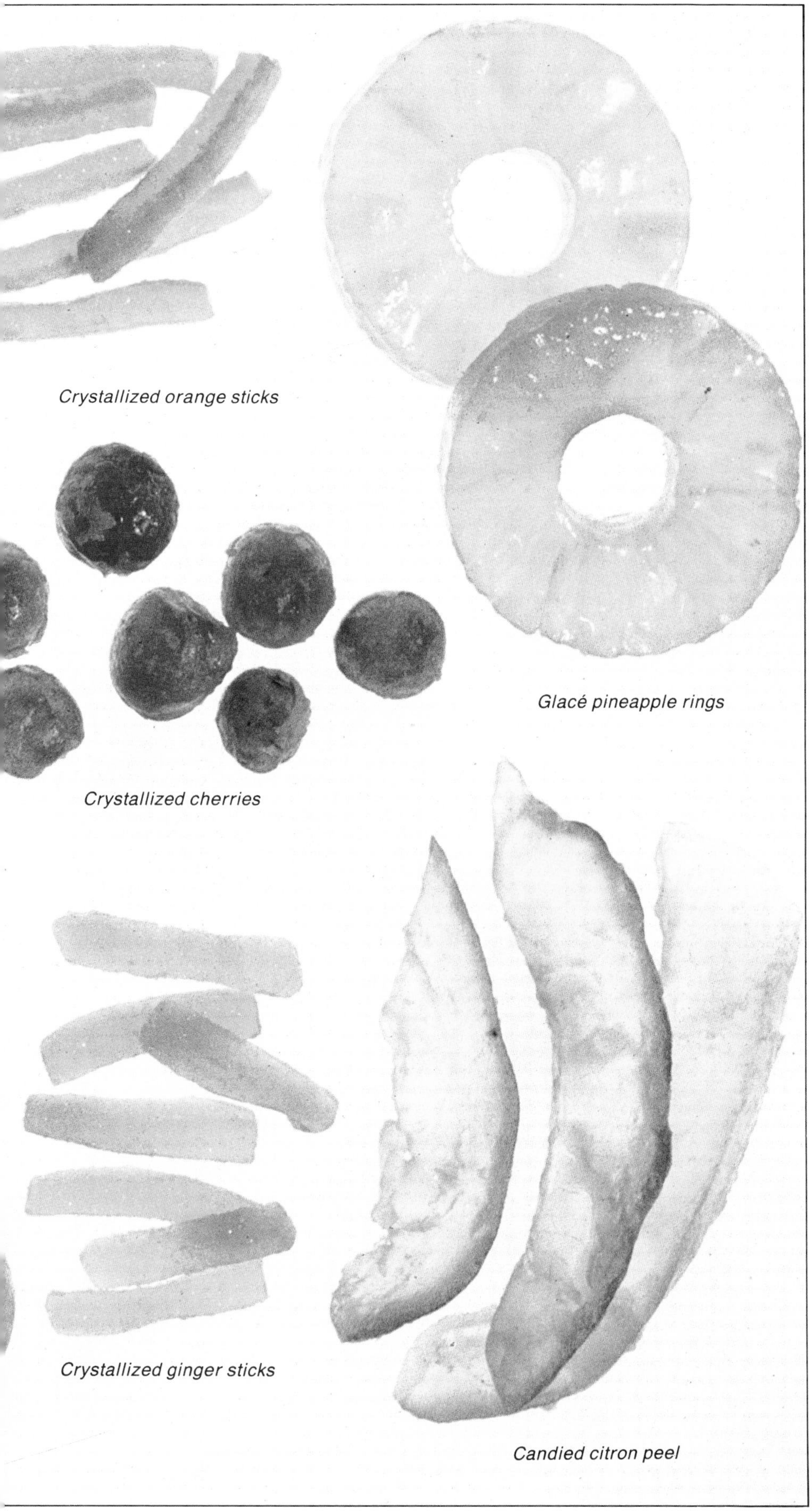

Crystallized orange sticks

Glacé pineapple rings

Crystallized cherries

Crystallized ginger sticks

Candied citron peel

RECIPE SUGGESTIONS

Christmas pudding

2 cups/225 g shredded suet
$1\frac{1}{4}$ cups/225 g light brown sugar
$1\frac{1}{3}$ cups/225 g raisins
$1\frac{1}{3}$ cups/225 g sultanas
$\frac{1}{2}$ cup/115 g candied peel
$\frac{1}{2}$ teaspoon mixed spice
$\frac{1}{4}$ teaspoon ground nutmeg
2 cups/225 g fresh white bread crumbs
1 cup/115 g flour
$\frac{2}{3}$ cup/115 g blanched almonds, cut in halves
$\frac{3}{4}$ cup/115 g glacé cherries
4 eggs
$\frac{2}{3}$ cup/1.5 dl milk
$\frac{1}{2}$ wine glass brandy

MAKES 2 PUDDINGS, EACH SERVING 8 OR MORE

Prepare all the dry ingredients and mix them together. Whisk the eggs well, add the milk and mix thoroughly with the dry ingredients. Let the mixture stand for 12 hours in a cool place, add the brandy, put into well-greased pudding bowls and cover tightly with foil or muslin.

Boil for 8 hours or longer. Before serving, reboil for 2–3 hours. Like all Christmas puddings, these are best made a month or so before, and improve with keeping.

This recipe is based on the English royal family's Christmas pudding.

Twelfth Day cake

4 cups/450 g self-rising flour
1 teaspoon each mixed spices, ground ginger and nutmeg
1 lb/450 g butter
$2\frac{1}{4}$ cups/450 g dark brown sugar
6 eggs
$1\frac{1}{2}$ cups/225 g candied peel, chopped
2 cups/340 g each of currants, sultanas and raisins—large seedless ones if possible
$1\frac{1}{2}$ cups/225 g halved glacé cherries
1 cup/115 g ground almonds
$\frac{2}{3}$ cup/115 g blanched almonds, cut in slivers
1 large glass Madeira or brandy

MAKES 2 LARGE CAKES

Preheat the oven to 350°F/180°C.

Sieve the flour and spices together. Soften the butter, but do not let it become oily. Cream the butter and sugar until light and pale, and beat in the eggs one at a time, adding a tablespoon of the flour and spices after each egg. Add the remaining flour, mix it in with a wooden spoon and then stir in the peel, fruit, almonds and Madeira or brandy. Turn the mixture into two lined and buttered pans and bake for $2\frac{1}{2}$–3 hours. Look at the cakes from time to time and turn them around if they are rising unevenly. Cover them with a sheet of foil when they are starting to brown and before they start to blacken.

Twelfth Day is 6 January and is, according to old custom, a day of kings, cakes and wassailing. A Twelfth Day cake was traditionally lavishly decorated with colored confectionery designed as stars, palaces and dragons, and should have a bean and a pea inside; the person who receives the bean is king for the night and the one who receives the pea is queen.

ALTERNATIVE: **Christmas cake**. *Cover the entire cake with marzipan and royal icing.*

NUTS

The cracking of nuts has always been a pleasant accompaniment to conversations: "after-dinner talk across the walnuts and wine," is Tennyson's description of the Northern nut ritual, while in the Middle East pistachio nuts and almonds are eaten before a meal as part of the varied mezze, the morsels that precede a meal, and are "savored accompanied by feelings of peace and serenity." As well as spreading serenity and tranquil enjoyment, nuts have also been used since earliest times in a huge variety of cooked dishes.

Egyptians and Persians, many of whose favorite recipes have changed very little for almost twelve centuries, use almonds and pine nuts to thicken their sauces, in stuffings for lamb, chicken and vegetables and in all kinds of pastries and sweets – dates stuffed with walnuts and almonds was one of the earliest sweets invented. In India, pilaus and rich rice dishes are decorated with almonds or cashew nuts, and coconut is an important flavoring of curries in many areas, particularly in Kerala in the south-west, while peanuts are used throughout Africa in all sorts of stews.

In Europe, chestnuts are much liked with turkey and with game of all sorts; the British love black pickled walnuts and the Italians use fresh pine nuts to make pesto – their superb green basil sauce for fresh pasta. The French serve wonderful green salads sprinkled with fresh walnuts, and enjoy almonds with trout, while Eastern Europe specializes in rich nut cakes with ground almonds or hazelnuts taking the place of flour. Pecan pie is one of the traditional great American dishes, and of course nut-flavored ice creams abound.

Since nuts are so rich in protein, vitamins, calcium, iron and oils (nut cooking oils are used everywhere) and are so extremely versatile, no good cook should be without them. Buy them in small quantities and often, preferably in their shells, and store them in a cool environment, since their high oil content makes them subject to dire alterations of flavor if they get hot or are kept too long. Make a particular point of enjoying fresh nuts in the autumn and early winter when they are sweet and milky.

CASHEWS
Anacardium occidentale
Kidney-shaped cashew nuts come from a tropical tree, which found its way from South America to the rest of the world by way of the early Portuguese explorers. Cas-

hews are widely eaten throughout South America, India and Asia and often appear – plain, roasted or salted – with drinks or as dessert nuts in the colder continents (they are easy to toast and salt yourself at home). In Brazil, they are also used for making wine and for the production of the famous anacard or cashew nut vinegar. In Chinese cooking, of course, they often appear as an ingredient, especially in chicken dishes. Use plain cashews for cooking, there is no need to go to the expense of buying toasted and salted "cocktail" nuts to put into the pot.

PINE NUTS
Pinus pinea
These nuts actually do come from the beautiful glossy cones of pine trees. They are contained inside hard little torpedo-shaped shells which are covered with a sooty dust. In the Mediterranean they can be found lying all over the sand or rocks in September, wherever the handsome umbrella-shaped Stone Pines grow, and more can be shaken out of the open cones if the weather is dry.

These are the classic pine kernels used in Mediterranean cooking. They are delicious in stuffed vegetables – eggplant, zucchini or vine leaves – and form part of the liaison in pesto sauce – the smooth green paste of basil that is so irresistible with fresh tagliatelle or linguine. They combine with rice and raisins in a rich stuffing for chicken, duck or turkey, and are mixed with prunes, dried apricots, pomegranate seeds and almonds in *khoshaf* – exotic dried-fruit salad, flavored with rosewater.

Pine nuts can generally be found in Italian delicatessens, but don't store them for too long because their resinous oil spoils easily and they start to taste musty.

MACADAMIAS
Macadamia ternifolia
Sweet and buttery, these are of the pre-dinner drinks and dessert-nut variety. Native

Peanuts

Pecans

to Australia, where they are also known as "Queensland" nuts, they are also grown in Hawaii, California and Florida; their hard shiny shells are cracked open and the kernels roasted in coconut oil before being marketed.

ALMONDS
Prunus dulcis

No other nut features as widely in old recipe books as almonds. Milk of almonds – the juice extracted from ground almonds steeped in water – used to take the place of milk on fast days or in hot weather (it is almost as rich in calcium). This technique of dealing with ground almonds is still used in such dishes as almond soup. Slivered almonds, fried golden, were much used for seasoning: they are still often scattered on fried river fish, particularly trout.

Ground almonds do more than provide their liquor. They can be used in the place of flour for rich, moist cakes and for crisp cookies. Sweet almonds are the chief ingredient of marzipan for coating cakes, and smooth sugared almonds, ovoids in silver, white, pink and pale blue, in silver baskets, traditionally grace French wedding feasts (and confectionery stores). "Burnt almonds," cooked in sugar, nobbly and the color of burnt sienna – the classic praline – are superb in ice cream. In delicate Mogul cooking they are combined with chicken in a variety of ways, while fresh almonds in their delicate green velvet coats form part of the early autumn *corbeille des fruits* in France and Italy.

Almonds can be bought in their shells or out of them, and also come ready blanched, flaked, shredded, diced and pounded. Good stores stock not only sweet but also bitter almonds (*Prunus amara*), which some recipes for cookies and candies may specify. The pungent taste of bitter almonds – like that of the crushed peach kernels you would add to jam – is due to the same enzyme reaction by which prussic acid is produced. Although they are inedible raw, bitter almonds, like peach kernels, are quite safe to use in cooking, because the poison is highly volatile and evaporates when heated. Once heated, they retain the flavor of ratafia (indeed, ratafia essence and the liqueur by that name rely on the essential oils of both sweet and bitter almonds). One bitter almond can bring out the flavor of a dish using sweet almonds, but store them in a jar apart, well marked to avoid confusion.

PEANUTS
Arachis hypogaea

Whether you know them as peanuts, ground nuts or monkey nuts, these are the success story of our age. Dry-roasted, salted, shelled

Cashews

Pistachios

Macadamias

Pine nuts

Chestnuts

Brazil nuts and whole husk

Filberts

Fresh giant filberts

Coconut

or unshelled, they come to more cocktail parties than any other nut. In North African countries you will find whole peanuts scattered over couscous; in Indonesia ground peanuts go into savory sauces; and all over the world pressed peanuts give peanut or arachide oil – a light, delicate oil for use in cooking and as a salad oil.

Raw peanuts have a faint taste of green beans – which is not surprising, as the peanut is a member of the legume family. These are the peanuts that can be so useful in cooking. You can roast raw peanuts by first tossing them in a little heated oil and a little salt, then toasting them to a light golden color in a moderate oven. To devil them, toss them in oil with a little chili powder instead of salt, or season the oil with ground coriander, cumin and red pepper.

When you buy peanut butter you may find the highly nutritious oil sitting on top – stir it in before you start spreading. You can make your own by grinding whole shelled peanuts, with their skins removed, together with a little peanut oil in a blender. Add a little salt and do not make too much at a time, as fresh peanut butter is inclined to go rancid. However, it will soon be used up if you make peanut butter cookies or use it as a foundation for peanut fudge, in which to encase chopped, blanched nuts.

PISTACHIO NUTS
Pistacia vera

These exquisite pale green nuts, with usefully half-open shells and papery skins marked with a rosy fingerprint, are the greatest luxury. They come from the Middle East and are usually roasted and salted – sometimes also flavored with rosewater – to eat between meals, or with drinks. They are also found, blanched and skinned, studding the galantines and terrines in good restaurants (you can use hazelnuts instead in duck pâté). The best Turkish delight and nougat contain pistachio nuts, and the nuts were originally used in ice cream making, although pistachio ice cream nowadays, unless made at home, probably owes more to almond essence and green coloring than to the nuts themselves.

BETEL NUTS
Areca catechu

These are the tough little nuts much beloved in India. Chopped and mixed with spices, pink-dyed coconut shreds, other nuts, or tiny candy balls, they are wrapped in betel leaves to make the small triangular packages called *paans* which Indian hostesses (and restaurants) may offer to guests after a meal. Chewing these little parcels is said to aid the digestion and sweeten the breath. It can also turn the mouth an alarming red. Betel nuts can be bought whole (in which case you need a special cutter called a *sarota*) or ready shredded at supermarkets.

*Walnuts:
green, pickled and mature*

Almonds

*Betel
nuts*

191

PECANS
Carya illinoensis

These are not so easy to find outside the United States, their natural home. Their very name is American Indian, and the nut was widely used in tribal cookery. Pecans, heavier in fats than walnuts, which belong to the same family and which pecans somewhat resemble in taste and in the appearance of their kernels, were particularly cherished for their oil. Their flesh, ground to a fine meal, was used to thicken soups and stews.

Nowadays, pecans are used to enrich cakes, confectionery and ice cream, but their proudest moment comes at Thanksgiving, in dark toffee-colored pecan pie – a rich sweet mixture of syrup, brown sugar, eggs, vanilla and nuts which traditionally follows the turkey. Pecans can be tracked down in the more elegant stores outside the United States, but if they prove to be elusive, walnuts can usually be substituted in recipes that specify pecans.

HAZELS, COBS AND FILBERTS
genus Corylus

These are the joy of the autumn countryside. If you don't have the chance to go gathering your own nuts – in England the terms hazel and cob are used for the same nut, known to Americans as filbert, and the nut known in Europe as the filbert is called in America the giant filbert – you can buy them, fresh, moist and juicy, in good stores. By Christmas, the pretty leafy husk will have shrivelled, the shells hardened, and darkened to the familiar hazel color. The kernels themselves will be less milky, but, in their own way, as good to eat and to use in the kitchen.

The ubiquitous peanut butter has rather overshadowed hazelnut butter, which is a very pleasant compound; and although almonds are the more usual garnish for fish, trout with hazelnuts is both good and interesting. But where hazelnuts come into their own is in the preparation of desserts, cakes and ice cream. To make cakes and cookies you need neither flour nor fat: hazelnuts have enough oil, balanced with mealiness, to provide it all. Just combine them, ground, with eggs and sugar and/or cream, as the case may be, and you have a whole repertoire of rich dishes and sweets. In grocery stores and supermarkets you can buy shelled hazelnuts whole, ground or chopped. In some shops they'll be sold complete with shells – the heavier the nut, the fuller the kernel and the better the buy.

CHESTNUTS
Castanea sativa

Edible chestnuts, also called Spanish chestnuts, are first cousins to horse chestnuts. They are a prettier shape, but have none of their cousin's flamboyant mahogany sheen. Their pointed shell encloses a truly delicious nut – good to eat with moist leafy vegetables such as brussels sprouts; wonderful for stuffings; warming – and a joy – roasted over the fire on a winter's day.

Marrons glacés are easy to make, and a great treat, although they do not often look as stunning as those bought, at some expense, sitting in individual frilled paper cups. Puréed sweet chestnuts make the basis for the creamy and delicious *marrons mont blanc* and for iced Nesselrode pudding (invented for the nobleman of that name by his gifted cook). In Italy, chestnuts are stewed in wine, and in France, these useful nuts, braised or puréed, provide garnishes for chickens, pigeons and young turkeys.

When shopping for fresh chestnuts, look for smooth, shiny shells and buy nuts that feel heavy for their size. Preserved chestnuts come canned in water, in syrup, or, of course, in the form of purée (which can also be bought in tubes). Chestnuts are also sold dried, ready to be soaked and then cooked to make chestnut purée, which makes a traditional accompaniment for roast game.

BRAZILS
Bertholletia excelsa

These are the seeds of a mighty tree that towers above the Brazilian jungle. The trees have never been cultivated: their seeds are gathered and buried by the cotia, the Amazonian hare, and those that the hare forgets to retrieve take root. The fruit the tree produces is as large as a coconut and a considerable weight; it falls to the ground when ripe, and inside the hard, woody shell are the twelve to twenty triangular seeds, packed tightly together like segments of an orange. These are the brazils that we buy in the stores, either in their shells (don't buy those that rattle or feel light) or shelled in packets. Rich and creamy fleshed, brazils are available all year, but are best in winter.

WALNUTS
Juglans regia

Fresh walnuts have flesh that is pearly white, soft, easily peeled inner skins, and shells that still have a trace of moisture about them. These are called green walnuts, perhaps because their husks – called "chucks" – are green at the time of harvesting. Green walnuts are a great delicacy, eaten raw and as soon as possible after you've acquired them so that their moisture has had no chance to evaporate. At an even younger age, when the shells are still not hardened, green walnuts are suitable for pickling in vinegar, which turns them black. They also make walnut ketchup.

After the first flush of youth, walnuts become both drier and more oily in consistency. It is in this state that their kernels, halved or chopped, are used in cooking. Chopped walnuts are good in stuffings, pressed into cream cheese, in buns, breads and cakes, and are an essential ingredient of a winter fruit salad of prunes, pears and dried apricots, cooked in spiced red wine. Walnut toffee (or taffy) and walnut fudge are delicious, and so are halved nuts, candied and threaded on a stick, and toasted around a bonfire, while nothing goes better with after-dinner port than a dish of fat walnuts (and a pair of nutcrackers).

Black walnuts (*Juglans nigra*) and butternuts, or white walnuts (*Juglans cinerea*), are the North American branch of the family. Black walnuts are inclined to be larger than the average European walnut and their shells are so hard that special nutcrackers need to be used. The kernels give a stronger taste to confectionery, ice cream and cakes than other walnuts. Butternuts are not as difficult to crack and have a rich flavor.

COCONUTS
Cocos nucifera

Coconuts, known to us as hard, brown, hairy objects, are harvested when their outer husks are green, their shells pliable and their flesh soft and moist. They grow in great clusters on giant palm trees, once found only in Malaysia, but now cultivated on tropical coasts all over the world. This is because, apart from providing useful ingredients for cookery, the coconut palm also supplies a huge range of products, from coir for matting to palm wine. And in our kitchens, the coconut proves its versatility in any number of ways.

By the time it arrives in the Western World, its shell is dark, its flesh thick, a great deal of the coconut juice – the thin white liquid present in the center of the unripe nut – will have been absorbed. When you buy a coconut, weight is the factor to watch – the heavier the nut, the juicier it will be. When you have opened it and extracted the juice, which makes a sweet, refreshing drink, you only have to pare away the brown skin with a sharp knife and grate your coconut meat to use in curry, pies, cakes, puddings and sweets. You can also mix fresh grated coconut with boiling water and then squeeze the liquid from the shreds to get coconut milk, the *sine qua non* of the true Indian curry. To make coconut cream, simply use less water, or you can skim the cream from coconut milk that has been allowed to stand for a while.

Coconut is also useful in its shredded form. This is made from copra – dried coconut meat from which most of the oil has been extracted for other purposes – and has less flavor than the fresh grated flesh, but it can be infused for a short time in hot water then squeezed to produce a quite reasonable coconut milk or cream.

RECIPE SUGGESTIONS

Pecan pie

shortcrust pastry made with 1¼ cups/170 g flour
¾ stick/85 g butter, softened
scant ½ cup/85 g soft light brown sugar
1 tablespoon vanilla sugar
3 eggs
4 tablespoons corn syrup
1¼ cups/170 g pecans
salt

SERVES 4–6
Preheat the oven to 425°F/220°C.
Line an 8 in/20 cm pie dish with the pastry and bake it blind. Cream the butter and the sugars together, either in a food processor or by hand, and then beat in the eggs one at a time. Stir in the honey, the nuts and a pinch of salt. Fill the cooked pie shell with the mixture and bake for 30 minutes. To test the filling, insert the point of a knife into the middle of the pie—if it comes out clean, the pie is ready. Eat it warm—not really hot or cold.

——————◆——————

Hazelnut cakes

3 egg whites
¾ cup/170 g sugar, preferably superfine
1¼ cups/170 g ground hazelnuts

MAKES 12–18
Preheat the oven to 350°F/180°C.
Whisk the egg whites to a stiff peak and fold in the sugar and ground hazelnuts lightly but thoroughly. Spread the mixture ½–¾ in/1–2 cm thick on a sheet of foil dusted with flour in a baking pan and bake for about 20 minutes or until brown and crisp on top. Cut into squares, turn them over carefully and put them back in the oven at 275°F/140°C to dry off for 10–15 minutes.
Hazelnut cakes have a delicious rich flavor and should be soft in the center but with a slight crunch to them.

PREPARING NUTS

1 BLANCHING ALMONDS

Plunge shelled almonds into boiling water for a few seconds until the skins expand and loosen. Drain, and then pinch the kernels free.

2 SKINNING HAZELNUTS

Toast shelled nuts under broiler until the skins begin to color and loosen, then put them all in a paper bag and rub them against one another to free the skins from the kernels.

3 PEELING CHESTNUTS

With a sharp, pointed knife score a cross on the side of each nut. Boil the scored chestnuts for a few minutes, drain them and then while still warm peel away the hard outer shell and the furry inner skin.

4 SPLITTING A COCONUT

Pierce two of the eyes with a strong, sharp instrument such as a robust kitchen skewer or, as shown here, a workshop bradawl.

Shake out the milk; bake the empty nut in a hot oven for 15 minutes.

Lay the hot nut down and give the center of the shell a sharp blow with a hammer; it should break cleanly in two.

HERBS

Each herb used in the kitchen has a special and well-known affinity with certain kinds of food – fresh basil with tomatoes, mint with new potatoes, rosemary with lamb, sage with pork – but there are no rules laid down about these harmonies, and one of the pleasures of preparing food is to find one's own combinations.

This is especially enjoyable for those who can stroll out into the herb garden for inspiration and cast their eye over the fresh greenery growing so pleasantly there. The judicious use of dried herbs, too, can lead to some memorable discoveries, so always keep a wide variety at hand – not simply a pot of mixed herbs to fling into everything.

Herbs from the garden can be dried at home, but they must be picked at the right moment, just before they flower, or they lose their strength. Gather them on a dry but grey day and wash them quickly.

Divide small-leafed herbs such as thyme, tarragon and savory into bunches and tie them loosely with string. Either hang them up in muslin bags or spread them on a cloth or on newspaper laid over a rack and leave them to dry in a warm place.

Large-leafed herbs such as bay, sage and mint can be tied loosely and dried in the same way, or dipped into boiling water for a minute, shaken dry and dried to a crisp in a very slow oven. Parsley is more difficult, as it is a very moist herb. Dry it on a rack in a hot oven (400°F/200°C) for one minute, then turn the heat right down and leave the parsley until it is quite crisp.

If you want to crush dried herbs for storage in glass jars, use a rolling pin or whizz them in a little grinder, which will turn them a nice green color again. Fill the jars loosely to the top and make sure the tops fit properly to preserve the aroma.

Most of the more tender herbs – mint, tarragon, parsley, chives, dill, basil, chervil and so forth – can be frozen. They will darken in color when they thaw, but the flavor is well preserved. Since herbs are extremely strongly scented, store them in airtight boxes or they will flavor everything in the freezer.

BOUQUET GARNI

Traditionally this is a few sprigs of parsley, some thyme and a bay leaf; tied with thread it goes into the soup. It can also be a mixture of dried herbs tied up in a little square or bag of cheesecloth, and a bouquet of fresh herbs to flavor a stock can simply be tied inside a stick of celery.

FINES HERBES

This is a delicate mixture of the more tender herbs – parsley, chervil, chives and sometimes tarragon – all chopped very fine. The alchemy of this mixture has a hundred and one uses, from flavoring all kinds of subtly cooked eggs to poached sole or any delicate fish with a cream and white wine sauce. *Fines herbes* are delicious, too, in melted butter with a squeeze of lemon, poured over roasted, broiled or fried chicken, or veal scallops. They go into tartare and bearnaise sauce, and can be mixed into mayonnaise to make an excellent sauce to accompany shrimps and, of course, hard-boiled eggs – the mayonnaise should be green with herbs.

PARSLEY
(Petroselinum crispum)

The most serviceable of herbs and one that you can always buy fresh, parsley seems to have just as much affinity with garlic and hard-flavored Sicilian dishes, salty with olives, anchovies, goats' cheese and capers, as it does with the potato soups and fresh cod of the north. Flat-leafed parsley is tastier than the curled, and parsley roots – the roots of Hamburg parsley – are good for flavoring stews. Use parsley in court bouillons, soups and of course parsley sauce. *Jambon persillé* – a dish of chunks of ham set in an aspic quite solid with green chopped parsley – is a Burgundian dish well worth trying.

CHERVIL
(Anthriscus cerefolium)

One of the classic *fines herbes*, chervil has a delicate, aniseedy flavor, so subtle that it needs to be used lavishly. It is good in green salads, with eggs and in a herb butter for steak or sole. It makes a very good light soup, and chervil and sorrel, both shredded fairly finely, are a traditional garnish for chicken soup.

CHIVES
(Allium schoenoprasum)

With a flavor faintly redolent of onions but far finer and more delicate, chives are best with eggs, especially omelets, with potatoes – particularly baked potatoes split open and piled with sour cream mixed with chopped chives – and with raw or cooked tomatoes. Chives freeze well but do not dry.

TARRAGON
(Artemisia dracunculus)

Like basil and dill, tarragon has an addictive flavor – that is to say, those who have eaten it fresh can't very well get through the summer without it, since it is so delicious. French tarragon tastes sweetly of vanilla and aniseed and harmonizes completely with all kinds of egg dishes, with cream and with chicken or ham. It is good in green salads, potato salad and with cold salmon or trout, and tarragon vinegar makes an excellent mayonnaise for potato salad or chicken. Dried tarragon takes on an uncharacteristic, hay-like flavor, but frozen tarragon is very good.

DILL
(Anethum graveolens)

Dill is the flavor that makes Scandinavian pickled salmon (gravlax) so delicious, and is used as a matter of course with boiled and mashed potatoes. With white fish, serve dill either in melted butter or made into a sauce rather like parsley sauce. To preserve dill, freeze it in plastic bags, or use dill seeds or dried dill weed when fresh dill is out of season.

FENNEL
(Foeniculum vulgare)

The sweet herb fennel – not to be confused with Florence fennel – is used both as an herb and for its seeds. A few small twigs are invaluable for bouillabaisse, bourride and with sardines. If crayfish are cooked with a jungle of fennel, it gives them a most delicate flavor and is a good alternative to dill. Burn a few dried twigs when you are grilling fish or lamb outdoors, and put twigs inside a fish and under it when you bake it in the oven. The anise-flavored oils permeate the food with a wonderfully sympathetic flavor. In Sardinia, wild fennel is often used to flavor a bean and pork stew.

Parsley

Hamburg parsley

Chervil

Chives

French tarragon

Dill

Fennel

Coriander

Sweet cicely

CORIANDER
(Coriandrum sativum)

The soft, floppy green leaves of coriander look like rather lacy, flat parsley. They don't smell particularly strong unless you bruise them, and their taste, on its own, is harsh with a green note quite unlike the warm flavor of the seeds. But chopped and used sparingly in meatballs and lamb stews, or with lamb or pork kebabs, coriander has a superb flavor. It is also an essential flavor in many types of curry, particularly shrimp and lamb, and a very good addition to meat or chicken curry is a paste made from fresh ginger, garlic, green chili pepper and fresh coriander all pounded together.

SWEET CICELY
(Myrrhis odorata)

A pretty, old-fashioned herb, also known as anise chervil, sweet cicely can be used like parsley in salads or as part of a bouquet garni. Both the leaves and the green seeds can be used – they taste fragrant and sugary, somewhere between anise and licorice.

BASIL
(Ocimum basilicum)

Sweet basil has large, tender leaves that bruise easily and smell sweetly of cloves. It should be picked young and eaten raw, or almost so, since the aroma and flavor are fugitive. Use it lavishly on tomato salad – it has a great affinity with tomatoes – and with eggplant, zucchini and other squashes. In the south of France, a few chopped leaves are sometimes thrust into a dish of ratatouille at the last moment. The famous pesto alla Genovese – basil and pine nut paste – is one of the greatest spaghetti sauces, and *soupe au pistou* would be no more than an ordinary vegetable soup if it were not for the "pommade" made with oil, garlic and basil pounded together and added to the bowl at the last moment.

To preserve basil, push the leaves into a jar, sprinkling a little salt between the layers, and fill the jar with olive oil. Both leaves (which become black) and oil are good, and carry the flavor into whatever they are added to. Basil can also be preserved by deep-freezing, after a brief blanching.

MARJORAM
(Origanum majorana)

Sweet or knotted marjoram smells very sweet, both when it is fresh and when it is cut, just after flowering, and dried in bunches like thyme and sage. Use fresh leaves in a salad or on lamb kebabs, roast lamb or in stuffing for chicken or guinea fowl, and put dried marjoram in spaghetti and tomato sauces and any tomato-based soup or stew.

Pot marjoram *(Origanum onites)* is slightly less warm flavored than sweet marjoram but can be used in the same ways.

OREGANO
(Origanum vulgare)

This wild Mediterranean marjoram has a wonderfully warm, heady scent and flavor. In Italy it is used for the same dishes as marjoram. The dried leaves give a strong, spicy flavor to an oil and lemon sauce for fish and roast meat, to pizza and spaghetti sauce, chicken broth, beef stews and broiled fish, especially red snapper.

ROSEMARY
(Rosemarinus officinalis)

One of the prettiest of shrubs, rosemary loves the baking heat and dryness of the Mediterranean, but will grow to quite a good size in northern climates if given a warm, dry, sheltered place. It particularly likes the seaside – its name comes from the Latin for "dew of the sea." It has a great affinity with veal, lamb and pork and also with rabbit – put a sprig under a rack or leg of veal or lamb before roasting or into the butter in which you are sautéing onions for a veal or rabbit stew, and drop a sprig into the fat or oil in which you are frying potatoes. Rosemary is better fresh than dried and fresh rosemary has the added advantage of staying in one piece in the cooking.

BAY
(Laurus nobilis)

Everybody who is familiar with cooking is familiar with the sweet, resinous smell of bay. The leaves and twigs go into court bouillons for fish, into stocks, broths and marinades, pickles and stews, daubes and spaghetti sauces. The best decoration for a terrine is a fresh bay leaf, and in the past bay leaves were used to flavor milk puddings – bay infused in boiled milk gives a very agreeable flavor, much nicer than synthetic vanilla. To dry bay leaves, spread them on newspaper and leave them to dry in the dark to preserve their color. In France, bay leaves are called laurier, dangerously translated as laurel leaves in many French cook books.

SAGE
(Salvia officinalis)

Sage was once believed to give wisdom and prolong life. It is certainly a powerful herb, harsh and dry but fragrant. The leaves go into stuffings for roast pork and goose, and sage is an important ingredient – usefully lessening the impact of the fat – in pork pies and sausages. Partridge is sometimes cooked with sage, and eel and bacon wrapped in sage and broiled makes an extremely good dish. In Italy, fresh sage is fried in the oil in which veal or calf's liver is to be cooked to give an interesting flavor.

THYME
(Thymus vulgaris)

Use it in every kind of long-simmered and red-wine dish, with rabbit, veal and chicken

Basil

Oregano

Sage

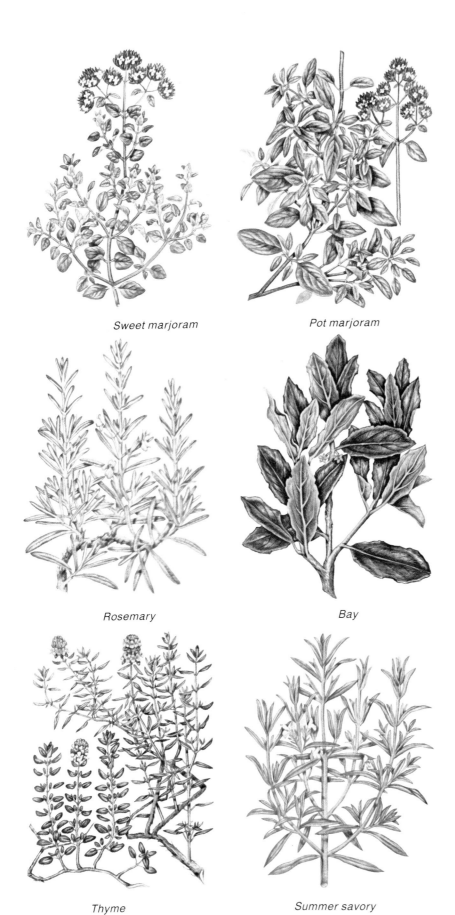

Sweet marjoram

Pot marjoram

Rosemary

Bay

Thyme

Summer savory

in all their tomatoey forms, in a bouquet garni and marinades and – instead of rosemary – with lamb. In Marseilles, thyme is sprinkled into everything including vinaigrette dressing, and over fish to be grilled on a wood fire. It gives pungency to pâtés, terrines and meatballs, and has an affinity with Mediterranean vegetables such as eggplant, zucchini and sweet peppers. Lemon thyme (*Thymus citriodorus*) is superb in stuffings for pork and veal. Home-dried or frozen thyme is incomparably better than commercially dried or powdered thyme – to dry it, hang bunches in a warm place, then rub the leaves off and store in a jar.

SUMMER SAVORY (Satureja hortensis)

Aromatic and pleasantly bitter with a scent a little like thyme, summer savory was used by the Romans to flavor vinegar in much the same way as the English use mint in mint sauce. In France, where it is called sarriette, it is used with thyme to flavor rabbit, and fresh sprigs are cooked with fava beans and peas. It dries well and is used with other herbs in stuffings for turkey and veal.

MINT (Mentha)

One of the oldest and most familiar of herbs, mint has almost as many varieties as it has uses. Spearmint *(Mentha spicata)*, with its pointed leaves and fresh taste, is the most commonly used, but apple mint *(Mentha rotundifolia)*, which is much prettier and has woolly, rounded leaves, has a superior flavor – its woolliness disappears when it is chopped.

In America, mint is best known as an accompaniment to roast lamb in mint jelly, but it is also used a good deal in the Middle East: finely chopped and stirred into yogurt it makes a dressing for cucumber salad.

Mint is often boiled with new potatoes, when it is delicious, and with garden peas, when it is a mistake. It is also used in the making of desserts that contain fresh oranges (with which it has an affinity) and with shellfish, particularly broiled shrimp. Sprigs of mint go into fruit drinks, wine cups and juleps, and in northern India chopped mint is used in fresh chutney – mixed with fresh green chili pepper and yogurt, it is good with Tandoori chicken.

BURNET (Poterium sanguisorba)

Salad burnet, with its grey-green leaves and cool cucumber flavor, was eaten a great deal by our ancestors. The young leaves are very tender and can be sprinkled into the salad bowl with the lettuce. Used a great deal in France and Italy, burnet can also be used, like borage, in cooling drinks, and is an excellent flavoring for vinegar.

ROCKET
(Eruca sativa)

This neglected salad herb with its pale yellow flowers looks like mustard and has a peppery flavor. The young leaves give a dry, aromatic taste to plain green salads, and in southern Italy wild rocket is used as an extra flavor in the mixed salads eaten with pasta or veal. But be careful which herb you use – the name rocket applies to a number of other plants some of them far too bitter to be eaten.

BALM OR LEMON BALM
(Melissa officinalis)

Beloved of bees – and of beekeepers, who use it to increase the honey harvest – balm was the vital ingredient of Paracelsus' *elixir vital*, designed to make man immortal. It now gives its essence to Chartreuse, that green and potent liqueur made by monks, who keep most of the other ingredients a secret. The fresh, lemon-scented leaves and small white flowers are delicious in white wine cups, and in a German claret cup made with cucumber, orange and soda water. A few freshly picked leaves can also go into a green salad.

BORAGE
(Borago officinalis)

A hairy, bristly plant which stings the fingers, borage makes up for the discomfort it inflicts by its flowers, which are a heart breaking blue and which, together with the cucumber-flavored leaves, complete that fruit salad of an English summer drink called Pimms. The flowers also make a pretty decoration for crab salad.

SWEET WOODRUFF
(Asperula odorata)

A small woodland herb, sweet woodruff has a ravishing hay-like perfume and is used in May, before it flowers, to flavor a delicate wine-cup. Steep the well-washed plants in a pitcher of white wine overnight in the refrigerator, add brandy and sugar or Benedictine and serve with a garnish of leaves.

LOVAGE
(Ligusticum officinalis)

This old-fashioned herb looks rather like immensely tall celery that has got out of hand. It has a very strange, pleasant but heavy smell and is called the Maggi plant in Holland because the flavor is reminiscent of stock cubes, with monosodium glutamate lurking somewhere in its nuances. It is a strong-flavored herb and should be used sparingly to season stocks or soups when a meaty flavor is wanted.

ANGELICA
(Angelica archangelica)

Nobody knows why angelica is associated with angels, although it has been helpful in

Mint

Salad burnet

Balm

Borage

Lovage

Angelica

Rocket

Sweet woodruff

Horseradish

its time for curing coughs, colds and colic. It is best known today as a candied stem used for decorating desserts and cakes, and freshly shredded leaves are a good flavoring for rhubarb and can be used in making jam, particularly rhubarb jam.

HORSERADISH
(Armoracia rusticana)

A fresh, stinging horesradish sauce with roast beef is one of life's pleasures and is very good, too, with hot boiled tongue. In Germany, horseradish is grated and mixed with vinegar as a sauce for fish, and it can be mixed with mayonnaise as a dressing for hard-boiled eggs. Commercially dried Swedish or American horseradish flakes are a reasonable substitute for the fresh root.

GARDEN LEAVES AND FLOWERS

Peach (*Prunus persica*)
Fresh peach leaves make a delicate flavoring for custard, more interesting than the usual vanilla and tasting faintly of almonds. Pick five or six fresh leaves and infuse them in the milk for 5–10 minutes, then proceed with the custard in the usual way.

Vine leaves (*Vitis*)
Every vine that produces edible grapes produces leaves that are edible when young. As dolmades and as a wrapping, with bacon, for little birds such as quail, partridge and snipe, they impart a delicious faint lemon flavor. Choose large, tender young leaves and blanch them in boiling salted water to soften them before they are used.

Geranium (*Pelargonium graveolens*)
The curling, slightly furry leaves of the rose-scented geranium add a delicate rose fragrance to a clear amber-pink crabapple jelly or to lemon water ice. Pick the larger leaves, just as they begin to turn yellow.

Marigold (*Calendula officinalis*)
This pretty golden flower used to be used a great deal to decorate salads – especially shrimp, crab or lobster – and to color and flavor fish soups and meat broth. It still sometimes colors butter and cheese, and can be used as a substitute for saffron if you don't like the strong flavor of the spice. The petals can be fresh or dried, but don't use the flower centers.

Nasturtium (*Trapaeolum majus*)
Almost every part of this tender plant has a place in the kitchen. The flowers and young leaves can be used in salads – the leaves taste like watercress, but don't use too many because they are very hot. The buds and seeds can be pickled to make false capers. Gather the seeds as soon as the blossoms have fallen, before they get hard, wash them in cold water and soak overnight in cold salted water. Drain and cover with cold spiced vinegar, seal and keep for twelve months before using.

Roses (fam. *Rosaceae*)
Much of life must have been far from rosy in medieval days, but it must have been a great pleasure, on a fine day, gathering dark red rose petals to make into rose syrup, rose candy and rose vinegar. In the Middle East roses are still definitely the domain of the cook, who will sprinkle rosewater into fruit salads made with pomegranates and make clear, rose petal jelly with nuts suspended in it. The Victorians made rose petal sandwiches – lay deep red petals on and under a large, flat piece of butter in the refrigerator, and the next day spread the butter onto thin slices of crustless white bread. Lay a few fresh petals on top and allow them to show around the edges of the sandwich. Cream cheese and cinnamon can also be added. Rose petals are also good in cherry pie.

RECIPE SUGGESTIONS
Omelet fines herbes

2–3 eggs
salt and freshly ground pepper
1 teaspoon each of chopped fresh chives, parsley, tarragon and chervil
½ tablespoon Parmesan, freshly grated
1 tablespoon/15 g butter for frying

SERVES 1
Whisk the eggs lightly in a bowl, just enough to break them down. Season with salt and pepper, add the herbs and cheese and whisk lightly once again to spread the herbs evenly through the mixture. Heat the butter in an omelet pan. When it starts to brown, pour in the egg mixture. Stir it around for a minute, tipping the pan and lifting the edges as they set, so that the liquid can run underneath.
When the egg is set and brown underneath, but still creamy and runny on top, flick one half over towards the middle of the omelet and then roll the omelet onto a heated plate so that it is folded in three. It should look like a plump golden cushion. Eat at once: speed is essential for both the cooking and the eating of omelets.

Horseradish sauce

3 tablespoons grated horseradish
⅔ cup/1.5 dl whipping cream
1 teaspoon Dijon mustard
1 tablespoon white wine vinegar
pinch of sugar

Whisk all the ingredients together in a bowl. Taste and add more vinegar or an extra pinch of sugar if you think it needs it. Eat with hot or cold roast beef. For a mild horseradish sauce omit the vinegar and add a little more sugar.

Mint sauce

3 tablespoons fresh mint, finely chopped
2 tablespoons boiling water
4 tablespoons vinegar
1–2 teaspoons sugar, according to taste

Put the chopped mint in a bowl and add the boiling water to moisten it. Let it get cold, then add the vinegar and sugar—malt vinegar is traditional, but white wine or cider vinegar will give a much better, mellower flavor. Allow to stand at least 1 hour before serving to give it time to develop its flavor. Eat with hot or cold roast lamb.

SPICES

The spices once used so effectively in Elizabethan dishes rather fell into disrepute as "good plain cooking" followed in the wake of the Puritans. Now the heady, aromatic smells of the bazaars are back, with the wave of new ethnic food shops, and with them a revived interest in the cooking of India and the Middle East.

Dill seeds

Sesame seeds

Cloves

Cassia

Buy spices in small quantities and use whole spices whenever possible, pounding or grinding them freshly for each dish that calls for ground spice.

ANISE
Pimpinella anisum

Also known as sweet cumin, the seeds give a sweet, aniseed flavor to fish and particularly to mussels, to sweets and creams and, in some parts of Europe, to cakes and bread. In the Middle East, anise flavors green figs and jam, and it is a flavoring in some Indian vegetable and fish curries.

STAR ANISE
Illicium verum

Star anise has the same essential oil that gives anise its characteristic flavor but is much stronger and more licorice like. It is used in Chinese cooking, particularly with pork and duck, and is an ingredient – together with anise pepper, cinnamon, cloves and fennel seeds – in Chinese five spice powder.

ANISE PEPPER
Xanthoxylum piperitum

Also known as Szechwan pepper, this comes from the Szechwan region in China. It has a peculiar delayed reaction: nothing happens when you bite it, then it floods your mouth with a strong, hot flavor.

DILL SEEDS
Anethum graveolens

Sprigs of dill complete with half ripe seeds are a familiar sight in jars of gherkins and dill vinegar. Dill seeds are also excellent in a court bouillon and as a flavoring in fish soups and stews. They can be used, too, to flavor cakes.

FENNEL SEEDS
Foeniculum vulgare

These have a sweet, aniseed flavor, and a few seeds chewed after meals will help the digestion and sweeten the breath. Try using them to flavor the milk in which fish is cooked for fish soup or pie.

JUNIPER BERRIES
Juniperus communis

The flavor of the juniper berry is strangely harsh and turpentiny on its own but when combined with game, red cabbage, fried pork fillets, stewed rabbit or beef they give a delicious, rather somber, spicy background flavor.

CELERY SEED
Apium graveolens

Although inclined to be bitter, celery seeds give a lift to soups and stews when fresh celery isn't available. They can also go into dishes that combine rice with tomatoes, and into savory bread, but are much more familiar in celery salt.

SESAME SEEDS
Sesamum indicum

The nutty taste of toasted seasame seeds is probably most familiar topping bread and cakes, but sesame comes in many guises. Tahina, the oily paste made from finely ground seeds, is used with chick-peas to make the Greek hummus. Halva, is a sweet, compressed, oily bar of crushed seasame seeds. *Gomasio* – a seasoning popular in macrobiotic cooking – is a mixture of lightly toasted seasame seeds and sea salt.

POPPY SEEDS
Papaver somniferum

The blue-grey seeds are scattered over loaves and rolls and have a bread crumb flavor themselves. The creamy yellow seeds used in India are ground to make a floury curry spice that adds texture rather than flavor. They are also sprinkled into the whole wheat flour from which puris and chapatis are made. Poppy seed chutney, made from the Indian seeds, is delicious freshly made and eaten with all kinds of curry.

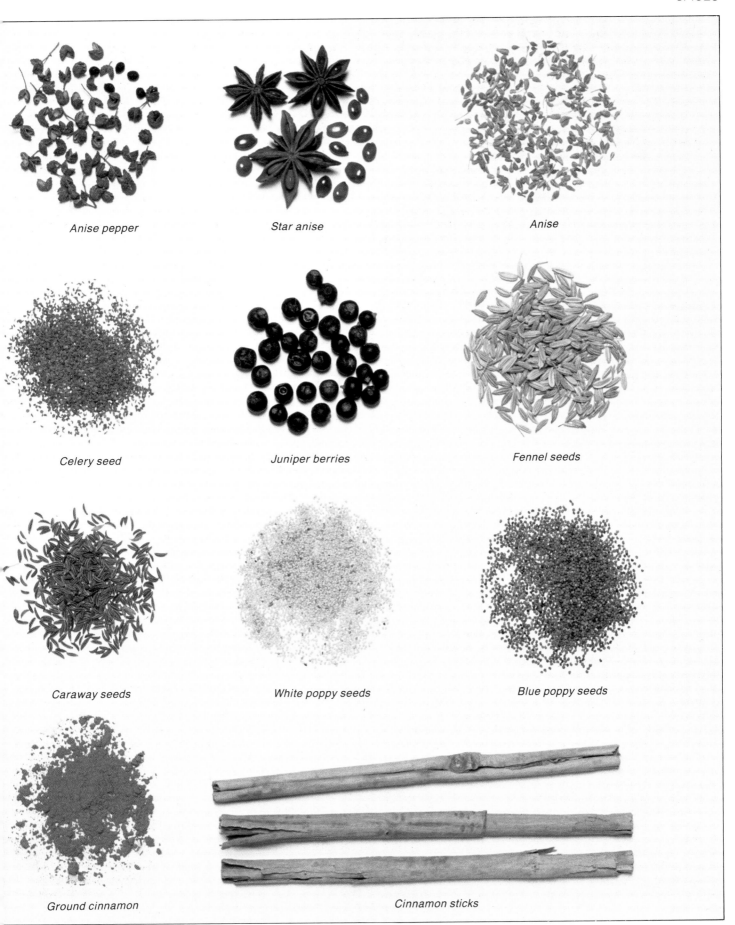

Anise pepper

Star anise

Anise

Celery seed

Juniper berries

Fennel seeds

Caraway seeds

White poppy seeds

Blue poppy seeds

Ground cinnamon

Cinnamon sticks

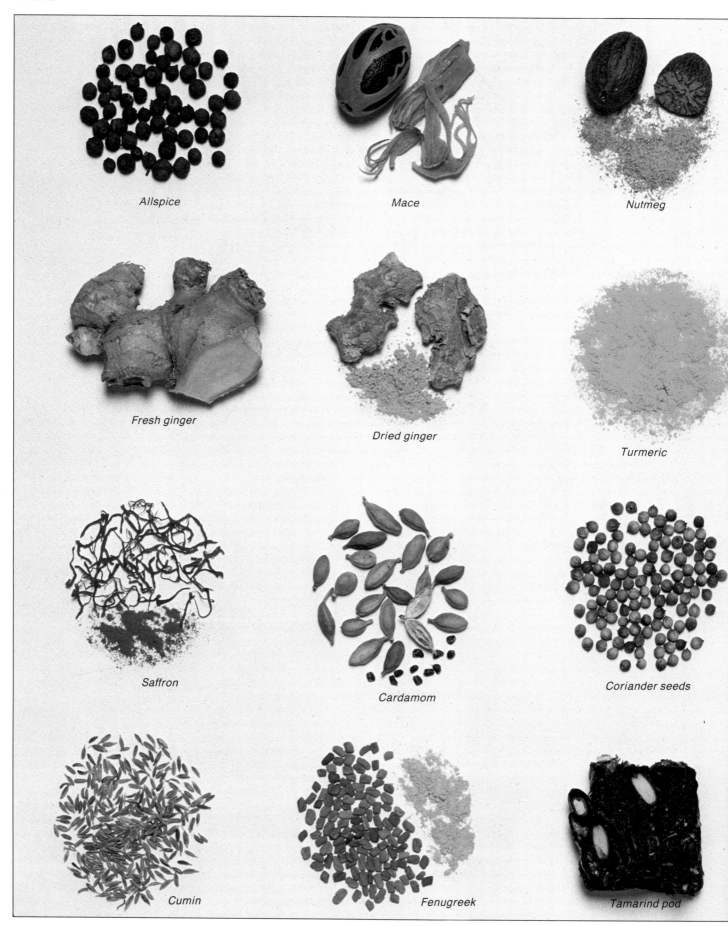

Allspice

Mace

Nutmeg

Fresh ginger

Dried ginger

Turmeric

Saffron

Cardamom

Coriander seeds

Cumin

Fenugreek

Tamarind pod

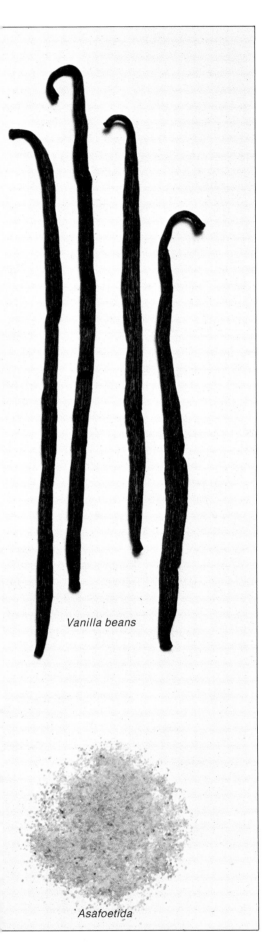

Vanilla beans

Asafoetida

CARAWAY SEEDS
Carum carvi
It could be the fact that they aid digestion that makes these an ingredient of so much heavy, delicious rye bread. They are also used when making seed cake and treacle sponge.

If you find caraway in a recipe for curry it is probably a mistranslation for cumin, and the confusion is not helped by caraway being known in France as *cumin des prés* – wild cumin – as well as by its correct French name *carvi*.

CLOVES
Eugenia caryophyllus
Cloves have the scent of the Spice Islands, sweet and warm, with a rather numbing quality that has also made them since the earliest days of medicine a sovereign remedy for toothache. They are not, however, particularly pleasant to bite on when found floating in the dinner, so are usually fixed firmly in an onion – for oxtail stew, jugged hare and other gamy, long-cooked meat dishes – or used ground. Cloves flavor the best bread sauce, spiced beef, hams, pilau rice and curry, and are traditional with cooked apples and pears, in mead, sweet spiced pickles, hot toddies and claret cups. The best cloves are large, dark and plump, and not easily broken.

CINNAMON
Cinnamomum zeylanicum
Cinnamon sticks` are curled, paper-thin pieces of the bark of the cinnamon tree, packed one inside the other. Use them for flavoring the milk for rice puddings and crème caramel, and put a few pieces in a pilau rice. The sticks are also used in mulled wine, hot punches and in sweet pickles.

Ground cinnamon is used in baking, in rum butter and cinnamon toast, and in spiced dishes all over the Middle East and India. In Italy it appears on doughnuts and in sweet fritters of ricotta cheese.

CASSIA
Cinnamomum cassia
In thicker rolls than true cinnamon, less delicate, more pungent and less expensive, cassia is better suited to stronger dishes such as spiced meats and curries. Dried cassia buds, which look rather like cloves, can be used in the same ways as the rolls.

ALLSPICE
Pimenta dioica
Allspice, or Jamaica pepper, is a hard brown berry, larger and smoother than a peppercorn. It tastes faintly of cinnamon, strongly of cloves and has a touch of nutmeg about it, which is why it is sometimes mistakenly thought to be a mixture of spices when it is bought ready ground. Pounded, it can go into pâtés, sausages and pork pies. It is also used in Christmas cake, in marinades, when pickling pork, with soused herrings and salt beef, and seems to impart something of a peppery as well as a spicy flavor.

MACE
Myristica fragrans
This is the frond-like outer coat, or aril, of the nutmeg, dried to an orange-brown. More delicate than nutmeg, it is used a great deal in potted meats or fish, in sausages, pâtés, terrines and pork pies, marinades and pickles. The sweet, spicy flavour of mace is delicious in cakes and puddings.

NUTMEG
Myristica fragrans
Nutmeg is equally at home in sweet and non-sweet dishes. It will keep, whole, for several months and sometimes for years. Buy a good-quality, large nutmeg rather than ground nutmeg, and grate it as you need it. Use it in sausages, terrines, pâtés and potted meat, in egg dishes, with mashed potatoes, spinach, and in sweet dishes.

Northern Italians use nutmeg in many of their stuffed pastas and in India it is a frequent ingredient of garam masala.

VANILLA
Vanilla planifolia
Vanilla was used to flavor chocolate by the Aztecs, the original chocolate addicts, and produces yellow beans that are picked unripe and allowed to cure to a dark brown. When you buy them the beans should be somewhat soft, ribbed, pointed at one end and have a frosting of crystals – the vanillin essence. A favorite way of using vanilla beans is to keep them in a jar of sugar, keeping the jar replenished as you use the sugar in rice puddings, crème caramel, and so forth. Another method, useful when making ice cream and crème brûlée, is to infuse the bruised bean in the milk or cream. The bean can then be gently washed and dried and stored for another time. It imparts a flowery and spicy aroma.

GINGER
Zingiber officinale
The fresh root is used a great deal in Chinese cooking with pork, fish and chicken, duck, shrimps, crab and beef. It has a delicious rosemary scent and a crisp texture, and if you can't buy fresh ginger root the best substitute in Chinese cooking, rather than dried ginger, is scallions. In India fresh ginger is a favorite curry ingredient. Dried root ginger needs to be bruised before it is used to break open its fibers and release the hot flavor. Powdered ginger – Jamaican is best – goes into ginger cookies, brandy snaps and gingerbread, and is mixed with sugar to sprinkle on chilled melon. Stem ginger preserved in syrup and packed in Chinese jars goes, with its syrup, into puddings, with rhubarb dishes and over – and sometimes into – ice cream.

TURMERIC
Curcuma longa

Turmeric has a harsh taste, bitter and somehow reminiscent of freshly scrubbed wood, but its color is indisputably useful – not as pretty and golden as saffron, but a deep yellow ochre that turns curries with dark spices to a warm mahogany color, and others made with yogurt and pale spices a sharp appetizing yellow. Use it in moderation and do not try to use it in place of true saffron – the flavor is quite different.

SAFFRON
Crocus sativus

True saffron is fabulously expensive – each red-gold shred is a crocus stigma, and each saffron crocus has only three stigmas to be hand-gathered and dried.

It is used a great deal in the south of France for soups, particularly fish soups, and is essential in Milanese risotto. But the Spanish must have it. They like their rice bright yellow, and they have saffron in their fish stews, in vegetable soups, with mussels and shrimps. Very little is needed: a pinch soaked in a little warm water or white wine will diffuse the liquid with its powerful flavor – which is somewhere in the realms of warm sap, varnish and flowers – and characteristic color. Saffron is almost always added with the liquid in which the dish is cooked, but sometimes is kept until the end of the cooking and then stirred in for a dish of many shades of yellow.

Saffron powder, also expensive and liable to be adulterated, is a poor substitute for saffron strands, and there is a strong Spanish powder, *colorante alimentario*, which adds color without flavor.

Saffron and turmeric are sometimes substituted for each other, but this is a mistake. Saffron is perfect with garlic, fennel, white wine, mussels and fish, while turmeric belongs with vegetables and meat.

CARDAMOM
Elettaria cardamomum

Genuine cardomom is costly and has a great many inferior relatives, so it pays to look carefully at what you are buying. The best cardamom pods are the size of peas, pale brown or greenish, and the tiny seeds, when you split a pod open, should be dark, shiny and richly aromatic. Larger hairy black pods are best avoided. The flavor of cardamom is essential in curry – it has a warm, oily but sharp taste, and an anesthetic effect on the tongue. You can buy powdered cardamom, but it has a much more floury flavor than the seeds.

CORIANDER SEEDS
Coriandrum sativum

These seeds are the basis of all that is delicious in home-made curries and vegetables *à la grecque*. They have a warm, faintly orangey fragrance that is enhanced if they are parched by gentle heating in an iron frying pan just before use. Coriander seeds, together with lemon peel, make a delicate substitute for vanilla in custards and ice creams, and an excellent flavoring for cooked apples. Their flavor harmonizes well with lentils.

CUMIN
Cuminum cyminum

Cumin is essential in curry. Its scent is hard to define; powerful, warm, sweet and slightly oily, but quite unmistakable – which is fortunate, because it looks rather like caraway and the two are often confused. In Spain, cumin is the traditional seasoning for chick-peas, in Mexican cooking it is part of the background in chili con carne and in the Canary Islands it flavors fish soup. In North Africa and the Levant it is used in couscous, on kebabs, with stewed lamb, and to spice rice and vegetable dishes.

FENUGREEK
Trigonella foenum-graecum

Floury, somewhat bitter and smelling of maple or fresh hay, the ground seeds of fenugreek are used as a curry spice and are a common ingredient of made-up curry powders. The hard seeds need to be lightly roasted before they are ground, but don't overroast them or they become bitter.

TAMARIND
Tamarindus indica

Sharply sour, the sticky, dried pods of the tamarind tree – also known as Indian dates – are used instead of limes or lemons to add an acid note to curries, and go into delicious fresh chutneys to eat with curry. To obtain tamarind juice, steep the pulp in a bowl of hot water until the sour brown juice can easily be squeezed out.

ASAFOETIDA
Ferula asafoetida

An ingredient in some curries and Indian vegetable dishes and pickles, asafoetida is an evil-smelling resin. It should be used in exceedingly small quantities or it can be omitted from recipes that call for it.

RECIPE SUGGESTIONS

Pilau rice

1¼ cups/225 g long-grain rice
4 cloves
8 cardamom pods
2 in/5 cm piece of cinnamon stick
1 onion
½ stick/55 g butter, clarified
2 bay leaves
scant ¼ cup/30 g blanched almonds
⅓ cup/55 g raisins
salt

SERVES 4

Wash the rice thoroughly under cold running water and leave to drain. Bruise the cloves, cardamom pods and cinnamon stick. Peel the onion and cut it into the thinnest of rings. Heat about a quarter of the butter and fry the onion rings, without stirring, until they are a cinnamon brown. Lift them out of the pan with a fork and keep them hot.

Add the remaining butter to the pan and stir in the spices and bay leaves and then the rice. Cook gently for 7–8 minutes, stirring the rice around until it becomes translucent. Add about 2 cups/4.5 dl water, stir it in and add the almonds and raisins. Season with salt, bring to the boil, cover and simmer for about 25 minutes over a gentle heat until the rice is tender, adding a little more water if it is necessary.

Serve, scattered with the browned onion rings, as an accompaniment to curries or with spiced chicken.

Soused herrings

6 plump herrings, each about ½ lb/225 g
1¼–2 cups/3–4.5 dl each cider vinegar and hard cider
2 bay leaves
4 sprigs thyme
12 black peppercorns
6 allspice berries
4 cloves
2 blades mace
salt and cayenne pepper
fresh fennel for garnish

SERVES 6

Preheat the oven to 350°F/180°C.

Scale and gut the herrings, cut off the heads and fins and trim the tails. If they have roes with them, put them back inside the fish.

Lay the herrings in an earthenware or enamelled iron pie dish or gratin dish and cover with the vinegar and cider (the amount of liquid needed depends on the size and shape of the dish used). Push the herbs and spices in among the fish and season with salt and cayenne. Cover the dish with a sheet of foil and stand it in a bain-marie or a large roasting pan. Pour in enough boiling water to come halfway up the gratin or pie dish and bake for 30 minutes. Allow to cool and garnish with fresh fennel. Eat soused herrings within a day or two.

Apple fritters

8 cooking apples
1 cup/115 g flour
3 tablespoons butter, melted
¼ cup/55 g sugar, preferably superfine
large pinch each of ground cinnamon and ground cloves
salt
beaten white of 1 egg
oil for deep frying

SERVES 4–6

Make the batter about an hour before it is needed. Mix together the flour and melted butter and gradually add 1 cup/2.5 dl lukewarm water. Let it stand in a cool place.

Peel and core the apples and cut into slices. Dust them with the sugar mixed with the cinnamon, cloves and a pinch of salt.

Fold the beaten egg white into the batter and dip the apple rings in it. Deep fry them in hot oil and drain on paper towels. Sprinkle the fritters with leftover spiced sugar and serve with cream.

SALT AND PEPPER

It has long been considered a measure of a cook's talent as to whether food can be sent perfectly seasoned to the table, and of all the condiments salt and pepper are the cook's greatest allies. There are, however, two important aspects to the proper seasoning of food. One is what goes into the food in the kitchen, the other is what goes onto it at the table.

SALT

One of the properties of salt – which is an invaluable preservative as well as a seasoning – is to draw the moisture out of foods. This is an advantage with vegetables such as eggplant that have bitter juices; they can be sliced and salted before cooking so that the bitterness is drawn out. Fresh meat, however, should not be salted before frying or roasting, as the moisture raised on its surface will prevent it sealing and browning.

Salt also toughens food, which can be an advantage when pickling with vinegar – food salted before being pickled will not go soft and soggy in the jar. But again this is a disadvantage when cooking meat, and with legumes such as dried beans, so start these in fresh unsalted water and do not add salt until at least 15 minutes after they have reached simmering point.

Sea salt

This is the best of all salts for both kitchen and table. It is made by evaporating sea water, either naturally by sun and wind or by artificial heat. The result is large crystals of pure salt which retain their natural iodine and have no bitter aftertaste. They can be sprinkled directly onto food, like Maldon salt, or ground in a salt mill or wooden mortar. This is also the salt to sprinkle over certain breads, rolls and pretzels before they go into the oven – the crystals dissolve so slowly that they will still be a sparkling presence after baking. Fine sea salt is the best to use in cooking.

Sel gris

This is a coarse, greyish, unrefined sea salt that contains traces of other minerals. It is for kitchen use rather than at table.

Common salt

Ordinary domestic salt is made by dissolving the salt found in underground deposits and then drying it in a vacuum. It can be coarse-grained for kitchen use or refined into table salt, in which case it has to be coated with magnesium carbonate or some other additive to prevent it absorbing moisture from the air. This type of salt, although useful because it can be sprinkled finely, has a decidedly bitter aftertaste, but it is better than any other salt for baking.

Iodized salt

This is domestic salt to which iodine has been added. It is useful in areas where the water and soils are lacking in this essential trace element.

Rock salt

Known in France as *sel-gemme*, rock salt is a hard, coarse, crystalline salt that needs a salt mill or mortar to make it manageable. At its best, it can be the finest flavored of all the salts, but it must not be confused with non-edible freezing salt, also called rock salt, which is often used in the United States when making homemade ice creams.

Block salt

This is also known as canning salt, it is pure, refined rock salt. It is good for all cooking and is the salt to use for pickling, because it has no additives that might spoil the clarity of the pickling liquid. Other names for it are pickling salt and dairy salt.

Monosodium glutamate

The sodium salt of glutamic acid, MSG is a chemical that "wakes up the palate." It accentuates other flavors already present in the food and is used extensively in Chinese cooking, but it is a lazy way of giving flavor to food and is not a good thing to have in the kitchen and is frowned upon by nutritionists.

Saltpeter

Potassium nitrate is a preservative, and has been used in the making of brines and dry salt mixtures for hundreds of years. It has the culinary quality of turning meat a beautiful pink – in France, many restaurateurs put a pinch of saltpeter in their pâté – and is present in bacon, ham, sausages, salt beef, salami and so on. It has been found to be harmful when eaten in large quanities, so it is probably wise to think twice before flinging an unmeasured amount into every pâté you make.

PEPPER

The vine that gives us peppercorns and chili peppers and sweet pepper plants that give us chili powders, cayenne and paprika are not related, although all these seasonings add a pungent savor to food.

Ready-ground pepper soon tastes dull and dusty, and inferior brands are sometimes adulterated with such things as powdered date stones, so buy whole peppercorns – they should be evenly colored, aromatic, free from dust and too hard to be crushed between the fingers.

Different peppers vary in pungency and size of corn. Usually they are called after their place of origin – Malabar black, for instance, is one of the best of the black peppercorns.

Black peppercorns

These are the dried, shrivelled berries of the pepper vine, *Piper nigrum*. They are picked before they are quite ripe and dried in the sun, where they blacken within a day or two.

White peppercorns

These are the ripened berries, soaked, rubbed to remove their husks and then dried. White pepper is slightly less warm and spicy, than black pepper, and it has a drier smell; it is useful when making pale soups or sauces.

Mignonette pepper

This also called shot pepper, consists of coarsely crushed black and white peppercorns. It is used in pâtés and terrines, to which it gives an aromatic flavor without bringing tears to the eyes, as happens when peppercorns are thrown in whole. It is also the pepper for *steak au poivre*.

Green peppercorns

Fresh, unripe pepper berries, green peppercorns are milder than dried peppercorns and with a nice crisp texture. Picked when green, they become black within a day or two and so are only found fresh in the very best and most expensive stores. Freeze-dried and canned green peppercorns, however, are a good substitute. Use them in a sauce for

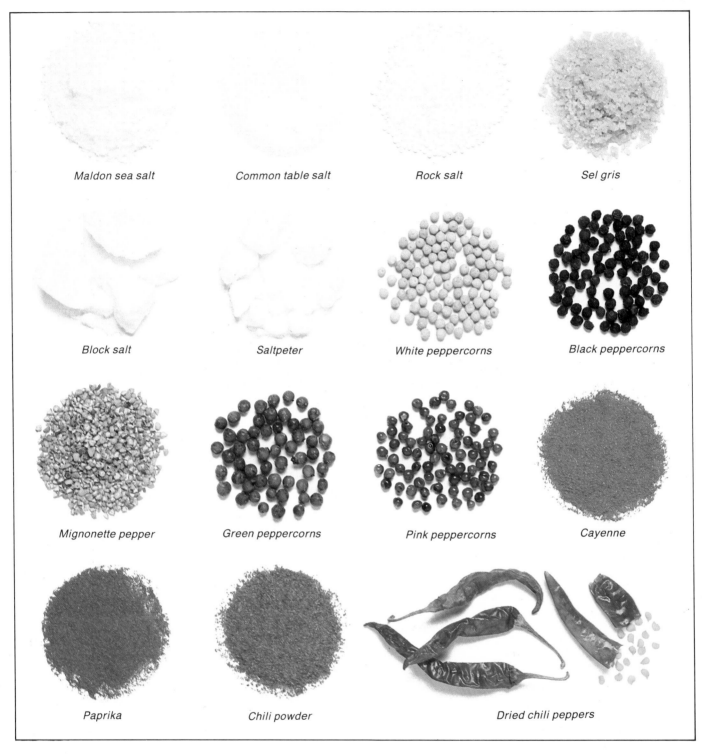

Maldon sea salt   Common table salt   Rock salt   Sel gris

Block salt   Saltpeter   White peppercorns   Black peppercorns

Mignonette pepper   Green peppercorns   Pink peppercorns   Cayenne

Paprika   Chili powder   Dried chili peppers

lamb, steak or duck, in pâtés, fish terrines, and with shellfish and smoked fish.

Pink peppercorns

More subtle than green peppercorns and with little of the hotness associated with pepper, these are much used in the south of France in fish dishes. Preserved in vinegar and sold in jars, they are quite soft and lend themselves to being mashed.

Chili powders

These are dried and ground chili peppers, either red or black, and they vary enor-mously. They can be pungent, mild, tasty or absolutely red-hot, and only by experience can you know what you are getting. Once you have found a good source of chili, or made your own powder at home by grinding a blend of dried chili peppers, and knowing how much or how little to add, it is a good idea to stick to that. Use chili powder in curry, chili con carne, with beans and chick-peas and in couscous – although authenti-cally for couscous you should use harissa, a very hot Tunisian mixture of crushed dried chili peppers, ground cumin and salt.

Cayenne pepper

This is made from ground dried chili peppers that give an orange powder, very hot and rather delicious. (It is the long red cayenne, which is easily dried, that is used in Tabasco sauce.) It is used in potted shrimps and in dishes such as devilled turkey and with devilled almonds, and in the gravy served with roasted wildfowl.

Paprika

Although it may be faintly hot, paprika by

nature has a sweet flavor and is made from sweet red peppers. In Spain and Portugal it is used in fish stews, potato and vegetable soups and with salt cod, as well as in most of the *chorizos* and *salsichas* (salamis and sausages). But it is in Hungary that paprika really comes into its own, so the best to buy is the original mild Hungarian paprika. The combination of paprika and sour cream has the most appetizing delicacy and, although chicken paprika and goulash may be somewhat overworked dishes, both are wonderful food.

RECIPE SUGGESTION

Béarnaise sauce

2–3 shallots
1 tablespoon tarragon vinegar
2 tablespoons wine vinegar
12 black peppercorns, coarsely crushed
2–3 sprigs fresh tarragon
3 egg yolks
1¼ sticks/140 g unsalted butter, cut into cubes
salt

Peel the shallots and chop them finely, put them in a small saucepan with the vinegar, peppercorns and tarragon and bring to the boil. Reduce rapidly over a brisk heat until you are left with no more than 1 tablespoon of liquid. Allow to cool, then beat in the egg yolks. Place the pan over a larger pan of hot water—a bain-marie—on a gentle heat and slowly increase the heat, whisking all the time. When the mixture has thickened a little and is creamy, start adding the butter, dropping in a piece at a time and whisking it in until it has been fully incorporated into the béarnaise before adding the next piece. When all the butter has been incorporated, season the sauce and keep it warm over the bain-marie—away from the heat so that it does not get too hot and coagulate around the edges. If the sauce gets too thick, add a few drops of cold water to cool it down. If the egg yolks do not seem to be thickening at all, increase the heat slightly. Serve with beef and lamb.

MUSTARD

Mustard has been adding its hot spiciness to food for thousands of years – the ancient Egyptians, Greeks and early Romans used to crunch the seeds between their teeth during meals, and the Romans used mustard to preserve vegetables – their pickled turnips in mustard were the forerunners of our fierce piccalilli.

Mustard as we know it is basically a paste made from the ground seeds of black mustard (*nigra*) and white mustard (*alba*), which is also called yellow mustard. *Nigra* is hot. *Alba* is cooler. It is *alba* which will obligingly grow on moist cotton to provide young mustard for mustard and cress sandwiches, and *alba*, mature, which yields the seeds that are used whole in pickling. There is a third, brown, variety in the mustard family called *juncea*, or Indian mustard. Less harsh than *nigra*, this is the whole mustard seed that is usually called for in recipes for curry.

FRENCH MUSTARDS

The most famous of these are the mustards of Dijon, Bordeaux and Meaux.

In Dijon, mustard center of the world, the mustard is blended with salt, spices and white wine or verjuice – an acid juice made from unripe green grapes. Some Dijon mustards rival English mustard in strength, but can be distinguished from it by their creamy grey-lemon color and by a more subtle flavor. Other Dijon mustards are milky pale and delicate rather than sharp. The famous

house of Poupon – one of the sights of Dijon – sells dozens of different blends and exports them all over the world.

Most cooks use Dijon mustard in preference to any other: for vinaigrettes, for mayonnaise (which mustard helps to emulsify), for the more delicate creamy sauces to go with kidneys, egg dishes and chicken or fish.

Blended with unfermented Bordeaux wine, Bordeaux mustard is strong, dark brown and both more acid and more aromatic than that of Dijon. It is unsurpassed for eating with steak, complementing rather than overpowering the flavor of the meat. When you are offered a choice of French or English mustard in a restaurant, the French variety is almost certainly Bordeaux, the darkest of them all and the one that differs most, in looks and taste, from the hot, bright yellow English type.

Moutarde de Meaux is an interesting mixture of ground and half-ground seeds, with a grainy texture and an attractive musty taste. It comes in wide-mouthed stoneware jars, their corks secured by sealing wax, and is

made to a formula that has been a closely guarded secret since 1760, when it was handed by the abbots of Meaux to the Pommery family, of Champagne fame.

There are, of course, other French mustards: sometimes tarragon is added, or a mixture of fresh herbs (which produce a pleasant tasting but rather alarming looking result). There is a mustard containing tomato purée, making a red-brown mustard that is designed to go with hamburgers; and a mustard this is basically mild, but with the bite of crushed green peppercorns.

ENGLISH MUSTARD

Its color is a hot yellow, it is made of blended seeds, finely ground, and its taste is straightforward and hot.

The famous Mr Colman began milling his mustard powder in the year 1814 and today you can buy Colman's mustard in powder form and also – convenient but not as good – ready-mixed. A straightforward blend of ground and sifted seeds, flour and spices, it contains no wine or vinegar to lessen the natural impact of the seeds.

To mix "common" English mustard, simply add cold water to the powder – the water must never be hot or it will release bitter oils that spoil the taste. To be at its best, the mustard should be freshly made up in a small quantity – a quarter of a teaspoonful of mixed mustard per person is usually sufficient. Allow it to stand, well covered, for about half an hour before use, to develop its full flavor and heat.

To make mild mustard, use milk, a teaspoon or two of cream and a few grains of sugar. To make a thick Tewkesbury-type mustard, which has a delicate flavor and a biting aftertaste, moisten the powder with wine vinegar, grape or apple juice, or with red wine or ale.

Common English mustard is perfect with roast beef, its classic partner, with other plain roast meat, gammon and ham, pork pie and beef or pork sausages. It goes well with Cheddar cheese, especially with welsh rarebit, and it is the proper mustard to use when making strong mustard sauce to go with richly flavored oily fish such as herring or mackerel. But simmered for any length of time in dishes that call for mustard, even English mustard loses some of its taste and piquancy, and mustard sauces benefit from being given a boost of a little more mustard shortly before the end of cooking.

There are other ready-made mustards, one contains honey (good with pork), and commercially made Tewkesbury mustard.

GERMAN MUSTARDS

Made from a blend of strong mustard flour and vinegar, German mustard – *Senf* – generally combines pungency with aroma, and comes halfway between hot, sharp English mustard and the earthy, aromatic flavor of that of Bordeaux. In northern Germany it is ladled out by the spoonful. Stronger palates go for mustard that is *scharf* or *extra scharf* – hot or extra hot.

A lot of mustard is consumed in Germany: it is specifically designed to be eaten with the profusion of sausages of the frankfurter type – knackwurst, bockwurst and dampfwurst, and of course with frankfurters themselves. So it is not surprising that the Bavarians and other South Germans, whose pale local sausage is made of veal and called weisswurst, have a mild, pale mustard to go with it.

AMERICAN MUSTARDS

Owing to the wide range of national tastes, every kind of mustard, plain and spiced, can be found in American supermarkets. What is thought of as the true American mustard, however, is yellow mild and sweet, and has a consistency rather more like a thick sauce than a mustard. It is made from *alba* mustard seeds, flavoured with sugar, vinegar or white wine, which accounts for its cool character and for the fact that it can be applied in such quantities to hot dogs that it oozes over the sides of the buns, and is even lavished on that other American specialty, the hamburger.

This is also the mustard that is frequently used when making mayonnaise, not only to speed up the emulsion of the egg yolks and the oil but also to give the mayonnaise a distinct mustard flavor, which improves any salad that contains hard-boiled eggs – potato salad and tuna fish salad being the main candidates.

ITALIAN MOSTARDA DI FRUTTA

This is a confection of fruits – figs and cherries, chunks of pears, lemons and peaches – preserved in a syrup containing mustard oil. Its delicate, strange, sweet-sharp flavor makes it an interesting relish for cold meats, particularly boiled beef.

MAKING YOUR OWN MUSTARD

To grind the seeds, use a small coffee grinder (clean it very well after use) or, for a coarser mixture, simply pound them in a mortar.

The first time you make your own mustard, use equal amounts of black and white seeds and, if necessary, gradually alter the balance according to taste. Moisten the ground mustard with water until just saturated, then add white wine vinegar, salt and the flavorings of your choice and then leave to ferment for several days. A little olive oil takes the edge off a hot mixture. Store in a cork-topped jar in a cool larder or in the refrigerator.

RECIPE SUGGESTIONS

Sauce grelette

4 tomatoes, skinned and seeded
1½ tablespoons fromage blanc
2 tablespoons heavy cream
1 teaspoon Dijon mustard
Juice of ½ lemon
4 sprigs parsley and 6 fresh tarragon leaves, chopped
salt and freshly ground pepper
few drops of Tabasco

Cut the tomatoes in small cubes and put them in a colander to drain. Put the *fromage blanc* in a bowl with the cream and mustard and whisk them together. Gradually add the lemon juice, whisking all the time, and finally the tomato, herbs and seasoning. Serve this *nouvelle cuisine* sauce with plainly cooked cold fish, shellfish or with fish pâté.

Potted cheese

½ lb/225 g Stilton or other blue cheese, or Cheddar
¼ stick/55 g unsalted butter, softened
¼ teaspoon ground mace
1 teaspoon hot mustard

Mash the cheese with the butter, season with mace and mustard and work to a cream. Pack into small earthenware or china pots, making sure that it is well pressed down. If you want to keep it for any length of time, cover the cheese with clarified unsalted butter.

Mustard seed: alba

American spicy brown mustard

German mustard with herbs

Extra-hot German mustard

Mustard seed: nigra

Moutarde de Meaux

Bordeaux mustard

Dijon mustard

American mild mustard

French mustard with tomato

French mustard with herbs

Dijon mustard with tarragon

Hot German mustard

Mostarda di frutta

Ready-made English mustard

Welsh mustard with honey

Bavarian mustard

Tewkesbury mustard

Green peppercorn mustard

English mustard powder

VINEGAR

Vinaigre, the French word for vinegar, means sour wine, and this is what wine vinegar is, being produced by an acid fermentation of fresh wine. By the same process, malt vinegar is made from malt liquor and cider vinegar from cider. Chinese and Japanese sweet-sour vinegars are made from fermented *sake* – rice wine.

"The grateful acid," as vinegar was called by a seventeenth-century writer, has had its abuses. In Elizabethan days salads were served swimming in malt vinegar – a condiment much loved by the British – without benefit of either salt or oil. But things have improved since then. Although vinegary pickles still go well with rich foods such as cold pork, the biting character of vinegar has been tempered – first by the increased use of wine vinegar, which is an altogether milder affair than malt vinegar, partly by reducing the quantity of vinegar used in such things as salad dressings and increasing the proportion of oil, and partly – which is rather a pity – by the increased use of sugar. (If you want to avoid using sugar as a seasoning for salad dressing, use sherry vinegar as a base for the dressing or mix red or white wine vinegar half and half with wine of the same color.)

Apart from its role in salad dressings vinegar can be used instead of lemon juice in mayonnaise, hollandaise and bearnaise, and is essential in mint and horseradish sauces. It is used in marinades for meat and game, and a little vinegar can improve the flavor of stews and welsh rarebit – a dash of vinegar certainly works wonders with a dull sauce or gravy. A little vinegar in the water when steaming food stops the pan from discoloring, but vinegar is corrosive, so when cooking food that includes vinegar use pots of stainless steel, glass or earthenware, or enamelled ones.

Good vinegars are always worth their price. Cheap vinegars are usually inferior, frequently synthetic and usually nasty.

Wine vinegar

The best wine vinegar is made by a slow,

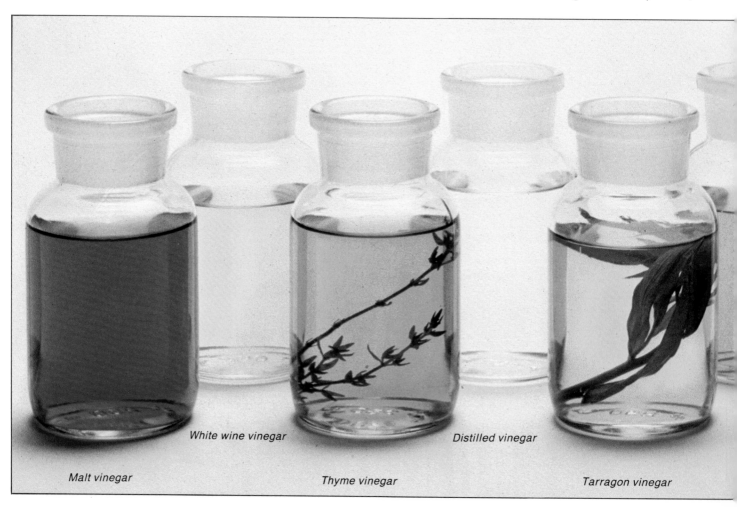

Malt vinegar

White wine vinegar

Thyme vinegar

Distilled vinegar

Tarragon vinegar

gentle process that allows it to mature naturally. Look for the French wine vinegars from Orléans, still probably the best and purest. Wine vinegar can be red or white and is sometimes very powerful, but it has a delicious flavor. If it is stronger than you like, dilute it, for salad dressing, with wine of the same color.

If you are offered a "vinegar mother," accept her with alacrity. She is a fungus that lives in wine and will turn all your leftover wine into excellent vinegar. Keep her in a warm place in an earthenware jar with a loose-fitting lid, so that air can get in, and give her wine as often as you have it to spare. If she is not very active, feed her a large dose of cheap wine and a pinch of sugar.

When the wine vinegar smells strongly acetic, decant it carefully into a bottle and let it stand for a month to mature and mellow before using it. Red wine seems to produce the best-flavored vinegar, but white is more useful in mayonnaise and even in most vinaigrettes, as the red turns them a curious pink color.

Cider vinegar
If we are to believe all we read about it, cider vinegar is a cure for all ills. As a seasoning, it has a strong, distinctive taste of cider and in sharpness is midway between wine vinegar and malt vinegar. Use it when making pickles and fruit chutneys, especially those with apples in them, and for a refreshing vinaigrette to use with fresh tomatoes.

Malt vinegar
Brewed from malted barley, malt vinegar is colored with caramel to varying shades of brown. The color is no longer an indication of the strength of the vinegar, although originally a deeper color probably did mean a well-matured vinegar, since it was kept in oak barrels, which colored the clear vinegar as it aged.

The best malt vinegar, with an acetic acid content of at least five percent, is excellent for pickling, which needs a strong vinegar.

Distilled vinegar
Being colorless, this is often labelled white vinegar and is the vinegar to use for pickling silver onions and for any pickling when color is important.

Spirit vinegar
This is strong and slightly alcoholic – flavored with lemon, it makes a good addition to a vinaigrette.

Sherry vinegar
A delicious vinegar made from sweet sherry, sherry vinegar used half and half with lemon juice in a vinaigrette tastes very nutty, almost like walnut oil. French chefs some-times use sherry vinegar in *poulet au vinaigre*.

Rice vinegar
This features in Japanese cooking, where its sweet, delicate flavor is used in *sushi* – vinegared riced – dishes.

Flavored vinegars
Wine vinegar can be flavored by putting fresh herbs – tarragon, basil, mint, thyme, burnet – into a jar, covering the herb with vinegar and keeping it in a warmish place – a warm kitchen, for example – for a week, giving the jar an occasional shake. Then decant the vinegar, keeping a token sprig of herb to show what's what. Three tablespoons of fresh herb to 5 cups/1 liter of wine vinegar is ample.

To make garlic vinegar, crush the garlic and leave it in the vinegar for 24 hours. For a really good chili vinegar, the chili peppers need steeping for ten days and should be given a daily shake.

Tarragon makes the best home-flavored vinegar, excellent for hollandaise sauce and on salads. Use chili vinegar with shellfish, especially lobster salad, burnet for mayonnaise to eat with fish, garlic vinegar for salad dressings when sharp flavors such as anchovies and capers are being used.

Spirit vinegar with lemon

Red wine vinegar

Cider vinegar

Mint vinegar

INDEX

ACKNOWLEDGEMENTS

Agricultural Attaché, American Embassy,
  London
A–Z Collection/Eric Soothill
W. Baxter & Sons
Billington (Edward) (Sugar) Ltd
British Egg Information Service
British Farm Produce Council
British Poultry Federation
Carolyn Brooke (who, with Caroline
  Conran, tasted all the recipes)
Robert Bruce
I. Camisa & Son
Cheese From Switzerland Ltd
Victor A. Shanley and Raymond Sargent of
  Clifton Nurseries Ltd
Diane Corless
Bryan Simpson, Technical Advisor,
  ESS-Foods (UK) Ltd Danish
  Agricultural Producers
W. Fenn Ltd
German Food Centre
Mary Ann Green
Harrods Ltd
International Food Store
Adrian Cullingford of Justin de Blank
Rocco Longo/Bruce Coleman
Mack & Edwards Ltd

Doreen Messant
Ministry of Agriculture, Fisheries and Food
Anna Monaghan
Dr Peter Moore
Arthur Myall & Sons Ltd
National Dairy Council
Natural Sausage Casing Association
Roberto Terzaga of Negroni (Pietro) Ltd
R. Portwine & Sons
Richards (Fishmongers)
Selfridges
Jack Shiells
J. O. Sims Ltd
Chris Sowe (Assistant to Clive Corless)
E. P. Spackmann
Marion Starr
John Steed
Sunwheel Foods Ltd
Swedish Embassy, London
Wendy Godfrey, Home Economist, Tate &
  Lyle Refineries Ltd
Van den Berghs & Jurgens Ltd
Pat Rance of Wells Stores
And many thanks to all stallholders at the
  Berwick Street and Rupert Street
  Markets, London.